I Am Cyrus

I Am Cyrus

Harry S. Truman and the Rebirth of Israel

Craig von Buseck

Straight Street Books
Lighthouse Publishing of the Carolinas

I AM CYRUS: HARRY S. TRUMAN AND THE REBIRTH OF ISRAEL
BY CRAIG VON BUSECK

Published by Straight Street Books
An imprint of Lighthouse Publishing of the Carolinas
2333 Barton Oaks Dr., Raleigh, NC, 27614

ISBN: 978-1-946016-98-0

Cover design by Elaina Lee
Interior design by AtriTeX Technologies P Ltd.

Available in print from your local bookstore, online, or from the publisher at ShopLPC.com.

For more information on this book and the author, visit vonbuseck.com.

Brought to you by the creative team at Lighthouse Publishing of the Carolinas (LPCBooks.com):
Eddie Jones, Ann Tatlock, Denise Loock, Shonda Savage, Elaina Lee, and Brian Cross

Library of Congress Cataloging-in-Publication Data

Von Buseck, Craig.

I Am Cyrus: Harry S. Truman and the Rebirth of Israel / Craig von Buseck 1st ed.

Printed in the United States of America

Praise for *I Am Cyrus*

The greatest proof that there is a God and that the Bible is His Word is the nation of Israel and the Jews. *I Am Cyrus* will allow anyone to never doubt God and the Bible again.

~ **Sid Roth**
Host, *It's Supernatural!*

I Am Cyrus is a detailed, inspiring read for anyone interested in learning about the historical scope of the Zionist enterprise: the suffering that went into its creation, the stubborn determination to make a miracle of a barren land, and the wonder of a tiny nation surrounded by implacable enemies that has become a beacon of light to nations greater in size. It's truly amazing.

Craig von Buseck must be applauded for his well-stocked and researched book. A must read for everyone interested in learning more about the Jewish State of Israel.

~ **Barry Shaw**
International Public Diplomacy Associate
Israel Institute for Strategic Studies

In *I Am Cyrus*, Craig von Buseck takes us behind the scenes into one of the greatest dramas in the past 2,000 years—the miracle story of Israel's rebirth. His meticulous research captures the drama, intrigue, and high-stakes history when Israel's fate hung in the balance. He shines an historical spotlight on Harry S. Truman, a man for his times, and also chronicles the amazing men and women such as David Ben-Gurion, Golda Meir, and Truman's best friend, Eddie Jacobson—men and women who played their part in history and who were born "for such a time as this." I highly recommend von Buseck's book as a rich addition to one's understanding of the times when prophecy came alive and a nation was born in a day.

~ **Chris Mitchell**
CBN News Middle East Bureau Chief, Jerusalem

What an amazing story—all of it true! The book reads like a novel, but it is well researched and carefully documented, giving the background to the miracle of modern Israel and the unique role played by President Harry Truman, the Cyrus of his day. What a timely and enjoyable read.

~ **Dr. Michael L. Brown**
President, FIRE School of Ministry
Host, *Line of Fire* radio program

I truly believe God's heart for Israel and the rebirth of His promises are powerfully revealed in this book, beyond my expectations. As a former Muslim, who was born and raised in the Middle East for the first twenty-five years of my life, I couldn't find a better source to make me understand the divine purpose of the Messiah for Israel.

While I was reading this powerful book, my heart was enlarged in a supernatural way and came into alignment and agreement with the sovereign will of God for the rebirth of Israel. I even felt like shouting my excitement. I'm in awe of how the Holy Spirit led each and every pen stroke to create such a masterpiece. I'm very grateful for this book's guidance and impact on my heart and life. I strongly recommend that every Christian who wants to know the truth about Israel and God's divine plan for its rebirth read this book.

~ **Isik Abla**
Founder and President of Isik Abla Ministries TV
Social Media Evangelist to the Muslim World

This book is a powerful read. I simply devoured its pages. Frankly, it captured my interest in a huge way, like few other books. While I thought I knew some things about the state of Israel, I found many gaps in my knowledge.

This is a profound book. I can't wait to tell my friends to read it.

~ **Dr. Cindy Jacobs**
Generals International

The account of how the nation of Israel came to be is one of the most fascinating stories in human history. God has never turned His back on His chosen people, and He always surprises us with how His promises to them are fulfilled. From pagan ancient kings to modern American presidents, God continues to bless the Jews. Read this book and be reminded that God does and always will intercede in the affairs of mankind. May you join the ever-increasing ranks of those who will continue to "pray for the peace of Jerusalem"!

~ **Janet Parshall**
Nationally syndicated Talk Show Host

The miraculous rebirth of Israel in 1948 was a pivotal moment not only in modern history but also in the history of the world. *I Am Cyrus: Harry S. Truman and the Rebirth of Israel* is the fascinating inside story of how God chose a Bible-believing farm boy from Missouri as His unlikely point man to make it all happen. In gripping detail, Dr. Craig von Buseck lays out President Harry Truman's journey from wartime president to modern-day Cyrus and the enduring special relationship between the United States and Israel that he helped spark. *I Am Cyrus* is an absolute must-read book for anyone who wants to know more about the prophetic times that we are living in and why Israel is—and always will be—at the center of God's divine plan.

~ **Erick Stakelbeck**
Host, TBN's *The Watchman*

The birth of Israel is one of the greatest miracles of modern times, and in *I Am Cyrus: Harry S. Truman and the Rebirth of Israel*, Craig von Buseck shows us how God put all the right people in place at the right time, including an American president, to pull off the impossible. A thrilling read!

~ **Wendy Griffith**
Co-host, *The 700 Club*

During the signing ceremony at the White House following President Trump's proclamation recognizing Israeli sovereignty over the Golan Heights, Prime Minister Netanyahu established the historical significance of the Golan decision. "In the long sweep of Jewish history," declared the prime minister, "there have been a handful of proclamations by non-Jewish leaders on behalf of our people and our land: Cyrus the Great, the great Persian king; Lord Balfour; President Harry S. Truman; and President Donald J. Trump."

As Dr. Craig von Buseck explains throughout his well-researched book, *I am Cyrus: Harry S. Truman and the Rebirth of Israel*, the comparison to the ancient Persian king has great significance. Truman's courageous decision to recognize the State of Israel—as outlined thoroughly by Dr. von Buseck in his extensive volume, deeply researched with over 1,000 footnotes—made him a hero. However, it was only the first step in the Edict of Cyrus.

We pray that Israel continues to grow and thrive as it has since May 14, 1948, and that it assumes its true spiritual significance with a "house of God" in Jerusalem as Cyrus the Great called for 2,500 years ago.

~ **Rabbi Tuly Weisz**
Founder of Israel365
Publisher of Breaking Israel News
Editor of The Israel Bible

This important book comes at a pivotal time in world history. In an age of the diminution of truth, von Buseck persuasively illustrates how the uncompromising stand for what is right can have both national and global impact. I encourage all churches, and especially seminaries, to include this book as part of their curricula of what moral leadership could look like in our world.

~ **Dr. Corné J. Bekker**
Dean, Regent University School of Divinity

Craig von Buseck's *I Am Cyrus: Harry S. Truman and the Rebirth of Israel* tells, with extraordinary detail, the complex, nuanced story leading up to Truman's dramatic decisions concerning Israel's rebirth. The result is an account that is so lucid, crisp, and moving that it reads like a page-turning suspense novel—except that every word is based on accurate research. Those who know the basic story of America's role in Israel's independence will discover new and unexpected things.

~ **Michael Robert Wolf**
Author
Senior Congregational Leader
Past President of the Messianic Jewish Alliance of America

In 1983, I received a prophecy that I would one day lead a ministry located on the property that President Harry S. Truman once lived on and that we would be inspired by his stand for Israel in that he was a political intercessor for Israel. Unknown to me, on January 29, 1958, a Jewish family purchased part of President Truman's farm in South Kansas City (Grandview, Missouri). In the fall of 2007, their adult children sold that property to the ministry I lead, the *International House of Prayer of Kansas City* (IHOPKC).

A dear friend of our ministry paid the entire cost of the property and gave it to us debt free as an amazing gift from the Lord. We closed on the property exactly fifty years (on the Monday after the weekend of September 29, 2008) after this Jewish family purchased that land from President Truman. We rejoice that it is like a Jubilee property, debt free and returned to its right owner, the intercession ministry for Israel. Today, the people of IHOPKC are spiritual intercessors for Israel on a daily basis, fulfilling this amazing prophecy.

As you can imagine, the story of President Truman's intercession during the critical period just before and after the rebirth of Israel is of great interest to me. This story is chronicled by Dr. Craig von Buseck in *I Am Cyrus: Harry S. Truman and the Rebirth of Israel*. To cut through the anti-Israel propaganda so prevalent in the news media and on college and public school campuses, von Buseck reaches back to the birth of the Zionist movement in the late nineteenth century to give a detailed description of how the Jews rebuilt this decimated land. Drawing on years of research, he carries the reader through World War One and the Balfour Declaration, then up to the Nazi Holocaust during World War Two, when six million Jews were brutally murdered.

At this critical moment in history, Harry S. Truman enters the White House and is called upon to help decide the fate of the 1.5 million homeless Jewish survivors in Europe—and the future of the one place most of them wanted to go, their ancient homeland in Eretz Israel. Facing overwhelming pressure to reject statehood for the Zionists, Truman courageously decides to do what he believes is best for America and for Jewish people worldwide. As a result, a people who had wandered the world for nearly 2,000 years returned with joy to their Promised Land. *I Am Cyrus* tells this remarkable story with details that will surprise and astonish the open-minded reader, challenging many of the assumptions made by today's media elite.

~ Mike Bickle
International House of Prayer of Kansas City

Craig von Buseck's *I Am Cyrus* helps fill in several gaps in the important story of the nation of Israel's reestablishment in the twentieth century. Well-written and thoroughly researched, it reveals the rationale behind the motivations, challenges, and ultimate decisions President Truman navigated to formally recognize the need of a national home for the Jewish people. These facts and insights will help politicians, scholars, and engaged citizens better understand the reasons for America's continuing support of Israel's place, security, and prosperity in the modern Middle East.

~ David J. Gyerston, PhD
Dean of the Beeson International Center of
Asbury Theological Seminary
Professor of Leadership Formation and Renewal

At a time when so much of Israeli and Jewish history is being twisted or subtly rewritten, a documented history book like this is right on time. We live in an era when biblical prophecy, history, and current events are colliding in Israel, and so few people seem to recognize the profound implications of what that means. For those looking into that convergence, *I Am Cyrus* should be on their reading list.

~ Doug Hershey
Author of *Israel Rising: Ancient Prophecy / Modern Lens*

Throughout history, God has been a miracle-working God. However, almost always, divine miracles have been performed with human participation of some kind. When God displays His sovereignty, the supernatural move of His Spirit normally involves natural, earthly elements as well. This miraculous divine/human partnership is beautifully illustrated in Craig von Buseck's outstanding book, *I Am Cyrus*. Few people realize the important role US President Harry S. Truman played in the rebirth of the modern nation of Israel. Despite formidable obstacles and unlikely human vessels, God performed a miracle that fulfilled His prophetic declarations from many centuries earlier.

Craig von Buseck has written much more than an excellent history book. This is a powerful testimony of God's faithfulness to His covenant people—and to each of us today.

~ Jim Buchan
Author
Director of Partner Communications, Inspiration Ministries

With *I Am Cyrus*, Craig von Buseck does more than shine a light on the role of one unassuming man from Missouri who became the world's most powerful leader just before Israel was reborn. He also skillfully weaves the story of how the Hand of Heaven has shaped leaders and governments for more than 2,000 years to bring to pass the words of Bible prophets concerning Israel. Read this book—you'll be encouraged.

~ John Waage
Senior Editor, Middle-East Reporter, CBN News

TABLE OF CONTENTS

To my father, Clemens von Buseck
Like the ancient partriarchs, you set us on a path
to knowing God
With much love and gratitude

Foreword

I first visited Israel with my father, Pat Robertson, in 1969, two years after the Six-Day War. I'll never forget being at the Western Wall and witnessing the sheer joy of people once again worshiping at the temple and dancing with Torah scrolls. I was just eleven years old, and I can't quite explain it, but I felt a bond to the place and the people of Israel. So, when my children turned twelve, I took each of them on a trip to Israel to be baptized in the Jordan River and to pray at the Western Wall.

Some people seem to bond with Israel, and some people seem to hate Israel. Regardless of your feelings, the birth of the modern state of Israel is one of the greatest dramas in history. No other people group has survived as a nation for 2,000 years in exile. Israel is proof that God keeps His promises.

When asked by the British Peel Commission if the Jews had a deed to the land of Israel, David Ben-Gurion held up the Bible that he had just used in swearing to tell the truth and answered, "This is my document. It is the most highly respected book. And I believe that you British respect it also. Our right in Palestine is not derived from the Mandate or the Balfour Declaration. It is prior to that. The Bible, which was written by us in our own language, in this very country, is our mandate. Our right in Palestine is as old as the Jewish people. We must have this land."

In May 1948, the British Empire ended their mandate and withdrew from Palestine. After decades of preparation, David Ben-Gurion stood in Tel Aviv and declared the establishment of the State of Israel. Hours later, President Harry Truman boldly led the United States to be the first nation to recognize the fledgling state. Jews around the world rejoiced and five Arab nations declared war.

One year after that first war, Israel's Chief Rabbi, Isaac Halevi Herzog, met President Truman in the White House. The president asked if the Rabbi knew how he had been involved in Israel's rebirth. The aged Rabbi looked intently at Truman and told him that "he had been given the task once fulfilled by the mighty king of Persia, and that he too, like Cyrus, would occupy a place of honor in the annals of the Jewish people."

This book tells that epic story.

That is why I am pleased to endorse *I Am Cyrus: Harry S. Truman and the Rebirth of Israel* by Dr. Craig von Buseck. In this thoroughly researched and documented book, Craig tells this story, reaching back into antiquity to make the case for the presence of the Jews in their homeland, Eretz Israel.

I believe it is important for people everywhere to know the full story, and the truth behind the rebirth of Israel in the land the Romans re-named Palestine. This book shows how God's hand was upon Israel at its rebirth, and then you will see how His hand remains upon Israel today.

Gordon Robertson
Chief Operating Officer, The Christian Broadcasting Network
Co-host of *The 700 Club*

Prologue

Birth Pains

"I had faith in Israel before it was established, I have faith in it now."
President Harry S. Truman, May 14, 1948

"Next year in Jerusalem ..."

MAY 1948—TEL AVIV, ERETZ ISRAEL

Five Arab armies stood poised on the borders as a wiry, white-haired man rose in the Tel Aviv Museum and proclaimed a new nation for the Jewish people in Eretz Israel after nearly 2,000 years of exile. The date was 5 Iyar 5708, or May 14, 1948. The grizzled leader of the World Zionist Organization, David Ben-Gurion, declared that this nation would be known as the State of Israel.

A radio station broadcast the ceremony and the news streaked like a meteor to the four corners of the globe within minutes. Instantly, Jews around the world reconnected with the ancient home from which their ancestors had been expelled by the Roman Empire in 70 CE. After that national catastrophe, the Jews were scattered to the ends of the earth. From that time forward, at the end of every Passover Seder, Jews collectively uttered their longing with the famous declaration, "Next year in Jerusalem."

With Ben-Gurion's Declaration of Independence, this ancient hope would not merely be a longing of the heart, but a concrete possibility for every Jew with the passion for the Promised Land and the drive to get there.

The Jews could not forget Jerusalem or the land promised by God to their patriarchs. They had been the majority in this Promised Land from the time of Joshua around 1,400 BCE[1] until the Babylonian exile in 597 BCE[2]—and then again after the return from Babylon until the destruction of the Second Temple in 70 CE.

PERSECUTION IN EXILE

During the 1,800 years that followed the destruction of Jerusalem, the Jews faced various forms of persecution—most notably the infamous Spanish Inquisition and the Russian pogroms. Yet despite the constant threat to their existence, God's chosen people endured. A remnant remained in the land they lovingly called Eretz Israel—what the Romans later renamed Palestine.

Then, beginning in the seventeenth century, a more liberal climate swept through Western Europe. In response, many Jews assimilated, embracing the clothing, language, and culture of their adopted nations. Exhausted by the age-old struggle, some even rejected their Jewish heritage and traditions. As a result of their integration into mainstream society, certain Jews rose to levels of wealth and power that previous generations could not have imagined.

The Rothschild family, for example, became prominent in the banking industry, and soon they were known and revered throughout the world. At the height of Queen Victoria's reign in Great Britain, Benjamin Disraeli ascended to the lofty position of prime minister, wielding worldwide power and influence.

But, as in earlier centuries, the illusion of peace and safety for the Jews in Europe eventually disappeared as old hatreds resurfaced toward the end of the nineteenth century. This was especially true in Tsarist Russia, where Jews lived in grinding poverty in what was called the Pale of Settlement under the cruel hand of the secret police. After the assassination of Tsar Alexander II in 1881, the Russian government blamed the Jews for his murder and unleashed a series of horrific pogroms that shocked the world. In response, many of the Jews of Russia embraced the *Hovevei Zion*, or Lovers of Zion, movement. Some of these brave souls were pioneers in what became known as the First Aliya—the initial wave of immigrants to Palestine beginning in 1882.

They were certainly not the first Jewish immigrants, as thousands of Jews had desired to recolonize Palestine for 1,800 years. But these were the first permanent, organized settlements with a dedicated group of pilgrims willing to do whatever was necessary for success. Soon their tenacity caught the attention of a group of wealthy, influential Jewish financiers from around the world willing to spend the significant cash needed to build a successful colony in Palestine.

The Russian Jews who entered Palestine at that time were young, energetic idealists determined to tame the land. The settlement of *Rishon LeZion*, or First to Zion, was founded on July 31, 1882, by ten pioneers who purchased 835 acres of land southeast of present-day Tel Aviv.

They faced mind-numbing difficulties. The soil was rocky or sandy, water was scarce, marshes were full of malaria, and the settlers had little or no agricultural experience. But after a well was dug, untapping an ample supply of fresh water, more pioneers began arriving—primarily from Russia—and the colony slowly started to grow.

Soon the powerful Baron Edmond James de Rothschild became aware of the settlement and was persuaded to become a benefactor. With his help, major progress was made in the planting of vineyards, in agriculture, and in citrus production. Under Rothschild's patronage, the Carmel-Mizrahi Winery was established and prospered, gaining fame around the world.

Baron Rothschild said of the project, "Without me, the Zionists could have done nothing. But without the Zionists, my work would have been dead."

The Jews were now a growing force in their ancient homeland, and soon tens of thousands would join this ragtag early group of settlers.

In 1883, a young Jewish poet from Rishon LeZion penned some verses that she called "*Hatikva*," or "The Hope." Sixty-five years later, her poem became the national anthem of the new State of Israel.[3] The words reflect the spirit of the Jewish people who never gave up the hope that they would someday return to the Promised Land of Eretz Israel.

> As long as deep within the heart
> The Jewish soul is warm

And toward the edges of the east
An eye to Zion looks
Our hope is not yet lost,
The hope of two thousand years
To be a free people in our own land
In the land of Zion and Jerusalem.
To be a free people in our own land
In the land of Zion and Jerusalem.

Around that same time, in the small village of Lamar, Missouri, far away in the middle of the United States, a horse and mule trader named John Anderson Truman rejoiced with his wife, Martha, at the birth of a healthy baby boy. The following day, a famous Baptist circuit rider, Rev. Washington Pease, paid a visit to see the new baby. Without warning, he lifted the newborn and carried him out of the small, dimly lit clapboard house and into the brilliant Missouri sunshine. Lifting little Harry S. Truman into the air, the preacher declared, "Yes, he will be a strong boy."[4]

Part One

THE PROMISE

Chapter One

THE JEWISH DIASPORA

597 BCE—JERUSALEM

The triumphant days of King David and King Solomon were distant memories when Nebuchadnezzar of Babylon conquered Jerusalem in 597 BCE.[5] The Hebrew kingdom seemed to be at an end. The glory of the nation of Israel had departed. It seemed to many that the unique relationship between the Hebrew people and *Yahweh*, their God, was irreparably broken. Most of the Jews were carried off to Babylon by Nebuchadnezzar. Those left behind in Eretz Israel were forced to toil among hostile neighbors with no organized government to provide protection.

It was the beginning of the Jewish Diaspora.

Seventy years passed, and then Cyrus the Great began his conquest of the lands surrounding Persia. As a follower of Zoroastrianism, Cyrus believed both good and bad gods existed. Yahweh was one of the good gods. He claimed that Yahweh visited him one night and commanded him to rebuild the temple in Jerusalem. Cyrus obeyed the heavenly vision, ordering the temple rebuilt and the Jews returned to their homeland.[6]

Judah became a protected theological state within the Persian Empire as Yahweh's temple was rebuilt. This was a monumental task, but after years of toil, the temple was completed and rededicated to the glory of Yahweh. Persia ruled the ancient Near East for the next two hundred years, and the Jews enjoyed peaceful worship in Jerusalem.

THE RISE OF THE GREEKS

Then in 336 BCE, a Greek ruler named Alexander of Macedon—or Alexander the Great—swept across Asia with his armies. When he conquered Persia in 331 BCE, Eretz Israel became a Greek state.[7] After the untimely death of Alexander in 323 BCE, three of his generals divided the Middle East among themselves.[8] For the next 125 years, the Ptolemies and the Seleucids fought for the valuable Land of Israel, the crossroads of three continents. Then in 198 BCE, Antiochus III defeated the Ptolemies of Egypt and annexed Judea.

Antiochus initially allowed the same religious and political autonomy the Jews enjoyed under the Persians. But after a military loss to the Romans in Asia Minor, Antiochus retaliated against the Jews, trying to force them to reject Yahweh and embrace Greek paganism. He banned many traditional Jewish religious practices and made possession of the Torah a capital offense.

His son, Antiochus IV, came to the throne in 176 BCE, pushing even harder to eliminate the worship of Yahweh. When the Jews rebelled, he outlawed the observance of the Sabbath and circumcision. He defiled the holy temple by erecting an altar to the god Zeus, allowing the sacrifice of pigs, and opening the temple to non-Jews.[9]

THE MACCABEES

These actions united the Jewish people against Antiochus and soon uprisings took place across Eretz Israel. In the village of Modiin, a Jewish priest named Mattathias the Hasmonean refused to worship the Greek gods. In a bold act of defiance, Mattathias killed a Hellenistic Jew who stepped forward to offer a sacrifice to an idol. Mattathias fled with his five sons into the wilderness, where they made plans for full-scale war. Mattathias' family became known as the Maccabees, from the Hebrew word for *hammer*, as their warfare skills struck hammer blows against their enemies.

When Mattathias died the following year, his son Judas took his place, destroying pagan altars across Judea. Antiochus underestimated the will and strength of these Jewish freedom fighters and sent a small force to put down the rebellion. When those troops were annihilated, he led a more powerful army into battle only to be defeated yet again. In 164 BCE, Jerusalem was recaptured by the Maccabees in a stunning victory. Immediately, the Maccabees moved to ritually cleanse the temple, reestablishing Jewish worship and installing Jonathan Maccabee as high priest.

The successor to Antiochus agreed to the Jews' demand for independence, and in the year 142 BCE, after more than 500 years of subjugation, the Jews were again masters of their own fate. Simon Maccabee, the last of the five sons of Mattathias to survive, ushered in an eighty-year period of Jewish independence in Judea.[10]

THE ROMANS

Independent Hasmonean rule lasted until 63 BCE when the Roman general Pompey conquered the Land of Israel. After gaining control of the region, Julius Caesar appointed Hyrcanus II as ruler of Judea, as he was the son of Alexander Yannai, the former Hasmonean king. The Hasmonean dynasty ended in 37 BCE when the Idumean, Herod the Great, was named king of the Jews by the Roman Senate.

Under Julius Caesar, Judaism was officially recognized as a legal religion. But unlike the Persians and the Greeks, who encouraged Jewish religious freedom, the Romans didn't understand how the majority of the Jews could cling to a religion that seemed so unusual—one that did not honor the deification of the emperor. Rome came down hard on its Hebrew subjects, levying steep taxes and persecuting those who resisted.

The emperor gave almost unlimited autonomy to Herod to govern the region.[11] Along with the construction of numerous architectural wonders, Herod's crowning achievement was the restoration and rebuilding of the temple of Jerusalem into one of the wonders of the ancient world. Herod had enclosed the original top of Mount Moriah with a rectangular set of retaining walls, built to support extensive substructures, and had filled the remaining space with dirt, sand, and stone. He then constructed a massive flat, paved area on which his magnificent temple stood.

Despite his skill at bringing prosperity to Judea and his construction of theaters, aqueducts, and other magnificent structures, Herod was an Arabian Edomite, and his Jewish subjects did not trust him. After his death, the Romans divided his kingdom among three of his sons and his sister. During the siblings' fractious rule, the Jews' growing anger against Roman suppression escalated into a full-scale revolt.

In 66 CE, the First Jewish–Roman War began. The revolt was put down by the future Roman emperors Vespasian and Titus. In the Siege of Jerusalem in 70 CE, the Romans destroyed much of the Second Temple and plundered many of the religious artifacts. Roman forces were finally victorious, defeating the last Jewish outpost at Masada in 73 CE.[12]

More than one million people were killed by the Romans during the uprising, and approximately 97,000 Jews were captured and sold into slavery.[13] From this time forward, Jews in the Roman Empire were only allowed to practice their religion if they paid a special tax.

THE BAR KOKHBA REVOLT

The Jews enjoyed one final short time of sovereignty as the result of the revolt of Shimon Bar Kokhba in 132 CE. For a brief period, Jerusalem and Judea were controlled by the Jews. The revolt was eventually put down by the overwhelming power of the Romans, and the vast majority of the Jewish population of Judea was killed, sold into slavery, or forced to flee. In an attempt to erase the historical ties of the Jewish people to the region, Emperor Hadrian changed the name of the Judean province to *Syria Palaestina* and Jerusalem to *Aelia Capitolina*. Temples were built to honor Jupiter and other Roman gods, and Jews were barred from Jerusalem, except on the day of *Tisha B'Av*.

To prevent the political regeneration of the Jewish nation and to sever the connection of the Hebrew people to their homeland, several Greek and Roman colonies were planted in Palestine by the Roman government. Heavy taxation, cruel discrimination, and social shunning further alienated the remaining Jews. Although a small group of Jews maintained their presence in Palestine, they became a people in exile—even within their own homeland.[14]

THE JEWISH EXILE

Jewish religious law and cultural traditions became the common bond among Jews in the Diaspora. These keepsakes were passed from generation to generation. Some of the most famous and important Jewish texts were composed at this time, including the Jerusalem Talmud and the completion of the Mishnah.

Although the temple had been destroyed, Judaism survived. Priests were replaced by rabbis and the synagogue became the focus of religious life.[15]

The small remaining Jewish community in Palestine gradually recovered, strengthened occasionally by returning exiles. By the sixth century, forty-three Jewish communities existed in Palestine.[16]

Despite continual persecution, a Jewish remnant remained in or near Jerusalem for all the years of the Diaspora. Known as *Neturei Karta*, these pious guardians of the Jewish Scriptures and culture lived as close to the sacred temple grounds as they were able.[17]

But the majority of Jews were scattered to the ends of the earth.

A glimmer of hope appeared for the Jewish people when Emperor Julian allowed exiles to return to "holy Jerusalem which you have for many years longed to see rebuilt." Sadly, Julian was killed in battle in 363 CE, and his plans for a Third Temple were abandoned. Control of the Holy Land passed from the Romans to the Byzantine Empire after the division of the Roman Empire into east and west in 395 CE.[18]

Although the Jewish people had been forced to leave their homeland, Eretz Israel and Jerusalem would never leave them.

Muslim Conquest

In 634 CE, the Muslim conquests began. Many Jews initially joined the Muslims against their Eastern Roman rulers. As a result, Jewish communities were largely expelled by the Byzantines from Judea and sent to various Roman provinces outside of Palestine.[19] Then in 636 CE, Muslim soldiers defeated the Byzantines to take possession of Palestine.[20]

Following the fall of the city of Jerusalem to the Arabs, Jews and Christians were designated "People of the Book," enjoying a level of protection in exchange for a "poll tax."[21] In 691 CE, construction was completed on the Dome of the Rock, built on the site of the Temple Mount. The Al-Aqsa Mosque was then erected nearby and completed in 705 CE.[22]

The Crusades and Saladin

Beginning in the eleventh century, Christians in Jerusalem were increasingly persecuted by the city's Islamic rulers, especially when control of the Holy City passed from the relatively tolerant Egyptians to the Seljuk Turks, a new group of Islamic warriors. The Byzantine emperor, Alexius

Comnenus, was also threatened by the Seljuk Turks and appealed to Pope Urban II for aid to fight off the Muslim invaders.

The result of this appeal was the Crusades, which began in 1095 CE. The Crusaders finally prevailed over the Turks in 1099 and set up four Christian states in Jerusalem, Edessa, Antioch, and Tripoli, calling their realm "The Kingdom of Jerusalem." The invaders built castles and fortresses throughout Palestine to defend their domain. The Royal Palace of the Kingdom was located in the Al-Aqsa Mosque, and the Dome of the Rock was converted into a church.[23]

The Crusaders held Jerusalem for nearly a century until 1187 when Saladin, the founder of the Ayyubid dynasty, recaptured the city. The Jews fought alongside the Muslims, and after the victory, Saladin invited them to return to the Holy Land.[24]

Control of Palestine next passed to the Egyptian Mamluk Sultanate in 1250.[25] The Mamluks ruled in Palestine until 1517 when the Ottoman Turks defeated them at the Battle of Marj Dabiq.

Under Turkish rule, Palestine became a forgotten desert in the vast Ottoman Empire. It remained a desolate wasteland for the next 350 years.

THE JEWS IN EUROPE

At the same time, Jews experienced both persecution and favor as the political and religious winds blew through the lands in which they were scattered.

In 1066 CE, at the invitation of William the Conqueror, Jews entered England with the Norman Invasion for the purpose of establishing banks.[26] At that time, the Roman Catholic Church prohibited the lending of money with interest, which created an opportunity, as Judaism permitted the practice. As a result, many Jewish bankers became wealthy and the subject of envy and suspicion among the general public. They also became a source of wealth for the monarchy, which levied steep taxes on Jewish moneylenders to line the royal pockets.

Soon rumors spread of the Jews in England as diabolical people who hated Christ and committed ritual murders to use the blood at Passover.[27] Hatred and persecution continued to grow against the Jews, and in 1218, England became the first European nation to require Jews to wear a marking badge.[28]

The tide turned under the "Statute of the Jewry" in 1275 CE when all lending at interest by Jews in England was outlawed.[29] Then in 1290, as a way of selling a steep tax imposed to reduce his debts, King Edward I offered to expel the Jews from England. Three days after the heavy tax passed, Edward issued the Edict of Expulsion, driving more than 2,000 Jews from the nation. They would not return to England until 1657 under Oliver Cromwell, more than 360 years later.[30]

THE SPANISH INQUISITION

One of the cruelest persecutions against the Jewish Diaspora began in 1491 with the launch of the Spanish Inquisition. This brutal tribunal was directed principally at Jews who had converted to Christianity and were suspected of leading secret Jewish lives. This was a tragic reversal for the Jews of Spain.

The Jews first settled in Spain after its conquest by the Arabs in the eighth century. These new Muslim overlords became known as the society of the Spanish Moors, a remarkable culture of scientific, literary, and artistic achievement. The Jews of Spain quickly became an important part of the Spanish intellectual aristocracy.

When European Christians once again gained control of Spain, both the Moors and Jews initially retained their positions of authority. Spanish monarchs depended on the Moors and Jews to serve as doctors, professors, and scientists. Despite persecution in other parts of Western Europe, Spanish Jews were allowed to own land and hold high rank at court. The wealthy and powerful Sephardic elite enjoyed a golden age of tolerance.

Then in 1492, these privileges ended abruptly when the final stronghold of Moorish Spain, Granada, fell to the troops of King Ferdinand and Queen Isabella. The financial problems of the Spanish government added to the rush to persecution. The long war had depleted the royal treasury, and confiscating the estates of banished Jews was a way to replenish the coffers.

Of Spain's 300,000 Jews, approximately 100,000 saved their property by embracing Christianity, although many practiced Judaism secretly. Many Jews caught by Inquisition spies died at the stake for their relapse into the forbidden creed. Tens of thousands of Jews were murdered in riots and massacres in this dark period.[31] Another 100,000 of the Sephardim abandoned homes and possessions and poured out of Spain in a new Diaspora.[32] Almost no one returned to Palestine, which had been mismanaged by the Turkish Ottomans to the point that it had become a wilderness of scorching deserts and malaria-plagued marshes.

NAPOLEON'S JEWISH STATE

The first hints of modern Zionism as a political and organic movement can be traced to French Emperor Napoleon Bonaparte's promise to establish a Jewish state in Palestine at the turn of the nineteenth century. Backing his words with action, Napoleon set out to establish a Jewish Sanhedrin.

In 1798, Napoleon, leading the French expeditionary force, invaded and occupied Turkish-controlled Egypt. The French would remain in Egypt for three years but never conquered Palestine. This was the beginning of the decline of the Ottoman Empire as European powers rose to dominate the world stage.[33]

THE DESOLATION OF THE HOLY LAND

In 1857, American writer Herman Melville, author of *Moby Dick*, toured Jerusalem and described it as "a pile of arid rocks where the emigrant Jews are like flies who have taken up their abode in a skull." As a result of persecution and Ottoman neglect, Jews and Arabs were living in absolute poverty.[34]

That same year, the British Consul in Palestine reported "the country is in a considerable degree empty of inhabitants and therefore its greatest need is that of a body of population." James Finn reported to the Earl of Clarendon from Jerusalem: "depopulation is even now advancing."[35]

At the same time, H. B. Tristram noted in his journal: "… North and south, land is going out of cultivation and whole villages are rapidly disappearing from the face of the earth. Since the year 1838, no less than 20 villages there have been thus erased from the map …"[36]

American author Mark Twain visited Palestine in 1867 and wrote his observations for newspaper readers in America. These collected reports would later become his book *The Innocents Abroad*. Twain described the Ottoman Empire's forgotten underbelly as a "… desolate country whose soil is rich enough, but is given over wholly to weeds—a silent mournful expanse …"[37]

Writing of the region around Tabor, Twain declared: "A desolation is here that not even imagination can grace with the pomp of life and action."[38]

"We never saw a human being on the whole route … There was hardly a tree or a shrub anywhere. Even the olive and the cactus, those fast friends of the worthless soil, had almost deserted the country."

"There is not a solitary village throughout its whole extent—not for thirty miles in either direction … One may ride ten miles hereabouts and not see ten human beings."[39]

As he prepared to leave the Holy Land, Twain wrote his final thoughts: "Of all the lands there are for dismal scenery, I think Palestine must be the prince. The hills are barren, they are dull of color, they are unpicturesque in shape. The valleys are unsightly deserts fringed with a feeble vegetation that has an expression about it of being sorrowful and despondent … It is a hopeless, dreary, heart-broken land."[40]

THE MONTEFIORE SETTLEMENTS

Yet in the midst of these dismal times for the people of Palestine, a Jewish leader with vision and determination rose up to plant seeds that would soon bloom into the literal fulfillment of the prophetic utterance of Isaiah:

> The Lord will surely comfort Zion and will look with compassion on all her ruins; he will make her deserts like Eden, her wastelands like the garden of the Lord. (Isaiah 51:3)

This leader was Sir Moses Montefiore, a remarkable Jewish businessman from England who started as an apprentice to a firm of grocers and tea merchants and ended up as a stockbroker for the Rothschild family.

In 1812, Montefiore married Judith Cohen. Her sister, Henriette, married Nathan Mayer Rothschild, for whom Montefiore's firm acted as stockbrokers. Nathan Rothschild headed the family's banking business in Britain, and in time, the two brothers-in-law became business partners. In the midst of his illustrious career, Montefiore amassed a fortune that allowed him to give financial assistance to his fellow Jews in the Holy Land. He was so successful that he was able to retire from business in 1824 and spend his time on civic and philanthropic ventures.

In 1854, his friend Judah Touro, a wealthy American Jew, died and left money in his will to fund Jewish settlement in Palestine. As executor of his will, Montefiore used these funds for a variety of pragmatic projects to help the Jews take root once again in the Holy Land. Montefiore's imagination was set afire, and for the remainder of his life, Jewish philanthropy in Eretz Israel was his passion. Montefiore donated large sums to promote industry, education, and health. These activities were meant to enable the members of the Old Yishuv—the term used for the Jews living in Palestine at that time—to become self-supporting in preparation for incoming settlers who would help reestablish a Jewish homeland.[41]

Montefiore developed a plan to acquire land and attempted to bring industry back to the country by introducing a printing press and a textile factory. In 1855, he purchased an orchard on the outskirts of Jaffa to provide agricultural training for the Jews.

He turned his attention to Jerusalem in 1860 when he purchased a piece of land outside the city walls from the mayor to develop a Jewish settlement. "They fleeced him sadly," Melville explained, "charging enormous prices for everything he bought."[42] From Montefiore's perspective, the cost was insignificant next to the opportunity to help his fellow Jews return to their ancient land. On this newly acquired property, he planted a community that he named *Mishkenot Sha'ananim*, or "peaceful dwellings," from the prophecy in Isaiah 32:18, "My people will dwell in a peaceful habitation" (KJV).

This became the first settlement of the New Yishuv.

Living outside the city walls was dangerous at the time, with roving bandits and a lack of law enforcement. To encourage settlement, Montefiore offered financial inducement to poor families to move outside the protective walls of Old Jerusalem. Jews reluctantly made the move but often sneaked back inside the city walls to sleep at night.

Next, Montefiore turned his attention to the lack of food, as there wasn't a single bakery in all of Jerusalem. If you wanted bread, you had to make it at home, but there were no stores that sold flour, and no mill to make flour. So he built a windmill to provide inexpensive flour to the Jews in and around Jerusalem.[43] The Jews of the Yishuv referred to their patron as "ha-Sar Montefiore," or "Minister Montefiore," a title of honor from Hebrew literature.[44]

Unlike Twain, who lamented the lost glories of yesteryear, Montefiore, in his first visit to Eretz Israel in 1827, looked to the future when the deserts would bloom again. His pilgrimages to Jerusalem had a profound religious effect on him, and from then until the end of his life, he became strictly observant. He traveled to Palestine seven times, sometimes accompanied by his wife, although these voyages were both dangerous and difficult. He made his final journey to Eretz Israel at the age of ninety-one.

KARL NETTER AND THE ALLIANCE ISRAELITE UNIVERSELLE

Another beacon of light was Karl Netter who, along with Adolphe Crémieux of France, founded the Alliance Israelite Universelle in 1860. Their goal was to give practical help to all who suffered because they were Jewish. In 1868, the Alliance sent Netter to study the condition of Jews in Palestine.

"The hungry ask for bread to eat," Netter reported, "a garment to don, but with the wages of their labor and not as charity. All the time I was in Jerusalem, not one single person of sound health asked for an outright gift." Netter proposed the founding of an agricultural school as a means to help the Jews of Palestine become productive and self-reliant.

"I present to you a plan for a new institution where you can educate the next generation in farming. Thus you will construct a refuge for our many brethren who, today or tomorrow, must flee from their dwelling places because their Gentile neighbors hate them. Little by little, you will resettle the Holy Land, to which the eyes of all Israel are ever lifted up, if farming truly expands there and our brethren come as settlers in their multitudes from the Diaspora. Then we will see the New Jerusalem with our own eyes."

The Alliance charged Netter to carry out his plan. He traveled to Istanbul and procured from the sultan a grant to build an agricultural school on 650 acres near Jaffa. In 1870, the doors opened to this new institution, which was named *Mikveh Israel*, with Netter serving as both principal and instructor. He lived to see a new agricultural settlement in Petah Tikva, and a thriving and diverse community in Rishon LeZion.[45]

Although scattered to the corners of the earth, the Jewish people somehow retained their national identity. Like Ezekiel's dry bones coming together to live again, the efforts of great Jewish leaders like Moses Montefiore, Karl Netter, and later Baron de Rothschild—along with thousands of brave Jewish pioneers willing to risk everything to rebuild their homeland—were breathing life into the barrenness of Eretz Israel.

But the groundswell that would grow into a tsunami was just beginning.

Chapter Two

Ben-Yehuda: The Language and the Land

1875—Luzhky, Lithuania

One night in 1875, a seventeen-year-old Jewish boy from Lithuania had a vision. "Light flashed across the sky, as if lightning struck. Then an incandescent light radiated before my eyes and I was transported to the passage of the Jordan where the Children of Israel crossed into the Promised Land. Suddenly a great voice rang in my ears and spoke three times the words, 'the return of the people to the language and the land.'"[46] He immediately understood the vision was a calling for him to restore Hebrew as the language in the Promised Land.

The boy was Eliezer Yitzhak Perelman. Later, as the vision became more focused in his mind, he adopted a Hebrew name, Eliezer Ben-Yehuda, and moved as a pioneer to Eretz Israel.

Early Life

Ben-Yehuda learned ancient Hebrew as part of his childhood religious studies—a common practice, although the language was used only for religious purposes. He was a gifted student, so his mother, hoping he would become a rabbi, sent him to a Talmudic academy. But like many young Jews of his day, his attention was drawn to the excitement of the secular world. He was accepted into a Russian high school in Moscow where he rose to the top of his class. As he grew to manhood in the bustle of Moscow, he was mesmerized by the modern world, forsaking many of his Jewish traditions. As graduation day approached, Ben-Yehuda told his mother he planned to be a medical doctor, not a rabbi.

That same year, the Russian Empire declared war on the Ottoman Empire to help their fellow Slavs, the Bulgarians, break free of Turkish rule. Ben-Yehuda suddenly saw the connection between the Bulgarians' struggle for an independent homeland and the Jews' desire to return to the land of their ancestors.

During the nineteenth century, several European ethnic groups, such as the Greeks and the Italians, had been given national sovereignty in the ancient land of their forefathers. It stood to reason, he concluded, that if the Bulgarians, who were not an ancient people, could be given a state of their own, then the Jews, whose roots went back more than 3,000 years, could petition for the same.

Ben-Yehuda knew Eretz Israel was mostly a barren wasteland, controlled by the same Ottoman Empire that held the Bulgarians in its grasp. He also understood that the scattered Jews didn't have a common spoken language. Then he remembered his childhood vision. His life's purpose became clear. He would go to Palestine to help revive Hebrew as a spoken language to unify his people under one common tongue.[47]

A Detour to Paris

After graduation, he left Russia in 1878 with a scholarship to study medicine in Paris. In addition to his linguistic work, he thought medical training would benefit the Jews of Palestine. While studying in Paris, Ben-Yehuda met fellow Jews who introduced him to a political movement that grew into Zionism. He was also introduced to the powerful Jewish leader Baron Rothschild.[48]

Ben-Yehuda's plans to be a doctor came to an abrupt halt when he started having coughing fits. After a thorough examination, his doctor gave him the devastating news that he had developed tuberculosis. The physician soberly predicted Ben-Yehuda would not live to celebrate his next birthday.

He immediately abandoned his studies and went searching for a cure. His newfound friend, Baron Rothschild, convinced him to travel to Algiers and sponsored his treatments. While convalescing in the Algerian sun one afternoon, Ben-Yehuda once again heard the call, "the land and the language." Again, he remembered his vision. "God doesn't want me to be in Paris," he realized. "He wants me to be what He showed me."

If God had truly given him this vision to revive the Hebrew tongue in Eretz Israel, Ben-Yehuda concluded, then He would keep him alive long enough to accomplish that goal. Returning to Paris, Ben-Yehuda shared his vision with Baron Rothschild. To his surprise, Rothschild agreed to help fund the young man's efforts in Palestine.

Before he left, he broke the news to his fiancée, Devora, through a letter to her father. "Dear Sir," he wrote, "I'm writing you this letter because I want you to break the news to your daughter that I have a mortal disease and I will not be able to marry her." But Devora refused to be jilted. Believing God had called them both to see this vision fulfilled, she insisted they be married.

On his arrival in the Holy Land, Ben-Yehuda was so filled with enthusiasm for his work he said it was like he was born again. "We have to bring God back to the land," he declared to his fellow Jews.

The few Jews who inhabited their ancient homeland were divided—not in spirit but because they spoke the various languages of the Diaspora. In an attempt to unify the people, Ben-Yehuda published a newspaper entirely in Hebrew.[49]

There wasn't even a Hebrew word for *newspaper*, or for many of the other common items used in modern life that didn't exist for the ancients. So Ben-Yehuda coined the new words himself using roots of ancient languages like Hebrew, Canaanite, and Arabic. The ancient Hebrew word *et* for *time* became *itone* for newspaper since a newspaper is a time-sensitive publication. A dictionary is a collection of words, and *word* in Hebrew is *mila*, so the dictionary became *milon*.[50]

Ben-Yehuda wrote about the pertinent news for the day, then in the back of his newspaper, he added a list of the new words used in that issue. He told the people, "I will only have the word listed once, so please cut out this list and keep it."[51] It wasn't long before the people clamored for a complete Hebrew dictionary.

THE HEBREW FIRST

But Ben-Yehuda didn't merely advocate Hebrew for the masses—he practiced what he preached in his own home. When his son, Ben-Zion, was born in 1882, Eliezer and Devora agreed to raise the boy as the first all-Hebrew speaking child in modern history. Ben-Yehuda insisted visitors speak only Hebrew so that when the child began to talk, he would be living proof that a revival of the language was possible.

This strict discipline caused strife between Devora and Eliezer. This was intensified by the fact that at age four, their son had not spoken a single word from any language.

Devora could no longer stand it, so one day while her husband was away she sang lullabies to the child in Russian. Eliezer arrived back earlier than he had intended and was outraged when he heard Russian being used in the house. He shouted at his wife to stop immediately.

"It caused a great shock to pass over me," young Ben-Zion later wrote, "when I saw my father in his anger and my mother in her grief and tears, and the muteness was removed from my lips." Crying out in Hebrew, the lad implored his father to stop yelling—and modern Hebrew was born.[52]

Because the child needed to speak about the common things in his life, Ben-Yehuda was forced to find new words on a continual basis. Soon he created words for everyday items like ice cream, jelly, omelet, handkerchief, towel, bicycle, and hundreds of other necessities. As the child grew, so did the modern Hebrew language.

Ben-Yehuda advocated a threefold plan for reviving Hebrew: "Hebrew in the home," "Hebrew in the school" and "Words, words, words."[53]

With the help of Nissim Bechar, principal of the Alliance Israelite Universelle in Jerusalem, Ben-Yehuda carried his crusade for Hebrew into the education system.

With the sudden influx of Jewish settlers, Bechar recognized the necessity of using Hebrew. For the first time, Jewish children from various nations studied in one common language. Within a short time, the children spoke the new language fluently.

"The Hebrew language will go from the synagogue to the house of study," Ben-Yehuda declared, "and from the house of study to the school, and from the school it will come into the home and become a living language."[54]

The task of reviving a language was monumental, so in 1890, Ben-Yehuda founded the Hebrew Language Council. This committee helped to solve problems raised in the writing of Ben-Yehuda's dictionary, including making decisions on final pronunciation, spelling, and punctuation. The group became the Hebrew Language Academy, the authority on all matters pertaining to the Hebrew language.[55]

A NECESSARY MIRACLE

Throughout Palestine, intelligent people soon began to see the wisdom in Ben-Yehuda's efforts. Collectively and spontaneously, Jews who were born and raised in various nations around the world decided to replace their own language with one that hadn't been spoken outside the synagogue for nearly 2,000 years.

It was a necessary miracle, but a miracle nonetheless.

The language provided unity, and unity provided common vision, and that common vision provided the human energy needed to bring a nation back to life.[56]

But the glory of this achievement was tempered by losses. In a tragic irony, the tuberculosis that Eliezer tried to keep from Devora took her life in 1891. Soon after his wife's death, tragedy struck again when three of their five children died of diphtheria.

Devora's final wish was that Eliezer marry her younger sister, Paula. Six months later, the two were married, and Paula took on a Hebrew name, Hemda. During the thirty years of their life together, she worked tirelessly with her husband. Together, their crowning achievement was the seventeen volumes of the *Ben-Yehuda Dictionary-Lexicon*.

Then, just one month before Ben-Yehuda's death in 1922, the British Colonial government officially recognized Hebrew as the language of the Palestinian Jews.

It was a time of pioneers in Palestine. Out of this persecution came the first giant wave of immigrants to Eretz Israel—and then a tidal wave that changed history forever.

Chapter Three

HERZL AND THE JEWISH STATE

1881—THE PALE OF SETTLEMENT

During the Diaspora, thousands of Jews were corralled into an oppressed region between the Baltic and the Black Seas known as the Pale of Settlement.[57] The majority of the world's Jews—more than five million—lived at this time in the Pale. Mostly forbidden to live in cities, they created their own villages called *shtetls*.[58] These tight-knit communities produced their own food and goods and traded mostly among themselves. In addition to Russian, they often spoke Yiddish, a combination of Hebrew and German.

Shunned by their hosts as a bizarre religious order, and often labeled "Christ killers," the Jews of Eastern Europe were subject to frequent violent and even deadly riots called *pogroms*—derived from the Russian phrase meaning "to destroy." This government-sanctioned force was a reminder to the Jews that they weren't truly Russian. They didn't belong.[59]

When Tsar Alexander II was assassinated in St. Petersburg in 1881 by a Russian left-wing terrorist organization, one Jewish girl was among the plotters. That was enough to unleash the hounds of hell on the Jewish population. Within a month, a tidal wave of violence against Jews washed across the Pale of Settlement.[60]

In response to this violent resurgence of anti-Semitic persecution, the First Zionist Aliyah to the Land of Israel began in 1882. This large-scale immigration continued from 1882 to 1903, and it included many members of a group known as Hovevei Zion.

The following year, the Jewish philosopher Nathan Birnbaum coined the term *Zionism* in a periodical promoting Hovevei Zion and the similar Bilu pioneer movement.[61] That same year, the design for the first Israeli flag was created in Rishon LeZion. Only four years later, in 1889, the first all-Hebrew school was established in Palestine.

Zionism became the engine of transformation in this dry and desolate land. In 1800, Ottoman Palestine was mostly a barren wasteland, with only 275,000 people. By 1900, that figure had doubled to half a million people.[62] In the following half century, the population of Palestine sky-rocketed as Jews poured in from the nations of the world, bringing with them their talent and their treasure. As time passed, Arabs and others also moved into Palestine attracted by the higher standard of living that emerged as a result of Zionist endeavors.

Early Settlements Emerge

In 1878, twenty-six Jerusalem Jewish families purchased a piece of land outside Jaffa and named the new settlement Petah Tikva, or "Gate of Hope." A leader of the group, Joel Moses Salomon, produced a periodical called *Judah and Jerusalem*, preaching the message, "Go out and work the land!" His vision was fulfilled with the help of two Hungarian Jews, Joshua Stampfer and David Guttman.

Stampfer recorded their humble beginnings. "The first chores were done collectively, with twelve yoke of oxen, five horses, and a few donkeys." The group dug a well and eventually hit water twenty meters down.[63]

The settlers had to temporarily evacuate when disease spread from a nearby malarial swamp. But with the financial help of Baron Edmond de Rothschild, they eventually drained the swamp and moved back in 1883. Other Russian immigrants also settled in Petah Tikva during this time, giving the settlement an important influx of human capital and energy.

In July 1882, the first group of fourteen Bilu pioneers arrived in Eretz Israel led by Israel Belkind. They joined Hovevei Zion members in establishing the settlement Rishon LeZion—an agricultural cooperative on land purchased from an Arab village.[64]

The settlers couldn't grow traditional crops in the sand dunes. If a plant took root, it was destroyed by a sandstorm. In desperation, the pioneers turned to Baron Rothschild for help. In addition to his financial contribution, he sent horticultural experts to discover which plants could survive in the harsh environment. They advised the settlers to plant citrus and grapes in the tropical climate.

It worked.

The settlers established a thriving citrus grove where Jews and Arabs worked side by side. Then Rothschild gave them grapevines from his own vineyard in France, the famous Chateau Lafite. These vines took root, and soon the Jews were making wine from their world-class vines. Rothschild sent experts to supervise the new Carmel winery, and eighteen years later, it won a gold medal at the Paris World's Fair.[65]

Other settlers arrived from Romania, Lithuania, Poland, and elsewhere. Settlements sprouted throughout the Holy Land in places such as Rosh Pina, Zikhron Yaakov, and Yesod Hamaala.[66] By 1900, Rothschild had invested in more than twenty agricultural settlements, earning the title, Father of the Yishuv.

THE SPREAD OF ZIONISM

As settlers built communities in Eretz Israel, Zionism took root around the world. The return to the land was in the heart of Jews everywhere.

The great Jewish leader Chaim Weizmann wrote of this time:

> In my early childhood Zionist ideas and aspirations were already awake in Russian Jewry. My father was not yet a Zionist, but the house was steeped in rich Jewish tradition, and Palestine was at the center of the ritual, a longing for it implicit in our life. Practical nationalism did not assume form till some years later, but the 'Return' was in the air, a vague, deep-rooted Messianism, a hope which would not die. We heard the conversations of our elders, and we were caught up in the restlessness.[67]

David Ben-Gurion observed, "Those great visionaries of Jewish revival did no more than give voice to the yearnings that pulsed in every Jewish heart in every generation."[68]

Theodor Herzl

Then in 1894, Theodor Herzl, an assimilated Jew and journalist from Vienna, witnessed what became known as the Dreyfus Affair. Suddenly, everything changed for him—and for Jewish people everywhere.

France had been the birthplace of Jewish emancipation, an outgrowth of the Enlightenment. But this scandal involved a Jewish army captain, Alfred Dreyfus, accused of espionage. The anti-Semitism that surrounded his arrest and trial shocked the Jewish world, including Herzl, who served as the Paris correspondent of the *Neue Freie Presse* of Vienna. As a reporter, Herzl had a front-row seat for the trial. The hatred directed toward this officer, simply because he was Jewish, awoke Herzl from years of daydreaming as an assimilated playboy and set him on the path toward Zionism.

An improbable prophet, Herzl was born in Budapest in 1860 to an upper middle-class family. At the time, the city was known as "Judapest" due to its large Jewish population.[69] Near their house stood the liberal reform temple that young Theodor attended with his father, Jacob, on Sabbaths and Holy Days. Jewish rituals were observed in the Herzl home, with particular emphasis on the celebration of Hanukkah and Passover.[70]

Theodor's grandfather, Simon, was an observant Jew, scrupulously following the ancient commandments. He sounded the Shofar on Rosh Hashanah and led his local congregation in the *Kol Nidre*, an Aramaic declaration recited in the evening service on Yom Kippur.

Theodor's father remained connected to his Jewish heritage but gave most of his attention to business. By age thirty-five, Jacob was a director for the Hungarian Bank in the city of Pest—before it merged with neighboring Buda, becoming Budapest.[71]

The strongest influence on young Theodor, though, was his mother, Jeannette. Educated in the classics, she quoted from German literature every day. Although a Jew, she imparted her German heritage to her children and passed on her sense of form, bearing, tactfulness, and simple grace.[72] In later years, these attributes helped catapult Theodor to a position of leadership in the Zionist movement.[73]

One day in 1866, one of Theodor's teachers read the story of the exodus from the Bible, but his features didn't show a spark of emotion. Theodor concluded from his teacher's demeanor that this was nothing more than a fairy tale. His first profound impression was replaced by dislike, and it planted a seed of skepticism.[74]

When he was twelve, Herzl read about the King-Messiah in a German book. Most Jews awaited this prophetic figure who would come riding like the poorest of the poor on a donkey. As he read this intriguing book, he remembered the exodus story. His creative mind wove the two tales together, inspiring him to concoct a wonderful story. But when he tried to write it down, he couldn't complete it to his satisfaction. A short time later, Herzl had a dream about this King-Messiah:[75]

> The King-Messiah came, a glorious and majestic old man, took me in his arms, and swept off with me on the wings of the wind. On one of the iridescent clouds we encountered the figure of Moses. The Messiah called to Moses: It is for this child that I have prayed. But to me he said: Go, declare to the Jews that I shall come soon and perform great wonders and great deeds for my people and for the whole world.[76]

Herzl never mentioned the dream to anyone until six months before his death when he shared it with fellow writer Reuben Brainin.

Herzl celebrated his Bar Mitzvah at the Reform Temple one year after having the dream. Herr and Frau Herzl invited relatives and friends to the "confirmation," as it had come to be called in European Reform congregations.[77] Despite this official passing from boyhood, Herzl had fallen into a state of discontent.

His parents enrolled him in a technical school after he expressed dreams of one day building a canal across Panama to connect the Atlantic and Pacific Oceans. Modern marvels fired young Herzl's imagination. But despite his power to dream, young Theodor soon discovered he didn't have the desire or technical ability to pursue engineering.

He displayed a dazzling imagination, but it was in the description of the technology, not in the invention of it. What interested him was not so much the machinery, but its ability to solve human problems.

Recognizing this aspect of his personality, Herzl decided to leave the technical school. For the next few months, he was instructed by private tutors. Freed from the distractions of his fellow students and the undercurrent of anti-Semitism from his teachers, he devoted himself to the study of ancient languages and culture. Within a year, he acquired a foundation in Latin and Greek. He enrolled in the Evangelical High School and pursued his interest in literature, language, and culture with vigor. He also began to write in earnest—essays, books, poems, and theater reviews.[78]

During this time, he drifted away from the Jewish community. Try as he may to break away from his heritage, though, anti-Semitism was a constant reminder of who he was.[79]

Among friends and colleagues, he was always elegantly groomed in the latest fashion, ever jovial, seemingly untouched by the troubles of the world. He often displayed a cynical air and a mocking demeanor. Eventually, he embraced the spirit of the Gilded Age, becoming a complete nihilist. It seemed nothing was sacred.

But Herzl's writing from the period revealed the compassionate side of his personality. "I have thought much," he wrote in 1878, "on the purpose of human existence, the highest manifestation of life on earth."

TRAGEDY STRIKES

This quest for life's meaning coincided with the tragic death of his older sister and best friend, Pauline, of typhoid fever. She had been an ever-present encouragement. After her death, Theodor guarded her every keepsake.[80]

Herzl's mother, Jeannette, couldn't bear the thought of remaining in the home that held so many memories of her daughter. Within a week of Pauline's death, the family packed everything and moved to Vienna. Theodor returned only once to Budapest to take his final examination at school. After that trip, Herzl never again went back to his boyhood home.[81]

Soon Herzl announced his decision to become a writer. A local rabbi, paying respects to the family, commented that writing was not really a profession. Herzl's parents agreed, though they encouraged him to write as a hobby. They felt a writer needed an economic basis in some other job, so they persuaded Theodor to enroll in law school at the University of Vienna.

There he became aware of the dramatic resurgence of anti-Semitism in the Germanic countries. Jews were accused of dominating national life, holding unhealthy control over finance, and conducting themselves in an alien, insufficiently German manner. In 1881, a group calling itself the Anti-Semitic League lobbied Chancellor Otto von Bismarck to disenfranchise the Jews and halt their further immigration. An Anti-Jewish Congress was held in Dresden.

Herzl's personal solution for anti-Semitism was assimilation. He believed if you dressed like a Gentile, talked like a Gentile, and lived like a Gentile, then they would accept you.

But then in 1881, he read Eugen Duhring's book *The Jewish Problem as a Problem of Race, Morals, and Culture*.[82] Herzl was shocked by Duhring's assertion that the Jews were a race without worth. Duhring believed those peoples that had permitted the Jews to live among them with equal rights had to be de-Judaized. Intermarriage with Jews should be forbidden, if possible—and if not, then severely ostracized. There was to be a complete reversal of the emancipation given to the Jews in the Enlightenment.[83]

Herzl wrote with indignation in his diary: "An infamous book ... If Duhring, who unites so much undeniable intelligence with so much universality of knowledge, can write like this, what are we to expect from the ignorant masses?"

The veil of illusion had been ripped from his eyes, and a lifelong preoccupation with the plight of his fellow Jews began.

A FULL-TIME WRITER

In July 1884, Herzl completed his studies and was admitted to the bar in Vienna. He went to work as a lawyer, but his heart wasn't in it. Then in 1891, after years of struggle, Herzl's feature article on St. Jean de Luz created a sensation after appearing in the *Neue Freie Presse*. The editors were so impressed they hired Herzl as their Paris correspondent.[84]

Herzl immediately moved to Paris.

The editors asked Herzl to cover French domestic and foreign politics, but he was free to submit articles on art and literature, finance, and even social events. Herzl had become a professional writer, and he had the salary and prestige to go along with it. Living in Paris, he became a connoisseur of opera and theater. By his own admission, he was a bit of a playboy.

But Herzl couldn't escape the virulent anti-Semitism re-emerging in France, just as it had in Germany and Austria. In 1885, the Frenchman Edouard Drumont published *La France Juive*, which sold more than one hundred thousand editions in its first year. According to Drumont, the emancipation of the Jews was a tragic blunder. The Jews of France weren't Frenchmen, but guests who exploited the economic system for their own benefit and for world domination. With their "unclean racial characteristics," they corrupted the spirit of France and were responsible for the decadence in the nation. As an alien people, their assimilation was impossible.

Drumont recommended Jewish emancipation be withdrawn, their possessions confiscated, and the proceeds applied to the creation of means of production for the exploited working classes.[85]

This renewed hatred for the Jews had a chilling effect on Herzl. His initial reaction was radical assimilation. The solution could only come through the complete disappearance of the Jews through baptism and intermarriage. "When I think of my son's future, I ask myself whether I have the right to make life so difficult for him as it has become for me. That is why we must baptize Jewish children while they can still feel nothing, either for it, or against it. We Jews must submerge in the people."[86]

Other Jews were shocked at these radical statements. Industrialist Baron Friedrich Leitenberger issued a harsh response: "... That all Jews without exception should get themselves baptized is really nothing more than charming salon chatter. It is not the kind of thing to be taken into serious consideration by earnest men who have made up their minds to proceed in all seriousness against the racial war."

The strong response surprised Herzl, but he continued promoting a plan of mass conversion.[87] He asked the editors of the *Neue Freie Presse* to reach out to the pope. "Help us against anti-Semitism," he proposed, "and I in return will lead a great movement amongst the Jews for voluntary and honorable conversion to Christianity."

Herzl's editor, Moritz Benedikt, responded like a father to a son. "Throughout one hundred generations your people has sustained itself as Jews. And *you* want to become the limit of that process. That is something which you cannot and may not do."[88]

After thorough reflection on Benedikt's advice, Herzl realized his proposed solution was unrealistic.

The Dreyfus trial further solidified Herzl's slow conversion to Zionism. At first, it looked like a cut-and-dried case of espionage. No one had reason to doubt Dreyfus was guilty, even though Drumont's anti-Semitic newspaper, *Libre Parole*, trumpeted his Jewish identity.[89] On December 6, Herzl wired his paper the final results of the preliminary investigation. Dreyfus denied having written the note on which the prosecution was basing its case, and the handwriting experts split on the actual authorship.

It was an important story, but the public interest and excitement surrounding the affair surprised Herzl. When the trial began on December 19, 1894, he posted his observations from the courtroom in the *Neue Freie Presse*.

Then came the verdict. The court-martial unanimously declared Dreyfus guilty.[90] On January 5, 1895, Herzl watched as he was stripped of his medals and publicly degraded. Crowds filled the streets yelling, "Death to the traitor!"

But then the mood changed, and many started chanting: "Death to the Jews. Death to all Jews."[91] Herzl's eyes were forever opened to the true state of the Jews in exile. He said that he left in a state "of curious excitement."[92]

"We are a people living perpetually in enemy territory," Herzl wrote after witnessing the ugly scene. The truth finally sank in—nothing could save the Jew from anti-Semitism. He now fully understood he was hated because he was different.[93]

> The Dreyfus case embodies more than a judicial error; it embodies the desire of the vast majority of the French to condemn a Jew, and to condemn all Jews in this one Jew. "Death to the Jews!" howled the mob, as the decorations were being ripped

from the captain's coat. Where? In France. In republican, modern, civilized France, a hundred years after the Declaration of the Rights of Man. The French people, or at any rate the greater part of the French people, does not want to extend the rights of man to Jews. The edict of the great Revolution has been revoked.[94]

Anti-Semitism had turned Herzl himself from a darling of Vienna's literary salons, at home in the non-Jewish world, into a man dedicated to the cause of a Jewish homeland.[95] But Dreyfus had been an assimilated Jew, proud of his military uniform, and in the end, this had made no difference.

Although Herzl believed him innocent, Dreyfus was on his way to prison on Devil's Island. Herzl finally concluded that assimilation could not be the answer. It could bring an end to Judaism but not to anti-Semitism. The only real solution to the problem was a modern exodus of Jews to a land where they could live their lives, practice their religion, and build a culture apart from Gentiles.

Herzl the literary playboy had transformed into Herzl the Zionist.

THE JEWISH STATE

With this newfound revelation, Herzl shut himself in his apartment and wrote his ideas for five straight days. As an assimilated Jew, he knew nothing of the Hovevei Zion or Bilu Pioneer movements settling Jews in Palestine. He hadn't read any of the pamphlets or theories of the back-to-Palestine faction. He had become so removed from the community of Jewish thought that he believed he needed to invent Zionism independently.

When a friend visited, he was alarmed by Herzl's disheveled appearance and the wild ideas he was spouting. He suggested they go for a walk to get some fresh air. As they walked, he advised Herzl to seek medical help before someone hauled him off to the madhouse.[96] Herzl paid no attention, and upon his return to the apartment, he continued writing the ideas that were boiling over in his head. From this manic episode, he produced what would become his manifesto, *Der Judenstaat*, or *The Jewish State*.[97]

In many ways, the booklet came across as simplistic, but it captured the imagination of the masses and became a significant step toward establishing a homeland in Eretz Israel.[98]

"I believe that a wondrous generation of Jews will spring into existence," he wrote. "The Maccabeans will rise again … The Jews who wish for a State will have it. We shall live at last as free men on our own soil, and die peacefully in our own homes. The world will be freed by our liberty, enriched by our wealth, magnified by our greatness. And whatever we attempt there to accomplish for our own welfare, will react powerfully and beneficially for the good of humanity."[99]

The Jewish world was rocked with the publication of *The Jewish State*. Recognizing this as a turning point in Jewish history, Chaim Weizmann described Herzl's work as "… an utterance which came like a bolt from the blue." Weizmann declared:

> Fundamentally, *The Jewish State* contained not a single new idea for us … That which so startled the Jewish bourgeoisie, and called down the resentment and derision of the Western Rabbis, had long been the substance of our Zionist tradition … If Herzl had contented himself with the mere publication of the booklet—as he originally intended to do, before it became clear to him that he was no longer his own master, but the servant of the idea—his name would be remembered today as one of the oddities of Jewish history. What has given greatness to his name is Herzl's role as a man of action, as the founder of the Zionist Congress, and as an example of daring and devotion … Yet the effect produced by *The Jewish State* was profound. Not the ideas, but the personality which stood behind them appealed to us. Here was daring, clarity and energy.[100]

In *The Jewish State*, Herzl called for a self-governing Jewish republic outside Europe. Palestine was a preferable location for historical reasons, but Herzl had no strong commitment to ancient Zion. He thought Argentina might be just as satisfactory.[101] "We shall take what we are offered," he wrote a friend. In Herzl's master plan, lower-class Jews would be shipped out first to build roads and houses. The middle class would follow when accommodations were ready. There would be a Jewish army of defense. Thrift and hard work were to be encouraged in every way. A corporation would be set up in London to handle the raising of capital for the project.

David Ben-Gurion wrote of the impact Herzl made on his generation:

> My father, a lawyer and a prominent member of the Jewish community, he called himself a "Lover of Zion." Before Herzl, he and his friends would meet frequently at our house and one would hear repeated over and over the phrase "The Land of Israel." But all the Jews of my age in Europe northeast of the Danube favored the idea of taking matters to the logical conclusion: emigration and active building of Eretz Israel rather than mere talk, dreams, or passive waiting for the magic fulfillment of prophecies.[102]

Through Herzl's efforts, the Jewish problem was raised to the level of an international question that must be given consideration by enlightened statesmanship.[103] The sentiments of *The Jewish State* might have remained no more than a dream, except for Herzl's newfound messianic fervor. A man of great presence, with formidable speaking abilities, Herzl was now charged with a sense of mission—and he devoted the rest of his life to seeing that mission to completion.

Chapter Four

HERZL AND THE ZIONIST MOVEMENT

1896—VIENNA, AUSTRIA

The year 1896 was a turning point for Theodor Herzl—and through him, Jews everywhere.

He was a different person. The cocoon of assimilation fell off and the Zionist emerged. *The Jewish State* soon became a worldwide phenomenon, thrusting Herzl into a position of leadership among Jews in Europe. He instinctively knew the Jews had to unify if they were to establish a homeland.

Herzl's ideas, rhetoric, and energy were so infectious he drew thousands of Zionists out of their lethargy. People who had harbored a theoretical hope for a Jewish homeland allowed themselves to dream it could be possible in their lifetime.

The Jewish State's success opened the door for him to meet influential people. One of them was Rev. William Hechler, chaplain to the English Embassy in Vienna. He had written *The Restoration of the Jews to Palestine According to the Prophets*.[104] At their first meeting in March 1896, Herzl explained the most important objective was to meet with government officials to advocate on the Jews' behalf. If he could build a list of high-level connections, then perhaps the Jews would follow him.

For Herzl, however, the grand prize would be meeting the German kaiser.

Hechler immediately agreed to help Herzl. Hechler had tutored the children of the grand duke of Baden—and he was a friend of the duke's nephew, the kaiser—so he immediately made plans to travel to Berlin.

The Grand Duke

After a week spent in suspenseful waiting, Herzl received a telegram from Hechler informing him that the grand duke would receive him. Herzl carefully prepared for this important audience.

When he finally stood in the grand duke's presence, Herzl was touched by his "quiet goodness … noble modesty, and … deep faith."

"If some of the royal heads of states were prepared to express their benevolent attitude toward the movement," Herzl explained, "The Society of Jews could start out with greater authority, and the migration could be organized more rapidly and with greater discipline."[105]

The duke was intrigued but suggested it would be better to create the Society of Jews first. He made it clear that his attitude was one of benevolence, but since the plan was to promote the migration of the Jews from Europe, he did not want to be seen as driving them out in an anti-Semitic push.

Hechler suggested the grand duke give Herzl permission to publicize his support of a homeland for the Jews in Palestine. Won over by Herzl, the duke agreed.

Not everyone was thrilled with Herzl's ideas, however. Some religious Jews thought it blasphemy to reestablish the nation of Israel without the Messiah.[106] Other assimilated Jews didn't want some rabble-rouser making trouble.

Despite this opposition, Herzl worked tirelessly to realize his vision. He labored to find a way to be introduced to the sultan of Turkey. His plan was to literally buy the Land of Israel, obtaining the money from wealthy Jews, so he decided to travel to Istanbul.[107]

His childhood vision of the King-Messiah began to make sense.[108]

Herzl reached out to a fellow journalist, Philip Michael Ritter von Nevlinski, a former Polish diplomat.[109] In June 1896, Herzl traveled with Nevlinski to Constantinople where they met with high-level government officials, including the vizier.

THE PLAN FOR PALESTINE

The finances of the Ottoman Empire had been in shambles since the middle of the nineteenth century, with the government owing more than £106 million to foreign lenders. To pay this debt, a group of creditors known as the Administrative Council of the Public Debt was empowered to collect taxes from profitable Turkish industries. This arrangement was an embarrassment for a sovereign nation, so Herzl proposed the elimination of this debt by giving Palestine to the Jews who, in turn, would pay off the creditors.

Despite Herzl's favorable meetings, the sultan refused to meet with him. It became clear that the Turkish leader would not give up sovereignty over Palestine. There was, however, a glimmer of hope when officials told Herzl and Nevlinski that if they could obtain financial backing from the Jews, they might obtain Palestine, not as an independent nation but as a vassal state within the Ottoman Empire.

Herzl left Constantinople satisfied with their progress. He moved on to England, where he would set in motion his plans to establish the Society of Jews.[110]

Despite an initially cool reception by wealthy Jewish leaders, Herzl secured a tentative agreement from Sir Samuel Montague and Colonel Goldsmith to work with him. They had specific conditions: if the international powers agreed; if the Baron de Hirsh Fund would place its £10 million at the disposal of the plan; and if Baron Edmund de Rothschild entered the executive committee of The Society of the Jews.

Herzl traveled to Paris to meet with Baron Rothschild. He promised Rothschild the leadership of the Society if he carried forward the work of securing Palestine for Jewish settlement. Rothschild was not moved. He did not believe it possible to oversee a mass migration of Jews to Eretz Israel. The baron believed it best to stay the course of slow colonization.

Rothschild's refusal carried with it the rejection of the Hirsch Fund and the leading Jews of London. This put an end to the hope of striking a deal with the sultan.

Herzl decided the time had come to move forward at the grassroots level. "There is only one reply to this situation," he wrote to his secretary in London. "Let us organize our masses immediately."[111]

The First Zionist Congress

Earlier in 1896, a doctor detected a problem with Herzl's heart. As 1897 commenced, Herzl sensed his strength waning as he suffered from cardiac arrhythmia.[112] After weeks of melancholy, Herzl finally looked death in the face and determined to use it as motivation to finish his life's work.

Herzl had contemplated the idea of a General Zionist Conference. Such a gathering would be a way to survey the current state of the human capital at his disposal and to gather information on the readiness of the Jewish people to make the move to Palestine.[113]

As a result of the popularity of *The Jewish State*, Jews from all over the world answered Herzl's call. The nascent movement had little money and virtually no political leverage. Yet in August, 197 delegates from seventeen countries arrived in Basel—the first representative Jewish assembly in nearly 2,000 years.[114]

Behind the podium hung a white flag with two blue stripes and a Star of David.[115] Dr. Lippe of Jassy, a member of Hovevei Zion since the founding of the first colony in Palestine, opened the congress by speaking the *Sheheheyanu* prayer: "Blessed art Thou, O Lord our God, King of the Universe, who has kept us alive and brought us to witness this day."

Herzl then rose and walked to the podium. "We are here to lay the foundation stone of the House, which is to shelter the Jewish nation." With this statement, wild applause broke out. The delegates cheered and stomped their feet for fifteen minutes.[116] One English delegate described the excitement of the crowd: "By the rivers of Babylon we sat down and wept as we remembered Zion. By the rivers of Basel, we sat down and resolved to weep no more."[117]

"The feeling of unity among us," Herzl declared, "was in process of dissolution when the tide of anti-Semitism rose about us. Anti-Semitism has given us our strength again. We have returned home. Zionism is the return of the Jews to Judaism even before their return to the Jewish land."[118]

He called for acquisition of an internationally recognized legal right to colonize Palestine, along with the formation of a permanent large-scale migration to Palestine.[119]

During the Congress, calls were made for the promotion of Jewish settlement in Palestine, the organization of Jews in the Diaspora, the strengthening of a worldwide Jewish consciousness, and the preparatory steps to attain the necessary governmental grants.[120]

Action during the Congress included the official founding of The Zionist Organization with Theodor Herzl serving as president. Out of this new institution, Herzl hoped a governmental structure would evolve to help lead the eventual state.[121]

As the Congress drew to a conclusion, Professor Max Mandelstamm, one of the oldest delegates, asked for the floor. In a quivering voice, full of emotion, he thanked all those who had contributed toward the creation and success of the Congress. "But above all," he continued, "to that courageous man who is primarily responsible for this gathering of Jews from all countries taking counsel on the future of our people."

The delegates sprang to their feet and shouts of admiration and gratitude rose for Herzl. When the applause subsided, Herzl pleaded with the delegates to carry out this mission to establish a homeland for the Jews in Eretz Israel in the face of all discouragement until their dream was fulfilled. With this, Herzl closed the Congress.[122]

After the First Jewish Congress ended, Herzl wrote in his journal: "At Basel I created the Jewish State. Were I to say this aloud I would be greeted by universal laughter. But perhaps five years hence, in any case, certainly in fifty years hence, everyone will perceive it."[123]

PERSUADING THE SULTAN

The consensus of the First Jewish Congress was that Turkey needed to be persuaded to give Palestine to the Jews. The Ottoman Empire was crumbling, the government was nearly bankrupt, and the sultan with his corrupt viziers had no vision for the future. It was unlikely they could be persuaded to give away any territory.[124]

To seek a solution, Herzl met with Ahmed Tewfik, the Turkish ambassador in Berlin. Tewfik made it clear the Turks opposed any type of settlement by Jews in Palestine that could lead to the growth of towns or cities. If there were colonization at all, it would have to be scattered. There could be no talk of a Jewish territory or Jewish autonomy. Herzl rejected the proposal outright.

In 1898, the Second Zionist Congress laid the foundations for the formation of the Jewish Colonial Trust, later the Anglo-Palestine Bank in London, which served as the agent for soliciting contributions from wealthy Jews and sympathetic Gentiles.[125]

Herzl finally arranged a meeting with the kaiser in Palestine. At Mikveh Israel, pupils assembled with Herzl and local settlers in front of the school to greet the German emperor. To the crowd's astonishment, the kaiser rode his horse directly to Herzl and greeted him.[126]

> "How are you?" he asked from the saddle.
>
> "I thank Your Majesty. I am taking a look at the country. How has Your Majesty's journey been till now?"
>
> "Very hot! But the land has a future," the kaiser responded.
>
> "For the moment, it is still sick," said Herzl.
>
> "It needs water," answered the German leader, "plenty of water."
>
> "Yes, Your Majesty, large scale irrigation."
>
> "It is a land with a future," repeated the kaiser. He extended his hand again to Herzl and, while the students sang the German Imperial hymn, he rode off.[127]

For a while, the kaiser seemed interested in pressuring the sultan, even offering German protection to a new Jewish state. But the German leader made an abrupt about-face that shocked everyone. On his way home from Palestine, Herzl received a German communiqué stating that the kaiser viewed with benevolent interest all efforts directed toward the improvement of agriculture in Palestine as long as these accorded with the welfare of the Turkish Empire, and were conducted in a spirit of complete respect for the sovereignty of the sultan.[128]

Herzl realized that Kaiser Wilhelm was a theatrical personality who spoke of plans and purpose with great interest. But after reflecting on the possible international consequences, the kaiser's convictions melted away.[129]

Herzl struggled on, but he felt time was running out as his heart continued to weaken. Drained by fatigue, confronted by opposition from inside and outside the Zionist Cause, he somehow found strength to soldier on. Then in May 1901, he finally obtained an audience with the sultan—not as a Zionist but as a journalist.

The sultan opened their meeting by telling Herzl he was a devoted reader of the *Neue Freie Presse* and was pleased by the friendly relations between Turkey and Austria. Herzl answered that he was devoted to the sultan, as the Turkish leader was a good friend of the Jews. The sultan answered that his empire had always been open as a refuge to Jews.

Herzl took advantage of this friendly opening from the sultan. "When I was informed that His Majesty would receive me, I could not help thinking of the charming old fable of Androcles and the lion. His Majesty is the lion, and I am Androcles. Perhaps there is a thorn which I could withdraw."[130]

"I consider the Public Debt the thorn," Herzl continued. "If this could be removed, then the life-strength of Turkey, in which I have great faith, would unfold anew." The sultan said he had tried in vain to remove this thorn, which had been left to him by his predecessor.[131]

Herzl proceeded. "What this land needs is the industrial initiative of our people. Other Europeans who come here become rich quickly and run away with their booty. Certainly one should make an honest and decent profit out of any enterprise, but one should remain in the country where one's fortune has been made." Herzl explained the general outline of his plan, and he highlighted what could be done through cooperation with the Jews. The sultan listened and agreed to continue discussions of possible cooperation.[132]

A few days later, Herzl continued his conversation with two leading viziers. Herzl's proposal of an official charter was taken to the sultan for his consideration. Soon an official returned with the sultan's reply and a fond farewell: "The sultan expects your positive proposals in the next four weeks."

At the Fifth Zionist Congress in December 1901, Herzl reported on his audience with the sultan. "The attitude and the language of His Majesty gave me the feeling that in the ruling Khalif, the Jewish people have a friend and protector."[133]

Herzl also announced the establishment of the National Fund, the Zionist Bank, and the overall structure of the Zionist Organization. "Our institutions are, to a large extent, only outlined—they are certainly subject to improvement—but they exist."[134]

After months of negotiations between Herzl and the sultan's officials, however, it became painfully clear that the Jews were not being offered unrestricted immigration into Palestine. The best they were able to get from Constantinople was a weak offer to settle in the wastes of Mesopotamia. Herzl abandoned the talks.

The British Offer

In October 1902, Herzl shifted his attention toward Great Britain, a powerful, tolerant, and progressive empire. Many British abhorred the anti-Semitism growing in Europe. Herzl surmised that surely they could spare a little of their global empire for the Jews. They could not give him Palestine since it belonged to the Turks, but the British did have a protectorate over Egypt as a result of their interest in the Suez Canal. Herzl wondered if this seemingly benevolent empire could be persuaded to cede the Sinai Peninsula.

Most of the Sinai was desert, but the Mediterranean coastal strip could be populated. This was especially true in the area around the town of El Arish. The Sinai was next door to Palestine, so work could continue nearby in pursuit of a return to the Holy Land.

The British government was willing to listen to Herzl because a potential problem was developing in London, where thousands of Jewish refugees from Russia were filling the tenements of the East End.[135] This situation created a resurrected fear of foreigners that had some people talking of limiting immigration across the board. If the government could help find a more permanent spot for persecuted Jews, it might be able to avoid a new round of anti-Semitism—something they considered to be un-British.

Herzl presented his proposal to Colonial Secretary Joseph Chamberlain, who thought El Arish had potential. He referred Herzl to the British Foreign Office, which investigated the possibility. Herzl immediately dispatched a Zionist committee to El Arish to see if it was suitable for habitation.

Like the spies in the days of Moses, the committee came back with a negative report. They believed El Arish lacked a reliable water supply for a large population. The British Foreign Office brought a second bit of bad news when it reported that it could not transfer the Sinai territory to anyone without the permission of Turkey, which nominally had sovereignty over Egypt. Beyond this, the Egyptian people were firmly against the idea of planting a Jewish state next door to them—especially if it meant giving up their own territory.[136]

THE KISHINEV POGROM

In the spring of 1903, the need became even more urgent as the world learned of a brutal massacre in Russia. On Easter Sunday, a group of Russian men entered the Jewish quarter of the village of Kishinev. Led by their priest, they shouted, "Death to the Jews"—the same cry Herzl had heard in Paris. Eyewitnesses described the bloody massacre that followed. Families were shot down together. Children had their brains beaten out in front of their parents. By the end of the day, the streets were filled with dozens of murdered Jews.[137]

The Jews of Kishinev were delivered up to the fury of a mob organized and supported by the government. After two full days of mayhem, the infamous Vyacheslav von Plehve, Minister of the Interior, ordered the military to intervene and halt the carnage. When the violence ended, forty-five Jews had been killed, eighty-six wounded, and 1,500 homes and shops destroyed.[138]

A wave of despair swept over the Russian Jewish community, augmented by feelings of both humiliation and impotence. "The Kishinev pogrom was the reply of Tsarist Russia to the cry of freedom of its Jewish subjects," Russian Zionist leader Chaim Weizmann wrote. "We knew intuitively that it was not to be the last, but was rather the signal for a whole series. The massacres were deliberately organized, carefully planned, and carried out under the eyes of the civil and military authorities, who stepped in only when they judged that the slaughter and pillaging had gone far enough."

Herzl was devastated when he received the news. With his heart growing noticeably weaker and painful attacks increasing, Herzl felt encircled by the shadow of death. He was anxious to bring a measure of practical accomplishment to the Jewish people, even if it necessitated a detour from the goal of a Jewish homeland in Palestine.

As the time for the Sixth Zionist Congress approached, rumors of political negotiations with England abounded. After the Kishinev pogrom, Joseph Chamberlain, Great Britian's colonial secretary, shocked Herzl by offering a huge tract of land to the Jews in British East Africa, now Uganda.

Fearing more pogroms, Herzl believed he had to accept the offer to give his people a safe haven. The British drew up a plan for a colony they called "New Palestine."[139] As the colonial secretary's word was binding, this was a bona fide offer. In August 1903, Herzl came before the Sixth Zionist Congress with a written commitment from the British government.

Since the First Zionist Congress, it had always been the custom to hang a map of Eretz Israel on the wall behind the president's chair. As delegates entered the hall, they immediately noticed this had been replaced by a map of Uganda.[140] This symbolic message set an ominous tone for many of the delegates.

Herzl opened his address by painting a picture of the rising persecution, which the delegates knew only too well. He proposed bringing immediate relief by enabling large-scale emigration for the Jews facing imminent danger. Emergency measures were needed, he insisted. Herzl didn't relinquish the idea of Palestine as the Jewish homeland. But as far as the immediate problem was concerned, something of great significance had developed. With great power in his voice, he announced that the British government had offered to give the Jews a large, fertile territory in British East Africa.

The announcement sent a shockwave through the delegates.

"Admittedly British East Africa is not Zion," Herzl said. This was only an auxiliary activity to give immediate protection to Jews who faced persecution. But times were harsh, Russian Jews were in distress, and this tract in Africa offered an immediate answer, a resting place on the road back to Palestine.[141]

Anticipating opposition on the floor of the Congress, Herzl didn't submit the proposition that the British offer be accepted, but he cushioned the proposal by suggesting the Congress send an investigative commission to the territory to report on its suitability.[142]

Like a dark, foreboding storm front sweeping in from the sea, anxiety spread through the Congress. It was one thing to talk of Uganda as a way station or as a temporary measure, but if the prospect were actually adopted, it would mean deflecting the energies of the Jewish people from the development and population of Eretz Israel to the building of a national home for the Jews in Uganda.

Despite Herzl's best intentions, this proposed relief effort for persecuted Jews would mean the practical dismantling of the Zionist Organization and its pursuit of building a Jewish homeland in Zion itself. Many Zionist leaders, particularly from Eastern Europe and Russia, wondered how Herzl could contemplate such a shift.

Everyone understood the symbolic significance of Herzl's plea. A deep and passionate division manifested itself. When the first session concluded, the delegates scattered to their caucuses. As the audience exited the great hall, a young woman ran up onto the platform and tore down the map of Uganda.[143]

Weizmann met with the caucus of the Russian delegation. Some favored the Uganda proposal: "What have we to lose by accepting Uganda? The British are a great people. It is a great government which makes the offer. We must not offend a great government by refusing."

Weizmann was not moved by these sentiments. "We know that Palestine cannot be obtained in short order, and that is why we do not despair if this or that particular attempt fails. If the British Government and people are what I think they are, they will make us a better offer."

This last sentence became a slogan for the anti-Ugandists. Weizmann's speech made a strong impression, and when the Congress reconvened, the anti-Uganda forces came in united.[144]

The vote on the resolution was by roll call. Every delegate had to say yes or no. The replies fell like hammer blows. Two hundred and ninety-five delegates voted yes, while one hundred and seventy-five voted no. One hundred members abstained.[145] The majority of negative votes came from the Russian delegation.

To the astonishment of many in the West, the delegates from Kishinev were firmly against the Uganda offer.

When the result of the roll call was announced, the Russian members of the Actions Committee stood and left the platform, followed by the majority of the Russian delegates. Some older statesmen wept openly. As the dissidents assembled in a different hall, some were so distressed they sat down on the floor in the manner of ritual mourning for the dead.[146]

"As we sat in caucus," Weizmann recalled, "depressed, our hearts filled with bitterness, a message was brought in that Herzl would like to speak to us. He came in, looking haggard and exhausted. He was received in dead silence. Nobody rose from his seat to greet him. He understood, he said, that this was merely a spontaneous demonstration and not a secession, and he invited us to return."[147]

Herzl reassured the group of his unswerving devotion to Palestine. "I don't have to tell you, of all people, of the urgent need for finding an immediate refuge for large masses of homeless Jews." He turned and left the room, but the Russians' silence sent a loud message.

Later, Herzl approached a group of delegates in the lobby. "These people have a rope around their necks," he said of the Russians, "and still they refuse!"

The young lady who had torn down the map of Uganda stood nearby and heard what he said. She exclaimed, "*Monsieur le Président, vous êtes un traître!*" Shocked, Herzl turned and rushed from the lobby in anger.

Herzl had a majority for the Uganda proposal, but it was clear that acceptance of the British offer would be futile. The vote had been too close.

Besides, the people for whom British East Africa was intended—the op-pressed Russians—did not want it. They would not give up the dream of Zion.

Herzl returned to the grand hall and closed the Sixth Zionist Congress by raising his right hand and reciting Psalm 137:5: "If I forget thee, O Jerusalem, may my right hand forget its skill." They were the last words he spoke at the podium of a Jewish Congress.

In the following months, his health declined rapidly. He told his friend Rev. Hechler, "Greet Palestine for me. I gave my heart's blood for my people." He died the next day, July 3, 1904, at the age of forty-four.[148]

It turned out Uganda was a mirage after all. The British settlers there were alarmed at the prospect of Jewish immigration. They sent up an outcry to the government in London. When Chamberlain left the Colo-nial Office, the offer was quietly withdrawn.[149]

Herzl was like a meteor streaking across the night sky to light the way and then disappearing from view. He had attempted great things for his people, and he had restored to them the vision of attaining their home-land in Eretz Israel. In a prophetic statement in *The Jewish State*, he de-clared, "If you will it, it is no dream."[150]

Chapter Five

WEIZMANN, BALFOUR, AND CHURCHILL

"Miracles sometimes occur, but one has to work
terribly hard for them."

Chaim Weizmann

1904—MANCHESTER, ENGLAND

Kishinev, Uganda, El Arish, the sixth Zionist Congress, and especially the death of Herzl—these events combined to bring a crisis among Jews across Europe. With the rejection of the Uganda proposal, Zionism stood at a crossroads. The movement would either learn patience and endurance, and the difficult lesson of what Chaim Weizmann called "organic growth," or it would disintegrate into irrelevance. Weizmann understood it was time to take a decisive step toward a new start in life.[151]

To Weizmann, the Uganda plan was a disaster, but in it he saw a small ray of hope. For the first time in nearly two thousand years, a world power saw the Jews as a national collective.[152] Weizmann wondered if the British might be the Jews' best chance to finally secure a state in Palestine. He abandoned Switzerland and moved to England.

Great Britain presented itself as a country where a Jew might be allowed to live and work without hindrance, judged on his merits not his ethnicity. Weizmann had no prospects in England whatsoever—not even a job opening. And he could barely speak the language. But on the same day that a delegation of students from Geneva set out for Vienna to attend Theodor Herzl's funeral, Chaim Weizmann left for Manchester, England.[153]

On his way to the train station, Weizmann mailed a letter to his sweetheart, Vera Khatzmann, writing that the death of Herzl had "left us a frightening legacy." He spoke of "a great weight on my heart," and he felt that in the face of the "difficult times that await me … a heavy burden has fallen on my shoulders, and the shoulders are weak and tired."[154]

His journey to England would be a continuation of the westward movement that Weizmann had begun as a teenager. Born in 1874 into an Orthodox Jewish family with fifteen children, Weizmann experienced Russian oppression firsthand. He grew up in the village of Motel in the heart of the Pale of Settlement.[155] The son of a timber merchant, fluent in Hebrew and deeply rooted in the traditions of Judaism, Weizmann was Herzl's antithesis. Modest and reserved, he had little patience for showmanship. He was passionately dedicated to the idea of a Jewish homeland in Palestine—nowhere else.[156]

Only a handful of Russian Jews were permitted to attend university. Weizmann concluded his best option was to study chemistry in Germany.[157] He escaped with thousands of Russian Jews in "a sort of educational stampede."[158]

He needed a foreign passport to travel abroad, but that was an expensive document, and Weizmann barely had enough funds to get to his university. To cross into Germany, he secured a job as a raft worker. This allowed him to make the round trip on the river to Danzig without a passport. At the German town of Thorn, Weizmann grabbed his bags, went ashore, and never looked back.

He enrolled in the Berlin *Polytechnicum*, one of the best scientific schools in Europe. Weizmann completed three years in Berlin, then he followed his favorite professor, Bistrzcyki, a distinguished Polish-German chemist, to Freiburg for his final year.

The nearby Swiss city of Bern had a large Russian-Jewish student population and had become a center for revolutionary thought. By the time Weizmann graduated summa cum laude with his doctorate, his political outlook, his Zionist ideology, and his life purpose had crystallized.

Weizmann was appointed a lecturer in chemistry at the University of Geneva. Although he was paid only a modest income, the position was the beginning of an academic career. Weizmann poured himself into both his research and his Zionism. "While my scientific work never intruded on my preoccupation with the Jewish problem," he later wrote, "the Jewish problem did pursue me into the laboratory."[159]

As he worked, the idea of a Hebrew university in Jerusalem was planted in his thinking. The Zionist youth were enthusiastic about the idea. But most Western Zionist leaders, other than Herzl, considered the idea utopian. In their eyes, the work at hand had to be political Zionism, postponing the practical work in Palestine until after a charter had been obtained.

The Zionist leaders continued seeking meetings with heads of state and discouraged work in Palestine. They considered it premature and dangerous because it could antagonize Turkey and jeopardize the chances of a charter. Weizmann and the Eastern Zionists disagreed and pressed on with the practical work of community building in Palestine.[160]

He and Vera Khatzmann agreed to marry, but his financial prospects were not sufficient to plan a wedding. Zionist activities interrupted his research and hindered him from pursuing potentially lucrative grants and patents. He saw no firm financial assurances in the German or Swiss academic world.

Lack of opportunity eliminated Palestine as a possibility at that time. But a move to America or England could open teaching and research possibilities where he could gain experience and status as a chemist. He could also carry his Zionist message to the growing Jewish communities in those countries.

His last days in Switzerland coincided with the ever-increasing persecution of Jews in Russia, with the shock of the Kishinev pogrom and the Uganda fiasco, followed by the death of Theodor Herzl.

"My youth did not close," he wrote. "It was closed for me." His flight to England in 1904 was, he said, "a deliberate and desperate step."[161]

Weizmann's academic mentors referred him to the University of Manchester, which had recently built state-of-the-art laboratories.[162] He carried a letter of recommendation for Professor William Henry Perkin.

Weizmann's research in coal-tar dye was similar to work done by Perkin's father.[163] Perkin received him warmly and arranged for Weizmann to use one of the university's older laboratories.

Weizmann went right to work, cleaning up the dingy basement facility and spending several hours a day studying English. Within a month, he had completed two technical articles in collaboration with Perkin's assistant, William Pickles. These were the first of several academic articles published under the name "Charles" Weizmann in British scientific journals.

Soon a fellow Zionist hired him to do research for his firm, which gave him desperately needed income. Then Professor Perkin asked Weizmann to deliver a weekly lecture on chemistry—the beginning of a teaching and research career in Manchester that continued for thirty years. Weizmann was appointed a research fellow and assigned as supervisor of Perkin's new organic chemistry laboratory.

Although these were important career steps, Weizmann still lacked the funds needed to start a family. He supplemented his income by working for Charles Dreyfus, a chemist and also a Zionist and local political operative. Professor Perkin introduced Weizmann to Dreyfus, and soon both Zionists saw advantages in their relationship, even though they differed on the Uganda proposal and other issues.[164]

The Zionist leadership in England was pro-Uganda and, therefore, anti-Weizmann. These leaders, based primarily in London, gave Weizmann the cold shoulder. A certain amount of bitterness lingered among many Zionists who blamed the untimely death of Herzl on the anti-Ugandists, and Weizmann was a leader among that faction. At the same time, they were awaiting a report on the Uganda territory itself. Most were certain it would be favorable; otherwise, why would the government have made such an offer? Weizmann was shocked by what he considered their naiveté.[165]

Weizmann's depression deepened when he traveled to Vienna, where the Actions Committee held its first meeting after the death of Herzl. It quickly became clear that the new leadership had little vision beyond an attempt to keep alive the work initiated by the late president.

When the unsuitability of Uganda as an option for the Jews finally became apparent to the Zionists of England, Weizmann was no longer shunned, and he was invited to speak at the Manchester Zionist Society. Younger Jews started to come to the meetings, where Weizmann answered questions and encouraged discussion and debate. The audiences grew as people discovered these free-flowing exchanges were both interesting and instructive.[166]

Manchester slowly became a center of Zionist thought, and after years of steady labor and persuasion, Weizmann's ideas and influence spread throughout the country. Dreyfus recognized Weizmann's gift of political persuasion and looked for an opportunity to introduce him to Manchester's leading politicians.

WEIZMANN MEETS BALFOUR

Due to his education, Weizmann was ideally suited to span the gulf between the eastern and western Jews. He was poised to follow in Herzl's footsteps as a mouthpiece to political leaders. In addition to his Yiddish and Russian, he spoke French, German, English, and Hebrew.

Dreyfus found Weizmann a useful ally in accessing the Yiddish-speaking voters in the district. He also recognized the value of Weizmann's foreign connections.[167] At that time, Arthur Balfour, the former prime minister, was a Conservative MP representing part of Manchester. Balfour supported the concept of a Jewish homeland in Palestine, but he believed there would be more support among politicians for Uganda.[168] Dreyfus arranged for Weizmann to meet Balfour, hoping the Russian's passion might sway Balfour toward a more public commitment to Zionism.[169]

Dreyfus also wanted Balfour to convince Weizmann to change his mind on Uganda. They met at his campaign headquarters in the Queen's Hotel on Piccadilly. Balfour opened the conversation by asking Weizmann why so many Jews were opposed to Uganda. The British government sincerely wished to alleviate Jewish misery, and he was puzzled by the angry debate over the proposal.

Weizmann plunged into a description of the spiritual nature of Zionism and its connection to Palestine. "Nothing but a deep religious conviction expressed in modern political terms could keep the movement alive, and this conviction had to be based on Palestine alone. Any deflection from Palestine was a form of idolatry. If Moses had come into the Sixth Zionist Congress when it was adopting the resolution in favor of the Commission for Uganda, he would surely have broken the tablets once again," Weizmann declared, eliciting a chuckle from Balfour, who was a strong Bible-believing Christian.[170]

"We knew the Uganda offer was well meant," Weizmann explained, "and on the surface it might appear the more practical road. But I was sure that—quite apart from the availability and suitability of the territory— the Jewish people would never produce either the money or the energy required in order to build up a wasteland and make it habitable, unless that land were Palestine.

"Palestine has this magic and romantic appeal for the Jews. We have never accepted defeat and have never forsaken the memory of Palestine. Such a tradition could be converted into real motive power, and we were trying to do just that, struggling against great difficulties, but sure that the day would come when we would succeed."[171]

Weizmann felt as if he may have become too emotional. "I was sweating blood," he later recalled, "and I tried to find some less ponderous way of expressing myself." With no further argument in mind, Weizmann stood and moved toward the door, but Balfour held him back.

"I've heard of Dr. Herzl," Balfour declared, "the man who founded and organized the Zionist Movement."

"Herzl had indeed placed the movement on a new footing," Weizmann responded, choosing his words carefully, "and had given the tradition a modern political setting. But Herzl had died young, and he had left us this legacy of Uganda, which we are trying to liquidate."

Balfour was shocked by Weizmann's bold response. The Russian Zionist decided it was all or nothing. "Mr. Balfour, supposing I were to offer you Paris instead of London. Would you take it?"

Balfour sat up, looked Weizmann in the eye with a sly smile, and replied, "But, Dr. Weizmann, we have London."

"That is true," Weizmann responded, then grinned. "But we had Jerusalem when London was a marsh."

Balfour sat back in his seat and pondered. Weizmann allowed the silence to hang in the air—he knew his arrow had hit the mark. Finally, Balfour responded with his own inquiry. "Are there many Jews that think like you?"

"I believe I speak the mind of millions of Jews who cannot speak for themselves," Weizmann answered somberly.

"If that is so, Dr. Weizmann"—Balfour leaned forward again—"then you will one day be a force."[172]

Balfour had gone into the meeting hoping to change Weizmann's mind about Uganda. Instead, the Jewish people gained an ally in one of the most powerful men in England.[173]

Balfour began to understand the Zionist cause for the first time and became Weizmann's first convert among the British ruling class. But that year the Conservatives lost the election, and Balfour lost his seat in Parliament. Nearly a decade would pass before he would be in a position to speak out on behalf of Zionism.

During those years, Weizmann continued his propaganda activities in England and became much more involved in the leadership of the World Zionist Organization. But there was little forward movement toward a Jewish national state in Palestine.[174]

CHURCHILL AND THE JEWS

Another powerful Englishman entered Weizmann's life during this critical time. In 1904, Winston Churchill accepted a seat in Parliament from another part of Manchester where a third of his constituents were Jewish. He won them over by opposing the 1904 Aliens Act, a bill that sought to limit the number of Jewish immigrants entering Britain.

Concern for Jews and their plight was strong in the Churchill family. His father, Lord Randolph Churchill, was widely known, and often mocked, for his circle of Jewish friends. Despite this, he inspired in young Winston a lifelong love for the Jewish people.[175]

Churchill had no Jewish ancestry, but his father surrounded himself with so many Jewish friends that some joked he did not have any Gentile comrades. Young Winston grew up playing with the children of Nathan Rothschild, Lord Churchill's close friend. His father was also close to philanthropist Baron Maurice de Hirsch. Another Jewish banker, Sir Ernest Cassel—a close friend of the Prince of Wales, later King Edward VII—became Winston Churchill's mentor after his father passed away.

After the death of Winston's father, Sir Ernest Cassel took over management of Churchill's finances—something he would do for the rest of his life, free of charge. Having made his first significant income through his writing, Winston encouraged Cassel's investments, urging him to "feed my sheep."[176]

Churchill embraced the biblical injunction that God deals with the nations as the nations deal with the Jews. Churchill believed God rewards both individuals and nations for the way they treat the Jewish people.[177]

After the massacre in Kishinev, Churchill spoke at a rally in Manchester to protest the ongoing Russian pogroms. Churchill had recently been named the Under-Secretary of State for the Colonies. Among the leaders on the platform was Chaim Weizmann, who worried for the safety of his family back home. Churchill expressed outrage at the barbarism of the attacks:

> Many thousands of weak and defenseless people had suffered terribly … That those outrages were not spontaneous but rather in the nature of a deliberate plan combined to create a picture so terrible that one could hardly distinguish it in its grim reality, even amid the darkness of Russia. We meet here to express, in no uncertain terms, how deeply moved the whole British nation were at such atrocious deeds.[178]

"Even Winston had a fault," his friend, General Sir Edward Louis Spears once told a journalist. "He was too fond of Jews."[179]

Tel Aviv and the Purchase of Land in Palestine

At the Fifth Zionist International Congress in 1901, the Jewish National Fund (JNF) was created to assist Jews interested in immigrating to Palestine. The JNF launched a worldwide fundraising campaign that included the distribution of donation cans, known as blue boxes, which were placed in Jewish schools, synagogues, businesses, and homes.[180] Soon money poured into the fund as Jews everywhere became excited about the idea of owning property in Eretz Israel. The fund kept title to all the land purchased because the Jewish pioneers did not permit private ownership.[181]

The next step was finding property for sale that was inhabitable. The Jews often paid as much as ten times the normal rate for land Arabs considered unusable. Turkish officials were bribed to turn their backs as Jews bought land. Arabs were persuaded that the newcomers meant no harm and might even bring prosperity for everyone. The Jews paid as much as was asked because they needed acreage for a future homeland. The settlers developed every square inch, draining the malarial swamps, exploding the rocks, and uprooting the stumps. In time, they drained water from swampland and then gathered it in basins to be used for irrigation.[182]

Weizmann persuaded many Jews to not wait for future events. "A state cannot be created by decree, but by the forces of a people and in the course of generations. Even if all the governments of the world gave us a country, it would only be a gift of words. But if the Jewish people will go build Palestine, the Jewish State will become a reality."[183]

While some settlers developed the farms, others focused on building towns. In 1906, one group of Jewish settlers purchased sixty plots on the Mediterranean coast north of Jaffa. Three years later, in 1909, sixty-six Jewish families gathered on a sand dune to divide the thirty-two-acre tract using a lottery of sea shells. Family names and plot numbers were written on the shells and drawn randomly from a box. This was the birth of the city of Tel Aviv—its name taken from the Hebrew title of Theodor Herzel's book *Old New Land*.[184]

In 1909, the first kibbutz, Degania, was founded by young Jewish pioneers on the shores of the Sea of Galilee, combining agricultural settlement with a collective way of life. After years of disappointment, rank-and-file Zionists began to understand that a state does not just rise in one day. Nation building requires patience, preparation, and faithful, focused work.[185]

The Jews who made their way to Palestine faced a harsh, desolate land and, often, unfriendly neighbors. But they slowly pushed back the desert and brought forth new life—planting trees, grasses, and eventually crops. New Jewish towns, villages, and kibbutzim appeared across Palestine. Soon farms and orchards emerged where none had grown in 2,000 years.[186]

By 1914, nearly 100,000 Jews lived in Palestine in fifty agricultural villages. As the population grew, the JNF began to draw a map for the future State of Israel. By the time World War One erupted, the Jewish national movement was thriving.[187]

WEIZMANN AND THE GREAT WAR

With the practical work of building a nation in mind, Weizmann set out for Palestine for the first time in 1907. He discovered both progress and stagnation among the colonies. The first wave of romantic colonizers had fallen into a malaise. They operated orange groves and vineyards where Arabs worked as laborers. The colonies were spread out and disorganized. They had become dependent on the bounty of Baron Edmond de Rothschild. Facing a bad harvest, a cattle plague, or any other calamity, they ran to the baron for aid rather than relying on their own ingenuity and research. Sparse unity, and little pioneering spirit, existed among them.

Weizmann realized a new spirit of enterprise had to be introduced if there was any hope of statehood. In spite of all the political and administrative obstacles, great possibilities lay before them—only the will was lacking.[188]

At the same time, there were hopeful signs. In settlements like Merchaviah, Ben Shemen, and Hulda, young settlers were establishing a foothold with scientific achievement and organization. A Jewish high school had been established in Jaffa, and the Bezalel Arts and Crafts School opened in Jerusalem. Enough enterprises had succeeded to show that more could be done.

One of the driving forces behind this work was Arthur Ruppin, the director of the Zionist Colonial Department. Ruppin worked to put Weizmann's fears to rest. He assured him that Palestine could absorb large numbers of Jews in agriculture. He must not allow himself to be frightened by the smallness of the territory.

Ruppin took him for a walk over the dunes to the north of Jaffa. They had walked a considerable distance to where the sands came over their ankles, then Ruppin stopped and said solemnly, "Here we shall create a Jewish city!"

Weizmann looked at him in some dismay and peppered him with questions. Ruppin answered carefully and exactly. "Technically," he explained, "everything is possible. In the first few years, communication with the new settlement would be difficult. The inhabitants would soon become self-supporting and self-sufficient. The Jews of Jaffa would move into the new modern city and would create a market for their products. The Gymnasium would stand at the center, attracting families from Palestine and abroad who would want their children to be educated in a Jewish high school in a Jewish city."

It happened exactly as Ruppin envisioned.

In time, Tel Aviv exceeded, in both size and economic importance, the ancient town of Jaffa, and it became one of the leading metropolitan centers on the Mediterranean.[189]

In Jerusalem, Weizmann was struck by both the glorious surroundings and the poverty. "From the Jewish point of view it was a miserable ghetto, derelict and without dignity," Weizmann observed. "All the grand places belonged to others. We had not a decent building of our own. All the world had a foothold in Jerusalem—except the Jews."

As he surveyed the Jerusalem skyline, he had an idea. "There was one hill still uncrowned by monastery or church, the Scopus, on which stood then only the small villa of Lady Grey Hill." Weizmann pledged this would be the future site of the Hebrew University.

Weizmann returned to England with more determination than ever. His patient toil in Britain over the years had convinced several governmental leaders to support Zionism.[190] But the dream of a renewed nation in Palestine still seemed far off.

Then on June 28, 1914, an event occurred that seemed little related to the problems of a Jewish homeland. The consequences shook the earth and led to a promise from the world's greatest empire that changed forever the history of the Hebrew people.

On that fateful day, in Sarajevo, Serbia, a Slav nationalist assassinated Archduke Franz Ferdinand, the heir to the Austro-Hungarian throne.

At Germany's urging, the Austro-Hungarian Empire served an ultimatum on Serbia, demanding heavy reparations for the assassination. Serbia ignored the ultimatum and called on her protector, Russia, for help. On July 29, Austria-Hungary declared war on Serbia, and when Russia moved to Serbia's aid, both Austria-Hungary and Germany declared war on Russia. On August 2, German troops invaded France without formal declaration, violating the neutrality of Belgium in the process. Great Britain, outraged by the entry of the Germans into Belgium, announced a state of war with Germany and Austria-Hungary.[191]

World War One had begun.

Zionist leaders in Europe were divided over which side to take since many of them lived in German territories. Prominent Zionist leaders fought in the German army, in the French army, and in the British army—shooting at each other. Weizmann insisted the Zionists had to choose one side to support—the British.[192]

What it all meant for the Jews, Weizmann explained, was that Turkey, which owned the Holy Land, was sympathetic to Germany. Although she attempted to maintain neutrality, Turkey was pulled into the war by early November when Russia, Great Britain, and France declared war against her.

A plausible outcome would be the defeat of Turkey and the dismemberment of her sprawling empire. Palestine, as a prize of war, could soon be under British control. If that occurred, England could then make part or all of the land available to the Zionists. Weizmann went to work making plans for that eventuality, remote though it might be.[193]

At a party in the autumn of 1914, Weizmann was introduced to the influential editor of the Manchester *Guardian*, C. P. Scott. After listening to Weizmann's vision of Zionism, Scott had an idea. "I would like to bring you together with the Chancellor of the Exchequer, Lloyd George." And he added, "You know, you have a Jew in the government—Mr. Herbert Samuel."

"For God's sake, Mr. Scott, let's have nothing to do with this man," Weizmann blurted. Samuel, who had held several cabinet posts in the Liberal Party under Prime Minister Herbert Asquith, seemed to Weizmann to be "the type of Jew who by his very nature was opposed to us." In this Weizmann was mistaken.

Before seeing Lloyd George, who was known for his support of the national rights of small countries, Weizmann provided Scott with maps and data on Palestine and educated him in Zionist history. He even dangled before Scott a bit of political bait to snare a Jewish homeland:

> Should Palestine fall within the British sphere of influence, and should Britain encourage a Jewish settlement there, as a British dependency, we could have in twenty to thirty years a million Jews out there, perhaps more. They would develop the country, bring back civilization to it, and form a very effective guard for the Suez Canal.[194]

On December 3, 1914, Weizmann met Scott early in the morning. "We're going to have breakfast with Mr. Lloyd George," Scott announced. When they arrived, Weizmann was dismayed to find Herbert Samuel present. Lloyd George began to question Weizmann about how many Jews were in Palestine, how many the country could support, and how secure the Zionist colonies were. Weizmann shrewdly described Palestine to Lloyd George as "a little mountainous country not unlike his native Wales" and won him instantly.

Lloyd George listened patiently and promised to give Weizmann's views serious thought. He suggested he confer with Balfour, once again the most powerful figure of the Conservative Party, and also that he see Prime Minister Asquith. At this point, Samuel astounded Weizmann, stating he was currently preparing a memorandum for Asquith recommending the establishment of a Jewish state in Palestine, when and if it was taken from the Turks.[195]

Asquith reacted coolly to Samuel's proposal, writing in his diary:

> He [Samuel] thinks we might plant in this not very promising territory about three or four million European Jews and that this

would have a good effect on those who are left behind. I confess I am not attracted by this proposed addition to our responsibilities, but it is a curious illustration of Dizzy's [Disraeli's] favorite maxim, "Race is everything," to find this almost lyrical outburst from the well-ordered and methodical brain of Herbert Samuel.

When the Samuel memorandum was circulated among Asquith's ministers, strong opposition came from Edwin Montagu, a Jewish member who saw Zionism as a threat to his own comfortable position. He labeled it treason to England. Montagu placed himself at the head of a group of wealthy, assimilated English Jews who would do all in their power to thwart the Zionist movement.

Weizmann asked his friend Professor Alexander to help set up a meeting with Balfour, who had become First Lord of the Admiralty. "Dear Sam," Balfour responded, "Weizmann needs no introduction. I still remember our meeting in 1906."

A few days later when Weizmann met him in his London office, Balfour hailed him. "Well, you haven't changed much since we met. You know, I was thinking of that conversation of ours, and I believe that when the guns stop firing you may get your Jerusalem."

The spirited conversation lasted for several hours. Weizmann explained how the focus must remain on the intolerable situation of the Jewish masses. The only solution of a definite status for the Jewish people was a homeland for the Jews in Palestine.[196]

Balfour promised to do what he could for the Zionists.

Weizmann saw a common thread between Balfour, Churchill, and Lloyd George—they were all deeply religious and believed in the Bible. To them, the return of the Jewish people to Palestine was a prophetic promise, so the Zionists represented to them a great tradition for which they had enormous respect.[197]

"It is a great cause you are working for," Balfour declared as the two men parted ways.

Chapter Six

ACETONE AND THE BALFOUR DECLARATION

1914—MANCHESTER, ENGLAND

The thunderclap of World War One came in August 1914 with all its terrors. As the guns blazed on the Western front and British Middle East forces moved into action against the Turks, the notion of Britain taking control of Eretz Israel had become a postwar possibility.

For Weizmann, this transformation meant his hour had come. "Thus hope begets action and justifies itself," he wrote of the amazing times. "It was a time of uncertainty; and I went about with my hopes, waiting for my chance."[198]

Following Weizmann's lead, Zionist leaders stressed the strategic importance of establishing a pro-British nation next to the Suez Canal. Many British leaders were painfully aware that France had designs on Syria, and she would take as much as she could get. By establishing a Jewish state in Palestine, Britain could block French ambitions.[199]

Weizmann found himself engaged with the British government both as a chemist and as a Zionist. This gave him additional leverage. For years he had been working on a new method for making acetone, a key ingredient in the production of explosives. At this critical moment, the element was in short supply at British munitions plants, which jeopardized the British ability to fight.

Weizmann was surprised when, in March 1915, he was summoned to the office of Winston Churchill, at the time the First Lord of the Admiralty. "Well, Dr. Weizmann," Churchill declared as they met, "we need 30,000 tons of acetone. Can you make it?"

"I was so terrified by this lordly request," Weizmann later confessed, "that I almost turned tail."[200]

Instead of running, Weizmann promised to do his best. Churchill gave him staff and a munitions plant, and the chemist went to work. Weizmann had already invented a way to create acetone by fermenting grains, potatoes, and chestnuts. But he had to figure out how to reproduce it in mass quantities. Eventually he unlocked the enigma, and the British were soon producing 90,000 gallons a year in breweries and distilleries.[201]

His acetone project was successful, keeping the British guns firing. As a result, his prestige among British leaders was enhanced. Weizmann moved his family to a new home in London, which remained a center for Zionism in England for years to come.

Another governmental shuffle produced a coalition cabinet. Balfour replaced Churchill at the Admiralty, and Lloyd George became head of the Ministry of Munitions. Weizmann worked in London and met almost daily with high government officials.

One of the most important officials to enter Weizmann's circle at that time was Sir Mark Sykes, chief secretary to the War Cabinet for Middle East affairs. In this capacity, Sykes was intimately involved in negotiating the design of the postwar Middle East.

Weizmann learned of Sykes by accident. Early in 1917, Sykes mentioned the details of his job to James de Rothschild as they talked about their mutual interest in horse breeding. Rothschild passed on the information to Weizmann. Within days, another mutual friend, James Malcolm, also contacted Weizmann to arrange a meeting with Sykes.[202]

He was, in Weizmann's words, "one of our greatest finds."[203]

On the Zionist front, Weizmann was elected president of the British Zionist Federation in February 1917. This enabled him to officially propose that the British government make a public commitment to support a Jewish homeland in Palestine. As an offensive against the Turkish forces in Palestine was being prepared, Weizmann decided to advance from general propaganda to political action. The time had come to press the British government for a definite declaration of policy in favor of a Jewish homeland in Palestine.

The Political Committee drew up the famous memorandum, "Outline of a Programme for the Jewish Resettlement of Palestine." This became a first draft of a Zionist Charter for a homeland in Eretz Israel. After several conversations with Sykes, Weizmann submitted the memorandum to the War Cabinet.

"With this move," he declared, "the battle is joined! We have stepped into the world arena. We have taken the plunge into international politics."[204]

It had occurred to Sir Edward Grey, the British foreign secretary and one of Weizmann's newly persuaded Gentile Zionists, that an Allied statement in favor of Jewish settlement in Palestine might win the world's Jews to the Allied side. Kaiser Wilhelm's government, which held a similar exaggerated view of the power of world Jewry to shape public opinion, was also considering a pro-Zionist declaration. In March 1916, Grey sounded the Russian government on the subject, and the Russians agreed that it might be a way to combat pro-German feeling among European Jewry.

No declaration emerged from Great Britain in 1916, despite the presence of Balfour, Grey, and Lloyd George in the cabinet. This was due partly to Asquith's indifference and partly to the hostility expressed by a group of anti-Zionist Jews in the government.

But some British leaders believed that backing the Zionists might be a tactical error. Certain experts on the Near East, notably T. E. Lawrence—known later as Lawrence of Arabia—pointed out that Britain could block France's ambitions in the Near East even more effectively by sponsoring an Arab state instead of a Jewish state.

Throughout the war, the British bought support from both sides by making promises of future nationhood to the Palestinian and Syrian Arabs as well as to the Zionists.

Late in 1916, though, Zionist sentiment among the cabinet ministers revived. Some thought British support of Zionist ambitions might bring the United States into the war on the Allied side. Justice Brandeis, the reasoning went, was a prominent American Zionist who exercised influence over President Wilson. Give Brandeis the hope of attaining Palestine for his people, and he might convince Wilson to ask for a declaration of war.

Weizmann didn't believe that Brandeis had such power over Wilson or that the United States would join a world war merely because the pet project of an American Jewish leader received British blessing. But he had other reasons to think the time was ripe to ask the British government for a pro-Zionist statement. Another cabinet upheaval in December of 1916 had made Lloyd George the prime minister in place of Asquith. Balfour was now the foreign secretary. The allies of the English Zionists were now in command.

Sykes-Picot

Weizmann's direct approach in these negotiations was a gamble, and he knew it. The trust he had built with the leaders of the British government was frail, subject to the ever-changing winds of war. The men considering support of a Jewish homeland in Palestine were at the same time facing the most critical year of the war. Losses from German submarine attacks were at an all-time high. The United States refused to take part in the conflict, and the Russians faced serious upheaval at home.

The fragility of their endeavor came into stark focus when Weizmann—along with Zionist leaders Herbert Samuel, Lord Rothschild, Dr. Gaster, and Harry Sachen—met with Sir Mark Sykes in February 1917.[205]

Although Sykes favored a Jewish state, he acted odd as he examined the Zionist document. Sykes voiced concerns over what he called awkward differences among Britain's allies, particularly the French. He suggested the Zionists needed to take their arguments directly to the French government. He also proposed that the Zionists aim at a much more limited charter—one that had them developing areas in Palestine they had already settled.[206]

What the Zionists didn't know was that Sykes had spent the last year hammering out the details of a secret agreement for postwar control of the Middle East between Great Britain and France. In return for French concessions to British interests in the area, the Sykes-Picot agreement stated that Palestine was to be divided right down the middle—the French controlling the north as a part of greater Syria, and the south controlled by a French-British partnership. The agreement awarded Lebanon, Syria, and northern Palestine—the fertile region from Acre to Tiberias—to France.

The arrangement severed some of the most valuable land from Palestine. The rest of the region was not placed under the control of Britain, with its sympathies toward the Jews, but under an unpredictable multinational body. However, the details of the agreement were known only to the inner circles of the British and French governments. Sykes acted as though the treaty did not exist when he conferred with Weizmann and his colleagues.

Sykes also warned of trouble with the Arabs, who constituted the majority of the population of Palestine at that time. On the verge of liberation from the Ottoman Empire, they were developing nationalistic thoughts of their own. Sykes still suggested the Arabs would cooperate with the Zionists if, in turn, they received Jewish support for Arab political demands.[207]

Weizmann and the other Zionist leaders were stunned. Sykes' change of attitude was bewildering.

Of course, this agreement was in complete opposition to the idea of Palestine as a Jewish National Home. The reality of the situation, however, was that Sykes was now out of step with the new prime minister, Lloyd George, who came to power after the negotiations were finalized.

On April 16, Weizmann received confirmation from C. P. Scott, who learned of the secret Sykes-Picot agreement from sources in Paris. Britain's hands were seemingly tied. Throughout the war, France and England raced to expand their postwar influence in the Ottoman-controlled territories. When Sir Henry McMahon promised British support to the Arab movement of independence, the French moved to protect their own interests.

As soon as he learned the details of the pact, Weizmann hurried to the Foreign Ministry to protest to Lord Robert Cecil, the assistant secretary for Foreign Affairs. Weizmann did not actually mention the Sykes-Picot agreement; he spoke only of "an arrangement which is supposed to exist."

As it was, the British government had second thoughts about the Sykes-Picot agreement. Sykes himself, who had been unable to tell Weizmann of the treaty's existence, had come to believe it treated the Jews unfairly.

Prime Minister Lloyd George, with his activist views about a British Middle East, did not like the terms of the agreement. Impatient with France's pretensions, he told Weizmann that the future of Palestine was a question that would be resolved "between Britons and Jews" and that Palestine "was to him the one really interesting part of the war."[208]

TROUBLE IN RUSSIA

Everything changed again in March 1917, when an uprising of Russian workers turned into a revolution. Tsar Nicholas II and his family disappeared into captivity and before long were executed. Some members of the new socialist government favored immediate withdrawal from the war.

The possibility that Russia's massive military machine might be withdrawn from the conflict left the Allies in a panic. Clutching at straws, the British government drew closer than ever to giving Weizmann his pro-Zionist declaration, hoping it would somehow induce millions of Jews in Russia to exert influence to keep Russia in the war.[209]

At the same time, Lloyd George ordered the British army in Egypt to invade the Turks in Palestine over the objections of the French. In response, the French government insisted on sending Picot to accompany the British troops as an observer. The British, in turn, sent Sykes to keep Picot from getting in the way. The prime minister instructed Sykes to make no pledges to the Arabs, particularly in regard to Palestine.[210]

The Zionists' whole campaign was based on the assumption that the Allies would capture Palestine. When troops under Sir Archibald Murray attacked Gaza on March 26, they had nearly surrounded the town by nightfall. But through failures in communication, the British officers inexplicably ordered a withdrawal instead of a final assault.

When Murray launched a second Gaza offensive on April 17, he was thrown back by the Turks, who had strengthened their fortifications. No additional opportunities to break through into Palestine came until the autumn of 1917. Summer heat in the Sinai Desert was considered an unsuitable environment for warfare.

AMERICA INTERVENES

The morale of the Allies was bolstered on April 6 by the United States' entry into the war. Many months passed before the American Expeditionary Force was ready to take the field, but the symbolic gesture of the declaration encouraged the war-weary British and French.

For the Zionists, it opened a whole new series of possibilities. No longer bound by the niceties of neutralism, President Wilson might take a public position on Palestine. Perhaps the United States would even participate in governing the conquered Turkish territories.

Weizmann met with Foreign Under-Secretary Robert Cecil, who agreed the Jews were morally entitled to a state in Palestine and that such a state would have strategic value to Britain. He was willing to help, but he suggested that Weizmann mobilize Jewish opinion throughout the world in favor of a British protectorate there—something he had already begun to do.[211]

Weizmann's focus shifted to the United States and Brandeis.

On May 6, Brandeis met with President Wilson and explained the problem that had arisen between Britain and France over future possession of Palestine. Wilson replied that he was wholly sympathetic to the Zionist aims and would see what he could do to persuade the French to permit a Jewish state in Palestine. In due time, Wilson said, he would release a public statement calling for a Jewish homeland there. He would ask Brandeis to draft that statement for him, but he wanted to consult privately with France before issuing the declaration.

Brandeis reported to Balfour a few days later that Wilson would eventually commit himself openly to the Jewish state. This eased Balfour's fears of trouble with France over support of Zionism, and he moved somewhat closer to releasing the British government's long-promised statement of backing for a Jewish Palestine.[212]

But then the anti-Zionist English Jews attacked the plan. Two of their leaders, David Alexander and Claude Montefiore, wrote a long letter to the London *Times*, opposing the Zionists. The Jews are merely a religious community, they argued, and have no right to a national home. The most that the Palestinian Jews might ask was religious and civil liberty, "reasonable" immigration, and colonization rights ... with no trappings of statehood.[213]

The *Times* itself replied editorially through a remarkable leading article written by Whickham Steed, chiding these assimilated Jews for their selfish fears:

> Only an imaginative nervousness suggests that the realization of territorial Zionism, in some form, would cause Christendom to turn round on the Jews and say, "Now you have a land of your own, go to it."[214]

At this crucial juncture, Edwin Montagu, India's newly appointed secretary of state, intensified his attack.[215] He saw the impending British recognition of Zionism as a mortal danger to his status as a British Minister of the Crown. His objections stalled the forward motion of the declaration as the government took time to consider the questions and concerns of such a prominent British leader.

France and the Zionist Movement

Unsurprisingly, opposition to the Zionist plans also came from the French government, which had not supported Zionism since the time of Bonaparte. Within the French Foreign Ministry, Zionism was mostly spoken of with scorn. But everything changed when the world learned that some of the key leaders of the Russian revolution were Jewish. Political leaders in Britain, France, Germany, and America concluded that Jews had powerful sway in Russia. Suddenly, it seemed desirable for the French to win Zionist support.

The French government did not support a homeland for the Jews in postwar Palestine, but in light of developments in Russia, they saw no harm in offering the Zionists words of encouragement, even if they were insincere. Opening negotiations with Zionist leader Nahum Sokolow, the French Foreign Ministry agreed to make a pro-Zionist statement in return for Sokolow's agreement to convince Russian Jews to keep the nation in the war.

On June 4, 1917, Jules Cambon, director-general of the French Foreign Ministry, gave Sokolow written formal assurance of French sympathy with the Zionist cause:

> … Consider that, circumstances permitting, and the independence of the Holy Places being safeguarded on the other hand,

it would be a deed of justice and of reparation to assist, by the protection of the Allied Powers, in the renaissance of the Jewish nationality in that land from which the people of Israel were exiled so many centuries ago.[216]

The Cambon letter was purposefully noncommittal, but it backfired. Since a French declaration of support for Zionism existed, the British felt free to publish an assurance of their own. With the Allies on common ground in support of Jewish aspirations in Palestine, the Zionists would have a role in choosing their protector, and they would choose Britain.

Armed with this written statement of support by the French, Balfour asked the Zionists in June to supply him with the draft text of the statement they desired. On July 18, 1917, the Zionist Political Committee submitted a draft form of the carefully worded Declaration to the Government:

> His Majesty's Government, after considering the aims of the Zionist Organization, accepts the principle of recognizing Palestine as the National Home of the Jewish people and the right of the Jewish people to build up its national life in Palestine under a protectorate to be established at the conclusion of peace following the successful issue of war.
>
> His Majesty's Government regards as essential for the realization of this principle the grant of internal autonomy to the Jewish nationality in Palestine, freedom of immigration for Jews, and the establishment of a Jewish national colonization corporation for the resettlement and economic development of the country.[217]

On August 17, Weizmann sent a cable to Judge Felix Frankfurter, a leading American Zionist, stating that the draft had met with the approval of the Foreign Office and of Lloyd George. It remained to be approved by the War Cabinet, but all indications were that this would be quickly accomplished.

But as it circulated among the cabinet members, Montagu exerted pressure for its rejection. It infuriated Weizmann that the only interference with the campaign for the Jewish homeland should come from a Jew.

On September 3, the Declaration was discussed at a cabinet meeting that Lloyd George and Balfour did not attend. In their absence, an impassioned plea of resistance by Montagu persuaded the other members to remove the Declaration from the agenda.

Looking for reassurance, the British turned to President Wilson. On September 4, 1917, Lord Robert Cecil cabled the president's adviser, Colonel House: "We are being pressed here for a declaration of sympathy with the Zionist movement and I should be very grateful if you felt able to ascertain unofficially if the President favors such a declaration."

House sent a memorandum to Wilson: "Have you made up your mind regarding what answer you will make to Cecil concerning the Zionist Movement? It seems to me that there are many dangers lurking in it and if I were the British I would be wary about going too definitely into that question."

Wilson was in a difficult spot. On the one hand, Justice Brandeis was pushing him to support Zionism. On the other, Colonel House was urging caution. A number of meetings took place between Brandeis and House, Brandeis and Wilson, and House and Wilson in an attempt to arrive at a satisfactory American policy.

Brandeis gradually overcame House's reservations about a declaration. In a cable sent on September 19, Weizmann told Brandeis, "May expect opposition from assimilationist quarters. Would greatly help if President Wilson and yourself would support text. Matter most urgent."

Brandeis replied, "From talks I have had with the President and from expressions of opinion given to closest advisors I feel I can answer you that he is in entire sympathy with declaration … I of course heartily agree."

Colonel House replied on Wilson's behalf to Lord Robert Cecil's query, stating the president did indeed favor a declaration backing the Zionists, but he did not think the proper time for making the declaration had come.

The problem was that when the United States declared war on Germany, it had not declared war on Turkey. Wilson hoped to convince Turkey to peacefully withdraw from the war. He also wanted the Turkish withdrawal to be accompanied by their surrender of Arabia, Syria, Palestine, and Armenia, which would give Brandeis the Jewish national home he desired. But it was diplomatically unwise for Wilson to make statements about the fate of the Turkish Empire while he was still trying to get Turkey to withdraw.[218]

THE RESTORATIONISTS

Weizmann worked to remind the British leaders of the plight of the Jewish masses scattered around the world. In this, Weizmann was aided by something that is difficult for some people to comprehend—the Bible.

Lloyd George was the only leader in his government that Weizmann did not have to convince regarding a national homeland for the Jews in Palestine. Unlike many of his colleagues who had been educated in exclusive schools that emphasized knowledge of the Greek and Latin classics, Lloyd George was brought up on the Bible. He objected to the division of Palestine in the Sykes-Picot agreement because he said it was not worth winning the Holy Land only to "hew it in pieces before the Lord." He declared that "Palestine, if recaptured, must be one and indivisible to renew its greatness as a living entity."[219]

Like many in the United States, Lloyd George came from a centuries-old tradition in British evangelical thought, going back to the Puritans, regarding the restoration of the Jews to their ancient home in Eretz Israel.

Lloyd George had tipped his hand in a secret session of the House of Commons on May 10 when he declared that Britain was not going to give back the German colonies in Africa captured during the war and that Turkey would not be allowed to keep Palestine. The prime minister also dismissed the Sykes-Picot agreement, declaring that physical possession was all that mattered. Regarding Palestine, he told the British ambassador to France: "We shall be there by conquest and shall remain."[220]

Balfour also had a lifelong interest in the Holy Land and its traditions stemming from knowledge of the Bible, as did Winston Churchill and Jan Christiaan Smuts, the South African member of the War Cabinet. These men deeply believed in Christianity's historic obligation to the Jews.[221]

This understanding hearkened back to the mid-seventeenth century, when two English Puritans living in Holland, Ebenezer and Joanna Cartwright, petitioned their government: "That this Nation of England, with the inhabitants of the Netherlands, shall be the first and the readiest to transport Izraell's [sic] sons and daughters in their ships to the Land promised by their forefathers, Abraham, Isaac, and Jacob for an everlasting inheritance."[222] The Puritans believed the advent of the Messiah would take place once the people of Israel were restored to their native land.

These ideas flourished throughout Great Britain and America, eventually embraced by President John Adams, his son, John Quincy, and later by Abraham Lincoln.[223]

In England, the Restorationist banner was raised by social reformer Anthony Cooper, who became Earl of Shaftesbury. He was inspired by a powerful evangelical movement within the Church of England promoting the return of the Jews to Palestine, thus hastening the second coming of Christ. Shaftesbury influenced Foreign Secretary Palmerston to extend British consular protection to Jews in Palestine.

But another reason to advocate for a Jewish Palestine was to strengthen the Ottoman sultan and the Egyptians against the French in the region. Palmerston sought to provide Britain with a client in the Middle East, and therefore an excuse for intervention in Ottoman affairs. The Russians claimed to defend the Orthodox faith in the Middle East, and the French defended the Roman Catholics. With a lack of a Protestant community, the British had to adopt some other protégé to make a similar claim.[224]

Palmerston's proposal to restore the Jews to the Promised Land was cheered by Christians advocating a homeland for the Jews in fulfillment of biblical prophecy. Throughout the nineteenth and into the twentieth century, a mystical idea remained in certain segments of society that Britain was to be the chosen instrument of God to return the Jews to the Holy Land.

When the Ottoman Empire joined forces with Germany against Great Britain and the Allies, the circumstances in which the Zionists' dreams could at last be fulfilled seemed possible—both to the Jews and the Restorationists. "What is to prevent the Jews having Palestine and restoring a real Judea?" author H. G. Wells asked in an open newspaper letter written when Turkey entered the war.[225]

Lloyd George privately held the same view. Although from a Welsh family, Lloyd George was born in Manchester, home of Britain's largest Jewish community. In 1903, he had been retained as the British attorney for the Zionist movement and its founder, Theodor Herzl. He saw in the Zionist movement the possibility that the words of the prophets would one day come true.

Lloyd George had grown tired of the delays on the proposed declaration and moved to place the topic back on the agenda for October 4. When the cabinet met that day, Montagu, close to tears, delivered an impassioned speech. The forcefulness of his words and his anti-Zionism amazed the assembled ministers. Lloyd George and Balfour felt they could not continue to withhold a pro-Zionist statement of some kind from the Weizmann faction, but the fury of Montagu's onslaught compelled them to abandon the July 18 formula that spoke of granting "internal autonomy" to the Jews of Palestine.

In addition to the opposition by Montagu, Lord Curzon argued that Palestine was too small and barren to accommodate the Zionists' dream of a homeland.

In response, Balfour produced a compromise statement promising "the establishment in Palestine of a national home for the Jewish race." This vague phrase could be interpreted almost any way at all, even that Great Britain was advocating nothing more than a Jewish colony within a Palestine run by Arabs.[226]

The new text included a specific guarantee of continued civil and religious rights for the non-Jewish inhabitants of Palestine, while omitting any reference to the Jewish National Colonizing Corporation that the Zionists had suggested as a quasi-governmental body. Then, as a gesture of conciliation to Montagu, the statement included a clause guaranteeing that nothing would be done to prejudice the rights of Jews of other countries "who are fully contented with their existing nationality and citizenship."

It was a painful moment when Weizmann finally read the actual text Balfour was offering. The flaws, ambiguities, and concessions to anti-Zionist Jews and pro-Arab British officials were all too evident. After anguished discussion, Weizmann and his colleagues decided to settle for the text as written.

"It is one of the ifs of history," he later wrote, "whether we should have been intransigent, and stood by our guns. Should we then have obtained a better statement? Or would the Government have become wearied of these internal Jewish divisions, and dropped the whole matter? Again, the result might have been such a long delay that the war would have ended before an agreement was reached, and then all the advantage of a timely decision would have been lost."[227]

Weizmann cabled the new text to Brandeis on October 9 and requested a statement of approval from Wilson, as well as an "enthusiastic message to us from American Zionists and also prominent non-Zionists." Brandeis and two other leaders of the American Zionist movement, Jacob de Haas and Rabbi Stephen S. Wise, were distressed by the text and unhappy with the willingness of the British Zionists to accept it. But the American Zionist leaders could do nothing about it.

Colonel House passed the statement along to Wilson when it arrived on October 10. Three days later, Wilson sent a note to House: "I find in my pocket the memorandum you gave me about the Zionist movement. I am afraid that I did not say to you that I concurred in the formula suggested from the other side. I do, and would be obliged if you would let them know it." In this offhand way, Wilson finally lent his support to the Zionist cause in a way that mattered. He still would not make a public statement, but he was at least willing to permit his confidant, House, to relay his expression of approval to the British government.[228]

On October 16, House cabled London that Wilson approved of the Balfour statement. The cable, Weizmann said afterward, "was one of the most important individual factors in breaking the deadlock created by the British Government to issue its declaration."[229]

Wilson later declared his full support for the Balfour Declaration. The son of a minister and well-versed in the Bible, he claimed he "had been influenced by a desire to give the Jews their rightful place in the world; a great nation without a home is not right."[230]

Lloyd George confided in Weizmann: "I know that with the issuance of this Declaration I shall please one group of Jews and displease another. I have decided to please your group because you stand for a great idea."[231]

On November 2, 1917, Lord Rothschild received a letter from London—the Balfour Declaration. At Weizmann's suggestion, it was in the form of a letter addressed to the nominal head of the British Jewish community.[232]

THE BALFOUR DECLARATION

Foreign Office
November 2nd, 1917

Dear Lord Rothschild,

I have much pleasure in conveying to you, on behalf of His Majesty's Government, the following declaration of sympathy with Jewish Zionist aspirations which has been submitted to, and approved by, the cabinet.

"His Majesty's Government view with favour the establishment in Palestine of a national home for the Jewish people, and will use their best endeavours to facilitate the achievement of this object, it being clearly understood that nothing shall be done which may prejudice the civil and religious rights of existing non-Jewish communities in Palestine, or the rights and political status enjoyed by Jews in any other country."

I should be grateful if you would bring this declaration to the knowledge of the Zionist Federation.

Yours sincerely,
Arthur James Balfour[233]

Balfour looked upon the declaration as the great achievement in his life. Viscount Robert Cecil, one of the founders of the League of Nations, considered the Jewish homeland to be of equal importance to the League itself.[234]

It was agreed to delay the public announcement until the following Friday, which was the publication date of the weekly *Jewish Chronicle*. By then, reports were coming in from Russia that Lenin and Trotsky had seized power. The British leaders who believed Russian Jews were powerful and could be valuable allies were driven to become even stronger supporters of the Balfour Declaration. Weizmann and Brandeis cabled friends in Russia, encouraging them to press the new Bolshevik government to remain in the war. The effort was a complete failure. The few Jewish Bolsheviks with any true influence in the government were hostile to Jewish nationalism.[235]

On November 9, the Declaration was announced by *The Times*. A few weeks later, on December 2, a gala celebration was organized by the British Zionist Federation at the London Opera House. In addition to the Zionist leaders, speakers at the event included Lord Robert Cecil, Sir Mark Sykes, and William Ormsby-Gore as well as a Syrian Christian, an Arab nationalist, and a spokesman for the people of Armenia. The speakers joined in their common hope that Jews, Arabs, and Armenians would move forward in harmony.

"The presence and the words of influential representatives of the Arab and Armenian peoples," *The Times* reported, "and their assurances of agreement and cooperation with the Jews, would alone have sufficed to make the meeting memorable. Its outstanding features were the Old Testament spirit which pervaded it and the feeling that, in the somewhat incongruous setting of a London theatre, the approaching fulfillment of ancient prophecy was being celebrated with faith and fervor."[236]

It was an appropriate statement, for biblical prophecy was one of the most significant motivations that moved the leaders of the British Empire in this promise to help restore the Jews to their ancient homeland— Eretz Israel.

Chapter Seven

WEIZMANN AND FAISAL: A DREAM OF PEACE

1917—JERUSALEM

Prime Minister Lloyd George foresaw a postwar peace treaty ensuring Palestine as a homeland for the Jews. To him, the importance of the Balfour Declaration was its contribution to the war effort, and then to the peace negotiations.

"When Clemenceau came to London after the War," Lloyd George wrote later, "I drove with him to the French Embassy through cheering crowds. After we reached the Embassy he asked me what it was I specifically wanted from the French. I instantly replied that I wanted Mosul attached to Iraq, and Palestine from Dan to Beersheba under British control. Without any hesitation he agreed."[237]

The Balfour Declaration was a public document issued by the greatest power on earth at the time—the British Empire—with the approval of the United States and France—and later Italy and the Vatican. It had been greeted with approval by the public and the press throughout the Western world. Most importantly for the Jewish people, it made a commitment that was difficult for the British, the Americans, the French, and finally the united nations of the world to ignore in the years to come.

"My personal hope," Balfour wrote, "is that the Jews will make good in Palestine and eventually found a Jewish State."

Lord Robert Cecil concurred. "Our wish is that Arabian countries shall be for the Arabs, Armenia for the Armenians, and Judea for the Jews."

In 1919, Smuts wrote of his vision for the rise of "a great Jewish State." Then in 1920, Winston Churchill spoke of "a Jewish State by the banks of the Jordan … which might comprise three or four million Jews."[238]

Lloyd George made the intention of his government regarding the Balfour Declaration's promise explicitly clear:

> It was contemplated that when the time arrived for according representative institutions in Palestine, if the Jews had meanwhile responded to the opportunity afforded them by the idea of a National Home and had become a definite majority of the inhabitants, then Palestine would thus become a Jewish Commonwealth. The notion that Jewish immigration would have to be artificially restricted in order to ensure that the Jews should be a permanent minority never entered into the heads of anyone engaged in framing the policy. That would have been regarded as unjust and as a fraud on the people to whom we were appealing.[239]

FIGHTING THE TURKS IN PALESTINE

The actual military conquest of the Holy Land unfolded in the weeks following the publication of the Declaration. The ineffective General Murray was replaced by Sir Edmund Allenby as British commander in Palestine. Allenby, who had distinguished himself in France, began a bombardment of Gaza on October 20. The British army seized Beersheba on October 31 and broke through into central Palestine by November 6. In the midst of the fighting, the Turks were divided into two groups; Allenby kept them separated while he captured the port of Jaffa on November 14. Then he began his inland march toward Jerusalem.

On December 9, 1917, the Holy City fell to the British, passing from Muslim control for the first time since Saladin had seized it from the Crusaders in 1187. Allenby accepted the surrender of Jerusalem from the Turks, who had controlled Palestine for more than 400 years.

When Allenby approached the Jaffa gate, he dismounted his horse and walked into Jerusalem on foot, declaring, "I come not as a conqueror, but as a pilgrim."[240] Allenby and his men prayed at the Western Wall, that ancient foundational structure of Herod's Temple, surrounded by rejoicing Jewish Jerusalemites.

"We experienced the thrill of those who make history," wrote British Brigadier Major Vivian Gilbert. "We were proud that Jerusalem, after languishing for 400 years, should be free at last. And above all, we had a great and abiding faith in God, whose mercy had granted us the victory."[241]

In his journal, Major Gilbert wrote the astonishing fact that Britain's liberation of Jerusalem had fulfilled the ancient prophecy of Daniel that God would "deliver Jerusalem in 1,335 years." Haggai added that the day of blessing would come on the twenty-fourth day on the ninth month of the Hebrew calendar. That date was December 9, 1917—the very day that the mayor of Jerusalem handed over the keys of the city to the British army.[242]

With Jerusalem and the Balfour Declaration in hand, the Zionists went to work to transform the promise into reality.

THE COMMISSION TO PALESTINE

The British government dispatched a Zionist commission to Palestine early in 1918 to inspect the country and make a report based on their findings. Chaim Weizmann was named chairman and the other Allied powers were invited to send representatives. The United States declined to participate due to the absence of a state of war between the US and Turkey, and, for the time being, Palestine was considered occupied Turkish soil. This gesture on the part of the Americans irritated Weizmann, but there was no persuading them. Russia, embroiled in its revolution, was unwilling to participate. When the commission finally got under way, it consisted of British, French, and Italian Jews. True to form, the delegate chosen by the French government was an ardent anti-Zionist.

Joining the group in an unofficial capacity was Mr. James de Rothschild, son of Baron Edmond who had done so much over the years to help the pioneers colonize Palestine. The younger Rothschild served as a liaison between the committee and the Palestine Jewish Colonization Association, founded by his father. He attended all the meetings of the commission but did not wish to be officially identified with the group. Some awkward encounters between the commission and Rothschild followed, but they were usually calmed by the diplomacy of Major Ormsby-Gore, the liaison officer with the British military.[243]

The commission collected information on what was needed to reconstruct the Palestinian economy. They worked to provide a link between the Palestinian Jews and the British occupation forces. They were focused on the plan for the future Jewish commonwealth, as well as the coordination of refugee resettlement.

Weizmann was particularly interested in the possibilities of founding the Jewish university he had dreamed of for years. He was eager to establish friendly relations with Arab leaders, hoping to build cooperation and mutual understanding.

Before departing, Weizmann was given an audience with His Majesty King George V, who showed great interest in the Zionists' endeavors. Knowing Weizmann was of Russian birth, the king spoke at some length about his deposed cousin, Tsar Nicholas, and the revolution in Russia. "I always warned Nicky about the risks he ran in maintaining that regime, but he would not listen," the king lamented. He then returned to the subject of the Holy Land and wished the committee success in their mission.[244]

The commissioners gathered in Tel Aviv, a town of only one hundred houses at the time. But they were not welcomed with open arms by the military. The British officers were focused on bad news coming from the European front and had little time for the commissioners. Most of the European troops in Palestine were being withdrawn to reinforce the armies in France. The train carrying the commissioners into Palestine was immediately loaded with British soldiers heading out. The majority of the British officers had not yet heard of the Balfour Declaration, and with the war raging, they had little interest in cooperating with the Zionists.

To many of the British military, the Jewish population, who spoke little English, seemed like the dregs of Russian and Polish ghettos. Fearing a massive counterattack from the Turks and Arabs—who were quick to sense the weakening in the British military position—British soldiers had little concern for the commissioners' welfare.

Palestinian Arabs understood that the British victories over the Turks meant major changes to the future of Palestine. With the arrival of the commissioners, they vehemently protested, "The British have sent for the Jews to take over the country."[245]

British officers were well aware of Arab opinions. In their insecurity, many became pro-Arab or took a cautious middle road. When Weizmann met with General Allenby, he handed him his credentials and letters of introduction from Lloyd George, Arthur Balfour, and others. The British commander was not moved. "Yes, but of course nothing can be done at present. We have to be extremely careful not to hurt the susceptibilities of the population."[246]

Weizmann and his colleagues felt decidedly unwelcome.

The one officer who was somewhat encouraging was General Wyndham Deedes. Weizmann spent his second night at British headquarters conversing with the general. They talked of the present situation and of the Zionists' vision for the future. "I told him of my hopes and plans," Weizmann recalled. "He listened patiently and benignly to it all, both critical and sympathetic. He warned me of the many obstacles I should have to overcome, but ended by reminding me that faith could move mountains."[247]

The next morning, General Allenby drove past Weizmann as he stood in front of his tent. He stopped and with a friendly greeting motioned for the Zionist leader to get into the car. "I'm going up to Jerusalem," he explained, "and I thought you might like to go up with me."

Weizmann was eager to "go up to Jerusalem," but something inside held him back. "I would like to come, but in the circumstances don't you think it would be better for me to go a little later? It might be embarrassing for you to be seen entering the capital with me."

Allenby got out of the car and stood silently by Weizmann, deep in thought. Then he smiled, held out his hand, and declared, "You are quite right, and I think we are going to be great friends."

This wise response won the trust of the general, and the two men formed a friendship. After this encounter, the commission was given freedom to travel throughout the British-controlled areas of the country. They also received a car, gasoline, and their own telephone—luxuries most Palestinian residents only dreamed of.

"I was determined that no action of mine should destroy the tender plant of confidence which had begun to grow up between GHQ [General Headquarters] and ourselves," Weizmann wrote.[248]

The Palestinian Jews also understood their way of life was about to change dramatically, and a feeling of uncertainty arose concerning the commissioners. The Orthodox Jews were far more concerned with the undisturbed continuation of their ritual observances than they were with the possible political realization of a Jewish state.

The Jewish community was, according to Weizmann, depleted, derelict, and disorganized.[249] Most of its leaders had been expelled by Turkish authorities. The Zionists' head of colonization, Ruppin, had been banished to Constantinople. The respected mayor of Tel Aviv, Meir Dizengoff, had also been ejected from the country. Many Jews had fled to Egypt and elsewhere during the war to save their lives. Without leadership, the Jews of Palestine were like sheep without a shepherd.[250]

All of these things tempered the euphoria of the Declaration and the taking of Jerusalem. Weizmann knew the task before the Zionists was monumental.

BRITISH ARMY SKEPTICISM

Many Jews who had fled Palestine slowly drifted back. As with any war, there was a scarcity of necessary goods, so as soon as the road to Egypt reopened, people pressed the military authorities for passes to go and buy the things they needed. Only one railway line connected Palestine with Egypt, and only one train traveled daily in each direction. The limited space was needed for military purposes, so it was not possible for civilians to use the train except in the most urgent circumstances.

In this atmosphere of tension, even trivial things rose to great importance. Over time, these necessary restrictions became a source of frustration and anger both against the commissioners and the British authorities.

Not only the frustrations of war were troubling. One day General Deedes handed Weizmann a few sheets of typewritten script and asked him to read them carefully. He read the first sheet and then raised his eyes at the general with a look of perplexity. "What could be the meaning of this rubbish?" he asked.

Deedes replied quietly but sternly. "You had better read all of it with care. It is going to cause you a great deal of trouble in the future."

It was the first time Weizmann had seen *The Protocols of the Elders of Zion*, a devious work of fiction being circulated around the world by anti-Semites to raise fear of the Jews and to create the illusion of a worldwide conspiracy of power.[251]

"How did this reach you? What does it all mean?" the Zionist leader asked.

"You will find it in the haversack of a great many British officers here," Deedes answered. "And they believe it!"

At a time when the horrors of the Bolshevik revolution were being revealed, the most fantastic rumors and slanders—motivated by preexisting anti-Semitism—were gaining adherents. The excerpts of *The Protocols* that Weizmann read had clearly been selected to cater to the tastes and prejudices of the British reader.[252]

The attitude of many British officers toward the Jews in Palestine was at best neutral, and at worst hostile and truly anti-Semitic.[253] Sadly, this prejudice often displayed itself in unfair treatment that pitted the Jews against the Arabs.

After much soul-searching, Weizmann requested an interview with the commander in chief. He was invited to dine with General Allenby that same evening. After dinner, the general suggested they find a quiet place to talk. Weizmann began to explain the situation.

Allenby asked his guest for a more detailed report on how he saw the relations between the Jewish population and his administration. Weizmann seized the opportunity. "While we understand that matters of high policy cannot be implemented at the moment, and the Balfour Declaration cannot find practical application until after the war, the continuance of strained relations between the Jewish population and the British military authorities is doing no good to anyone at the present—and it might seriously prejudice the future."

It was not simply a matter of relations between the Jews and the British, Weizmann explained, nor was it any immediate questions of particular rebuffs or setbacks. It was rather the effect on the Arab mind.

The local administration seemed bent on ignoring the home government's attitude toward Zionist aspirations in Palestine, or, what was worse, was going out of its way to show definite hostility to the policy initiated in London. "The outlook for later relationships between Jews and Arabs was," Weizmann said, "in these circumstances, not a promising one."[254]

Allenby, like most of the English officers in Palestine, was not necessarily hostile to the Zionist cause, but he was skeptical of the Jews' future in Palestine. It was not because he feared trouble with the Arabs. Most leading Arabs at the time had more or less accepted the reality of coexistence with the Jews. With some Arab leaders, the Zionists had established quite friendly relations. The primary leader of the Arab world at the time, the Emir Feisal, was actually enthusiastic about the possibility of working side by side with the Jews to bring modernization and prosperity to the people of the region.[255]

The work of the Zionists at this key moment was to overcome the skepticism regarding the practicality of the plan for a Jewish homeland among the British officers. Weizmann spoke to the general of the untapped resources of energy and initiative lying dormant in the Jewish people and how it would be released by the impact of a return to their ancient homeland. He reminded Allenby of the villages founded by Baron Edmond de Rothschild, which were oases of fertility in the surrounding dunes of sand—standing in stark contrast to the Arab villages dotted with mud hovels and dunghills.

Toward the end of this long discussion, Weizmann sensed the general's resistance yielding slightly, so he pressed his point:

> You have conquered a great part of Palestine, and you can measure your conquest by one of two yardsticks: either in square kilometers—and in that sense your victory, though great, is not

unique: the Germans have overrun vaster areas—or else by the yardstick of history. If this conquest of yours be measured by the centuries of hallowed tradition which attach to every square kilometer of its ground, then yours is one of the greatest victories in history. And the traditions which make it so are largely bound up with the history of my people.

The day may come when we shall make good your victory, so that it may remain graven in something more enduring than rock—in the lives of men and nations. It would be a great pity if anything were done now—for instance by a few officials or administrators—to mar this victory.

The general seemed a little taken aback by Weizmann's strong words, but when he finished, Allenby responded, "Well, let's hope it will be made good."[256]

WEIZMANN AND FAISAL

After this meeting, relations between the commissioners and the administration improved slightly, but on the whole, the attitudes and actions of the British officers were not conducive to building cooperation.

At the same time, two important developments were under way. The first came in June 1918, when the commissioners undertook their most delicate and potentially significant task: an attempt to win support for the new Jewish homeland from Emir Faisal, would-be king of Syria and Iraq as well as leader of the Arab nationalist movement.[257]

The second was laying the foundation stones for the Hebrew University.

At General Allenby's request, the commission reached out to the premier Arab leader.[258] In Allenby's opinion, Faisal was the only representative Arab whose influence was of more than local importance. As commander in chief of the Arab army, then in revolt against the Ottoman Empire, he carried great weight with both the Arabs and the British.[259]

Weizmann and the other commissioners saw Allenby's suggestion as a sign of his desire to pave the way for good relations between the Jews and the Arabs, and they were eager to get under way.

Faisal was based in Amman, east of Jerusalem on the far side of the Jordan River. Because the Jordan Valley was still controlled by the Ottoman army, Weizmann and his colleagues were forced to spend ten miserable days on a journey that should have lasted only a few hours.[260] They set out by rail along the coast to Suez, then embarked on a harrowing sea journey around the tip of the Sinai Peninsula to Aqaba, where Major Ormsby-Gore fell ill with dysentery. He could not continue the journey, so Weizmann left him in the care of a British doctor.

Weizmann continued by car with a British officer and an Arab guide. From the seaport, they moved north through the scorching Negev Desert toward Amman—with no trace of vegetation, no shade, no water, and no villages where they could stop and rest. All they could see were the mountains of Sinai on the horizon, surrounded by a wilderness of burning rock and sand. The car lasted three hours and then gave up. The group was forced to continue by camel and then on foot until the travelers reached the Royal Air Force station at the base of the Negev Mountains. There they stayed the night, grateful for British hospitality and shelter.

They set out again the next morning with a fresh car and an English driver who planned to take them up the mountain via a track made for army lorries. The car made it halfway up the slope when it too broke down, forcing the travelers to once again continue on foot to the top of the Trans-Jordan plateau. Happily, a fresh breeze greeted them at the top of the hill, and the countryside was a mix of desert and patches of green with small brooks here and there. They reached a British camp nearby and secured a third car to drive the rest of the way to the headquarters of the Arab army. On their arrival, Faisal's officers greeted them with thirst-quenching water and fruit.

Weizmann was received by Colonel Joyce, who advised him to take a good rest and not to attempt to see the emir until the next day. Wandering around the camp that evening, Weizmann looked down from Moab into the Jordan Valley and the Dead Sea. On that brilliant, moonlit night, he could make out the Judean hills in the distance. As he stood there, he felt as if three thousand years had vanished. He realized he was standing on the identical ground, with the identical errand of the Children of Israel who had come out of Egypt—to negotiate with the ruler of the country for a right of way so they could return to their home.

"Dream or vision or hallucination," Weizmann explained, "I was suddenly recalled from it to present-day realities by the gruff voice of a British sentry saying, 'Sorry, sir, I'm afraid you're out of bounds.'"

The next morning, Weizmann found Faisal surrounded by Arab and British soldiers listening to an Arabian band playing some sort of fantasia. Among the officers was T. E. Lawrence, the famous Lawrence of Arabia, chatting with various chiefs and seemingly making plans for the next raid. Weizmann was soon invited to follow the emir into his tent. [261]

Faisal was a member of the house of Hashem, a proud Arab dynasty tracing its ancestry to Mohammed himself. For centuries, the Hashemites held the hereditary post of emir of Mecca, maintaining it even under Turkish rule. In 1916, Lawrence had persuaded Faisal's father, Emir Hussein, to cast off his allegiance to Turkey and join the Allied cause. [262] Hussein dreamed of an Arab empire embracing all of Arabia, Iraq, and Palestine, so he saw cooperation with the Allies as the best route. He provided an army of Arab guerrillas to be commanded by his son Faisal, with Lawrence as chief adviser.

These irregulars won much attention by blowing up Turkish rail lines in Arabia and capturing the port of Aqaba. In return for this help, the British secretly promised Hussein that Faisal would become king of a Damascus-based state comprising Syria and Palestine and that Hussein's second son, Abdullah, would be crowned king of Iraq. [263]

Weizmann was warmly received by the desert chieftain, an intelligent and far-seeing man. He refused to regard Zionism as a threat to his family's dream of an empire. With the help of an interpreter, Weizmann explained the goals of the commissioners in Palestine and their desire to do everything in their power to allay Arab fears. "It is our hope that you will lend us your powerful moral support."[264]

Faisal asked a great many questions about the Zionist program, although he was already well informed. At the time, both eastern and western Palestine—later to become Trans-Jordan—were united as one province in the Ottoman Empire. Weizmann stressed that there was a great deal of room in the country if intensive development was applied. In time, the conditions of Arabs in the region would be greatly improved through cooperation. The emir agreed with Weizmann's proposals—a fact confirmed to him in a letter from Lawrence not long after the meeting.[265]

Toward the end of the two-hour conversation with Weizmann, Faisal expressed a desire for harmony between Arabs and Jews in Palestine. He promised the Hashemites' full assistance in implementing the Balfour Declaration.[266]

Faisal was altogether sincere. He saw no reason his people and Weizmann's could not work together for mutual benefit. As long as the great powers permitted Hashemite rule over most of the Arab world, he would not begrudge some or all of Palestine to the Jews. The emir promised to communicate the gist of the talk to his father, the Sharif Hussein, who was, he said, the ultimate judge of all his actions and carried the responsibility for Arab policy.[267]

No one yet knew whether Palestine would become a sovereign Jewish state or merely a place where Jews might settle under Arab oversight. An ominous warning had already come from Major Ormsby-Gore, a strong ally of the Zionists, who felt it was premature to talk of a Jewish state or commonwealth in Palestine and that any such expression of nationalistic sentiments by the Zionists only made the British government's diplomatic task more difficult.

Lawrence believed the Jews would be of great help and that the Arab world stood to gain much from a Jewish homeland in Palestine. Weizmann had met Lawrence in Egypt, then later in Palestine. When he was in England, Lawrence was an occasional visitor at the Weizmann home in London. Lawrence had mistakenly been represented as anti-Zionist, but, according to Weizmann, his relationship to the movement was positive in spite of his strong pro-Arab stance.

THE SEAT OF LEARNING

Weizmann had secured from Mr. Balfour his consent in principle to lay the foundation stones of the Hebrew University on the plot of land acquired for that purpose on Mount Scopus. In May 1918, the commissioners approached General Allenby on the subject. He was, at first, quite surprised. "But we may be rolled back any minute," he protested. "What is the good of beginning something you may never be able to finish?"

"This will be a great act of faith," Weizmann replied, "faith in the victory which is bound to come, and faith in the future of Palestine. I can think of no better symbol of faith than the founding of the Hebrew University, under your auspices, and in this hour."

"You have chosen almost the worst possible time," Allenby shot back soberly. "The war in the West is passing through a most critical phase. The Germans are almost at the gates of Paris."

"We shall win this war," Weizmann declared. "The present crisis is only one episode." [268]

Allenby agreed to send a telegram to the Foreign Office asking for advice. He soon received word that the government favored moving ahead with the ceremony.

Perched on the one last hill in Jerusalem without a significant structure or religious monument, a modest but memorable ceremony took place as the foundation stones of the Hebrew University were laid on Mount Scopus. [269] Joining the Zionists for the solemn occasion were General Allenby and his staff along with Muslim, Christian, and Jewish dignitaries from Jerusalem. [270]

As the ceremony proceeded, the setting sun flooded the hills with golden light. "It seemed to me that the transfigured heights were watching, wondering, dimly aware perhaps that this was the beginning of the return of their own people after many days," Weizmann wrote. "Below us lay Jerusalem, gleaming like a jewel." [271]

The small group of dignitaries could hear the gunfire on the northern front as Weizmann spoke briefly, contrasting the desolation the war was bringing with the creative significance of the act in which they were engaged. [272] He reminded them that only a week before they had observed the Fast of the Ninth of Ab, the day on which the temple was destroyed and Jewish national political existence was seemingly extinguished. But they were there, he declared, to plant the germ of a new Jewish life. He spoke of the Zionists' hopes for the university—hopes which, at that moment, seemed as remote as the ancient catastrophe of the Roman conquest.

The ceremony lasted an hour and concluded with the singing of "Hatik-vah" and "God Save the King."[273] But the laying of the foundation stones was yet another vital, symbolic piece of the growing picture of Palestine as a national homeland for the Jews. And that picture was coming into focus.

Chapter Eight

SAN REMO AND THE MANDATE FOR PALESTINE

1919—VERSAILLES, FRANCE

For more than 400 years, the Ottoman Empire ruled a territory that at one time stretched from the gates of Vienna to the tip of the Arabian Peninsula. After World War One, European victors were intent on dividing one of history's largest empires for the sake of the peoples long oppressed under the Turks—and for their own strategic interests.

On January 30, 1919, the Paris Peace Conference took up the subject. President Woodrow Wilson had come to Europe with what he called his Fourteen Points, hoping they would be the guiding principles for the peace negotiations. Europeans generally welcomed Wilson's points, but his main Allied colleagues—Georges Clemenceau of France, David Lloyd George of the United Kingdom, and Vittorio Orlando of Italy—were skeptical.

The Fourteen Points speech was made without prior coordination or consultation with Wilson's counterparts in Europe. After hearing of the Fourteen Points, Clemenceau declared sarcastically, "God himself was content with ten commandments ..."[274]

Since Wilson's efforts had helped to establish the conditions for the armistice, he felt an obligation to play a prominent role at the peace negotiations. Across the globe, there were high expectations for Wilson to deliver. Once the president arrived at the peace conference, however, he found "rivalries, and conflicting claims previously submerged." Wilson's attempts to gain acceptance of his Fourteen Points ultimately failed after France and Britain refused to adopt its core principles.

In the Middle East, negotiations were complicated by competing European colonial claims. Neither Britain nor France was willing to give up its territorial claims after the long, costly war. However, Wilson was determined to defend the claims of nationalities long held captive under the Ottoman Turks. "The United States intends to completely ignore these [European secret] agreements," read one of Wilson's guidelines, "unless by chance, they happen to contain certain provisions which we consider to be just and proper."[275]

The European Allies refused to apply Wilson's understanding of self-determination or to relinquish their claims to territory they felt was their right as the victors. Wilson accused the powers of seeking to annex the Middle East and undermine his envisioned League of Nations.

The Wilsonian principle of open covenants compelled the Allied Powers to put their cards on the table. When that happened, the backroom Sykes-Picot agreement faded into obscurity.[276]

So without a working treaty in the Middle East and in the face of world pressure against the expansion of their empires, the European powers had to find a way to maintain their strategic interests in the region.

The impasse was broken by a member of the British delegation from South Africa, Jan Smuts. He had been a combatant of the English in the Boer War, so he understood the nationalistic impulse of people under colonial rule. He proposed the concept of a "mandate" under which the League of Nations would bestow control over the former enemy territories to various powers, which would then prepare those populations for self-rule.[277]

Asserting that not all parts of the Middle East were ready for full independence, mandates were established for the government of three territories: Syria and Lebanon, Mesopotamia, and Palestine. In each case, one of the Allied Powers was assigned to implement the mandate until the territories could "stand alone."

The idea appealed to European officials eager to acquire colonies from the defeated Turks and Germans—and under a system sanctioned by the League of Nations. A council of representatives from ten Allied nations voted to create mandates for Armenia, Syria, Mesopotamia, Palestine, and Arabia.

Wilson was subjected to intense lobbying by ethnic, religious, and political interest groups across America, asking him to adopt their cause. He was already supportive of the Zionists in what they were calling a Jewish Commonwealth in Palestine. They argued that with the defeat of the Turks, who had curtailed Jewish immigration for hundreds of years, as many as 80,000 Jews would likely move to Palestine annually—quickly becoming a majority and qualifying for Wilson's criteria for self-determination.[278]

SAN REMO

An unofficial understanding already existed that France would receive the mandate over Syria. Great Britain would administer the mandate for Palestine, and presumably the British Mandatory officials would welcome Jews in accordance with the Balfour Declaration. But grave difficulties arose regarding the boundary line between the two mandates. France still clung to the Sykes-Picot agreement. This would create serious economic consequences for Palestine.

In February 1920, Louis Brandeis reached out to British Foreign Secretary Arthur Balfour to make sure Eretz Israel would have an ample supply of water: "We are deeply concerned at information that it is proposed to carry out the Sykes-Picot agreement to mutilate historic Palestine and render all future developments impossible." He also wired Andre Pierre Tardieu, France's representative at the peace conference, asking for "quick reassuring words" regarding this critical decision.

On February 4, Brandeis wrote President Wilson to say that negotiations on the future of Palestine "have reached so critical a state … as to compel me to appeal to you." He shrewdly reminded Wilson that the Sykes-Picot agreement was a secret treaty, something the president particularly detested. "The Balfour Declaration, which you made possible, was a public promise," Brandeis continued. "Your word to Miller [David Hunter Miller of the British delegation to the peace conference] and Lloyd George at this hour may be decisive."

Wilson didn't hesitate. He immediately cabled the US ambassador in Paris, directing him to see the French and British delegates to express the president's support for the Zionist position. Wilson's intervention helped in persuading the French to relinquish their claim to northern Palestine.[279]

In April, representatives of Great Britain, France, Italy, and Japan, along with the United States as a neutral observer, met at the Villa Devanchan in San Remo. Their deliberations would decide the future of the Middle East. Known as the City of Flowers, San Remo sits on the coast of the Italian Riviera.[280]

The delegates debated the various claims throughout the former Ottoman Empire to determine the precise boundaries for territories captured by the Allies. Delegates finalized the British Mandates over Palestine and Mesopotamia (renamed Iraq) as well as the French Mandate of Syria and another newly named country, Lebanon.

At San Remo, the Allies confirmed the pledge contained in the Balfour Declaration concerning the establishment of a Jewish national home in Palestine—and established this promise in international law.

The British delegation to San Remo was headed by Prime Minister David Lloyd George and Lord Curzon, who had replaced Lord Balfour as foreign minister in 1919. Balfour, however, was also present at the conference as a consultant.

The conference was also attended by Zionist leaders Chaim Weizmann, Nahum Sokolow, and Herbert Samuel who presented a memorandum to the British delegation on the final settlement in the Eastern Mediterranean region. Palestine went to the British with the controversial watershed attached, and Syria to France.

The Jews were to have their Zion at last.

The final San Remo resolution, including the Balfour Declaration, was a turning point for the Zionists. What was once a dream was now international law. They would finally have a state, and the British would be responsible for helping them create it. Britain's foreign minister later referred to the resolution as the Magna Carta of the Jewish People.[281]

Britain was made responsible "for putting into effect the declaration made … by the British Government and adopted by the other Allied Powers, in favor of the establishment in Palestine of a national home for the Jewish people; it being clearly understood that nothing should be done which may prejudice the civil and religious rights of existing non-Jewish communities in Palestine, or the rights and political status enjoyed by Jews in any other country."[282]

Everyone understood there must be some legitimacy more than the Jews' biblical attachment to Judea and Samaria—as profound and sacred as that was. On April 25, the Supreme Council conferred the Mandate for Palestine on Great Britain in the San Remo Resolution. This document created the Middle East we know today.

In San Remo, Israel received its legitimacy under international law.[283]

The draft peace agreement with Turkey signed at the conference became the basis for the 1920 Treaty of Sèvres. Germany was then called upon to carry out its military and reparation obligations under the Treaty of Versailles. The precise boundaries of all territories were left unspecified, to "be determined by the Principal Allied Powers," and were later confirmed by the Council of the League of Nations on July 24, 1922.

The resolution at San Remo was celebrated by mass rallies of Jews around the world.[284]

To underscore its commitment to the Zionist aim of establishing a national home in Eretz Israel, the British government, after consulting with Weizmann, appointed a Jew, Herbert Samuel, as the first high commissioner for Palestine.

But the question remained: would the Arabs agree to the Jewish colonization of Palestine?

THE WEIZMANN-FAISAL AGREEMENT

Weizmann and Faisal signed the written agreement that bears their names on January 3, 1919. The next day they both traveled to Paris, where Weizmann represented the Zionist delegation and Faisal led the Arabs at the peace conference.

Faisal became the face of oriental intrigue at the conference—eliciting images of Aladdin and *The Arabian Nights*. American Secretary of State Robert Lansing described Faisal as an "ancient seer and Moslem paladin."

The president's wife, Edith Wilson, remarked on the prince's "startling resemblance to pictures of the Christ." Wilson adviser William Westermann, normally a stoic academic, exclaimed, "Great is Faisal. I am a convert."[285]

The new agreement committed both parties to conduct all relations between the groups by goodwill and understanding, to work together to encourage immigration of Jews into Palestine on a large scale while protecting the rights of the Arab peasants and tenant farmers, and to safeguard the free practice of religious observances.

The Muslim Holy Places were to be under Muslim control.

The Zionist movement agreed to assist the Arab residents of Palestine and the future Arab state to develop their natural resources and to establish a growing economy. Disputes were to be submitted to the British government for arbitration.

Weizmann signed the agreement on behalf of the Zionist Organization, while Faisal signed on behalf of the short-lived Arab Kingdom of Hedjaz.

Two weeks prior to signing the agreement, Faisal had stated:

> The two main branches of the Semitic family, Arabs and Jews, understand one another, and I hope that as a result of interchange of ideas at the Peace Conference, which will be guided by ideals of self-determination and nationality, each nation will make definite progress towards the realization of its aspirations.[286]

For Weizmann, it was a triumphal moment, as this accord climaxed years of negotiations and ceaseless shuttles between the Middle East and the capitals of Western Europe. The landmark agreement promised to usher in an era of peace and cooperation between the Arabs and Jews.

Faisal also met with Felix Frankfurter, president of the Zionist Organization of America, in his villa outside Paris. Frankfurter reiterated Weizmann's assurances that the Jews had no desire to deprive the Arabs of their national rights and that the two movements could coexist peacefully to their mutual advantage.

On March 3, 1919, Faisal wrote to Frankfurter:

Dear Mr. Frankfurter:

I want to take this opportunity of my first contact with American Zionists, to tell you what I have often been able to say to Dr. Weizmann in Arabia and Europe.

We feel that the Arabs and Jews are cousins in race, suffering similar oppressions at the hands of powers stronger than themselves, and by a happy coincidence have been able to take the first step toward the attainment of their national ideals together.

We Arabs, especially the educated among us, look with the deepest sympathy on the Zionist movement. Our deputation here in Paris is fully acquainted with the proposals submitted yesterday by the Zionist Organization to the Peace Conference, and we regard them as moderate and proper. We will do our best, in so far as we are concerned, to help them through.

We will wish the Jews a most hearty welcome home ...

I look forward, and my people with me look forward, to a future in which we will help you and you will help us, so that the countries in which we are mutually interested may once again take their place in the community of civilized peoples of the world.

Yours sincerely,
Faisal[287]

Faisal conditioned his acceptance on the fulfillment of British wartime promises to the Arabs, who had hoped for independence in a vast part of the Ottoman Empire. He appended to the typed document a handwritten statement:

Provided the Arabs obtain their independence as demanded in my [forthcoming] Memorandum dated the 4th of January, 1919, to the Foreign Office of the Government of Great Britain, I shall concur in the above articles. But if the slightest modification or departure were to be made [regarding our demands], I shall not be then bound by a single word of the present Agreement ...[288]

Disappointment

On October 5, 1918, Faisal claimed an "independent Arab constitutional government with authority over all Syria" and a Syrian Congress in Damascus, which confirmed Faisal as king.[289]

On July 2, 1919, the Syrian Congress passed resolutions calling for a completely independent constitutional monarchy with Faisal as king, asking for assistance from the United States, and rejecting any rights claimed by the French.[290]

But despite the pleas of Faisal, any hope they may have had that the British or Americans would come to their aid and counter French moves quickly faded. This came into focus after the Anglo-French Agreement for the withdrawal of British troops and the end of the British military government in Syria.[291]

For France, the Faisal government would have to either submit to French Mandate rule, or it would be defeated militarily. Flying in the face of the French and British, the Syrian Congress asserted Faisal's claims to Syria, Palestine, and Lebanon. When Faisal also demanded independence for Mesopotamia, British interests were also threatened.

Britain would not allow Syrian nationalism to disrupt British control over Mesopotamia and Palestine. As a consequence, British and French foreign secretaries quickly drew up terms of a joint declaration condemning the Syrians' claims.[292]

In October, Faisal was called to London and instructed to settle with France on the best terms he could obtain. To add persuasion to their argument, the British government cut his monthly subsidy by half, leaving France to pay the rest.[293] Under this pressure, Faisal arrived in Paris on October 20 for a discussion with Premier George Clemenceau.

On January 6, 1920, France agreed to recognize the partial independence of Syria with Faisal as king if it remained under French control. Syria was to accept the French Mandate and to recognize the independence of Lebanon under the French Mandate and the independence of Palestine under the British.[294]

From Clemenceau's point of view, these were generous terms. "No other French politician would have agreed to let Arab Syria retain a certain measure of independence or offered to let the pro-British Faisal remain in Damascus, let alone as Syria's monarch."[295]

Faisal saw the writing on the wall. He bowed to pressure to sign an agreement.[296] When news of this compromise reached the people, Faisal's anti-French and independence-minded supporters were outraged. Syrian nationals immediately pressured Faisal to reverse this decision, which he did.

On January 20, 1920, the interventionist Alexandre Millerand came to power in France, replacing Clemenceau. Millerand immediately called a halt to the friendly relations that had begun to develop between Faisal and the French.

In response, the Syrian Congress declared unconditional independence from France. The following day, Faisal was once again declared king of the "United Syrian Kingdom," which was to include Palestine and Lebanon, rejecting a Jewish national home in Palestine.[297]

This move was immediately rebuked by both the French and the British.

Violent attacks broke out against French forces throughout the region. French military commander General Henri Gouraud gave an ultimatum to Faisal on July 14, 1920, ordering him to surrender or fight. Worried about the results of a long, bloody fight with the French, King Faisal surrendered.[298]

The Syrian Minister of Defense, Yusuf al-'Azma ignored the king's surrender and led a small army to confront the French. Equipped mostly with small firearms, the Syrians were no match for French artillery. At the Battle of Maysalun, the Syrian army was easily defeated, and General al-'Azma was killed.

The French Mandate for Syria and the Lebanon was immediately put into effect. After the occupation of Damascus, Millerand proclaimed Syria would be held by France: "The whole of it, and forever."[299]

After surrendering to French forces, Faisal was expelled from Syria and went to live in the United Kingdom. One year later, in August 1921, he was offered the crown of Iraq under the British Mandate.[300]

Despite the high hopes surrounding the landmark Weizmann–Faisal Agreement, in the end, the British—under pressure from France—didn't uphold their end of the bargain. The decision of the peace conference itself refused independence for the vast Arab-inhabited lands that Faisal desired, mainly because the British and French held on to many details of Sykes–Picot.

And so the Weizmann-Faisal Agreement survived only a few months.

The British Mandate in Palestine

The idea of a British protectorate over a Jewish homeland in Palestine was also attractive to London, as it gave Britain an ongoing presence in the Middle East. The League established the Jewish Agency to administer Palestine and supervise its relations with both Britain and world Jewry. Soon the nations of the world were making their approval for Jewish sovereignty in Palestine known. By 1922, fifty-two governments had endorsed the major goals of world Zionism.[301]

In theory, the Mandate represented the standing instructions to the British from the League of Nations. In reality, however, Great Britain, as one of the two dominant partners in the League in the immediate postwar period, was in a position to draft its own instructions.

And it did.

But as the later Peel Commission noted, "... The primary purpose of the Mandate ... is to promote the establishment of a Jewish National Home." Not only did the Balfour Declaration become an "integral part of the Mandate," but the Mandate actually reinforced the commitment to build the Jewish National Home in Palestine.[302]

When Palestinian Arabs protested this recognition, the British Colonial Office, led by Winston Churchill, responded in what became known as the 1922 White Paper: "It is essential that it [the Jewish Community] should know that it is in Palestine as of right and not of sufferance. That is the reason why it is necessary that the existence of a Jewish National Home should be internationally recognized and that it should be formally recognized to rest upon ancient historical connections."[303]

Although there were numerous failures in the postwar peace process—some that would lead to another world war only a generation later—there were also long-lasting achievements.

The Ottoman Empire was no more, though a sovereign Turkey was preserved. In the east, the Allies decided on independence for an Armenian state after the genocide of 1.5 million Christian Armenians, mostly Ottoman citizens within the empire, although it would not come for several decades. Under a League of Nations Mandate, Great Britain would oversee the development of what would become the nations of Iraq and Trans-Jordan. The French would detach the Maronite-Christian-dominated Lebanon from Syria, granting it eventual self-determination.[304] And the foundations of the future Jewish state were established in British-administered Palestine.

The building of a Jewish National Home in Palestine—with international legal recognition—could officially begin.

Part Two

THE MANDATE

Chapter Nine

THE HABERDASHERY

1919—INDEPENDENCE, MISSOURI

On April 9, the soldiers of the US Army 129th Field Artillery Regiment boarded a captured German passenger liner, the *Zeppelin,* for the voyage back to civilian life. The eleven-day passage was miserable for everyone aboard. The stevedores had overloaded the ship at the front, and the bow continually plunged beneath the water, then wallowed from side to side as it emerged. Piloted by American officers unfamiliar with the vessel, the *Zeppelin* pitched and rolled violently most of the way across the Atlantic. Captain Harry S. Truman, constantly seasick, lost nearly twenty pounds. Mercifully, the ship landed in New York on Easter morning, April 20.[305]

As his train rattled across the continent toward Missouri, Harry had time to reflect on his war service. He had been gone barely a year, yet it seemed like a decade. He had left as an insecure farmer and returned with the confidence of a proven leader. "I've always been sorry I did not get a university education in the regular way," he said later. "But I got it in the Army the hard way—and it stuck."[306]

Truman had come home with his biggest, best "gang" ever—battery "boys" who looked up to him as they would an older brother. He was the captain who brought so many sons of Jackson County home safe. Beyond his decision to avoid farming, he had no idea how to earn a livelihood.[307]

The war had made him a somebody in the eyes of all kinds of people, including, most importantly, his childhood sweetheart, Bess Wallace. By coincidence, the signing of the Peace Treaty at Versailles and their wedding took place on the same day.[308]

Birth of a Haberdashery

As America celebrated the end of the war, Harry Truman was just another soldier in search of a job. One morning in July, he went to Kansas City to look for work. By chance, he ran into an old army buddy, Eddie Jacobson, who had helped him manage the regimental canteen at Camp Doniphan. While every other canteen on the base had gone bust, the Truman-Jacobson operation made a profit and brought Harry to the attention of his superiors, which eventually led to a promotion.

"Maybe we ought to go into business together, and have a partnership again," Truman blurted.

Eddie didn't like the idea of returning to his old job of selling shirts on the road. "Why don't we set up a sort of civilian canteen," he responded, "like a men's furnishings store?" It sounded like an excellent idea, and they shook hands on it.[309]

From his years in the retail business, Eddie knew merchandise, and there was no doubt Truman could use his leadership skills to become an outstanding salesman. Besides, he also knew how to handle the books from his years as a bank clerk and as manager of his family farm.

On May 27, only three weeks after being mustered out of the army, Harry and Eddie signed a five-year lease at $350 a month on a choice downtown site on the ground floor of the Glennon Hotel.

Truman & Jacobson was in the center of the bustling business and entertainment district. Nearby was the Dixon Hotel, with two wide-open gambling parlors in play around the clock. A half-dozen large movie houses were within a few blocks, and nearby live theaters offered entertainment for every taste.

Times were prosperous, and conventioneers poured in and out of the nearby Muehlebach and Baltimore hotels. The hottest thing in the downtown district was jazz, which blared from the clubs. Prohibition did not keep alcoholic beverages from fueling the downtown nightlife; saloons did a brisk business.

Downtown Kansas City was a bustling commercial center during the day, and then there was something for everyone after dark—late-night shopping, burlesque, vaudeville, and craps games.[310] Day or night, sales-men, businessmen, secretaries, shoppers from outlying towns—nearly everybody seemed to have money to spend.[311]

Harry and Eddie secured bank financing, built an inventory, and pur-chased equipment.[312] Eddie invested his savings in the business. To raise his share, Truman arranged to sell his stock and equipment on the family farm for $20,000, giving his mother, sister, and brother a quitclaim on his quarter share. He used $5,000 to buy a Kansas City flat, which he rented out, and invested the remaining $15,000 in the store.

On November 15, in the middle of the Christmas rush, they opened their haberdashery selling "Gents Furnishings." Times were good, and they ex-pected little difficulty in moving the $35,000 worth of men's furnishings that filled the cabinets. Their war buddies, along with the Twelfth Street crowd, purchased the silk shirts at sixteen dollars apiece. [313]

Harry and Eddie made a good team, taking turns with the customers. They worked hard from eight in the morning until nine at night.[314] "We were not only business partners, but close friends," Eddie recalled.[315]

"There were no conflicts and they were good buddies," said Jacobson family friend Ruth Gruber. "They played poker every Saturday night. Truman called Eddie, 'You bald-headed S.O.B.' They were cut from the same mid-western cloth—except that the religious background was not the same."

Although Harry and Eddie were pals, Harry couldn't bring his Jewish friend home for dinner. His wife's overbearing mother—in whose home he now lived—would not allow a Jew in her home.[316]

The men of "Dizzy D" found the store a haven for swapping wartime reminiscences, and they walked out with ties, socks, and underwear. "The boys who had been in the 129th used to come into the store to see Harry," Eddie remembered. "He was their financial adviser, legal adviser and everything else."

During the first year of operation, the store sold more than $70,000 worth of goods, and the two owners earned a high return on their in-vestment. With visions of still greater profits to come, they plowed their earnings back into stock.

The store was a six-days-a-week operation, so there was little time for homelife during this hectic period. Even on Sunday, Truman's only day for relaxation, he seldom stayed home. Usually, he took Bess to the Grandview, Missouri, farm to visit his mother. After dinner, he and his sister Mary Jane played classical duets on Martha Truman's upright piano.[317]

Eddie's wife, Bluma, said her husband never worked as hard as he did that first year. There were no signed agreements between the two owners—never a need for it. "They just felt that close to one another that they could trust each other, which they did all through their lives."

During their second year in business, however, the happy glow of prosperity abruptly vanished. After the Harding administration took office, farm prices fell drastically.[318] In a postwar recession, prices of other goods soon dropped. Truman and Jacobson, who had bought their inventories at the high prices prevailing before the slump, were gradually forced to cut prices until their margin of profit disappeared.[319]

By 1921, the silk shirt that had been a symbol of the postwar boom became the item Truman & Jacobson could no longer sell. By midyear, their flourishing business had evaporated. To keep their stock up-to-date, they were forced to borrow more money.[320] But they fell steadily behind in payments to suppliers, many of which cut off credit. The Christmas season failed to provide the hoped-for sales needed for a bailout.

In January 1922, the business negotiated a $2,500 loan from the Twelfth Street Bank. This was soon in the hands of creditors. Truman then negotiated a $5,000 loan from the Security State Bank. In 1921, he had sold his Kansas City flat to make a $5,000 down payment on a $13,800 farm of 160 acres in Johnson County, Kansas. The Security State Bank insisted he put up the farm as security on the $5,000 loan.[321] Truman and Jacobson hoped in vain for a good Easter season. At last, the day came when the money from the Security State Bank was paid out, and they could not continue in business. They hung on through the summer, but in September, they held a going-out-of-business sale and closed their doors for good.[322]

Neither Truman nor Jacobson wanted the stigma of bankruptcy. Instead, they wrote to each creditor and explained their situation. Rather than go through a costly liquidation, Truman proposed returning the remaining stock to the creditors, deducting the value from the total bills, and making future payments on the balance until all debts were wiped out. The creditors agreed.

Their predicament was made worse by the fact that their landlord refused to waive what was left of their five-year lease. In total, Truman estimated that his haberdashery experience had cost him about $30,000, including the $15,000 he originally put into the business.

The price for refusing bankruptcy was steep. By the end of 1924, the two had paid off the $2,500 loan from the Twelfth Street Bank, paid the Security State $1,200, and had made small payments to merchandise suppliers. Eddie had gone back on the road as a shirt salesman, but by February 1925, he could no longer stand the pressure of his continuing debts. That month he filed for bankruptcy, listing the total remaining store debts as $10,058.50. After the failure of the haberdashery, Eddie and Bluma lived with her parents. [323]

Lawyers advised Truman to file at the same time as Eddie, but he refused. Instead, he insisted on paying off all the debts he and Jacobson had incurred, although Eddie was now free of them. [324] The ethic by which he had been taught to conduct his life told Truman that the formal, legal renunciation of debts was disgraceful. Better to live with the burden of his obligations and the possibility of their redemption than to commit the sin of renunciation.

A pragmatic consideration was also in play. Bankruptcy would hinder his move into another occupation that had always been in the back of his mind: politics. [325]

Harry and Eddie were victims of circumstances beyond their control. [326] Truman was thirty-eight years old and deep in debt. "Went into business all enthusiastic," he wrote at the time. "Lost all I had, and all I could borrow. Feeling fairly blue." [327]

AN OPEN DOOR TO POLITICS

Although a friend had offered to take him into his profitable building-and-loan business, thus solving Truman's financial problems, he had decided on a new career, so he rejected the offer. Other veterans were winning elections in Missouri and elsewhere. Politics seemed to be a promising field for ex-soldiers.

Politics wasn't new to Harry, who had served as a Democratic clerk at every local election since 1906. But to enter politics in Jackson County, a man had to be sponsored and supported by one of the political machines.

Truman had begun to consider a run for office during the war and had shared his thoughts with a friend and fellow officer, Lieutenant James Pendergast. Jim was the son of Mike Pendergast, who headed the Pendergast political machine in the rural part of Jackson County.

Mike's brother, Thomas Pendergast, was the "Big Boss" of the machine. A thick-necked, spat-wearing Irishman, Tom was a hard drinker and a reckless gambler. In time, he lost up to $6 million on the ponies. But in the political arena, he built a political machine so strong that pundits called Kansas City "Tom's Town."

Pendergast made money selling concrete to the county, monopolizing the market and lining his pockets with lucrative kickbacks. In Kansas City in the 1920s, there were many ways to get rich, and Pendergast had a hand in all of it—gambling, bootleg liquor, prostitution, and narcotics. [328]

Mike Pendergast had produced the heir apparent, Jim. Pleasant-mannered Jim suggested to his father that Harry Truman run for judge of the Eastern District of Jackson County. Jim brought his father to see Harry at the haberdashery.

Truman was standing behind the counter feeling depressed when Mike and Jim Pendergast walked through the door. After an introduction and some small talk, Mike asked Harry point-blank: "How would you like to be county judge?"

"I don't know," Truman answered shrewdly.

"If you would, you can have it," Mike said. [329]

"He didn't know I was busted," Harry later admitted. The meeting took place months before the final collapse of Truman & Jacobson, but well past the point when Harry knew the business was doomed.

Under the Missouri system, the position of county judge was not a judicial post, but the equivalent of a county commissioner. It was a prime spot politically, which Harry already understood. With three judges on the court—an eastern judge for the outlying county, a western judge for Kansas City, and a presiding judge—having one vote of the three was worth a great deal. The judges controlled the county purse strings. They controlled the road overseers, as well as road gangs, county clerks, and other employees numbering in the hundreds. They could also determine who was awarded county contracts.

Mike Pendergast gave his consent even before meeting Harry because, in part, of what he knew of Harry's father, John Truman. If Captain Truman was all Jim said, and he was John Truman's son, then, providing he had no link to the Ku Klux Klan or any other anti-Catholic faction, he was all right with Mike.

At a meeting of the Tenth Ward Democratic Club, Harry sat quietly as Mike got up to introduce him. "Now, I'm going to tell you who you are going to be voting for, for county judge. It's Harry Truman. He's got a fine war record. He comes from a fine family. He'll make a fine judge." He described Truman as "a returned veteran, a captain whose men didn't want to shoot him."[330]

For the Pendergast political machine, Harry Truman, a war hero, was a dream candidate. Had he wished, Mike could also have stressed that Harry Truman was a Baptist who could talk farming with farmers as no big-city Irish politician ever could. He could have explained Harry was of old pioneer stock—the son of an honest farmer and well-known and well-liked road overseer, who happened to be an enthusiastic, lifelong Democrat. Harry had proven he could lead men under the most difficult circumstances. He was a fresh face in Jackson County politics and an honest man.

"Old Tom Pendergast wanted to have some window-dressing," Truman's friend Harry Vaughan later explained. "He could say, 'Well, there's my boy Truman … Everybody thinks he's okay.'"

For Harry, the timing could not have been better. He badly needed rescuing. In later years, it would be stressed that his interest in politics was longstanding and that the Pendergasts had come to him, not he to them.

Yet to Truman himself there was never much question about the actual state of his affairs or to whom he owed the greatest debt of gratitude. "Mike Pendergast picked me up and put me into politics and I've been lucky." Mike was nothing less than his "political mentor," he continued. "I loved him as I did my own daddy."

His army friends gave nearly unanimous support for the idea. Ethel Noland, Harry's cousin, explained his willingness to take up with the Pendergasts. "They always like to pick winners, and they endorsed him. And, indeed, if he hadn't been endorsed by the machine he couldn't have run."[331]

But Pendergast didn't control all of Jackson County, so Harry needed to campaign hard. He counted on his war record, the boys from Battery D, and Pendergast to help him.[332] Candidate Truman opened his campaign on March 8, 1922, at a rousing, foot-stomping rally of war veterans. About three hundred people turned out for the speeches, free cigars, and music.

When introduced by Colonel E. M. Stayton, another veteran of the Argonne, Harry had stage fright so bad all he could say was he was willing to run. "I was scared worse than I was when I first came under fire in 1918," he recalled. But his few words were all the crowd wanted, and they cheered him on.[333]

In the beginning, Harry's speeches were blunt, his voice tinny as he spoke through his nose, and his style as rough as his dirt-farmer background. But throughout the campaign, Harry's army pals campaigned hard for him. They cheered at every rally, trying to whip up enthusiasm for good old Captain Harry.

One fellow veteran, Eddie McKim, persuaded a pilot to take Harry up in a World War One biplane above the biggest political picnic of the summer. With Truman in the back seat, the pair came sailing through the air, bombarding the local farmers with Truman leaflets. The pilot landed in front of the cheering crowd but had trouble stopping. He finally brought the aircraft to a halt only three feet from the pasture's barbed-wire fence. Harry climbed out of the plane, staggered over to the fence, and threw up in front of everybody.[334]

"Our candidate," McKim later recalled, "got out as green as grass. But he mounted the rostrum and made a speech."[335]

Like his father before him, Harry Truman liked politicking with the people of Jackson County. He was tireless on the campaign trail, and he won in November 1922 by a plurality of 300 out of a total of 11,664 votes cast.[336]

Truman, declared the *Independence Examiner*, had made a clean campaign and would go into office with no promises to compromise him.

"We are safe in predicting that Truman will make good and help give Jackson County a real business administration," wrote the *Lee's Summit Journal,* "one that will be open and above board."[337]

After years of drift and failure, Harry Truman had found his calling, and he gave it everything he had.

Chapter Ten

THE ARAB REVOLT

The British Mandate over Palestine created at Versailles in 1919 spoke of the historical connection of the Jews to Palestine and their need to re-constitute a national home there.[338] There had always remained a Jewish remnant in Palestine, but now the Yishuv was growing rapidly. At the end of World War One, 50,000 Jews lived in Palestine. But under the terms of the British Mandate, the doors of immigration into Palestine were opened. By 1928, the Jewish population ballooned to 160,000 and made up 20 percent of the total population, with 70 percent Muslim and 10 percent Christian.[339]

Although Jews and Arabs had lived for centuries in an uneasy peace under the Turks, with the defeat of the Ottoman Empire, both Semitic peoples thirsted for nationhood. Despite the peaceful agreement of Prince Faisal and Chaim Weizmann, most Arabs opposed massive Jewish immigration into Palestine—especially the Palestinian Arabs who wanted to rule the entire region.

The original homeland plan offered to the Jews by the British in the Bal-four Declaration included the entire province of Palestine under the Ot-toman Empire—on both the western and eastern sides of the Jordan River—the borders reaching Egypt, Syria, Iraq, and what would become Saudi Arabia.

In a meeting between Louis Brandeis, Felix Frankfurter, and British Foreign Secretary Arthur Balfour in June 1919, Brandeis presented the American Zionists' desires regarding Palestine.

First, "that Palestine should be the Jewish Homeland, and not merely that there be a Jewish homeland in Palestine." He argued that this was the real commitment of the Balfour Declaration, and the foreign secretary did not disagree. Second, Brandeis asked for "economic elbow room for a Jewish Palestine," meaning "adequate boundaries, not merely a small garden within Palestine." Specifically, he meant the well-watered Galilee and as much of fertile Lebanon as could be obtained from the French. The eastern border of the Jewish homeland, said Brandeis, should be set as far east of the Jordan as Faisal would allow.[340]

After their meeting with Balfour, Brandeis and Frankfurter traveled to Palestine to scope out the land for themselves. Brandeis had never been to the Holy Land, and like so many other first-time visitors, he was in awe of what he saw.

Despite his wonderment, Brandeis was confronted with the reality of the political situation when they met with the Zionist Commission. The acting chairman, Dr. Eder, reported that Lieutenant Colonel Hubbard, the British governor in Jaffa, had said before witnesses: "If the Arabs will massacre the Jews in Jaffa I will not do anything to protect them; I will stand at the window, looking on, and laugh at them."

Sir Ronald Storrs, governor of the District of Jerusalem, told American Zionist Robert Szold he had received no instructions from his government on implementation of the Balfour Declaration and was ready to "go either way—the way of the Arabs or the way of the Jews."

Brandeis investigated further and found these statements to be true. Returning to London after his visit to Palestine, he informed Balfour of the situation. Angered, Balfour replaced the military commander, General Sir Gilbert Clayton, with a Zionist sympathizer, Colonel Richard Meinertzhagen.

In a groundbreaking agreement with Chaim Weizmann, Prince Faisal had been generous and brotherly to his "cousins" the Jews in their quest for a homeland in Palestine. But by the middle of 1920, the Hashemites were losing the gains they thought they had won. The prospects for peace and harmony between the Arabs and the Jews were seriously endangered.

In Arabia, Faisal's father, Emir Hussein, was challenged by a rival prince, Ibn Saud. Since 1906, Saud had been master of much of Arabia, excluding Hejaz, the center of Hussein's power, and two other provinces under direct Turkish control. In 1919, Ibn Saud's army annihilated Hussein's forces; eventually the Hashemites were driven from Arabia altogether.

When the French deposed Faisal and expelled him from Syria by force, then went on to separate the coastal territory of Lebanon from the rest of Syria, setting up a separate state, the Arab world believed the British had agreed to these French actions. Any good feelings that had existed for allowing Jews to enter Palestine in accordance with British wishes disappeared.[341]

From the ashes of these broken promises emerged Arab hatred for Jews. And violence soon followed.

THE ARAB UPRISING

On June 30, 1920, Sir Herbert Samuel, a Jew of English birth, arrived in Palestine as high commissioner. Some noted he was "the first Jewish ruler of Palestine since Hyrcanus II," the last of the Maccabees. The Jews received him, one writer said, "with an enthusiasm appropriate to a herald of the messianic dawn ..." The Arabs showed unexpected restraint, most likely due to the French move to depose Faisal in Syria only a month after Samuel took office.

Samuel went right to work, passing a Land Transfer Ordinance in August that made possible the sale of land to the Zionists. In September, an Immigration Ordinance opened Palestine to legal Jewish immigration for the first time. Visas were granted to all persons recommended by the Zionist Organization. These two ordinances brought into effect the substance of the charter Herzl had dreamed of and worked for to his dying day.[342]

Samuel then issued a decree of amnesty for those involved in the Jerusalem riot of 1920—both the Arab instigators and the Jewish militia defenders. In March 1921, the Muslim spiritual leader of Jerusalem, the Grand Mufti, passed away. Samuel decided to appoint one of the Arab rioters, a convicted conspirator, Haj Amin al-Husseini, to the prestigious and powerful post. Samuel's idea was to balance the power of another Arab family, the Nashasabis, one of whom had just become the mayor of Jerusalem.

In the process, the high commissioner handed a position of enormous prestige to a man determined to destroy the Jewish homeland Samuel had been sent to Palestine to develop.

By April 1921, nearly 10,000 Jews had entered Palestine under Samuel's Immigration Ordinance the previous September. The Arabs grew restless. These immigrants were, for the most part, idealistic young Zionists who had eagerly waited for this opportunity. Their immigration was part of the Third Aliyah, which occurred between 1919 and 1923—a wave that revived collective farming under advanced agricultural training. In time, the people of the Second and the Third Aliyahs would become known as "the founding fathers of Israel."[343]

On May 1, 1921, rival socialist and communist Jews clashed during their May Day rallies near Jaffa. Arab onlookers, seeing the confusion, rushed to join the fight, and a riot ensued. An angry Arab crowd stormed the Zionist Immigration Depot in Jaffa and killed thirteen newly arrived Jews. At the same time, Jewish-owned shops were looted and destroyed.

The rioting spread into Tel Aviv, where Jews gathered to defend themselves with sticks and stones. Over the next few days, Arabs attacked Jewish settlements, burning homes, destroying orchards and crops, and stealing livestock. The British proclaimed martial law but made little attempt to intervene to stop the violence. After a week of rioting, forty-eight Arabs and forty-seven Jews were dead, and hundreds on both sides were wounded. Property losses were enormous.

British authorities blamed Arab resentment of Jewish immigration and the Zionist goal to build a commonwealth in their ancient home.

After reviewing the situation, Samuel shocked the Zionists with his announcement: "I am distressed that the harmony between the creeds and races of Palestine, which I have desired most earnestly to promote, has not yet been attained." He offered a "clarification" of the Balfour Declaration concerning the meaning of "a national home for the Jewish people." The British government, he said, had never intended that a Jewish government would be set up in Palestine to rule the Muslim majority, nor would the Jews be permitted to transform themselves by immigration into a majority themselves.

The Mandate's policy, said Samuel, would be "that the Jews, a people that are scattered throughout the world but whose hearts are always turned to Palestine, should be enabled to found here their home, and that some among them, within the limits that are fixed by the numbers and interests of the present population, should come to Palestine in order to help by their resources and efforts to develop the country, to the advantage of all the inhabitants."

Jews around the world were devastated by Samuel's decree. By this declaration, Samuel imposed sharp limits on future Jewish immigration under the British Mandate.

Privately, Samuel tried to clarify that he was acting according to a long-range plan to appease the Arabs. He believed he was keeping them calm until they realized the Jewish immigrants were no threat to them. Then the building of Zion could resume. The ruse worked for the next eight years. The new immigration restrictions were not strongly enforced, and Jews managed to trickle into Palestine at a rate of a few hundred a month, with the numbers gradually increasing once Arab suspicions had been lulled.

But two dangerous patterns were first revealed in the 1921 riots: First, the Balfour Declaration was shown to be a deliberately ambiguous document that could be interpreted to suit the needs of the moment; and second, the British had no stomach for civil disorder in Palestine and could be forced to reshape their policies by a few hundred marauding rioters.[344] The Arabs and Jews both learned these lessons, which shaped nearly thirty years of British occupation of Palestine.

IRAQ AND TRANS-JORDAN

After the French expelled Faisal from Syria, he angrily turned to the British and demanded compensation. At the same time, his elder brother, Abdullah, who had been promised the throne of Iraq, threatened to avenge the dual insult to his family through a holy war against France in Syria. In January 1921, Abdullah led his army north out of Arabia into the district of eastern Palestine known as Trans-Jordan, planning to move on Damascus to drive the French from Syria.

That same month, British government oversight of Palestine was transferred from Curzon's Foreign Office to that of the Colonial Office under

Winston Churchill. According to diplomat Christopher Sykes, Churchill "wished Zion well from his heart." He was also influenced by T. E. Lawrence and by the idea of ruling the Arab Middle East through the Hashemite dynasty, which had legitimized the British-instigated "Revolt in the Desert" against the Turks. The Colonial Office now had Iraq as well as Palestine under its care.[345]

In response to the Syria crisis, Churchill called for a conference of all senior British officials in the Arab world at Cairo. To appease Faisal, the British conference awarded him the throne of Iraq as king under the British Mandate. Sadly, his Syrian experience had so embittered the moderate Faisal that within a few years he denied ever having made promises to the Jews at all.

The British move on Faisal's behalf in Iraq left them with an extra Hashemite prince, Abdullah, with no available kingdom. Abdullah had temporarily called off his march on Damascus and was still camped at Amman in Trans-Jordan. The Arab population in and around Amman claimed him as their ruler. The glaring problem was that Trans-Jordan was part of Palestine, which had been promised to the Jews. Abdullah was not pleased that the British had promoted his younger brother to the Iraqi throne, which had previously been promised to him.

Late in March 1921, Churchill traveled from Cairo to Jerusalem to meet with Abdullah, High Commissioner Samuel, and Lawrence of Arabia. Within a half hour of sitting down with them, Churchill agreed to carve Trans-Jordan free from Palestine and set it up as an autonomous kingdom under British protection and Abdullah's rule. While the Hashemites were now placated, Palestine had been reduced in size by 80 percent—from a territory the size of Pennsylvania to a tract of land the size of New Jersey.[346]

Weizmann called the deal with Abdullah "a serious whittling down of the Balfour Declaration" that created a potentially dangerous situation. A sparsely settled region had been turned into a political entity under the control of an Arabian dynasty with no previous claim to Palestinian soil. That entity was so bleak, so far from viable, that there would surely be jealousy of western Palestine with its seaports, rivers, growing cities, orchards, and farmland. Caught between the British heavy-handed restrictions and the birth of an unexpected Arab kingdom to the east, the Jews of Palestine had reason for anxiety.

Despite these fears, the 1920s and 1930s saw unprecedented growth in the Jewish community in Palestine. Weizmann helped develop a plan to mine phosphates at the Dead Sea and a hydroelectric power plant on the Jordan River. In 1921, he joined his friend and fellow scientist Albert Einstein to raise money for what later became the Teknion Institute in Haifa.

THE CHURCHILL WHITE PAPER

As the British government prepared the actual text of the Mandate, the document that would serve as a temporary constitution for Palestine, Zionists pushed to make explicit the terms for a Jewish homeland that the Balfour Declaration had left vague. To ensure Jewish rights would not be minimized, the Zionists needed to keep a close watch over the British Foreign Office, which would write the text. The Foreign Secretary, Lord Curzon, was not considered a friend of Zionism.

Curzon's secretary, Eric Forbes-Adam, was assigned to write the Mandate's text. The Zionist representative who examined the emerging document was a twenty-eight-year-old American, Benjamin V. Cohen. Concerned with the strength of the language, Cohen wanted the preamble of the Mandate to acknowledge "the historic rights of the Jews to Palestine," but Curzon would not have it. "If you word it like that," he said, "I can see Weizmann coming to me every other day and saying he has a right to do this, that, or the other in Palestine!"

Balfour suggested referring to a "historical connection" rather than "rights." The final text read: "Recognition has thereby been given to the historical connection of the Jewish people with Palestine and to the grounds for reconstituting their national home in that country."

The final text of the Mandate was completed early in 1922, approving "Jewish immigration under suitable conditions" and "close settlement by Jews on the land ..." Hebrew, Arabic, and English were to be official Palestinian languages, completing the revival of Hebrew as a secular language. The Mandatory power was directed, "so far as circumstances permit," to "encourage local autonomy."

The only significant omission, from the Zionists' point of view, was a specific formula for the ultimate evolution of a self-governing Jewish state out of the Mandate. Despite this, Zionists around the world were satisfied with the language.[347]

The Arabs, on the other hand, were greatly alarmed by the text Great Britain was about to present to the League of Nations for ratification. To avoid more rioting in Palestine, the British government issued a White Paper—an official statement of policy—as a gesture of reassurance. It was a masterpiece of double-talk, declaring that the Balfour Declaration did not apply to the territories east of the Jordan. This amounted to a formal ratification of Churchill's creation of Trans-Jordan as a kingdom for Abdullah.[348]

The paper emphasized that the Balfour Agreement did not support "the disappearance or the subordination of the Arabic population, language, or culture in Palestine," and that the British intended to "foster the establishment of a full measure of self-government in Palestine."

In response, the paper called for both a limitation of Jewish immigration to "the economic capacity of the country to absorb new arrivals" and the restriction of the sale of land to Jews to reduce tensions between the Arabs and Jews in the region. This was considered a great setback to many in the Zionist movement.

After much wrangling back and forth, the League of Nations finally ratified the Mandate text on July 24, 1922.

THE JEWISH AGENCY

At the annual World Zionist Conference the following month, a militant faction confronted Weizmann over his acceptance of the Mandate text, calling it a sellout. The group, led by Vladimir Jabotinsky, argued Weizmann should have insisted on a formal pledge of eventual Jewish autonomy. Weizmann defended his actions on the grounds of realism and expediency. Jabotinsky eventually organized the Revisionists, with the goal of "revising" the boundaries of Palestine back to their pre-White Paper lines and incorporating Trans-Jordan into a sovereign Jewish state.

Moving beyond this protest, the delegates officially accepted the invitation to serve as the "appropriate Jewish agency" to advise the British authorities in Palestine.

During this time, leaders of the Yishuv formed the *Haganah*, a clandestine Jewish defense organization. After the first major Arab riots, Jewish leaders realized it was unwise to depend on the British authorities for security. After British troops refused to intervene in the rioting, the Yishuv leadership created this independent, clandestine force, completely free from foreign authority.

Another important organization, the *Histadrut*, or General Federation of Labor, was founded in December of 1920—"uniting all workers in the country who live on the fruits of their own labors." It embraced both the trade unions and the cooperative agriculture movement, including the kibbutzim. It was, in fact, the organizational embryo of the Jewish state. The Histadrut accepted responsibility for the Haganah on behalf of the Yishuv.[349]

David Ben-Gurion dominated the Histadrut from the early 1920s. Its aims were to mobilize all pioneers, farmers, and workers for a future Jewish state. The Histadrut constituted the only large-scale political body in Palestine and functioned as a pre-state Jewish government.[350]

On the Arab side, the British named Haj Amin al-Husseini president of the newly founded Supreme Muslim Council. In addition to his religious powers as Grand Mufti, al-Husseini would also have the powers of patronage in Muslim and legal affairs that had belonged to the Ottoman rulers. This made al-Husseini the most powerful Arab in Palestine.

By 1923, a tripartite system of government—British, Jewish, and Arab—had emerged in Palestine that would remain throughout the Mandate period. The British left each of the major communities to look after its own affairs in its own way.

Despite the controversy, Jewish immigrants streamed into Palestine, and the homeland was being built. By 1924, Jewish population in Palestine had risen above 100,000 for the first time since the destruction of the Second Temple. Jews entered Eretz Israel so fast the fledgling economy had a hard time keeping up. Unemployment became a serious problem.

Starting in 1924, Mandate officials agreed to permit the entry of "capital-ists"—anyone who could prove possession of $2,500. This plan was de-signed to encourage middle-class Russian Jews who had been stranded in Poland after the war. Normally, this merchant class would have emigrat-ed to the United States. But in 1924, the US government put the brakes on immigration for the first time in history. This deflected thousands of Eastern European Jews toward Palestine.

Weizmann and other old-time Zionists were uneasy about these new merchant immigrants. "True, a considerable amount of capital was being brought into the country," Weizmann explained, "but openings in indus-try, trade and commerce were as yet limited, and the numerous small shops which seemed to spring up overnight in Tel Aviv and Haifa caused me no little worry … Many of them had no knowledge of Hebrew, and, it was soon being said, rather ruefully, that at this rate Tel Aviv would soon be a Yiddish-speaking town. Even to the casual observer, the new immigration carried with it the atmosphere of the ghetto."[351]

Despite the obstacles, Jewish villages founded in the late 1800s grew into towns. The coastal plain bloomed once again as orange groves and vineyards replaced sand dunes. Jewish settlers organized marketplaces to sell their goods. They harnessed the Jordan River to create electricity. They drained swamps and diverted water to farmlands for irrigation. Across Palestine, the Jews worked with the British to introduce modern sanitation and medical care for every resident—Jew or Arab, Muslim or Christian.

Often, however, one step back followed every two steps forward. More than 34,000 Jews immigrated to Palestine in 1925, the peak year for the decade. But this great inflow caused massive unemployment with a sharp economic decline. As a result, two out of every ten Jews who came to Palestine in the 1920s failed to stay. In 1927, more Jews left the country than entered it.

At the same time, as the Zionists had predicted, Arabs from surrounding countries were attracted to the rising standard of living in Palestine and immigrated in droves. The Arab population, unfettered by immigration restrictions, doubled during the 1920s to 800,000.

Meanwhile, the Zionist movement also experienced a decline around the world. Excitement for the cause had ebbed after the ratification of the Mandate for Palestine, as it seemed the movement's most important objectives had been achieved. This was especially true in the United States, where membership in the Zionist Organization of America was one-fourth what it had been the previous decade.[352]

Weizmann was justifiably alarmed. He was even more certain that non-Zionists needed to be included in the Jewish Agency to support the Yishuv and also to keep the lines of communication open among the international Jewish community. For the sake of Palestine, Zionism had to abandon its ideological purity. The nation-builders and political activists would have to embrace those who were humanitarians and philanthropists.

For years, Weizmann had built relationships with Jewish philanthropic leaders, working to convince them that all of Palestine, Jews and Arabs, were worthy of their investment. Finally, in 1929, at the Sixteenth World Zionist Congress, Weizmann announced that of the 224 members of the Jewish Agency's governing body, half would be named by the Zionists and the other half would be appointed by various non-Zionist Jewish groups.

Zionists and non-Zionists signed a formal agreement of cooperation on behalf of their Jewish brethren around the world. Labeled "the Pact of Glory," the ceremony brought together prominent Jews, including Albert Einstein and Sir Herbert Samuel.

THE BIRTH OF THE HEBREW UNIVERSITY

In 1925, the Hebrew University of Jerusalem opened on Mount Scopus. Lord James Arthur Balfour, now seventy-seven years old, attended the ceremony at the invitation of Chaim Weizmann. It was Balfour's first and only visit to Palestine.

Protests appeared in the Arab press against Balfour, and the Arabs put on a display of public mourning. He either ignored or did not notice. "He passed through the silent streets in the old city of Jerusalem and assumed that friendly salutations addressed to his companion, Ronald Storrs, were addressed to him."[353]

Weizmann had carefully steered the university toward practical, academic achievement and away from romantic idealism. As a chemist, Weizmann was particularly fond of the burgeoning science and mathematics departments. "I felt … that the sciences had to be encouraged at Jerusalem, not only for their own sake, but because they were an integral part of the program for the full development of Palestine—and also because opportunities for Jewish students in the leading universities of Europe were becoming more and more restricted."

The most popular academic department was the Institute of Jewish Studies, which was endowed by Sol Rosenbloom of Pittsburgh. Baron Edmond de Rothschild, Felix Warburg, and others took a personal interest in this branch of the university. The Rothschild Hospital in Jerusalem would be the home base for medical research. The Jewish Agricultural Experimental Station already had a large number of researchers, and they became the initial members of the agricultural faculty.

"At that early stage no students had been accepted," Weizmann explained, "but a body of research workers was gradually assembling and the various institutes were taking shape … We sent out invitations for an opening ceremony to be conducted by Lord Balfour. I need not say how much his instant and enthusiastic acceptance of the invitation meant to us."[354]

The fledgling university had no hall to accommodate the massive crowd of visitors coming in from dozens of countries. The only place for a ceremony was a natural amphitheater facing a deep wadi on the northeast slope of Mount Scopus. Across this amphitheater, workers arranged tiers of seats, following the natural rock formation. "Everything was rather rough and ready," Weizmann remembered, "but the setting had such natural beauty that no art could have improved on it."

To face the audience, the platform was built as a bridge over the chasm itself. "The gorge was deep, sheer and rocky; the bridge was an improvised wooden affair which inspired—in me at least—little confidence," Weizmann explained. "I was told that it had been repeatedly tested, but my blood ran cold at the thought that something might give way at the crucial moment."

The builders assured Weizmann and the other leaders that the platform could safely bear as many as 250 people. To prove its safety, 200 young *chalutzim*—Jews who immigrated to Palestine after World War One to work the land—volunteered to perform an energetic *hora*, a folk dance, on the stage. A close inspection after the energetic dance confirmed the platform was sound.

Despite the integrity of the platform, the danger of sabotage by terrorists remained. Throughout the night before the ceremony, young Haganah volunteers camped in the wadi and conducted frequent inspections—the last only minutes before the guests arrived.[355]

At the appointed time, the dignitaries walked together, many wearing their academic robes, through the university grove and onto the platform. Lord Balfour's appearance set off a tremendous ovation.

Later that evening, at a dinner party arranged for the dignitaries, Vera Weizmann sat next to General Allenby. Turning to the conqueror of Palestine, she asked, "Did you think my husband completely harebrained when he asked your permission for the laying of the foundation stones [for the Hebrew University] in 1918?" Allenby thought for a moment, then replied, "When I project my mind back to that day—as I often do—I come to the conclusion that that short ceremony inspired my army, and gave them confidence in the future."[356]

Taking Balfour on a tour of Palestine, Weizmann drove through the countryside to sites of interest. Balfour wanted to see as much of the country as possible and was warmly received wherever he went. He said the tour reminded him of a general election campaign, but with everyone on the same side.

One of the most moving but harrowing parts of the journey was the day spent in and around the growing metropolis of Tel Aviv. The party drove into the city in the early afternoon in an open car, Lord Balfour in the back seat shaking hands and waving at the massive crowds.

"The enthusiasm with which Lord Balfour was received was indescribable," Weizmann recounted. "In Herzl Street stood a group of Jewish women from Poland, weeping for joy; now and again one of them would press forward and gently touch either the body of the car or Lord Balfour's sleeve, and pronounce a blessing on him. He was obviously deeply affected. The car moved forward slowly. Complete order prevailed, and in due course we reached 'Balfour Street,' which Lord Balfour was to open. Here he was greeted by representatives of the municipality, and the short ceremony followed."

Balfour went on to Syria by train, where, unfortunately, he was greeted by a violent demonstration of Arabs angry over the ouster of Faisal. Crowds of angry Syrians tried to storm the Victoria Hotel, and Balfour had to be whisked away by car to the dock where his ship was waiting. All plans for touring Syria were called off, and the party set sail for Alexandria, Egypt.

Lord Balfour wrote a parting letter of thanks to Weizmann for his visit to the Holy Land. "The main purpose of my visit was the opening of the Hebrew University. But the highest intellectual and moral purposes can be only partially successful if, parallel with them, there is not a strong material development. This is why I was particularly happy to see the flourishing Jewish settlements which testify to the soundness and strength of the growing National Home."[357]

Chapter Eleven

BEN-GURION AND THE HAGANAH

1928—PALESTINE

After nearly eight years of relative peace in Palestine, the current British high commissioner, Lord Plumer, made a decision that impacted the Holy Land for years to come. Assuming the harmony between the Arabs and Jews—and the British—would continue indefinitely, Plumer cut back severely on the armed forces available. Not long after this, Plumer retired, and his successor, Sir John Chancellor, took control in the midst of a crisis caused in large measure by the cultural and religious insensitivity along with the outright anti-Jewish bias of some of his top administrators.

Many British political leaders, military officers, and soldiers had a romantic notion of the Arabs from the tales told by Lawrence of Arabia and from their childhood reading of *The Arabian Nights*. Without thoroughly examining the political, religious, and historical facts, some of these officials became decidedly pro-Arab and anti-Jewish. Of course, some were just the opposite. But the Arab leadership, and particularly the Grand Mufti, was quick to use any anti-Semitic attitude or action to their advantage to stir up division.

The trouble began on the eve of Yom Kippur in 1928 when the British district commissioner of Jerusalem, Edward Keith-Roach, inspected the Temple Mount with police officer Douglas Duff. They came to the Haram esh-Sharif in the court attached to the Dome of the Rock, the chief Muslim Holy Place in Palestine. From this vantage point, they looked down on the Western Wall, also known as the Wailing Wall—a surviving section of Herod's Temple sacred to Orthodox Jews and venerated by other Jews.

This area of the Wall is also sacred to Islam. According to Muslim tradition, the Prophet Mohammed tethered his miraculous horse, Buraq, at the wall after his flight from Mecca to Jerusalem and before his ascent to heaven. Muslims call the area al-Buraq, after the horse. Jews have prayed at the Wall since the destruction of the temple in 70 CE, but their approach to it had been strictly restricted in the period of Muslim rule. It remained regulated under the British Mandate.

One of the driving philosophies under the Mandate was to maintain the Anglo-Ottoman status quo for the Holy Places. But as the commissioner looked down on the area in front of the Wall where the Jews were gathered, he noticed an object "made of lath and cloth exactly like an ordinary bedroom screen." The simple barrier had been placed there by the Jews to separate the men and women at prayers. Keith-Roach asked Duff whether he had seen such a screen there before. The police officer had, in fact, seen such a screen before, but he didn't say so. The commissioner then set off a firestorm: "This is an infringement of the status quo ante."

"Some of the religious sheikhs belonging to the Mosque had entered the room," Duff later wrote. "The District Commissioner turned to them and asked whether they had noticed the screen. The crafty old gentlemen had not, but, always willing to make capital at the expense of the Jews, immediately assumed miens of righteous indignation."[358]

The following day was Yom Kippur, one of the most important religious holidays for the Jews. The British police disrupted prayers at the Western Wall to remove the "infringement of the status quo." A clash ensued with some of the worshipers, who were shocked at the police action during the High Holy Days of the Jewish religious calendar. Anger against the British spread throughout the Jewish community. Ironically, Jewish accusations had an eye-opening effect on the Palestinian Arabs who suddenly realized the British authorities may not be as pro-Jewish as their leaders in London.

"It opened up new possibilities," wrote Christopher Sykes, a consistently neutral observer and commentator of the British situation in Palestine. "Suppose these accusations were true, they asked themselves, then, if they were, what were Arabs waiting for? Perhaps the British were their friends after all."[359]

The high commissioner's first significant move was to propose the establishment of a legislative council. Some leading Arab politicians had concluded that participation in representative institutions offered the best hope of blocking future Jewish immigration and of killing the Jewish National Home.

The newly elected British Labour government under Ramsay MacDonald also favored the abandonment of promises made in the Balfour Declaration. For the first time, a government in London had no past ties to the promise. The new colonial secretary, Lord Passfield, Sidney Webb, had little sympathy for the Jewish National Home.

After the Yom Kippur incident, the Mufti launched a propaganda campaign in the mosques and the Arab press charging that the Holy Places were in danger from the Jews. He had observed a marked sensitivity on the part of the Mandatory to Muslim religious sensibilities, while at the same time showing a lack of consideration to Jewish religious institutions. With the move toward representative government by the new high commissioner, the Mufti believed the British were ready to abandon the Jewish Home and hand power to the Arabs. He knew he was liked by the British officials, and he also understood they could be persuaded through unrest.

The Jews organized counterdemonstrations at the Western Wall, which fed right into the Mufti's argument of a threat to the Muslim Holy Places. The firestorm was released in August 1929 through the most innocent of offenses—a Jewish boy kicked a ball into an Arab garden.

A fight ensued between Jews and Arabs, and the boy was stabbed to death. After the boy's funeral, the Jews staged a demonstration at the Western Wall. This was followed by an inflammatory sermon from the Mufti in the Al-Aqsa Mosque, prompting large crowds of Arabs to enter Jerusalem armed with clubs and knives.

The British authorities did not have enough men to control the situation, and they refused the request of the Zionists to arm a large number of Jews. The violence continued for several days, spreading beyond Jerusalem. The worst clash occurred at Hebron, a town sacred to both Arabs and Jews as the burial place of their common ancestor Abraham.

By the time reinforcements arrived from Egypt, 133 Jews had been killed by Arabs and 339 wounded. In quelling the riot, the police killed 110 Arabs, with 232 wounded.[360]

Most Palestinian Jews concluded that a peaceful settlement with the Arabs was no longer possible. The policy of armed preparedness promoted by Vladimir Jabotinsky seemed to be fully vindicated.

The rift between the Histadrut-Haganah movement, led by Ben-Gurion, and the militarist Revisionist-Irgun movement, led by Jabotinsky, grew for years to come. Several Haganah members had formed this radical splinter group to avenge Arab attacks on Jews, while at the same time terrorizing the British in an attempt to force them out of Palestine.

As conflict increased between the Jews, Arabs, and British, the Yishuv generally followed Ben-Gurion's policy of *havlagah*, "self-restraint." It confined itself to the defense of the Jewish settlements. Ben-Gurion agreed with Jabotinsky's concept of the "iron wall"—a much tougher stand against the Arabs and British regarding Jewish security—although he differed with him over the plan's language and implementation.

Despite the differences between the two groups, Ben-Gurion believed confrontation with the Arabs was inevitable.

BEN-GURION'S BEGINNINGS

Born David Gruen in Plonsk, Russia, in 1886, Ben-Gurion was the son of Zionist Avigdor Gruen—a lawyer and a leader in the Hovevei Zion movement. Following his father's Zionist footsteps, young Ben-Gurion dreamed of life in the Holy Land. "I can hardly remember a time when the idea of building the Land of Israel wasn't the guiding factor of my life," he explained. "… From my tenth year on, I never thought of spending my life anywhere else."

David's grandfather taught him Hebrew. "He would sit me on his knee and I would repeat words after him. Within a few months, I became quite fluent, actually learning to speak and to love the Jews' ancient tongue before I could read in any language." For David, it was a living, breathing part of being Jewish.

Listening to his grandfather telling stories of Jewish history, he thought, *Plonsk isn't my real home. Here we live among strangers. I must go to the Land of Israel.*

Ben-Gurion's passion for the Holy Land was ignited when Theodor Herzl visited Plonsk. "Everyone went around saying 'The Messiah has come,' and we children were much impressed. It was easy for a small boy to see in Herzl the Messiah. He was a tall, finely featured man whose impressive black beard flowed wide down to his chest. One glimpse of him and I was ready to follow him then and there to the land of my ancestors."[361]

David's mother, Scheindel, died when he was ten years old. "…Life seemed to have lost all meaning … Then, when I was fourteen, I suddenly emerged from this tunnel to throw myself heart and soul into the Zionist movement."

For Ben-Gurion, there was only one land and one language for the Jewish people. Hebrew was the language of the Bible, and he wanted the nation to embrace its own language. For him the Bible was the essence of life—the story of the Jewish people. Many times he demonstrated that he knew the Bible better than the rabbis.[362]

His father insisted he attend university to finish his education before emigrating. But all of that changed in 1904 with Herzl's Uganda proposal. The Jewish youth of Europe were mostly against the Uganda scheme and were determined to fight it. In David's mind, the only true weapon at his disposal was immediate departure for Palestine.

ALIYAH

At age nineteen, David set out on a lifelong mission to rebuild ancient Israel. He and his friend Zemach shipped out on a Russian freighter, sleeping on the deck. "We did not mind the filth, bad fare or the hardship for we knew that in just fourteen days we would be anchoring in Jaffa."[363]

The port of Jaffa had only one main street lined with small shops and stalls with all sorts of exotic knickknacks. In those narrow, cobblestone alleys, people of every origin traded their wares and their stories. The town brimmed with people from around the globe—Turkish, French, and English traders; Armenian and Arab shopkeepers and dockworkers; Catholic and Greek Orthodox monks; and a few Jews, some whose families had lived there since the time of King Saul.

The day he landed in Jaffa was the happiest of his life. But his joy would soon be tempered by the reality of life in this Ottoman backwater.

In 1906, Palestinian villages were dominated by Arabs, so the only places for Jewish immigrants to go were a few settlements started by Baron Rothschild.[364] The two young men immediately set out on foot for Petah Tikva. After a three-hour walk, they arrived at the gates of the settlement around dusk. Exhausted from their journey, they laid down in a nearby field to rest.

Too excited to sleep, David wrote to his father:

> The howling of the jackals in the vineyards, the braying of the donkeys in the stables, the croaking of the frogs in the ponds, the heavy scent of acacias, the sound of the sea in the distance, the shadows of the orange trees in the half-light, the stars twinkling in a dark blue sky that glistened and seemed unreal, everything was so wonderfully strange as in some legendary realm. I thought of all the stages of my journey, the farewells, the sea passage and the approach to the coast of Palestine. And now I was in Eretz Israel. Was it really true? I sat up all night communing with these new skies.[365]

While the Holy Land sky was beautiful, the rocky land still yielded little to the inhabitants. To survive would take all the energy and ingenuity he possessed.

The Jewish farmers were the sons of the pioneers from the First Aliyah who had become comfortable landowners. They were repelled by the newcomers with their talk of socialism, collective living, and the sharing of wealth. "We frightened them with theories and annoyed them with our lack of farming competence. They turned their back on us, preferring Arab workers who were more efficient, demanded less pay, and most of all, didn't presume to social equality with the employer."

At Petah Tikva, David literally starved. Having never worked in agriculture, he was small and frail. He was passed over by the farmers who took the time to feel each candidate's arm to determine whether there was sufficient muscle for the work. It took ten days to get his first assignment—carting wheelbarrows of manure for the orange groves. The pay was barely enough for him to survive. He left Petah Tikva and wandered from settlement to settlement.

"I stayed a few weeks on the plateau of Kfar Saba and spent another pe-riod in the vineyards of Rishon-Le-Zion, where I planted vines, shifted manure, dug irrigation ditches, ploughed, helped carry away the end-less rocks and boulders that plagued all attempts to farm this earth." The weather changed abruptly from boiling heat to the cold drizzle of winter. The land turned to mud, and David's clothing and diet were inadequate to protect him from the elements. He soon contracted malaria.

His temperature spiked to 104 degrees, and he was often delirious. This went on for three or four days, then the fever subsided, leaving him weak and shaken. Work was scarce, so as he fought malaria, he also starved. A friend arranged for him to see a doctor who told David he would never shake the disease. Staying in Eretz Israel meant death.

Well-meaning friends pointed out that this was hardly a disgrace, as many immigrants who came to Palestine in those early days returned to their homes after only a short time. But David didn't listen. "I hung on grimly trying to let the disease and the lack of food hinder me as little as possible in the course I had determined my life should take."

His father wrote, begging him to come home, sending money for the voyage. David returned the money. "You know I won't leave this country."

"There was nothing here," he later wrote of these difficult times and why he chose to stay. "It was literally a forgotten corner of the Turkish Empire and of the globe. Nobody wanted it, certainly not the Palestinian Arabs who were placidly vegetating in their poverty under the Turks … When I came here, no one could have cared less about the place. Anyone was free to come and create afresh … We held clear title to this country. Not the right to take it away from others (there were no others), but the right and the duty to fill its emptiness, restore life to its barrenness, to re-create a modern version of our ancient nation … I felt we owed this effort not only to ourselves but to the land as well."

When spring arrived, the malaria became less acute. Rishon-LeZion was celebrating its twenty-fifth year, and though he had a fever of 102 degrees, David wanted to be present for this tribute to one of the first modern Jewish settlements. "We drank wine and danced through the night and suddenly, I felt well. The attacks didn't come back so strongly after that. A few months later, when I moved up to the hills of Galilee with a group of young people, they [the symptoms] disappeared almost totally."[366]

With his health restored, David joined a group of pioneer laborers as a ploughman with two oxen. He lived the life he had always dreamed of. The work was hard, with insufficient food and sparse living conditions, but he enjoyed every minute of it.

> My group was engaged in what we called "the conquest of labor." We would go out as a collective and work on land which the Jews themselves had bought and paid for through the Jewish National Fund or the Jewish Colonization Association. We would prepare a large patch of ground, making it ready for planting so that it could be settled rapidly by permanent settlers following on behind us. Then we would move off to work a new tract, perhaps a valley swamp or a boulder-strewn hillside. The idea was that we, who prepared the ground, would be permanent pioneers, moving from place to place on reclamation tasks, making the land fit for Jewish farm settlers.[367]

In 1909, a similar group working in the Jordan valley decided to plant a permanent collective settlement on a tract they themselves had prepared. This became Degeniah, the first communal village—in Hebrew, *kibbutz*—where everyone was equal no matter what his or her task. They all shared title both to the land and whatever its yield.[368]

David's group worked in Sejera and the surrounding area for the next two years. Although the work was difficult, their greater worry was marauding Arabs. "We were an isolated community surrounded by nomadic Bedouins. Their intent was not to hurt us or to drive us away, but plain theft. They bothered the Arab settlements as much as they did us."

The group organized its own defense called *Hashomer*, or "The Watchmen." At night, each person took a round at guard duty. As long as the Bedouins knew the Jews were vigilant, they kept their distance.

"There was complete anarchy up there in the Galilee. Defense of the settlements certainly didn't depend on the Turkish government since it had to all intents abandoned the country to its own devices. The only interest Turkey had in Palestine was the collecting of taxes."

At this time, David adopted a Hebraicized version of his birth name. "Hebraicizing one's name seemed to my generation a way of underlining our feeling for the country and our affinity with our ancestors. We were, in effect, indicating our purpose of taking up where they had left off." So David Gruen became David Ben-Gurion, which means "Son of the Lion" in Hebrew. This was in homage to a Jewish hero called Ben-Gurion who died defending Jerusalem against the final siege of the Roman legions in 70 CE.[369]

Arriving in Jerusalem, Ben-Gurion quickly realized that the Jews had no hope of a state without a leader. When he had questions, and nobody could give him the answers, he decided, "I've got to give the answers."

After World War One, Ben-Gurion entered politics by launching a campaign for workers' unity. The Jewish settlements in the country were in a state of decay after the war, and much of the work accomplished in the previous fifty years was in ruins. Ben-Gurion recognized a serious lack of leadership among the Yishuv, even though immigration of Jews was on the rise. He went to work to create a cohesive organization among the Jews of Palestine.

In 1925, Ben-Gurion's elderly father finally moved to Eretz Israel. As he built the Histadrut, Ben-Gurion and his family lived in near poverty in Jerusalem. At the same time, he represented the Palestine Jewish workers in the Zionist movement of Europe, where he advocated for financial support of immigrants and the creation of jobs and pioneering opportunities. He also served as the Histadrut's representative in the World Zionist Organization and the Jewish Agency.[370]

Ben-Gurion was elected chairman of both organizations in 1935. The Histadrut Union supervised massive waves of immigration, plus the creation of hospitals, schools, sanitation, and public works. But more Jewish immigrants meant more trouble with the Arabs. In the 1920s, widespread Arab riots rocked Palestine, and the British did little or nothing to stop them.[371]

As the head of the Histadrut, Ben-Gurion led the initiative to develop Hashomer into a countrywide clandestine army—the Haganah. The mission was to protect the Jewish communities from ever-increasing Arab hostility—much of which was fostered and promoted by the infamous Mufti of Jerusalem.[372]

Volunteers were mostly veterans of the Jewish Legion and Zion Mule Corps, who had fought for the British in World War One, and the Hasho-mer guards that had been formed to guard Jewish settlements. Friction soon developed between the army veterans, who wanted a tight-knit professional group, and the Hashomer people, who wanted a popular militia. The Haganah was illegal, it had few sources of weapons, and training was sparse. So in the May 1921 riots, the Haganah was not ef-fective. The political leadership wanted the Haganah to become a legal body subordinate to the British. But the soldiers objected, arguing they would lose their independence and, most likely, their arms. In the end, everyone agreed that the British would never allow independent Jewish self-defense.[373]

The Arab riots in 1929 brought about a complete change in the Haganah's status. The Zionists realized the force had to be expanded into a much larger organization encompassing nearly every Jewish adult. A compre-hensive training program was established for members and officers. It established central arms depots into which a continuous stream of light arms flowed from Europe.[374] The Haganah also developed clandestine factories to manufacture hand grenades and simple military equipment.

In some kibbutzim, munitions factories operated secretly in sub-base-ments beneath other facilities, such as bakeries or laundry rooms. Deep underground, kibbutz workers created small arms while their comrades worked the fields. To keep the operation a secret, the workers took breaks throughout the day to sit under sun lamps so they too looked like they had been in the fields. One worker was assigned to picking out metal shavings from the shoes of each worker as they finished their day of work and climbed the winding staircase up to the ground level.

Soon the Haganah was transformed from a poorly trained militia into a capable underground army.[375]

Passfield and the MacDonald Letter

After the 1929 riots, Colonial Secretary Lord Passfield along with High Commissioner Chancellor concluded that a Jewish National Home in Palestine was impossible due to the fury it caused among the Arabs. When Chaim Weizmann reached out to Passfield after the massacres, he initially would not even agree to a meeting.

Later, when Passfield finally agreed to meet, he made it clear he was against mass immigration of the Jews.[376] The political winds had shifted, and the Jewish National Home was in danger of being stillborn.

Passfield began a campaign to convince the League of Nations to make a major change in the interpretation of the original Mandate. The colonial secretary initiated two Royal Commissions, the first headed by Sir Walter Shaw and the second headed by Sir John Hope Simpson.

The Shaw report found that the attacks on the Jews were "unpremeditated." It blamed the Mufti for "not having done more to stop the riots" but came short of blaming him for instigating them. It recommended that the government should greatly restrict Jewish immigration to prevent provoking the Arabs to further rioting. In response, on May 12, 1930, the Colonial Office suspended the latest Jewish immigration schedule of 3,300 Labor Certificates.

In the second commission, Sir Hope Simpson used the criterion of "absorptive capacity" in Churchill's White Paper of 1922 to determine that Palestine could not absorb more than a total of 50,000 extra Jewish immigrants—a finding that, if true, would slam the brakes on the Jewish homeland.

Passfield took the findings of these two commissions to the Permanent Mandates Commission of the League of Nations, noting the existence of "a twofold duty" and of "a conflict of interests"—highlighting the differences between the Arabs and the Jews in Palestine. Passfield then incorporated the essential elements of the Shaw and Hope Simpson reports into an official White Paper, published on October 21, 1930. The document proposed a legislative council with an Arab/Muslim majority and a Jewish minority. The Passfield White Paper made no mention whatsoever of the Balfour Declaration and even suggested that Great Britain's commitment to a Jewish National Homeland had already been discharged.

The colonial secretary explained that his plan for British policy would move in the direction of an independent Arab Palestine with some form of "guarantees" for the Jews already there and severe restrictions on further Jewish immigration.[377]

In one bold move, Britain signaled a reversal of its support for the Balfour Declaration and its opposition to the Zionists' goal of a Jewish homeland in Palestine. Jewish trust in the British was shattered. England had its own aims for the Middle East—to create a permanent colonial outpost and to establish a pan-Arab union dependent on Great Britain. A Jewish state would be uncontrollable and independent; therefore, it had to be jettisoned.

Although greatly discouraged by these developments, Chaim Weizmann launched a campaign in defense of the National Home. In a symbolic and tactical move, Weizmann resigned as president of the Zionist Organization on the same day as the publication of the Passfield White Paper. His resignation personalized the government's betrayal of the Balfour Declaration and became the rallying cry of the opposition, led by Lloyd George, in the House of Commons debate.

Opponents of the White Paper from both the Conservative and Liberal sides denounced Passfield's actions as a betrayal of Britain's promise to the Jews.

Prime Minister MacDonald quickly realized the White Paper was a political blunder. He invited Weizmann to lunch and promised that the "errors" in the White Paper would be "put right" in a letter from him that would be made public.[378] Weizmann recognized MacDonald's parliamentary weakness and insisted that the letter of "clarification" be a retraction communicated to the League of Nations as an official document. He requested that the letter be included in a dispatch to the high commissioner in Palestine and publicized as an "authoritative interpretation" of the Passfield White Paper.

MacDonald acquiesced.

On February 13, 1931, the prime minister read his letter to Weizmann in the House of Commons. "The obligation to facilitate Jewish immigration and to encourage close settlement by Jews on the land remains a positive obligation of the Mandate," MacDonald declared, "and it can be fulfilled without prejudice to the rights … of all sections of the population of Palestine."

MacDonald's letter to Weizmann became known among the Arabs of Palestine as the Black Letter.[379] The violence against the Jews continued, spurred on by the Mufti.

In response to this ongoing Arab violence, along with growing British indifference, many Haganah fighters objected to the official policy of hav-lagah that Jewish political leaders had imposed on the militia. Fighters had been instructed to only defend communities and not initiate coun-terattacks against Arab gangs or their communities. This policy appeared weak and defeatist to some who believed the best defense was a good offense. In 1931, the more militant elements of the Haganah splintered off and formed the *Irgun Tsva'i-Leumi*, better known simply as the *Irgun* and also by its Hebrew acronym, pronounced "Etzel."[380]

THE RISE OF HITLER AND THE NAZIS

With the release of the MacDonald letter, immigration of Jews into Palestine reached levels undreamed of by the Zionists. Then, with the emergence of Adolf Hitler and the Nazis in Europe, Jewish immigration skyrocketed to more than 30,000 in 1933. In 1934, there were 42,359 immigrants, the greatest influx of Jews into Palestine since the return from the Babylonian captivity.

When the infamous Nuremberg Laws were passed in 1935, an astound-ing 61,854 Jewish immigrants fled to the Holy Land. Most of the sci-entists and artists escaping from Germany fled to the urban centers of the West. Nearly half of the immigrants of this Fifth Aliyah, the "Hitler Aliyah," were Polish Jews who saw the writing on the wall and chose to flee to Eretz Israel while the route was still open.[381]

Observing the growing threat of Adolf Hitler and Nazi Germany, Ben-Gurion spoke in eerily prophetic terms concerning the future—not only of the Yishuv but also of Jews around the world:

> The disaster which has befallen German Jewry is not limited to Germany alone. Hitler's regime places the entire Jewish people in danger, and not the Jewish people alone … Hitler's regime cannot long survive without a war of revenge against France, Poland, Czechoslovakia … and against Soviet Russia. Germany will not go to war today for she is not ready, but she is preparing for the morrow … Who knows; perhaps only four or five years, if not less, stand between us and that awful day.

Then, as leader of the Jews in Palestine, Ben-Gurion drew a hope-filled conclusion but also a call to action:

> In this period—the four or five years remaining—we must double our numbers, for the size of the Jewish population on that day may determine our fate at the postwar settlement.[382]

Chapter Twelve

HITLER AND THE NAZIS

The idea of a mass annihilation of the Jews wasn't new. It had been discussed for centuries. What Hitler did was transform the talk into heinous government-led action.[383]

During the 1920s, anti-Semitic propaganda spread throughout Germany. The *Protocols of the Elders of Zion* had been translated into German, selling 120,000 copies. This forgery was fabricated by the secret police of Tsarist Russia to justify that government's persecution of Jews. Even though the document was a work of fiction, people throughout Russia and Germany—including Adolf Hitler—believed it to be real.[384]

MEIN KAMPF

In an attempt to overthrow the government, called the Beer Hall Putsch, Hitler and some associates were incarcerated in the Landsberg Prison. While serving out his sentence, Hitler dictated his political manifesto, *Mein Kampf*. It was an autobiography, ideological white paper, and political party manual.[385] In Hitler's thinking, race was the central principle of human existence, highlighted by the age-old struggle between two world adversaries—the Aryans and the Jews.

According to Hitler, the Aryan race was the "bearer of human cultural development." The Aryans, therefore, by their nature—or as he put it, their " blood"—were chosen to rule the world.[386]

The obstacle to the fulfillment of this millennial vision, according to Hitler, was the Jew. The Aryans represented the perfection of human existence, whereas the Jews were the embodiment of evil. Hitler wrote of Jews being so wicked "that no one need be surprised if among our people the personification of the devil as the symbol of all evil assumes the living shape of the Jews."[387]

Hitler described Jews as parasites and vampires, contaminating the Aryan race and sucking the life from the nation. He invented the myth that the Jews had no language or culture of their own, that they sapped, drained, and ultimately destroyed other cultures and races. By that means, Hitler maintained, the Jews would achieve dominion over the world.[388]

By 1939, the book had sold 5.2 million copies in eleven languages, making Adolf Hitler a rich man.[389]

The Great Depression

Hitler realized he needed to use the democratic process to achieve power. Fortunes changed for the Nazis when the American stock exchange crashed in October 1929, plunging the world into a global depression. During the winter of 1929–30, more than three million Germans—14 percent of the population—were unemployed. That figure climbed to five million jobless by January of 1933.[390]

Economic distress contributed to an explosion in support for the Nazis. It was an era driven by hate and paranoia, and the Nazis told the public that a Jew lurked behind every problem. In 1923, the National Socialists had won 800,000 votes. In 1930, they won 6.5 million. In 1932, nearly fourteen million out of forty-five million voted for the Nazis in the last free election of the Weimar Republic.[391]

The Nazis now occupied 230 seats in the *Reichstag*—a total higher than the combined results of their two closest rivals, the Communists and the Social Democrats.[392] Hitler refused to join any coalition government, which forced new elections in November. Again, the Nazis had the most seats but not enough to form a government.

Faced with the prospect that no sustainable government would emerge after the November elections, German president Paul von Hindenburg used his constitutional authority to reluctantly appoint Hitler, a man he despised, as chancellor of Germany. Hitler had not seized power—it was handed to him by those who thought he could be controlled.

National Socialism was the consummation of German anti-Semitic efforts over the previous 150 years.[393]

With power in his grasp, Hitler set out to destroy the constitution and the laws he had sworn to protect. He set out to annihilate democracy, freedom, political pluralism, and, most of all, the Jewish people.

On August 2, 1934, von Hindenburg died. Within an hour, the government announced the offices of president and chancellor would be merged. Hitler became the nation's ultimate authority. On that same day, German soldiers were compelled to take a personal oath of loyalty—not to the nation but to Adolf Hitler.

Less than three weeks later, the German people were given the opportunity to ratify Hitler's new position and title: *Fuhrer* and Reich chancellor. Thirty-eight million Germans—90 percent of the votes cast—said yes.[394]

The following year, Hitler sent three vice-tightening laws against the Jews to the *Reichstag*, which passed them unanimously. The Law for the Protection of German Blood and Honor stated "the purity of German blood" was essential for the ongoing existence of the German people. The Nuremberg Laws found Jewish "blood" to be inferior and dangerous. Jews needed to be segregated, isolated, and removed from the mainstream of German society. These laws were used to identify the targets for persecution and, eventually, death.[395]

On June 17, 1936, Hitler appointed SS Chief Heinrich Himmler head of all German police units. The Gestapo—or German secret state police— was placed under Himmler's control. Responsible for state security, the Gestapo had the authority to send individuals to concentration camps.[396] In the months after Hitler took power, Gestapo agents went door to door looking for Hitler's enemies.

Democracy was dead in Germany. The Nazi police in the SS—a paramilitary force under the direct control of Adolf Hitler— set up hundreds of makeshift "camps" in empty warehouses and factories across Germany, where they held political opponents. One of these camps was set up on March 20, 1933, at Dachau, an abandoned munitions factory. Located near Munich, Dachau would become the model concentration camp.[397]

In 1937, the German Interior Ministry required Jews to carry special identity cards for travel inside the country. That summer, the Nazi camp system expanded, most significantly with the opening of Buchenwald. The camp initially housed political prisoners, but it was enlarged in 1938 to take in large numbers of Jews. The camp soon became a torture and killing center as tens of thousands eventually perished—victims of disease from overcrowding and poor sanitation, hard labor, torture, medical experiments, firing squads, and gassing.[398]

THE DRUMS OF WAR

On March 12, 1938, German troops crossed the Austrian border as the *Anschluss* pulled Austria into the Third Reich. Thousands of enthusiastic Viennese greeted Hitler's triumphal arrival. "As *Fuhrer* and chancellor of the German nation and Reich," Hitler proclaimed from the balcony of the Hofburg Imperial Palace in Vienna, "I now report to history that my homeland has joined the German Reich."

To raise the pressure on Jews to emigrate from Austria, a young second lieutenant, Adolf Eichmann, was tasked with finding various means of persuasion. In six months. Eichmann expelled nearly 45,000 Jews from Austria, and by May 1939, some 100,000 Jews—more than 50 percent of Austria's Jewish population—had fled.

In an effort to keep Jews out of their countries, many European nations started revoking the citizenship of those living abroad. On November 1, 1938, Poland revoked the citizenship of Polish Jews living in Germany.

The family of Herschel Grynszpan was among the Polish Jews who ended up in a concentration camp near the border town of Zbaszyn. Living in Paris at the time, Herschel received word from his sister that his family had been forced to leave their home in Hannover, Germany. At that time, they were among some 17,000 Polish Jews—most longtime residents of Germany—whom the Nazi government had deported to Polish territory. When the Polish state refused them entry, most of these hapless Jews ended up in this miserable refugee camp.

In reprisal, Grynszpan went to the German Embassy in Paris on November 7 and asked to see an official. He then shot and fatally wounded Ernst von Rath.

As Rath lay dying, Nazi plans made in advance of such an event were unveiled, giving free rein to the "spontaneous" eruption of "popular anger" that news of the shooting had provoked. After Rath's death, Propaganda Minister Joseph Goebbels gave the signal, sanctioned by Hitler himself, for a nationwide pogrom against the Reich's Jews.

These November pogroms came to be known collectively as *Kristallnacht*—Night of Broken Glass. A telegram from Gestapo chief Heinrich Muller was sent to all police units on the evening of November 9: "In shortest order, actions against Jews and especially their synagogues will take place in all Germany. These are not to be interfered with ..."

The "actions" were devastating. Throughout the Reich, Jewish synagogues, cemeteries, hospitals, schools, businesses, and homes were looted and set aflame. Scores of Jews were killed.

The German neighbors of the Jews inflicted much of this damage while police followed Muller's orders not to interfere. Meanwhile, fire brigades followed their orders to let torched synagogues burn but to protect nearby Aryan property. Jews were blamed for the pogrom and forced to pay for the damages. A fine of one billion *Reichsmarks*, equal to $400 million—was imposed on the Jewish community.

Kristallnacht ended the illusion that anything resembling normal Jewish life was still possible in the Third Reich.[399]

In 1939, two-thirds of the world's Jews lived in Europe and three-fourths of them—half of all world Jewry—were concentrated in Eastern Europe.[400] On January 30, Hitler spoke to the *Reichstag* about the future of Europe and the fate of European Jewry in particular. The evening's two-and-a-half-hour speech included familiar anti-Jewish tirades, but on this occasion Hitler's menacing forecasts were more ominous than usual.

"If international Jewish financiers inside and outside Europe again succeed in plunging the nations into a world war," Hitler insisted, "the result will not be the bolshevization of the earth and with it the victory of Jewry, but the annihilation of the Jewish race in Europe."[401]

Before the German attack could be launched, the Nazis needed to check potential opposition from the Soviet Union. On August 23, the foreign ministers of Nazi Germany and the USSR signed the German-Soviet Non-Aggression Pact, agreeing that Poland would be partitioned between them. Without fear of Soviet intervention, Nazi Germany invaded Poland on September 1.

Two days later, Britain and France responded to the plight of their Polish ally by declaring war on Germany. Before September ended, however, German forces had crushed Polish resistance.

MODERN MECHANIZED DEATH

On September 21, Reinhard Heydrich, the head of Nazi Germany's Security Police, dispatched a secret message to the chiefs of special task forces in Poland—the *Einsatzgruppen*. The subject of the message was the "Jewish Question in Occupied Territory." Jews would be concentrated: moved from the countryside and villages into large cities where railroad transportation was readily available. Certain parts of occupied Poland would become *Judenrein*—cleansed of all Jews—to facilitate the resettlement of ethnic Germans.

He also ordered the ghettoization of Polish Jewry, a deadly decision that eventually doomed millions of Jews. Under the cover of conventional war, a different war—one against all of Europe's Jews—was waged.[402] Jews were gassed by the hundreds of thousands.[403]

The Jewish Holocaust was under way.

Chapter Thirteen

THE 1939 WHITE PAPER

1936—PALESTINE

The Fifth Aliya, from 1933 to 1939, included many academics and professionals who settled in towns and cities, bringing with them a large influx of capital and technical expertise. In the beginning, the purchase of land was based on what was available for sale. Then, in the 1930s, it became clear the area would be partitioned into a Jewish state and an Arab state. The Jewish National Fund concentrated the purchase of land on the edges of Palestine to broaden the borders of the future Jewish state.[404]

Violence again erupted in Palestine in April 1936 when six prominent Arab leaders overcame their rivalries and joined forces to protest Zionist advances.

The Arab High Command, as the group was known, was led by the Grand Mufti, Haj Amin al-Husseini, and represented Arab interests in Palestine until 1948. Their protest began when they called for a general strike of Arab workers and a boycott of Jewish products. These actions quickly escalated into the "Arab revolt" with terrorist attacks against both the Jews and the British.[405]

On April 15, 1936, a group of armed Arabs took two Jews off a bus in the Nablus Mountains and murdered them. Two days later, members of the Irgun murdered two Arabs near the Jewish settlement of Petah Tikva. This led to a series of incidents that escalated into a widespread conflict.

Major disturbances occurred in Jaffa, Nablus, and other locations across Palestine after Arab strike committees unleashed an outbreak of armed violence. Leaders of the Jewish communities could barely restrain the young people in the Haganah from fighting back and starting a civil war.

In general, the Yishuv followed Ben-Gurion's policy of havlagah and confined itself to the successful defense of the Jewish settlements.

In the first weeks, the Jews were the main victims of the attack. But with the Mufti's instigation, the movement became an insurrection against British rule, and soon both the Jews and the British became Arab targets. The British government dramatically increased the number of troops by August.

The Arab Higher Committee, a loose coalition of recently formed Arab political parties, was created in the midst of the uprising with the Mufti becoming the head. The Supreme Muslim Council joined the uprising—a move that risked al Husseini's position as Grand Mufti, which the British Mandatory government had granted him.

According to his viewpoint, the Jews had refused offers of a national home in other places, such as Uganda, only "for a religious idea which they maintain and which aims at the reconstruction of the Jewish Temple of Solomon" in the place of the Mosque of Al-Aqsa. The British, in refusing the Muslim demands, were viewed as Jewish supporters in this endeavor.[406]

But the main Arab demand, and the key to everything else, was cessation of Jewish immigration. In one of history's great tragedies, as Hitler's murderous reign of terror was closing in on the Jews of Europe, the gates to Palestine—the Jews' ancient homeland—were slammed shut by the British. After record immigration by Jews to the Holy Land in the early 1930s, by the second half of the decade the numbers slowed to a trickle. As a result, millions of Jews faced the gallows, the firing squads, and, eventually, the gas chambers.

With the approach of another war, the British priority was keeping the goodwill of the Arab rulers to maintain the flow of oil for military use. At the same time, the British wanted to ensure that their Arab allies would not be overthrown. This was accomplished, according to the British government, by trying to keep the Arab people happy. For many in the Foreign Office and the Colonial Office, the way to please these rulers and make them more popular was to downplay, or even reject, the Jewish National Home in Palestine. The Arab leaders confirmed this was indeed the case. As a result, the total authorized immigration into Palestine in

THE 1939 WHITE PAPER

1936 was 29,727—less than half the figure for 1935, and the lowest since 1932.

In the summer of 1936, three Arab princes from the surrounding nations put pressure on the British to transform Palestine policy to favor the Arabs at the expense of the Jews. Haj Amin al-Husseini astutely read the shifting political realities in the Middle East and made an appeal to King Ibn Saud, the leader Saudia Arabia, which had recently entered the League of Nations. He also contacted Ghazi, king of Iraq, and Abdullah, the vassal emir of Trans-Jordan. The Mufti had been trying, since 1928, to make Palestine, and Jerusalem in particular, a Pan-Muslim concern.[407] His appeal to the three Arab princes was meant to bolster his influence and prestige both in the Arab world and among the British.

At the request of both the British Foreign Office and the Higher Arab Committee, the Arab princes were encouraged to issue a joint appeal to help quell the unrest so the British could send in a commission to study the unrest and make recommendations to the League of Nations. The Foreign Office assured the princes they could expect a report that would be favorable to the Arabs in Palestine. With these assurances in mind, the princes released their appeal on October 10, 1936:

> … We have been much distressed by the present situation in Palestine. In agreement with our brothers the Arab Kings and the Emir Abdullah we appeal to you to restore tranquility in order to prevent further bloodshed, relying on the good intentions of our friend the British Government to see that justice is done. Be assured that we shall continue our endeavor to help you.[408]

THE PEEL COMMISSION

Once order was restored, a royal inquiry was sent to Palestine to seek a solution to the problems fueling the uprising. Known as the Peel Commission, it arrived in November 1936 and held sixty-six meetings. Jewish evidence dominated most of these meetings since the Arabs boycotted the proceedings until the fifty-sixth meeting.

The most moving testimony was given at a public hearing in Jerusalem by elder statesman Chaim Weizmann, who spoke of the challenge of sharing the land with the Arabs. His words and tone carried a hint of sadness and pain:

> I think I can say before the Commission, before God and before the world, that in intention, consciously, nothing has been done to injure their position … On the contrary, indirectly, we have conferred benefits on the population of this country. I should like to be perfectly frank, we have not come for that purpose. We have come for the purpose of building up a National Home for the Jewish people, but we are happy and proud that this up-building has been accompanied by a minimum of suffering, by a minimum of servitude and by considerable benefits to the country at large.[409]

The commissioners seemed to fall under Weizmann's spell.

David Ben-Gurion spoke before the commission in a much different tone. His basic thesis was that the commission, its recommendation, and even the British Mandate were insignificant things in light of the title deed of the Jews to the Land of Israel.

> I say on behalf of the Jews that the Bible is our Mandate, the Bible which was written by us, in our own language, in Hebrew in this very country. That is our Mandate. It was only the recognition of this right which was expressed in the Balfour Declaration.[410]

The Grand Mufti gave testimony a week later and agreed that the Jewish claim to a National Home in Palestine was fundamentally religious, but he drew a sharply different conclusion, reiterating the controversial statement that was in large measure behind the Arab rioting over the previous decade.

> The Jews' ultimate aim is the reconstruction of the temple of King Solomon on the ruins of the Harm ash-Sharif, the El-Aqsa Mosque and the Holy Dome of the Rock.[411]

The report of the commission, which was issued in July 1937, described the Arab and Zionist positions and the British obligation to each as irreconcilable and the existing Mandate as unworkable.

The disease is so deep-rooted that, in our firm conviction, the only hope of a cure lies in a surgical operation ... An irrepressible conflict has arisen between two national communities within the narrow bounds of one small country ... About 1,000,000 Arabs are in strife, open or latent, with some 400,000 Jews ... But while neither race can justly rule all Palestine, we see no reason why, if it were practicable, each race should not rule part of it ... Partition seems to offer at least a chance of ultimate peace. We can see none in any other plan.[412]

As the Peel Commission put it: "Twelve years ago the National Home was an experiment, today it is a going concern."[413]

According to this plan, the Jews would establish a wholly autonomous and independent state in the Galilee and Valley of Jezreel, an area comprising about one-fifth of western Palestine. The Jewish state would be assigned a coastal strip from south of Jaffa to north of Haifa, together with Galilee from the sea to the Syrian border. The Arabs would get almost the entire remainder of the country, which would be incorporated into the newly created state of Trans-Jordan, owing its existence to the Churchill White Paper of 1922. The British would keep Jerusalem, Nazareth, and a corridor to the Mediterranean, including the port of Haifa.

In 1937, the Twentieth Zionist Congress agreed in principle to partition, although it rejected the specific boundaries. Histadrut joined the Zionist movement in accepting the commission's proposal on the grounds that, small as the designated Jewish territory was, it nevertheless constituted a basis for the formation of a Jewish state in Palestine.[414]

Weizmann and Ben-Gurion both favored partition because it carried with it the Jewish state, even in a small territory. The Zionist Executive was authorized to negotiate with the Mandatory for the purpose of "ascertaining the precise [British] terms for the proposed establishment of a Jewish state."

Despite the Palestinian Arab nationalists' rejection of any kind of partition, the British government approved the idea. In a White Paper issued simultaneously with the published report, the British government expressed general agreement with the Peel Commission's findings, and stated specifically "that a scheme of partition on the [Peel recommend-ed] lines … represents the best and most hopeful solution of the dead-lock."[415]

But just when it seemed there was a glimmer of renewed hope, the Brit-ish backed away in the face of universal opposition by the Palestinian Arabs. The tactic used was to allow the idea to die slowly through yet another royal commission—this one sent to establish precise partition lines. In reality, the Woodhead Commission came to Palestine to demon-strate that partition was impracticable.[416]

At the same time, diplomats tried to assure Arab princes of an inde-pendent state to be established at some time in the future. The British Foreign Office worked diligently to destroy the partition plan and the Jewish state.

The option the Foreign Office had hoped for, an independent Arab Pal-estine with "guarantees" for the Jews already there, was no longer viable. With the Yishuv now standing at 400,000 people, and with Jews being hunted down and killed by the Nazis in Europe, it was not realistic for Britain to jettison their promise of a National Home for the Jews in Pal-estine. It became obvious that the Jews would fight rather than be forced into an Arab-majority state. For Britain, the only realistic options left were to impose partition or to pull out and leave the Jews and Arabs to fight it out.

Arab anger and frustration over the situation reached a boiling point again in the autumn of 1937. In this second phase of Arab revolt, clashes with the British forces became much more severe, as did the attacks on Jewish settlements. On September 26, 1937, Lewis Andrews, the British acting district commissioner of Galilee was murdered by Arab marauders. This was the first successful assassination of a high level official by the Arabs, and it was regarded as a declaration of rebellion against British rule.

The British had no choice but to put down the revolt using harsh measures. They put out warrants for the arrest of the Arab High Command members and removed Haj Amin from his position as head of the Supreme Muslim Council. Fearing that the British might violate his sanctuary on the Hara mesh-Sharif, Haj Amin dressed as a Bedouin and secretly descended the wall. He made his way to Lebanon, where the French gave him asylum.

Against this full-scale revolt, the British applied severe military repression, including marshal law, military courts, capital punishment of offenders, and reprisals against rogue villages.

As war with Germany became imminent, Britain's dependence on Middle-Eastern oil, and therefore the need for Arab goodwill, loomed increasingly large in its strategic thinking. The pro-Zionists Balfour and Samuels had left the Foreign Office, and the new administration was not inclined toward the Zionist position. The Jews had little choice but to support Britain against Nazi Germany, losing any leverage they might have had otherwise.

Thus, Britain's commitment to a Jewish homeland in Palestine dissipated, and the Mandate authorities pursued a policy of appeasement toward the Arabs. The surrounding Arab states became advocates of the Palestinian Arabs. Britain had previously tended to deal with its commitments in Palestine as separate from its commitments elsewhere in the Middle East; by 1939, pan-Arab pressure carried increasing weight in London.

In the Yishuv, the Palestinian Revolt reinforced the already firm belief in the need for a strong Jewish defense network. The new Arab uprising was so formidable that the British finally sanctioned the arming of the Haganah to help quell the violence. The two groups cooperated until the disturbances ended in 1939.

The end of the revolt was partly due to the work of British intelligence officer Charles Orde Wingate, a pro-Zionist Christian officer in the British army who organized special night squads of Jewish volunteers to combat the attackers. Wingate had been dispatched to Palestine because of his fluency in Arabic and his presumed rapport with the Arab community. What the authorities were not aware of was Wingate's deeply held belief in New Testament biblical prophecy, which quickly transformed the young captain into a passionate supporter of Zionism.

"I count it a privilege to help you to fight your battle," he told a Jewish friend, David Hacohen. Soon Wingate became a close adviser and confidant to Weizmann and Jewish Agency leaders.

As he studied the tactics of the Arab guerrillas, Wingate noticed their ability to strike and escape from heavily armed government columns. He

developed fast patrols to hunt for these terrorists. He developed tricks of
decoy and feint to carry out surprise raids against the guerrillas—what
he called "active defense." Soon he gained the admiration of his Jewish
troops. During forays and ambushes, the Jewish Special Night Squads
inflicted heavy casualties on the Mufti's rebels, greatly diminishing their
effectiveness.

Soon Wingate's pro-Zionist views were communicated to British leadership in Palestine, and the young Scot was sent back to England. His
superiors wrote in his file: "A good soldier but a poor security risk. Not
to be trusted. The interests of the Jews are more important to him than
those of his own country."

The effects of these raids demoralized the Arabs but infused new confidence into the Jewish population.[417]

THE 1939 WHITE PAPER

For nearly a year, the Arabs fought against a policy of partition that was,
in the mind of the British government, already dead. Conversely, the
British soldiers fought the Arab insurgency so their government could
replace the defunct policy in a dignified manner that would help them
save face on the international stage.[418] All the while, the Jews held on to
the original promise of the Balfour Declaration.

In November 1938, the British government, having announced its abandonment of partition and the Jewish state, invited Middle East governments to a conference in London to discuss the future of Palestine. Held
in St. James' Palace, the conference was attended by representatives of
Egypt, Saudi Arabia, Iraq, Yemen, and Trans-Jordan, along with a Palestinian delegation and the Zionist Executive. The British met with the Arabs in one room and with the Jews in another because the Palestinians
refused to meet with the Jews.

Some joint meetings between the Zionists and the Arab states were held
without the Palestinians. At one of these meetings, Aly Maher of Egypt
made a courteously worded appeal to the Zionists to stop, or at least limit, immigration into Palestine. Ben-Gurion replied that an appeal to the
Jews in 1939 amid Hitler's atrocities to stop immigration into Palestine
was like asking a woman in labor to stop birth.[419]

In the end, the St. James conference had no other function but to prepare the way for an imposed solution in the form of a unilateral statement from the British government. Ultimately, the British military suppressed the Arab revolt, but on May 17, 1939, the Chamberlain government rewarded the Arabs with the publication of the 1939 White Paper. The infamous document severely restricted Jewish immigration just as Hitler unleashed his murderous rampage against the Jews of Europe.

Chaim Weizmann called on Prime Minister Chamberlain at 10 Downing Street on March 21. "I pleaded once more with the Prime Minister to stay his hand and not publish the White Paper." With the coming war, Britain needed American support, and Weizmann stressed the power of the American Jewish community. But the argument that had such a powerful effect in World War One proved less convincing in 1939. "The Prime Minister of England sat before me like a marble statue," Weizmann explained. "His expressionless eyes fixed on me, but he never said a word."

Early in May 1939, Weizmann was invited to visit former Prime Minister MacDonald at the Englishman's country home. He drove out to the estate with his political secretary, Yechazkal Sacharoff. Two hours later, Weizmann stormed out of the house, pale and trembling. "He broke into strong, violent, unrestrained language against MacDonald," Sacharoff recalled.

"That he could do this," Weizmann exclaimed. "He who made me believe he was a friend." He told his secretary that he had often heard that the English were double-faced and disloyal, but throughout his long experience with Englishmen, he had never believed it until then.[420]

The White Paper in effect abrogated the Balfour Declaration and the obligations assumed by Britain under the Mandate. The document declared its abandonment of the Zionist policy, stating that 75,000 more Jews would be allowed into Palestine over the next five years, and then the gates would be permanently closed.

Under the policy, Jews could purchase land only within an area encompassing 5 percent of the country. Then, after an interval of ten years, a Palestinian state, led by the Arabs, would be established.[421]

When Britain implemented the White Paper's provisions, it trapped untold numbers of Jews in Nazi Europe who might have otherwise escaped.

The policy was supported by the Conservative majority and approved by the House of Commons on May 23, 1939. The document was strongly opposed by the Labour Party, as well as by dissenting Conservative leaders such as Winston Churchill and Leopold Amery.[422]

While the Arabs saw the White Paper as a promise to stop the Zionists, whom they viewed as intruders taking over their land, the Jews saw it as a betrayal of the Balfour Declaration and the Mandate established by the League of Nations. The League's Permanent Mandates Commission refused to sanction it, saying that Britain's new policy was not in accordance with their interpretation of the Palestine Mandate."[423]

The League's consent was required under Article 27 of the Mandate for any change in its terms. But the outbreak of war put an end to the League's active life and the Council never met to consider the matter.[424]

The Anglo-Egyptian Treaty of 1936 enabled the British to keep troops in Egypt for only an additional twenty years. The concept of unlimited British presence in Palestine suddenly seemed like a necessity in the minds of British military strategists in the late 1930s.[425]

To ensure their policy was carried out, the British Royal Air Force and Navy instituted a blockade around Palestine. No Jewish immigrant was allowed to enter without British permission. A courageous few made it through, but most were turned back to Europe.[426]

The Jews had no other choice but to side with the British against the Nazis.[427] Consequently, the Yishuv would have to think in terms of defending its National Home not only against the Arabs but also possibly against the British.[428] The Haganah began supporting illegal immigration and organized sporadic demonstrations against the British anti-Zionist policy.[429]

The Twenty-First Zionist Congress

At the Zionist Congress in August 1939, strong opposition was expressed against the White Paper and support for illegal immigration. Dr. Weizmann declared:

> During the three years of Arab terror, which began in April 1936, the Yishuv has established fifty new settlements, built a Jewish port overnight, organized large-scale defense, and achieved a

greater measure of economic independence. The Jews will stand united in defense of their rights in the Land of Israel, rights based on international agreements and the eternal link between the people and their Homeland.

The Congress declared its unremitting hostility to the policy of the White Paper, at the same time proclaiming its unwavering support of Britain against the Nazis. Ben-Gurion's statement to the Congress set the tone and policy of the Yishuv throughout the war:

> The White Paper had created a vacuum which must be filled by the Jews themselves. The Jews should act as though they were the State in Palestine, and should so act until there would be a Jewish state there.[430]

The British responded partly by police efforts and partly by deducting estimated "illegals" from the already reduced quotas. The British also ended their military cooperation with the Haganah, driving the Jewish militia underground for the duration of the Mandate.[431]

The Jewish Agency repudiated the new British immigration policy. The Jewish people, they declared, regarded the suspension of immigration "as devoid of any moral justification and based only on the use of force … It is not the Jewish refugees returning to their homeland who are violating the law but those who are endeavoring to deprive them of the supreme right of every human being—the right to live."

Ben-Gurion was the leader of the Zionist movement, both within the Yishuv and as the chairman of both the Zionist Executive and of the Jewish Agency. Weizmann remained as the acting foreign minister of the movement. It was Ben-Gurion who had been a driving force behind bringing him back as the president of the World Zionist Organization.

At the same time, Ben-Gurion made it clear to American Jewish leaders that Weizmann—despite his eloquent defense of Zionism during the Peel Commission hearings—would not be the supreme leader of the Zionist movement as he had been in the past. "Weizmann will not be the ruler and leader and he knows it," Ben-Gurion explained. "The Executive will lead."[432]

Britain fully embraced the role it had tried to hide—that of a power which was in Palestine by right of conquest and whose authority to determine the future of the territory rested ultimately on use of force. By taking this position, the British invited both the Arabs and the Jews to think of force as the legitimate and only means of challenging them when the time came.[433]

As Ze'ev Jabotinsky wrote from Warsaw: "Even the Jewish sigh 'Next year in Jerusalem' becomes anti-British."

After the release of the White Paper, Ben-Gurion changed his policy toward the British. He believed a peaceful solution with the Arabs had no chance and soon began preparing the Yishuv for war: "Peace in Palestine is not the best situation for thwarting the policy of the White Paper." Through his campaign to mobilize the Yishuv in support of the British war effort, he strove to build the nucleus of a "Hebrew army."

As chairman of the Zionist Executive, Ben-Gurion declared: "We will fight with the British against Hitler as if there were no White Paper; we will fight the White Paper as if there were no war."[434]

Chapter Fourteen

WORLD WAR TWO

SEPTEMBER 1, 1939—POLAND

The Twenty-First Zionist Congress ended earlier than planned when the news of the Hitler-Stalin Pact arrived—an unmistakable harbinger of the tragedy about to unfold. It was now clear that the three million Jews of Poland were caught in a trap that would likely lead to mass tragedy and death.

Closing the Congress, President Weizmann prepared the delegates for the struggle to come. "It is my duty at this solemn hour to tell England … we have grievances … But above our regret and bitterness are higher interests. What the democracies are fighting for is the minimum … necessary for Jewish life. Their anxiety is our anxiety. Their war our war."[435]

Two days after the Germans attacked Poland on September 1, 1939, Britian and France declared war on the Nazis.[436] That same day, Chamberlain brought Winston Churchill back into the cabinet as First Lord of the Admiralty after ten years of exclusion. This appointment came after countless warnings from Churchill for Britain to take Hitler seriously and to prepare for war. Chamberlain's government had ignored Churchill's cautions so long that Britain found itself in an extremely vulnerable position against an enemy bent on world domination.

A NEW LEADER

Chamberlain remained prime minister during the early period of sporadic military action, but after the failure of a British expedition to Norway in April 1940, he lost the support of Conservatives in the House of Commons. On May 10, 1940, German forces struck simultaneously at Holland, Belgium, and Luxembourg, with the goal of invading France. In the wake of these hammer blows, Chamberlain was forced to resign, and King George VI acted to make Churchill the new prime minister.[437]

In Tel Aviv, a student named Ben Gale was listening to a speaker in a large lecture hall. Suddenly, the chairman of the conference interrupted to read a note handed to him by a messenger. "Chamberlain has stepped down and Winston Churchill is now Prime Minister." Everyone in the hall stood and cheered wildly. They instinctively understood the renewed hope for the Jews of Palestine with Churchill in charge.[438]

As the war progressed, Churchill focused mainly on defeating the Nazis, but he kept a constant eye on the Jewish people. Throughout his career, Churchill protected and defended the Jews and the Balfour Declaration with great vigor, although he was often in the minority.

On September 19, Churchill invited Weizmann to dine with him at the Admiralty House. During their talk, Weizmann brought Churchill up to speed on the position and spirit of the Jews of Palestine, noting that 75,000 Jewish men and women had registered to fight as part of the British armed forces wherever needed. Churchill asked if they were armed, and Weizmann told him they were not.[439] Churchill promised to arm them immediately. If the Jews were armed, Churchill replied, it would be possible to take British troops away from Palestine.

It was "an extraordinary position," Churchill concluded, "that at a time when the war was probably entering its most dangerous phase, we should station in Palestine a garrison one-quarter the size of our garrison in India"—for the purpose of enforcing a policy which, in his judgment, was unpopular in both Palestine and in Great Britain.[440]

Churchill continued to challenge the White Paper and to speak in cabinet meetings against the unreasonable restrictions on future Jewish land purchases. If it had been within his power, Churchill would have nullified the 1939 White Paper on his first day in office. Sadly, his objections to the White Paper restrictions were overruled. Churchill had the tortuous task of opposing the White Paper and seeking to delay its implementation until it could be overturned while also enforcing the parts of it that became the law of the Empire.

The Yishuv had hoped that the White Paper—what they saw as another of Chamberlain's appeasements—would be discarded once Churchill became prime minister. But this nefarious document was more than just appeasement. It represented the still-dominant strategic thinking of most

British politicians, military leaders, and diplomats when it came to Palestine and Great Britain's position of influence in the Middle East.

In December, Churchill once again met with Weizmann, who thanked him for his unceasing interest in Zionist affairs. "You stood at the cradle of this enterprise; I hope that you will see it through."

Churchill was somewhat put off by the remark and asked Weizmann to clarify what he meant by the phrase "see it through." Weizmann replied, "… After the war, the Zionists would wish to have a State of some three or four million Jews in Palestine." To this Churchill replied, "Yes, indeed. I quite agree with that."[441]

Publicly, Churchill had to maintain a certain degree of official dignity and solemnity; privately, however, he was emotional about what was happening to the Jews. On one occasion, the prime minister, with tears on his cheeks, approached a colleague saying, "Look what they're doing to my Jews."

He was terribly upset about the Holocaust, which he knew about through reports from British intelligence. Churchill held this ghastly secret for many months before it was revealed to the world. Although his first priority was Britain's survival, in his heart, Churchill continued to be concerned about Zion.

On June 27, Churchill asked the cabinet to arm the Jews of Palestine to free up the British and Australian troops in the Holy Land for other service. Secretary of State Lloyd remained immovable, and Churchill had no authority to overrule him. The troops remained in Palestine, and the Jews remained unarmed while the Arabs both inside and outside Palestine were fully armed.[442]

Despite this inequity, in September 1941, fifteen battalions of Palestinian Jewish volunteers—almost 20,000 men—were added to the British army and sent to join the defense of Egypt against Italian and German attack. Following Ben-Gurion's declaration that Jews should fight both the Nazis and the White Paper—and with the thought of their imprisoned brethren behind German lines in Europe—the Jews were eager to fight.

That same month, a wave of Italian warplanes bombed Tel Aviv, killing one Australian soldier and four British soldiers as well as ninety-five Jews, including fifty-eight children. As soon as Churchill learned of the raid, he telegraphed the mayor of Tel Aviv, the city he had visited two decades earlier. "Please accept my deep sympathy in losses sustained by Tel Aviv in recent air attack. This act of senseless brutality will only strengthen our united resolve."[443]

THE *PATRIA*

Ben-Gurion's battle was both foreign and domestic. The Haganah furnished the majority of the 30,000 Jewish volunteer men and women from Palestine who fought under the British. It also cooperated with British intelligence units and sent its personnel out on various commando missions. In 1943, more than thirty Jewish parachutists dropped behind enemy lines in coordinated military missions in the Balkans, Hungary, and Slovakia.[444]

Ben-Gurion also waged war against the White Paper, allowing both legal and illegal immigration of thousands of European Jewish refugees into Palestine.

In an effort to expel all Jews from Nazi territories, leading Holocaust architect, SS Lieutenant Adolf Eichmann, chartered three Romanian ships in the autumn of 1940. He packed 3,600 Jews on these vessels and sent them from the Black Sea port of Tulcea bound for Palestine. The goal of the SS was to bring international embarrassment to the British government over their White Paper policy of restricting Jewish immigration while they condemned German aggression against the Jews.

The Jews arrived off the coast of Palestine and were intercepted by the British Royal Navy. The haggard passengers were transferred to the *Patria*, a French vessel seized by the British in Haifa harbor after France fell to the Germans. The British planned to transport the refugees to the British Indian Ocean island of Mauritius, not far from Madagascar, to be interned with other "illegals."[445]

To protest the British White Paper policy and keep the ship from leaving Palestine, the Haganah rigged explosives on the *Patria* in Haifa harbor. The charge was more potent than intended; the explosion not only disabled the ship but also killed 267 of the refugees.[446]

When British authorities in Palestine moved forward with their plan to transport the *Patria* survivors to Mauritius, Churchill stepped in. "I hold it would be an act of inhumanity unworthy of British name to force them to re-embark."[447] The *Patria* survivors were allowed to remain in Palestine.

After the incident, the cabinet insisted that all illegals be sent to Mauritius. Churchill hesitantly agreed, "provided … these refugees are not sent back to the torments from which they have escaped and are decently treated."[448]

Immigration into Palestine was on the cabinet agenda again on Christmas Eve. Churchill moved to temper the measure, explaining that the British government "have also to consider their promises to the Zionists, and to be guided by general considerations of humanity towards those fleeing from the cruelest forms of persecution."[449]

The issue of arming the Jews inside Palestine arose again as German and Italian forces advanced deep into Egypt in 1941 and 1942, threatening to reach the Suez Canal. Churchill's spies informed him that the Nazis were pressuring the Turks to allow the passage of German troops to also threaten Palestine from the north. With the danger of a German pincer attack from both north and south, the Jewish community prepared for self-defense, building fortifications on the crest of Mount Carmel, high above Haifa.

Churchill wrote to the British colonial secretary in the Black Sea port of Tulcea concerning the need to protect the Jews in Palestine. "I have always been most strongly in favour of making sure that the Jews have proper means of self-defense for their Colonies in Palestine. The more you can get done in this line, the safer we shall be."[450]

CHURCHILL AND THE FUTURE OF PALESTINE

On May 19, 1941, Churchill dictated a note for the War Cabinet, stating that at the same time that Great Britain was giving "great advancements to the Arab world"—postwar independence for both Syria and Lebanon—"we should, of course, negotiate with Ibn Saud a satisfactory settlement of the Jewish problem; and, if such a basis were reached, it is possible that the Jewish State of Western Palestine might form an independent Federal Unit in the Arab Caliphate. This Jewish State would have to have the fullest rights of self-government, including immigration and development, and provision for expansion in the desert regions to the southward, which they would gradually reclaim."[451]

At their first wartime meeting in August 1941, President Franklin Roosevelt presented Churchill with the Atlantic Charter, his vision of the postwar world. Roosevelt proposed that Britain and the United States pledge themselves "to respect the right of all peoples to choose the form of government under which they will live."[452] Churchill supported such a promise, but he also wanted to make sure the promises of the Balfour Declaration were upheld for the Jews. He explained to Roosevelt that "the Arabs might claim by majority that they could expel the Jews from Palestine, or at any rate forbid all future immigration … I am strongly wedded to the Zionist policy, of which I was one of the authors."[453]

At a meeting of the War Cabinet on October 2, Churchill insisted that if Britain and the United States "emerged victorious from the war, the creation of a great Jewish State in Palestine would inevitably be one of the matters to be discussed at the Peace Conference."

The Minister of Labor and National Service, Ernest Bevin, responded in a manner that he later disavowed, but it reflected the position of the Labour Party in 1941. "If an autonomous Jewish State could be set up, the question of regulating the flow of immigration thereto would be a matter to be settled by the authorities of that State. This would greatly ease our difficulties in the matter."[454]

Early Reports of Genocide

By 1941, news of atrocities against the Jews was being reported to the Allies, but no direct action was taken to stop the death camps. On June 21, Germany betrayed its agreement with Stalin and launched Operation Barbarossa, a full-scale invasion against the Soviet Union. As the Nazis advanced into Russian territory, SS killing squads followed with the systematic mass murder of Jews in every captured town and village. British Intelligence soon intercepted top-secret German police radio messages confirming these atrocities and passed them along to Churchill. He had to keep this information confidential, being careful not to reveal his source for fear of alerting the Germans to the fact that their secret communications had been compromised by British code-breakers.

Churchill was heartbroken.

Then, as multiple sources reported the genocide against the Jews, there was no longer the need to withhold the information from the world. On August 24, 1941, Churchill broadcast the news of the unfolding Holocaust: "Whole districts are being exterminated. We are in the presence of a crime without a name."[455]

On August 27, Churchill received the German police decryption reporting the execution of 367 Jews in South Russia. On September 1, the report arrived of the shooting of 1,246 Jews; on September 6, the shooting of 3,000 Jews; on September 11, more than 5,000 Jews near Kamenets-Padolsk. After this massacre, Churchill was told by his Intelligence service, "The fact that the Police are killing all Jews that fall into their hands should by now be sufficiently well appreciated. It is not therefore proposed to continue reporting these butcheries specially, unless so requested."

On November 14, 1941, Churchill sent a signed message to the *Jewish Chronicle*, which the weekly newspaper printed in full:

> None has suffered more cruelly than the Jew the unspeakable evils wrought on the bodies and spirits of men by Hitler and his vile regime. The Jew bore the brunt of the Nazis' first onslaught upon the citadels of freedom and human dignity. He has borne and continues to bear a burden that might have seemed to be beyond endurance. He has not allowed it to break his spirit; he has never lost the will to resist. Assuredly in the day of victory the Jew's sufferings and his part in the struggle will not be forgotten.[456]

Yet despite Churchill's love for the Jewish people—and despite knowledge of these Nazi atrocities—he was not able to persuade his colleagues to change the official policy of the British government in the White Paper that continued the restricted immigration of Jews into Palestine.[457]

This decision kept tens of thousands of Jews trapped within the grip of the Nazi death machine.

The Struma

As the Nazis bore down harder on the Jews, those who were still able tried to escape Europe any way they could. An increasing number of Jews set out for one of the last remaining possible safe havens, Palestine, even though entry was technically illegal to most of them.

By the end of 1941, German troops had achieved dramatic victories throughout Europe as they marched eastward into Russia. Fearing for their lives, Jewish refugees from Poland, Austria, Hungary, and Czechoslovakia fled to Romania on riverboats and barges. Their destination was the port city of Constantza in Romania, where they hoped to depart for Palestine via the only route open, the Black Sea and Turkey.[458]

On December 12, 1941, the *Struma*, an aging cattle barge carrying Jewish refugees bound for Palestine, escaped the Nazis.

A shipping agency had advertised a voyage to Palestine on a luxury liner. Their posters and brochures even featured a picture of the *Queen Mary*. In reality, the vessel was a seventy-four-year-old ramshackle riverboat measuring only fifty feet long and twenty feet wide. The Nazis considered her too old to transport cattle and other supplies. Instead, the ship's owner made cursory repairs and placed her under Panamanian registry. Within a short time, 769 Jews responded favorably to the offer.

When these people saw the ship, they were overcome with disappointment. The *Struma* had only 100 bunks and not a single toilet. The ship's owner had anticipated their response, and he soothed the passengers' worries by saying that because the advertised ship carried an American flag, she had to remain anchored outside the territorial water of Romania. The *Struma* was merely a transport vessel to get them to the real ship.

In the midst of all the confusion, the passengers received word on December 7 of the attack on Pearl Harbor. The world seemed to be heading for a widespread conflagration, and most of the Jews desired to leave as soon as possible for the Holy Land. In haste, the *Struma* sailed from Constantza on December 12, 1941. When they reached the open sea, the passengers faced the harsh reality that there was no luxury liner waiting for them. At this point it was too late, as there was no way they could go back to Romania.

They arrived in Istanbul on December 15, 1941, with the engine malfunctioning and a leak in the hull. The captain of the ship requested a permit to stay in the harbor until repairs were completed. The Turkish authorities, considering a recent catastrophe that befell the *Salvador*, a wooden ship that sank with 350 Jewish passengers aboard in the Sea of Marmara, granted permission to stay beyond what the transit regulations provided.[459]

In view of the unbearable conditions on the ship, Turkish authorities allowed the passengers to disembark while it was repaired. Soon it became known that none of the passengers had entry visas to Palestine. The Turkish Foreign Office contacted the British ambassador in Ankara, requesting that all the passengers be issued visas to Palestine.

Once again citing White Paper restrictions, the British refused to grant the visas, leaving the Jews without any options. The *Struma* remained in the Istanbul harbor for seventy-one days, during which time the Turkish government conducted intense negotiations to find a viable solution. The British were reminded that the yearly quota of 10,000 allowed by the White Paper was still unfilled. Could they be allocated for the passengers of the *Struma*? The British dismissed this possibility claiming that these passengers, as Romanians, were enemy aliens and thus did not qualify for this quota.

The Turkish Foreign Office then contacted the Romanian ambassador in Ankara, proposing that the *Struma* be allowed to return to Romania. The ambassador responded that the Jews had left the country in an illegal manner, and therefore it was impossible to readmit them to Romania.

When the United States entered the war, Panama followed suit, joining the Allies. With this development, the captain, who was Bulgarian, declared that he and his crew could not stay on a ship that belonged to an enemy country. Besides, he claimed, the Mediterranean was dangerous to travel with a crippled ship and a large number of Jews on board. The port authorities refused to relieve the captain from his post in such a critical time.

After two months of quarantine in the Istanbul harbor, the *Struma* was refused further sanctuary. The Turkish government exhausted all means to overcome British intransigence. On February 23, 1942, the captain of the *Struma* was ordered to leave the harbor. Although the vessel remained unseaworthy, a tugboat towed the *Struma* to the Black Sea. The following day, still within sight of the harbor, an enormous explosion ripped through the doomed ship, and the *Struma* sank with 769 souls aboard.[460]

Rescue teams were immediately dispatched, arriving at the scene in the midst of high winds and treacherous seas. They found only one survivor, a twenty-one-year-old Romanian Jew named David Stoliar. He was later granted admission to Palestine.[461]

The *Struma* incident was an eye-opener for the Romanian authorities. They perceived that instead of exterminating the Jews, they could let them buy their own freedom. The World Jewish Congress discovered this prospect and appealed to the US State Department to allow money to be transferred through Switzerland to ransom Jews out of Europe, especially from Romania. The State Department agreed on condition that those freed would be admitted to Palestine by the British.

To raise money for this likelihood, the Jews in the United States launched a fundraising campaign to buy freedom for their brethren. A Jewish American organization ran the following full-page advertisement in *The New York Times* on February 16, 1943:

For sale to humanity.

70,000 Jews!

Guaranteed human beings at $50 a piece.[462]

The British refused any cooperation, and the venture came to nothing.

The *Struma* incident was only one of thousands of tragic examples of Jews doing anything they could to escape the death trap that Europe had become. And still the war dragged on and on with no end in sight.

Chapter Fifteen

TRUMAN'S NATIONAL ASCENT

After serving three successful terms as county judge, Harry Truman was elected to the United States Senate in a hard-fought election. With America caught in the grip of the Depression, Truman fell in line with Franklin Roosevelt's New Deal. He called Roosevelt "the greatest of the greats." But Roosevelt had no use for the junior senator from Missouri, considering his affiliation with the corrupt Pendergast political machine a liability. More than five months passed before Truman was finally invited to meet with the president.

"Actually," said Vic Messall, Truman's Senate office administrator, "Senator Truman only wanted to meet Roosevelt to say hello and for no other reason. I went along with the Senator to the West Wing of the White House the day of his appointment. When we got to the appointments secretary's office, outside the president's office, Harold Ickes, Henry Wallace, and other cabinet members were sitting around on the sofas and chairs and talking government business. We were both impressed. However, none of them said hello to the Senator, and he sat in silence while we waited. Finally, Pa Watson, who handled FDR's appointments, told Truman he could go in to see the President." A fifteen-minute appointment had been scheduled, but he was out in seven minutes.[463]

"I was practically tongue-tied," Truman admitted. He puzzled over this reaction for a long time and finally realized it was not caused by awe of Roosevelt personally but of the presidency and the tremendous role it played in the American republic. "I was before the greatest office in the world."[464] "He was as cordial and nice to me as he could be," Truman said of Roosevelt. "It was quite an event for a country boy to go calling on the President of the United States."[465]

But despite the official courtesy shown to Truman in this initial visit, Roosevelt continued to have little to do with him.[466] After three years in office, Roosevelt remained unwilling to give Truman any federal patronage, the bread and butter of any senator's home support. When it came to making appointments to the federal bench, federal attorney, marshal, collector of internal revenue, or even home-state river or harbor projects, Roosevelt pointedly ignored Truman. Instead, FDR worked with Senior Senator Bennett Clark, even though he was both an isolationist and an anti-New Dealer.

Eventually, Roosevelt grew annoyed with Clark's obstructionism and barred him from any further patronage. Even then FDR did not transfer such favors to Truman. Instead, he distributed them through Missouri Governor Stark. In addition to Roosevelt's feeling that Truman was tainted by Pendergast, FDR also took Harry for granted because he tended to vote as an ardent New Dealer.[467] Following the advice of Senator Carl Hayden of Arizona, Truman decided to be a workhorse rather than a show horse.[468]

Roosevelt's treatment began to irritate Truman. "The explosion came in 1938," Vic Messall remembered. "That summer he was driving back to Kansas City when Jimmy Byrnes called me. Byrnes said that the New Dealers had only a tie vote on a major bill and FDR needed Truman back at the Capitol to break the tie. I called the highway police and they picked Truman up and brought him back to Washington. He was mad clean through when he walked into the office. 'Who do those so-and-sos think they are?' he yelled. 'I haven't been recognized by the White House, but they think they can use me to vote for Roosevelt! Get Steve Early on the phone.'"

Early tried to mollify Truman. "What's troubling you, Senator?"

"I'm sick and tired of being the White House office boy!" Truman shouted. "This is the third time I've come back here to bail you guys out on a vote. You tell that to the President!" Not long afterward, Truman told reporters he did not favor three terms for any president.[469]

But even as he became more and more independent, he remained loyal to Tom Pendergast and kept a framed portrait of his friend in his office. But the Big Boss was in trouble. Pendergast was seriously ill, his gambling out of control, and his debt in the millions. In 1939, a grand jury indicted him for tax evasion. Convicted, he was sentenced to prison for fifteen months and banned from politics for five years.

The scandal tainted Truman, and it couldn't have come at a worse time. In 1940, he was up for reelection.

1940—WASHINGTON, DC

Most political pundits believed Truman would not run again for the Senate in 1940 with the Pendergast machine in disarray. Harry's opponents chided him as a fraud, elected by ghost votes. The *St. Louis Dispatch* called him "Ambassador of the defunct principality of Pendergastia."[470]

Truman worked to convince voters that Roosevelt supported him, but the president kept his distance. With Truman's ties to the disgraced Pendergast machine, Roosevelt considered him an embarrassment to the Democratic Party.[471] To lure him away from a reelection campaign, Roosevelt hinted he would give Truman a lucrative job with the Interstate Commerce Commission. But Harry balked at the idea of being bought off. He believed he had done a good job for the people of Missouri and that he should be returned to the Senate.[472] "I sent him word, however, that if I received only one vote, I intended to make the fight for vindication and re-election to the Senate."[473]

Roosevelt made it clear that he preferred Governor Stark as the next senator from Missouri. During 1938 and 1939, Stark's name showed up among those invited on the presidential yacht for cruises down the Potomac. In September 1939, Stark announced himself as a candidate for Truman's seat.

Without the support of the president or Tom Pendergast, Truman had to go it alone. Most observers didn't give him a chance, but that aroused the senator's fighting spirit.[474]

Truman declared his independence from FDR and the national Democrats in a letter to Bess:

> I don't care much ... what they do or don't, from here out I'm going to do as I please—and they can like it or not as they choose. I've spent my life pleasing people, doing things for 'em, and putting myself in embarrassing positions to save the party and the other fellow, now I've quit. To hell with 'em all.[475]

Despite the downfall of Boss Tom, young Jim Pendergast did what he could to keep the organization together in Kansas City. Vic Messall visited with Truman's old war buddy to check on the level of his support for the reelection campaign. Pendergast said, "Tell Harry that if he only gets two votes he will get my vote and my wife's vote."

The remnants of the Pendergast machine would back Harry—and that meant 100,000 votes. That was enough to convince him to file for reelection.[476]

Truman's eighty-eight-year-old mother sat proudly on the platform in front of the Sedalia Court House on June 15 as he officially launched his reelection campaign. The campaign strategy was to speak to every segment of the Missouri population, and Truman began with African-Americans in the first speech:

> I believe in the brotherhood of man, not merely the brotherhood of white men, but the brotherhood of all men before the law. In years past, lynching and mob violence, lack of schools and countless other unfair conditions hastened the progress of the Negro from the country to the city. They have been forced to live in segregated slums, neglected by the authorities. Negroes have been preyed upon by all types of exploiters. The majority of our Negro people find but cold comfort in shanties and tenements.[477]

Truman was carving out a position for himself in the Democratic Party based on his own principles and deeply held beliefs. Although he was not raised to embrace all people as equals, his life experiences brought him to this turning point in his political philosophy. He was ready to lead his fellow Missourians and his fellow Americans forward.

Stark delayed launching his campaign, and his reason soon became obvious. From conversations with Roosevelt, he got the impression the president wanted him as his next running mate. Soon *The New York Times* reported that FDR had approved Stark, James Byrnes, Sam Rayburn, and Supreme Court Justice William O. Douglas as possible vice-presidential nominees.

When the Democratic National Convention got under way in Chicago on July 15, both Truman and Stark served in the Missouri delegation.

While Truman worked with his colleagues on the Resolutions Committee, Stark made it clear he had "consented" to run for vice president. He even established a campaign headquarters, and his supporters passed out "Stark Delicious" apples to all the delegates.

On the floor of the massive convention hall, Stark's people staged a demonstration for their man. But the stunt backfired when Mrs. Henry Clay Chiles, head of the women's division of Truman's campaign organization, marched through the "Stark for Vice President" crowd holding high a "Truman for Senator" banner, reminding delegates that Stark had first promised to run for senator.[478]

Stark's dream imploded when Roosevelt officially accepted the Democratic nomination for a third term and chose Secretary of Agriculture Henry Wallace as his running mate. The spectacle of a man running for both the Senate and Vice Presidency annoyed Missouri voters, although Stark remained the front-runner when he returned to launch his Senate campaign.

Truman's campaign routine was to make a short speech, shake as many hands as he could, then catch a nap in the car on the way to the next stop. He made his pitch to as many segments of the population as he could. Harry counted on large support from veterans, but Stark also had a distinguished war record. Truman also had to share the farm vote, since Missouri was covered in apple orchards whose fruits were distributed by the Stark Corporation.

Coming down to the wire, the Truman campaign started to run out of cash. Harry had to borrow $3,000 on his life insurance policy to help meet expenses. He refused to give up, and, in the end, he eked out a narrow 8,000-vote victory. In November, Truman defeated his Republican contender, Manvell Davis, to become senator in his own right.[479]

When Truman walked onto the Senate floor following his grueling ordeal, his colleagues gave him a standing ovation. A reporter on the scene noted, "They behaved like boys greeting a popular schoolmate who had just got over the measles."[480]

With his Senate victory, he determined to be accepted for his own abilities and principles. Once again, Truman revealed his strength as a leader, catapulting him onto the national stage.

THE TRUMAN COMMITTEE

By July 1940, Great Britain stood as the only free country remaining in Europe. That month, Hitler unleashed the greatest air battle in history as the *Luftwaffe* crossed the English Channel to bomb Britain's cities, ports, airfields, and military installations. As Royal Air Force Spitfires and Hurricanes rose to meet them in battle, Hitler promised that his air blitz would bring the English people to their knees.

In an effort to shore up the Brits, President Roosevelt delivered one of his radio speeches, known as his "fireside chats." Describing the destructive force of the Nazi onslaught across Europe, Roosevelt warned that American civilization was in deeper peril than at any time since Jamestown and Plymouth.

It was not war that he sought at that time, but massive production for war to supply nations like Great Britain under Nazi attack. "We must become the great arsenal of democracy."

Roosevelt addressed a joint session of Congress on January 6, 1941, delivering a call to support those nations fighting in defense of what he called the Four Freedoms: freedom of speech, freedom of religion, freedom from want, and freedom from fear. Truman later said that speech was Roosevelt at his very best. Within days, Roosevelt proposed his Lend-Lease plan to send arms, ships, tanks, and other military equipment to the British on credit.[481]

Congress responded to Roosevelt's plea by appropriating $10.5 billion in defense contracts—a sum greater than the entire budget of the United States for any of the Depression years of the 1930s.[482]

With these large sums of money being allocated, it didn't take long for corruption to seep into the process.

Early in 1941, stories of widespread contractor mismanagement reached Senator Truman. He decided to see for himself. Setting out from Washington in his own Royal Club coup, Senator Truman embarked on a 10,000-mile tour of military bases and manufacturing facilities across the United States.[483]

He discovered contractors being paid a fixed profit no matter how inefficient their operations proved to be. He found that most military contracts went to large corporations, while mid-sized and smaller qualified businesses were overlooked. Truman met with President Roosevelt on February 3, 1941, to plead the case of the small businesses. He left feeling as though he had received FDR's usual "cordial treatment" but little else.

Convinced the waste and corruption hindered the nation's efforts to mobilize itself for the war in Europe, Truman conceived the idea for a special Senate committee to investigate the national defense program.

Truman understood the government contracting process from his years as a judge in Independence. "I have had considerable experience in letting public contracts, and I have never yet found a contractor who, if not watched, would not leave the Government holding the bag."[484]

Senior military officials opposed the idea, recalling the Civil-War-era problems that the congressional Joint Committee on the Conduct of the War created for President Lincoln. Robert E. Lee said he considered the joint committee's harassment of Union commanders to be worth at least two Confederate divisions. But Truman had visited the Library of Congress for the Civil War records to verify for himself what mistakes the committee made—and to avoid them.

Despite opposition within the White House and the War Department, one influential voice cautioned against a "resentful attitude" toward such a committee—Chief of Staff George Marshall, who said it "must be assumed that members of Congress are just as patriotic as we."[485]

Roosevelt was against the proposal when he first heard it, fearing that congressional meddling would hamper the war effort. But Democratic congressional leaders advised the president it would be better for such an inquiry to be in Truman's sympathetic hands than to let it fall to those who might use it to attack his administration. They also assured the president that the committee would not be able to cause much trouble with a budget of only $15,000 to investigate billions in defense spending.

On March 1, by unanimous vote, the Senate created the Senate Special Committee to Investigate the National Defense Program, which came to be known as the "Truman Committee." There were seven members—five Democrats, two Republicans.[486]

The first hearing of the Truman Committee was conducted on April 15, with Secretary of War Henry Stimson as debut witness. A dozen of the highest-ranking military and civilian officials came before the committee that day, including Chief of Staff Marshall.[487]

Committee members and investigators soon fanned out across the country. War plants and military bases were inspected, and hearings were held in local hotels.[488] In only a few months, the committee produced results and gained attention from the press and public. In response, the Senate raised the appropriation from $15,000 to $50,000 and added one Democrat and two Republicans to the committee.

When presiding over the committee, Truman was both well prepared and in charge, though not domineering. He went out of his way to give other senators the stage. Truman could be tough and persistent with witnesses, but he was always fair. One reporter wrote of a "studious avoidance of dramatics, no hurling of insults or threats of personal violence that characterize so many other congressional hearings."[489]

On January 15, 1942, the Truman Committee presented its First Annual Report to the Senate. The findings helped induce President Roosevelt to replace the Office of Production Management with a new, more powerful War Production Board. Truman soon reported that savings attributable to the work of the committee estimated at $11 billion.

In recognition of his leadership and the tremendous financial saving, Truman's portrait appeared on the cover of *Time* magazine on March 8, 1943. The story characterized him as "a personally honest, courageous man" untouched by scandal, though still a Pendergast loyalist because he would not kick a friend who was down, and a crusader for an effective war effort.[490] In May 1944, Truman was selected as one of the ten most useful officials in Washington, DC, in a poll of fifty-two correspondents conducted by *Look* magazine.[491]

Earning nearly universal respect for his thoroughness and determination, Truman erased his earlier public image as an errand-runner for the Kansas City Pendergast machine. Harry Truman was now a known public figure across America—and in this time of war, he took seriously the responsibility that came along with notoriety.

By the summer of 1944, he was widely considered a possible vice-presidential candidate.

TRUMAN AND THE JEWS

During Harry Truman's childhood, Independence was a prejudice-ridden small Missouri town where many, if not most, of the residents looked with suspicion on those who were not white protestants. Truman's direct ancestors identified strongly with the slave-holding South—his grandparents received slaves as a wedding present. All four of his grandparents were born in Kentucky, and when they migrated to Missouri in the 1840s, they brought their slaves with them. One of his grandfathers owned two dozen slaves on his 5,000-acre plantation.

His parents, Truman recalled, were "a violently unreconstructed southern family."[492] As a result, Harry Truman came slowly to his support of civil rights for African-Americans and of a homeland for the Jews in Palestine.

But during Truman's two terms as a US senator, from 1935 to 1945, Nazi persecution against the Jews grew from old-fashioned "Jew-hating" to what the Nazis called the "Final Solution"—the murder of six million Jews in the death camps. This forced Harry to rethink his views.

Truman's ideas about Jews were complex. Although his private language regarding Jews could be salty, he had a long friendship with Eddie Jacobson, and that certainly influenced his later positions regarding the Jews and Israel.

Truman's first public support on behalf of Jewish settlement in Palestine came on May 25, 1939, eight days after the British announced the infamous White Paper. He asked that a newspaper article be printed as an appendix in the *Congressional Record*, along with remarks he had attached to it.

The article, which appeared in *The Washington Post*, had the provocative title "British Surrender—a Munich for the Holy Land." The author, Barnet Nover, argued the new British policy was a betrayal of the Balfour Declaration. Truman added in his attachment that the British government "has made a scrap of paper out of Lord Balfour's promise to the Jews," which amounted to nothing less than another addition "to the long list of surrenders to the axis powers."[493]

Two years later, Senator Truman joined the American Palestine Committee, a pro-Zionist political action group. Rabbi Stephen Wise thanked him "on behalf of hundreds of thousands of organized Zionists" who expressed their "deep appreciation of your action in agreeing to join … lending your support to the Zionist cause." Organized in 1932 by Emanuel Neumann, with the support of Supreme Court Justice Brandeis, the committee was a vehicle through which prominent politicians, mostly devout Christians, could offer support for the Zionist cause.

Speaking to the American Palestine Committee, Chaim Weizmann noted that at the war's end Jewish survivors would be "impoverished, dislocated, crushed and torn out of the economic fabric of which they had been a part." Only Palestine could be the place to give them refuge and a new homeland. Others had advocated exotic areas as a substitute—the first of many being Uganda—but these places did not have "the ties which bind an ancient people to its ancestral home." Pausing to emphasize the importance of his remarks, Weizmann explained, "Fate, history, call it what you may, has linked the national destiny of the Jewish people with Palestine."[494]

Truman joined sixty-eight other senators, known as the Wagner Group, in signing a statement that called for "every possible encouragement to the movement for the restoration of the Jews in Palestine." They endorsed a 1922 congressional resolution supporting the creation of a national home for the world's Jews in Eretz Israel.

Since Hitler had taken power in 1933, the statement read, 280,000 more refugees had come to the Holy Land. They were "streaming to its shores despite restrictive measures" enforced by Great Britain. To seek a home for them in Palestine was "in accordance with the spirit of Biblical prophecy."[495]

After Churchill's push to make the Nazis' atrocities against the Jews public in December 1942, several of Truman's Jewish constituents wrote, appealing to him to speak out. Truman received an invitation from the national chairman of the United Jewish Appeal stressing the need for rescue efforts.

Truman's reply was a mixture of official courtesy with a slightly condescending tag at the end about the war effort. "You are doing great work in endeavoring to keep up the morale of the Jewish refugees and also in your endeavor to unify the efforts of the American Jews for the proper care of their brethren in distress … In doing this extra war work however, remember that the main effort is now for the United States to win the war as quickly as possible."[496]

But as the evidence of the extermination of the Jews at the hands of the Nazis became overwhelming, Truman finally made a strong public statement of support for the Jews. In 1943, leaders of the American Jewish community launched mass rallies in twenty different states to "publicize the Holocaust and to mobilize public opinion behind the rescue proposals …"

On April 14, 1943, Senator Truman prominently participated in a Chicago mass meeting, the "United Rally to Demand the Rescue of Doomed Jews," which was called to protest Hitler's Final Solution. In his speech, he declared:

> Through the edict of a mad Hitler and a degenerate Mussolini, the people of that ancient race, the Jews, are being herded like animals into the ghettos, the concentration camps, and the wastelands of Europe. The men, the women and the children of this honored people are being starved, yes, actually murdered by the fiendish Huns and Fascists. Today these oppressed people, still with spirit unbroken look for succor to us, we people of the United States, whose flag has always stood for liberty, freedom and justice for all.
>
> No one can any longer doubt the horrible intentions of the Nazi beasts. We know that they plan the systematic slaughter throughout Europe, not only of the Jews but of vast numbers of other innocent peoples. The streets of Europe, running with the blood of the massacred, are stark proof of the insatiable thirst of the Nazi hordes.

Today—not tomorrow—we must do all that is humanly possible to provide a haven for all those who can be grasped from the hands of the Nazi butchers. Free lands must be opened to them. Their present oppressors must know that they will be held directly accountable for their bloody deeds.

This is not a Jewish problem. It is an American problem—and we must and will face it squarely and honorably.

Truman received immediate praise from the Jewish community for such a powerful public pronouncement. James H. Becker, chairman of the program committee and a member of the American Jewish Committee wrote: "Our hopes were buttressed by the glowing, trenchant words spoken by you."[497]

Privately, Senator Truman assured national Zionist leaders he felt no difficulty supporting the "Jewish Commonwealth" idea. "When the right time comes I am willing to make the fight for a Jewish Homeland in Palestine."[498]

Chapter Sixteen

THE MUFTI AND THE NAZIS

NOVEMBER 1941—BERLIN

Haj Amin al-Husseini was absolutely committed to expelling every Jew from Palestine and setting up an Islamic caliphate to govern the region and, in time, the world.[499]

Born in Jerusalem in 1895, at a time when Palestine was a province within the Ottoman Turkish territory of Syria, al-Husseini came from a wealthy, prominent Jerusalem Arab clan. Several members of his family had been mayors of Jerusalem.[500] Mustapha, his grandfather, and Kemal, his half brother, preceded him as mufti of Jerusalem.

Members of his family had served the Ottoman Turks as civil servants for generations preceding the arrival of the British. The prefix "Haj" signified that al-Husseini had completed the Islamic obligation of performing a pilgrimage, or hajj, to Mecca, which he fulfilled with his mother in 1913.[501]

With the outbreak of World War One in 1914, al-Husseini joined the Ottoman army, where he received a commission as an artillery officer. When he observed the Turks attempting to impose their language and culture on their Arab subjects, al-Husseini returned to his native Jerusalem. There he assisted in both the 1916 Arab revolt against the Ottomans and the effort to form an Arab nation. The Arabs were taking their first steps toward sovereignty after more than 400 years under Ottoman rule.[502]

Al-Husseini was a fanatical follower of the pan-Arab caliphate concept. He fervently opposed the League of Nations' Mandate to break Palestine away from Syria to develop a Jewish state in the ancient Land of Israel. For the rest of his life, he remained focused on the establishment of an

Arab-Muslim caliphate and the complete eradication of Jewish settlers in Palestine.[503]

He refused to compromise with the Jews of Palestine, insisting that every one of them be expelled. In 1918, al-Husseini stated plainly to I. A. Abbady, a Jewish coworker at the Jerusalem governorate, "This was and will remain an Arab land ... the Zionists will be massacred to the last man ... Nothing but the sword will decide the future of this country."[504]

He would tolerate Jews in Palestine only if they accepted *dhimmi* status, which under sharia law is a second-class citizen with no rights. Al-Husseini believed in an imperialistic utopian Muslim notion that the disciples of the Prophet Mohammed must work toward the creation of a single, united Arab caliphate. The establishment of this caliphate would lead to *Dar el-Islam*, a world under Islam, a concept found throughout Islamic history.[505]

Al-Husseini expressed the Islamic belief that any land conquered by Muslims, at any time in history, is part of the *waqf*, or the holy trust, to be controlled forever by Muslims. Since Palestine was subdued as part of the great Muslim conquests of the 630s,[506] al-Husseini—and other Muslims who hold the same beliefs—consider it to be Muslim land forever.[507]

After returning from Turkey, al-Husseini converted these beliefs into actions, helping to instigate the first large-scale pogrom against Palestinian Jewish settlers in 1920. This was the first time in hundreds of years that innocent Jews were slaughtered en masse by their Arab cousins.

Al-Husseini was indicted by the British for the incitement that led to the murders and riots, although he had already jumped bail and taken refuge in Syria.[508] He was tried and convicted in absentia and sentenced to ten years in prison.

In 1921, Sir Herbert Samuel, the first British high commissioner of the Palestine Mandate, pardoned al-Husseini and most of his co-conspirators. Soon after, Samuel appointed him as Grand Mufti of Jerusalem.[509] This historic appointment was made in spite of vigorous protests from both Jewish settlers and the majority of Palestinian Arabs.

The Muslim High Council considered al-Husseini a hoodlum and opposed his appointment as Grand Mufti. Before the appointment by Samuel, the Palestine Arab leadership had held a vote for the post of mufti, and Amin al-Husseini had come in a distant fourth.[510] But in a bid to offer an olive branch to Palestinian rival families, Samuel offered him the post, hoping it would placate the energetic al-Husseini.

The ploy backfired with disastrous results.

Turning a blind eye to the inner-Arab political struggles, Samuel also appointed al-Husseini to head the political Supreme Muslim Council in Jerusalem in March 1922. With both political and religious leadership in his hands, al-Husseini proceeded to harass and intimidate Arabs who favored cooperation with the Jews and the British.[511]

He quickly consolidated his power through terrorism and by assassinating moderate Arabs who opposed him. He immediately declared a *fatwa* of jihad—a declaration of holy war—against the Zionists. Any Muslims maintaining friendly relations with the Jews were to be considered infidels. Al-Husseini sponsored the first modern Muslim *fedayeen* suicide squads in Palestine, with the primary target being moderate Arabs.[512]

From 1936 to 1939, with the help of the Muslim Brotherhood and Nazi financing, al-Husseini played a key role in the Arab revolt against both the British and the Jews of Palestine.[513]

On July 15, 1937, six days before the outbreak of some of the worst rioting, al-Husseini met with the Nazi Ambassador Doehle, the German consul in Jerusalem. "The Grand Mufti stressed Arab sympathy for the new Germany," Doehle wrote of the meeting, "and expressed the hope that Germany was sympathetic toward the Arab fighting against Jewry and was prepared to support it."[514]

HITLER AND THE GRAND MUFTI

Al-Husseini was one of the first political leaders to send a congratulatory letter to Adolf Hitler upon his election in 1933.[515] Then in 1937, he became the highest-ranking Arab leader to become directly involved with the Third Reich when he met face-to-face with Nazi *Hauptscharfuhrer* Adolf Eichmann and SS *Oberscharfuhrer* Herbert Hagen during their secretive visit to Palestine.[516]

Eichmann wrote glowingly of "the national and racial conscience" that he observed among the Arabs. He reported that "Nazi flags fly in Palestine and they adorn their houses with Swastikas and portraits of Hitler."[517]

Al-Husseini wrote to the Nazis, promising that if Germany would "support the Arab independence movement ideologically and materially," then he would arrange for "disseminating National Socialist ideas in the Arab-Islamic world, combating Communism, which appears to be spreading gradually, by employing all possible means."[518]

In 1938, Nazi Admiral Wilhelm Canaris, a senior director of German Intelligence, placed al-Husseini on his payroll. He would serve as an agent for Nazi political, financial, and military interests throughout the Middle East.[519]

After the British implicated al-Husseini in the violent Arab revolt, he escaped from Jerusalem. He traveled to Lebanon and then to Iraq, where he played a behind-the-scenes role in a pro-Nazi Rashid Ali officers' coup against the British government in 1941.[520] Al-Husseini was welcomed into Baghdad at the time with cheering crowds hailing him as a pan-Arab hero and defender of the faith. He immediately took control of the pro-Nazi Iraqi Arab National Party. The party's agenda was to link up with radical Muslims in Syria, Trans-Jordan, and Palestine, overthrow the colonial powers, and form a united Muslim caliphate across Arabia.[521]

Early in 1941, al-Husseini's German-speaking envoy, Uthman Kamal Haddad, embarked from Iraq on a secret mission to Berlin with a letter that he personally delivered to Hitler. Presenting himself as the only leader in a position to speak to the Nazis on behalf of all Arabs, al-Husseini requested that Hitler issue a public declaration of support for Arab independence.

On April 1, 1941, the pro-Nazi coup d'etat was launched, bringing General Rashid Ali al Gailini to power in Iraq.[522] At this pivotal juncture in the war, al-Husseini arranged for German funds and fighter-bombers to be employed in the support of the coup plotters. Nazi fighter-bombers would take off from airfields in Vichy French Syria on their way to Iraq on bombing missions.[523]

Al-Husseini issued a fatwa on May 9, 1941, declaring Great Britain to be "the greatest foe of Islam." The British responded to the coup by releasing

Jewish Irgun members from prison and sending them to Iraq in an unsuccessful attempt to assassinate al-Husseini. The pro-Nazi coup collapsed at the end of May under a British-Arab counteroffensive.[524]

Fleeing Iraq, al-Husseini publicly declared the Nazis and their Axis allies would have "… to settle the question of Jewish elements in Palestine and other Arab countries in accordance with the national and racial interests of the Arabs and along the lines similar to those used to solve the Jewish question in Germany and Italy."[525]

At the invitation of the Nazis, al-Husseini arrived in Berlin on November 6, 1941. The Mufti resided in the luxurious surroundings of a mansion confiscated from a wealthy Jew. The Nazis set al-Husseini up as though he were head of a Nazi-Muslim government-in-exile. They gave him access to what they called the *Sonderfund*—money and property confiscated from imprisoned and murdered European Jews.[526] Al-Husseini regularly communicated by diplomatic pouch with Hitler, Mussolini, high-ranking Nazi officials, and pro-Nazi governments.[527]

The Germans promoted the Mufti at a reception given in his honor by the *Islamische Zentralinstitut*—the Nazi-Islamic Institute. Al-Husseini was greeted by fellow Muslim exiles and European Muslim leaders who honored him as the "Fuhrer of the Arab World."[528]

On November 28, 1941, Adolf Hitler met with al-Husseini in Berlin with all the pomp of a visiting head of state. Hitler promised al-Husseini, acting in his capacity as a Palestinian pan-Arab leader, that once the Nazis secured a dominant military position in Europe, they would proceed to send the *Wehrmacht*, the Nazi war machine, on a blitzkrieg across the Caucasus and into Arabia.[529]

According to notes taken at the meeting, as well as from al-Husseini's diary, Hitler promised he would help in the creation of a united Nazi-Muslim Middle East. He also said the time would come when the Final Solution against the Jews would be implemented in Palestine—and eventually in the entire Islamic world.[530]

The plan created by and agreed to by Hitler and al-Husseini was for the Mufti to recruit European Muslims to fight for the Nazi cause. Once they were trained, the Mufti would lead these Nazi-Muslims across the Caucasus Mountains and into the Middle East, where they would subdue the nations before them and establish a Nazi-Muslim caliphate.[531]

Germany stood for uncompromising war against the Jews, Hitler said. That naturally included active opposition to the Jewish national home in Palestine. Germany would furnish positive and practical aid to the Arabs involved in the same struggle. Germany's objective was the destruction of the Jewish element residing in the Arab sphere. In that hour, the Mufti would be the most authoritative spokesman for the Arab world.[532]

The Mufti thanked Hitler profusely.

Hitler and al-Husseini agreed to set in motion a secret fomenting of pro-Nazi Arab revolts in the Middle East at a time determined by Hitler. Both agreed on the immediate establishment of pro-Nazi Arab legions made up of indigenous European Muslims trained in Europe. They also agreed on carrying out the Final Solution on the Jews of Palestine and throughout the Arab world.

THE GROSSMUFTI AND MUSLIM-NAZI SOLDIERS

Throughout the war years, al-Husseini, known as the *Grossmufti vom Jerusalem,*[533] conducted aggressive recruitment and training of Muslim soldiers for the Bosnian Muslim Hanzar brigade to fight for the Nazi Wehrmacht under Nazi insignia. Approximately 100,000 European Muslims fought for the Nazis during the course of the war.[534] He initiated espionage and sabotage in the Middle East against both the Allies and the Jews.[535]

The Mufti toured the death camps and encouraged every aspect of the Holocaust against the Jews. And he did all this using money confiscated from Jews on their way to the death camps.[536]

Immediately after the Nazi occupation of the Balkans in 1941, a Nazi-Muslim unit was established called the *Deutsch-Arabische Lehr Abteilung* (DAL), which began operations in Nazi-occupied Greece. Al-Husseini referred to the DAL as the "Arab liberation force." The unit was transferred to the Russian front in the summer of 1942 in anticipation of crossing the Caucasus, defeating the British, and retaking the motherland. The unit wore the inscription "Free Arabia" on their sleeves.[537]

In May 1942, al-Husseini began a series of regular radio broadcasts to the Arab world. One such address occurred after the Allied victory against Field Marshall Erwin Rommel at El Alamein, Egypt—a key turning point in the fight for North Africa. Despite the Nazi loss, the Mufti promised a grand return at the vanguard of a Nazi-Muslim army with the goal of establishing a death camp for the Jews outside of Nablus.

"Arise, oh sons of Arabia," he proclaimed, "fight for your sacred rights. Slaughter Jews wherever you find them. Their spilled blood pleases Allah, our history and religion. That will save our honor."[538]

Thousands of Muslims throughout the region responded to the Mufti's pleas, joining various Nazi-sponsored military units. These included the infamous Nazi mobile genocide brigades, the *Einsatzgruppen*.[539]

In postwar testimony at Nuremberg, Dieter Wisliceny, who served as a deputy to Adolf Eichmann, stated of al-Husseini's Holocaust-related activities:

> The Mufti was one of the initiators of the systematic extermination of European Jewry and had been a collaborator and advisor of Eichmann and Himmler in the execution of this plan … He was one of Eichmann's best friends and had constantly incited him to accelerate the extermination measures. I heard him say, accompanied by Eichmann, he had visited incognito the gas chamber of Auschwitz.

Wisliceny testified that al-Husseini chastised the Auschwitz authorities for not being efficient in their work.[540] In his own memoirs, al-Husseini wrote:

> Our fundamental condition for cooperating with Germany was a free hand to eradicate every last Jew from Palestine and the Arab world. I asked Hitler for an explicit undertaking to allow us to solve the Jewish problem in a manner befitting our national and racial aspirations and according to the scientific methods innovated by Germany in the handling of its Jews. The answer I got was: 'The Jews are yours.'[541]

Part Three

THE REBIRTH

Chapter Seventeen

THE VICE PRESIDENT

1944—WASHINGTON, DC

As the presidential race heated up, Democratic leaders understood that with the war raging, President Roosevelt would have to run for an unprecedented fourth term. Their fundamental concern was Roosevelt's rapidly declining health.

The question on everyone's mind was who would be the candidate for vice president—because he would likely be the next president.

The race for the vice presidency would primarily be fought by political bosses. They would then have to convince an exhausted, seriously ill president.[542]

Roosevelt's personal physician, Vice Admiral Ross T. McIntire, described the president's trouble as bronchitis and told the White House that Roosevelt was reasonably healthy—as good as one might expect for a man his age.

What he didn't tell them was that on March 27, 1944, FDR had been examined by a cardiologist at Bethesda Naval Hospital, Lieutenant Commander Howard G. Bruenn, who discovered that McIntire had misdiagnosed the president. Roosevelt was suffering from heart failure.

Bruenn later described FDR's condition as "God-awful."

He prescribed rest and digitalis, which could help for a while. But the president's cardiovascular disease was so far advanced that almost any treatment would have only a temporary effect.[543]

Roosevelt never asked and was never told the extent of his illness.

The bosses were certain that FDR could not survive another term, but they still needed him to run in order to keep the White House in Democratic hands. A Gallup poll in July showed Roosevelt beating the Republican candidate, Thomas E. Dewey, by only 51 to 49 percent of the popular vote. No other Democrat could beat Dewey.[544]

The Treasurer of the Democratic National Committee, Ed Pauley of California, put it bluntly: "You are not nominating a vice president of the United States, but a president."[545]

The current vice president, Henry Wallace, was unpopular with many party leaders. They disliked his ultra-liberal politics and considered him unreliable and somewhat eccentric. An intensely shy man, he seemed aloof and failed at the most important service a vice president can provide to the president, which is building bridges of trust with individual senators.[546] Influential leaders joined forces to keep Wallace off the ticket.

The first meeting with Roosevelt to discuss the possibility of replacing Wallace took place at the White House in January of 1944. Among the possible choices discussed was James Byrnes, a former senator and Supreme Court justice. He was currently the director of the Office of War Mobilization. Some called him the "assistant president."[547] Other possibilities included Senate Majority Leader Alben Barkley, Speaker of the House Sam Rayburn, Supreme Court Justice William O. Douglas, and Senator Harry Truman.

The soon-to-be National Chairman of the Democratic National Committee, Robert E. Hannegan, was a friend of both President Roosevelt and of Senator Truman. Hannegan said he could support Harry Truman for vice president, but he was also enthusiastic about Byrnes.[548]

Roosevelt refused to reveal whom he favored. He understood the need to conserve his strength for the issues of highest importance at the moment—fighting the war.

Truman, on the other hand, was not interested in the job.

He had at last found a comfortable, distinguished place in the United States Senate. His work investigating waste in the defense industry had made him a popular, nationally known politician. He had also become a part of the Senate's insider club, and he liked it.

He adored his daughter, Margaret, "Miss Skinny" as he liked to call her. She and Bess spent the majority of their time with Truman in Washington. The senator was content.

Then in the summer of 1943, he heard rumbles that certain people wanted him to run for vice president. Truman called them "blow-hards." Publicly, Truman said Sam Rayburn was the best nominee.

In April, Roosevelt was diagnosed with "walking pneumonia" and would convalesce at a friend's estate in South Carolina for two weeks. The actual illness was not disclosed by Roosevelt's doctors. When he returned to the White House a month later, Ed Flynn, a top Democratic political boss from New York, was so alarmed by the president's appearance he urged Mrs. Roosevelt to use her influence to keep him from running.

But the war pulled on all of the president's energies.[549] In the Pacific, differences in strategy between Admiral Nimitz and General MacArthur caused sleepless nights for FDR.

Yet the upcoming election—and particularly his choice for a running mate—was a growing concern. Meeting with the president on June 27, Hannegan told Roosevelt that Wallace would likely be a hindrance to his reelection. He had to come off the ticket. All Roosevelt had to do, Hannegan declared, was to agree to James Byrnes, and they could "sail through" the convention and the election.

"That suits me fine," Roosevelt responded. "He was my candidate for the vice president four years ago, but religion got messed up in it." Byrnes had been raised Roman Catholic, then became an Episcopalian when he married his wife. Big City party bosses, such as Ed Kelly of Chicago and Frank Hague of Jersey City, had warned FDR they could not deliver their heavily Catholic constituencies for Byrnes because he had abandoned his Catholic faith.[550]

Late in June, the Republicans nominated Governor Dewey of New York for president. In response, Roosevelt dispatched Flynn on a cross-country trip to find out what leading Democrats thought of the current vice president. Flynn returned and told the president that with Wallace on the ticket, he could possibly lose states like New York, Pennsylvania, or California.

Flynn then shared with the president his concerns about Byrnes' record on racial issues. In 1938, Byrnes had led the charge of Southern senators who opposed the proposed federal anti-lynching law.

FDR had been doing some of his own research, speaking to key leaders across the country about the VP pick. Sidney Hillman, chairman of the powerful CIO Political Action Committee, told him leaders of the labor movement were strongly opposed to Byrnes.

With the Democrats divided, party leaders were searching for a candidate. As Roosevelt and Flynn went over the list of possible candidates, they kept coming back to Truman. Flynn later wrote:

> His record as head of the Senate Committee … was excellent, his labor votes in the Senate were good; on the other hand he seemed to represent to some degree the conservatives in the party, he came from a border state, and he had never made any "racial" remarks. He just dropped into the slot. [551]

Truman emerged as "the Missouri compromise." He had conservative friends, and Southerners liked him. But he had also been a good New Dealer with labor union contacts. Suddenly Harry became the person everyone could agree on.

In May, Roosevelt sent Henry Wallace on an extensive mission to China and Mongolia. Many thought the assignment was meant to get him out of the way while Roosevelt considered his options.

Fifty-one days later, Wallace returned and met with Roosevelt to report on his journey. Roosevelt eventually changed the subject to the upcoming political convention. The president assured Wallace he was his choice as running mate and that he desired for the fourth term to be "really progressive." Then he shared that his political advisers were warning that Wallace might mean a loss of two or three million votes.

"Mr. President," Wallace responded, "if you can find anyone who will add more strength to the ticket than I, by all means take him." [552]

The next day, July 11, President Roosevelt officially announced his intention to run for an unprecedented fourth term, "reluctantly but as a good soldier." Although his physician declared FDR to be "in excellent health," journalists at the press conference saw the president's hands trembling as he read his speech.[553]

That night following dinner, the political bosses met with Roosevelt in the president's blue oval study on the second floor of the White House. It was a hot, humid night. The tall French doors were open, letting in what little breeze there was. They sat perspiring with their shirtsleeves rolled up, debating the choice for vice president. The bosses were in agreement against Wallace and Byrnes.

Alben Barkley was ruled out next, this time by Roosevelt because he thought at age sixty-six Barkley was too old. The Republicans' nominee was forty-two-year-old Thomas E. Dewey. The president perceived age could become an issue in the campaign. Roosevelt proposed fifty-three-year-old Supreme Court Justice William O. Douglas, but no one else in the room was enthused by the suggestion.

The conversation turned to Harry Truman. Roosevelt agreed he was able, loyal to the administration, and wise to the way of politics. The president thought Truman had done a commendable job with the defense industry committee. The question of Truman's association with the Pendergast machine was thoroughly discussed but dismissed as irrelevant. At the end of the evening, Roosevelt turned to Hannegan and said, "Bob, I think you and everyone else here want Truman."

At that point, Ed Pauley rose and suggested they break up the meeting, then hurried everybody out of the room before Roosevelt had a chance to say anything more.[554]

Before Hannegan left, he got Roosevelt to scribble a note on the back of an envelope: "Bob, I think Truman is the right man, FDR."[555]

The president instructed Hannegan to see Vice President Wallace, and Walker to see Byrnes—to tell them both they were out. The meetings took place the next morning, but because of what the president had previously told them, neither man believed it. Wallace said he would only withdraw if the president told it to him—something FDR couldn't bring himself to do.[556]

Roosevelt later told his son Jimmy that, in fact, he really didn't care. He was a tired, sick man, and what energy he had was concentrated on the war.[557]

On Thursday, July 13, Vice President Wallace met for lunch with Roosevelt to plead his case. Roosevelt told him the professional politicians advocated for Truman as "the only one who had no enemies and might add a little independent strength to the ticket." Wallace pulled out the latest Gallup Poll showing 65 percent of Democratic voters favored him as their candidate, with Byrnes at 3 percent and Truman at only 2 percent.

The president said he planned to send a letter to the chairman of the convention, Senator Samuel Jackson, declaring that if Roosevelt were a delegate he would vote for Wallace. Roosevelt then extended his hand to the vice president. "While I cannot put it just that way in public, I hope it will be the same old team."

What FDR had not shared with Wallace is that earlier that same day he had told Byrnes he was certain Wallace could not win at the convention, but he would endorse no candidate. He said he wanted an open convention, which Byrnes took to mean he had every chance for the nomination. "You are the best qualified man in the whole outfit and you must not get out of the race," Roosevelt exclaimed. "If you stay in you are sure to win."[558]

Byrnes then phoned Harry Truman in Kansas City and asked if he was serious when he told the press he did not want the vice-presidential nomination. "Yes," Truman replied. "Absolutely. I am not a candidate." Byrnes said he had been given the "go sign" from Roosevelt and would like nothing better than to have Truman make the nominating speech for him in Chicago. "I said surely I'll do it if the President wants it done," Harry later explained.

Walker told Byrnes point-blank the previous Wednesday he was not Roosevelt's choice. But Byrnes pushed Truman to commit to him anyway, hoping that somehow the convention would draft him, and the president would accept it.

Only a few minutes later, Alben Barkley called Truman with the same request. According to Barkley, Truman replied, "Why, Alben, I'd be tickled to death to do it, but I've already promised Jimmy Byrnes I would nominate him."

"Well, if you've promised Jimmy," a dejected Barkley replied, "that ends that."[559]

THE DEMOCRATIC NATIONAL CONVENTION

Going into the convention, the unspoken consensus was that the delegates were there to pick not one but two presidents. Everyone knew Roosevelt was the first, but the identity of the second was not yet clear.

Wallace was favored by the delegates—and also by Eleanor Roosevelt. As the convention began, Wallace had more than half the votes necessary to secure his renomination. But as a moderate border-state senator, Truman was being touted by the Democratic Party leadership.

Hannegan arrived in Chicago on July 14, giving himself five days to maneuver before the convention officially began. Mayor Kelly, the Chicago party boss, provided Hannegan with an apartment on Chicago's North Side, where the other bosses could meet.

Truman consistently told everyone—even his daughter, Margaret—he was not a candidate.[560] When Truman's friend Max Lowenthal pressed him to run, Truman replied, "The Madam doesn't want me to do it."[561]

Bess had none of her husband's ambition. She had no desire to see him become president. She certainly did not want to be First Lady. Years later, Margaret Truman disclosed that one of the key reasons her father didn't want to run was that he feared word would get out about the suicide of Bess' father, David Wallace.

In addition, Truman didn't want to be president after Franklin Roosevelt. He didn't want to try to fill those legendary shoes.

Truman arrived in Chicago on Saturday, July 15, four days before the convention began. He had asked some Kansas City friends to join him at the convention for the supposed purpose of helping him to fend off the nomination. But after arriving, all of them quickly realized Harry was a leading candidate. They understood this meant he could eventually become president of the United States. They corralled the senator into a hotel room and tried to reason with him. After each shared his opinion, Eddie McKim hit him right between the eyes. "I think, Senator, that you're going to do it."

"What makes you think I'm going to do it?" Truman snapped back.

"Because, there's a little, old ninety-year-old mother down in Grandview, Missouri, that would like to see her son President of the United States." Truman said nothing more, but with tears glistening in his eyes, he stood and left the room.[562]

The day Truman arrived in Chicago, the president's westbound train made an unscheduled stop in the Windy City. Roosevelt was heading for San Diego where a Navy cruiser would take him to Hawaii for meetings with General MacArthur and Admiral Nimitz. Bob Hannegan climbed aboard the president's new armor-plated private railroad car, the *Ferdinand Magellan*, to discuss the vice-presidential choice. They spoke for a half hour, and when he emerged from the train, Hannegan carried with him a letter on White House stationery, postdated for July 19:

> Dear Bob:
>
> You have written me about Harry Truman and Bill Douglas. I should, of course, be very glad to run with either of them and believe that either one of them would bring real strength to the ticket.
>
> Always sincerely,
> Franklin Roosevelt[563]

Hannegan kept Roosevelt's letter a secret at first. He needed to convince Truman to take the job, and he didn't like that FDR had also mentioned Douglas.

Later, Margaret Truman explained: "The addition of William O. Douglas's name was designed to make it appear that he [FDR] was not dictating anything to the convention. At this point Mr. Douglas had no organized support whatsoever, and the nomination was totally beyond his grasp."[564] In fact, Justice Douglas didn't know he was under consideration and was hiking in Oregon at the time.

On Monday night, Hannegan leaked the letter Roosevelt had written for Wallace to the press. It was addressed to the chairman of the convention, Senator Jackson of Indiana.

I have been associated with Henry Wallace during his past four years as Vice-President, for eight years earlier while he was Secretary of Agriculture, and well before that. For these reasons, I personally would vote for his re-nomination if I were a delegate to the convention.

At the same time, I do not wish to appear in any way dictating to the convention.

The noncommittal letter had the effect Hannegan desired. It became known as the "kiss of death" letter. When labor leaders saw that Roosevelt was not for Wallace "do or die," his support started to erode.[565]

THE CALL TO DUTY

Hannegan met Truman at his hotel suite and laid out his strategy to make him the vice-presidential nominee. Truman interrupted to announce his intention to nominate Byrnes since the president wanted him on the ticket. Hannegan was floored and left the room in shock.[566]

When New York boss Ed Flynn arrived in Chicago the next day, Hannegan pulled him aside. "It's Byrnes!" he exclaimed.

Flynn exploded in frustration and demanded a meeting of the select committee. When they all gathered, Flynn let them have it. There was only one man to nominate, he insisted, and that was Truman.

"I browbeat the committee, I talked, I argued, I swore," he later wrote of the encounter. Flynn said Byrnes would cost no less than 200,000 Negro votes in New York City alone. He was a "political liability." Hillman added that Byrnes was unacceptable to organized labor.

Everyone in the room agreed that with Byrnes on the ticket Roosevelt could lose the election. Flynn put through a call to Roosevelt's train in San Diego. One by one, each of his political advisers got on the phone and agreed that Byrnes could hurt the president.[567] After hearing that Jimmy Byrnes would bring political disaster to the party, the president reiterated that Truman was his final choice.[568]

It was time for the professional politicians to make their move.

Hannegan called a press conference and passed out mimeographed copies of the letter given to him on the presidential train. Hurrying to a bank of telephones to call in the news to their home papers, the reporters drew the obvious conclusion: Roosevelt wanted Truman first and Douglas second.[569]

Within a short time that evening, Hannegan told both Byrnes and Truman what the president had decided. Meeting in Truman's room at the Stevens Hotel, Hannegan showed him FDR's hand-scribbled note. An hour later, Truman went to the Royal Skyway to meet with his friend Jimmy Byrnes. In light of the changing circumstances, he asked to be released from his promise of support. Byrnes said he understood perfectly. When Truman asked if he would stay in the race, Byrnes said he would have to sleep on it.

After Harry left, Byrnes tried to get through to Roosevelt by phone. He was told the president was unavailable.[570]

The following morning, Truman had breakfast with Sidney Hillman of the CIO. He told the powerful labor leader he wanted his support for Byrnes. Hillman shook his head. "Labor's first choice is Wallace. If it can't be Wallace, we have second choice, but it isn't Byrnes."

"Who, then?" the senator asked.

"I'm looking at him," Hillman retorted.

Truman received the same response from other labor leaders that day, including William Green, head of the American Federation of Labor. "The AFL's for you," he said bluntly, "and will support no one else."[571]

Within a day of Ed Flynn's arrival in Chicago, everything had changed. As talk spread throughout the convention that the bosses had killed his candidacy, Byrnes dropped out of the race. In a press release, Byrnes said he was withdrawing "in deference to the wishes of the President," but he departed for home enraged that Roosevelt had betrayed him.

Hearing the news, Alben Barkley was also furious over Roosevelt's double-talk and threatened to tear up his nominating speech. He told a reporter he was tired of trying to determine which shell the pea was under.[572]

Now the race was down to Truman and Wallace. Meeting with reporters in a press conference, Wallace sat on a table with his long legs swinging under him. He said he was there to fight to the finish. His supporters were claiming 400 votes on the first ballot.

But momentum was building for Truman. On July 20, the party bosses summoned him to Hannegan's suite in the Blackstone Hotel to listen in on a phone call that, unknown to the senator, they had rehearsed in advance with the president. It was political theater at its best. Barkley would later refer to Hannegan as "the stage manager" in Chicago. Hannegan said he wanted Truman to speak to the president, but the senator's "Missouri dander" was way up by now, and he refused. [573]

They placed a call to Roosevelt in San Diego. As Truman sat nearby on a bed, Hannegan held the phone so the senator could hear. But the president's voice boomed so loud, everyone in the room heard him clearly.

"Bob, have you got that fellow lined up yet?" Roosevelt bellowed.

"No," Hannegan replied. "He is the contrariest Missouri mule I've ever dealt with."

"Well, you tell the Senator that if he wants to break up the Democratic Party in the middle of the war, that's his responsibility," Roosevelt declared and slammed down the phone.

"What do you say to that?" Hannegan asked as Harry sat in stunned silence.

Truman finally stood and paced the floor. "Well, if that's the situation, I'll have to say yes. But why the hell didn't he tell me in the first place?" [574]

The call to duty did the trick. Truman agreed to run.

SHOWDOWN ON THE FLOOR

A crowd far beyond the auditorium's capacity had pressed into the arena to witness President Roosevelt's nomination for an unprecedented fourth term. The heat rose to 120 degrees, and people started to collapse. Delegates listened as Roosevelt addressed them from his train car in San Diego. As the president's voice boomed through the amplifiers, the massive crowd sat watching an empty podium.

"What is the job before us in 1944?" the now-feeble FDR asked. "First, to win the war—to win the war fast, to win it overpoweringly. Second, to form worldwide international organizations, and to arrange to use the armed forces of the sovereign nations of the world to make another war impossible …"[575]

No one in the massive convention hall knew it, but earlier that day, Roosevelt had suffered a seizure in his railroad car. Turning deathly pale, with a look of agony on his face, FDR called out to his son Jimmy. "I don't know if I can make it. I have horrible pains." His son helped him lie down on the floor and watched over him in terror for ten minutes. Finally, the pain subsided, and his father asked to be helped to his feet again. No one but the president and his frightened son knew that this near-death experience took place.[576]

DAY OF DESTINY

The final session of the convention began early the following day. As the drama of the vice-presidential race intensified, Truman entered with the Missouri delegation. Bess and Margaret sat in a box just behind the podium. As Wallace waited out the session in his hotel room—as was the custom—Truman sat in full view of the delegates, eating hot dogs and thoroughly enjoying the political circus unfolding before him.

The first ballot began at 4:30 in the afternoon. Wallace remained in the lead throughout the count, tallying 429 votes to Truman's 319. But Wallace did not have enough votes to win, so the delegates were released from any promises they had made to candidates before the convention.

Truman made his way up to the box seat with Bess and Margaret as the excitement of the second ballot began to build. Wallace was ahead for a while, and then Maryland's Governor O'Connor threw his eighteen votes to Truman. After this, the New York delegation withdrew their support and gave seventy-four and a half votes for Truman with only eighteen for Wallace. The Missouri senator moved ahead.[577]

Things tightened again for a few moments, with Wallace coming within five votes of Truman. But the floodgates opened when Alabama's favorite son candidate, Senator John Bankhead, withdrew his name and cast twenty-two votes for Truman. Across the convention hall, delegates rose to their feet.

Suddenly, South Carolina switched eighteen votes from Bankhead to Truman, and the flood began to rise. Photographers gathered around Truman's box, flashbulbs popping. Margaret Truman was jumping up and down like a cheerleader, rooting for her father, who sat next to her, grinning from ear to ear.

Senator David Walsh of Massachusetts announced his delegation was throwing thirty-four votes to Truman, and that put him over the top.

At 8:14 p.m., Chairman Jackson rose to formally make the announcement. "Senator Harry Truman has received more than a majority. I do now declare him to be the nominee of the Democratic Party and the next Vice President of the United States."[578]

A small army of policemen seized Truman and fought their way through the roaring crowd to the platform. Bob Hannegan held up Truman's arm while the convention hall went wild with delight. The pandemonium went on for several minutes until the new vice-presidential candidate seized the chairman's gavel and banged it. "Give me a chance, will you please?" he pleaded. Finally, the noise subsided, and he began a characteristically humble speech.

> You don't know how very much I appreciate the very great honor which has come to the state of Missouri. It is also a great responsibility which I am perfectly willing to assume. Nine years and five months ago I came to the Senate. I expect to continue the efforts I have made there to help shorten the war and to win the peace under the great leader, Franklin D. Roosevelt. I don't know what else I can say except that I accept this great honor with all humility. I thank you.

"My father fought his way off the platform," Margaret Truman remembered, "and … soon reached the box where we were sitting. There we were practically besieged by a horde of shouting, sweating photographers, who begged us ad infinitum for 'just one more' until Dad had to call a very firm halt and concentrate on getting us out of the stadium alive. The crowd was still frantic with excitement, and he was genuinely concerned for our safety."[579]

"Thankfully the police formed a kind of phalanx around us and we were able to get into a waiting car outside, where Mom looked at Dad, glared at him and said, 'Are we going to have to go through this for all the rest of our lives?'"[580]

Campaign by Train

The next morning, Truman received a telegram from President Roosevelt:

> I SEND YOU MY HEARTIEST CONGRATULATIONS ON YOUR VICTORY. I AM OF COURSE VERY HAPPY TO HAVE YOU RUN WITH ME. LET ME KNOW YOUR PLANS. I SHALL SEE YOU SOON.
>
> FRANKLIN D. ROOSEVELT[581]

The *St. Louis Post-Dispatch* called him an excellent choice. Writing of the nomination in his private diary, reporter Allen Drury observed:

> On the credit side, the Senator is a fine man: no one would do a better job of it in the White House if he had to … I think Senator Truman is one of the finest men I know. [582]

On August 18, Truman sat down for lunch with President Roosevelt beneath a magnolia tree said to be planted by Andrew Jackson on the White House lawn. Due to the heat, Roosevelt suggested they take off their jackets. Seated in their shirtsleeves at a small round table set with crystal and silver from the Coolidge administration, the two men posed together for photographers for the first time. The contrast in appearance between the two men was striking. Only two years younger than the president, Truman looked healthy and robust. The president had dark circles under his eyes, and his shoulders sagged.

Truman had not seen the president in more than a year and was shocked at FDR's frail and sickly appearance. Writing of the meeting, Truman noticed that when Roosevelt poured cream into his coffee, more went into his saucer than his cup. Even at this private luncheon, Roosevelt told Truman nothing of importance, posing for reporters and making small talk.

Meeting with reporters on the way out of the White House, Truman dutifully added to the fiction upheld by the president's aides. "The President looked fine and ate a bigger lunch than I did."

But when he arrived at his Senate office, he shared his concern with Harry Vaughan. "It doesn't seem to be any mental lapse of any kind. But physically he's just going to pieces."

Truman kicked off his campaign with a rally at his Missouri birthplace, Lamar. Nine senators escorted him to the rally where 35,000 people gathered on a steamy full-moon night in front of the old redbrick courthouse, just up the street from the house where he was born. Harry's ninety-year-old mother sat on the platform beaming with pride.[583] "You can't afford to take a chance," Truman declared. "You should endorse tried and experienced leadership."[584]

Truman campaigned with his usual energy and determination. He traveled thousands of miles, skipped meals, and washed his socks in the basin of his sleeping car. One night, Harry awoke in a cold sweat. He had dreamed that Franklin Roosevelt had died, and he, Harry Truman, was president of the United States. "In all my life," Truman later told a reporter, "I have never had such a terrifying nightmare."

Bess and Margaret joined Truman for the final leg of his whistle-stop campaign. "We paused for an exciting torchlight parade at Parkersburg, West Virginia," Margaret wrote. "At Pittsburgh, we had a twenty-six man motorcycle escort for a dash to nearby McKeesport for lunch. I was awed by the crowds …"

As the campaign concluded, the Trumans reserved a suite at the Muehlebach Hotel in Kansas City to wait out the returns on election night. Harry joined the Battery D boys and other political friends and supporters for a victory celebration. He played the piano for the crowd while they huddled around the radio, nervously listening to the results. The Republicans took an early lead, but as the night wore on, Roosevelt and Truman surged back. Dewey finally conceded defeat at 3:45 a.m.[585]

Not long after being nominated as vice president, Truman took his friend Eddie McKim to a White House reception. McKim was so shocked by the president's appearance he wondered if Roosevelt would live long enough to be inaugurated. As the two men exited through the wrought-iron gates, McKim told Truman to turn and look back, because that was where he would be living before long. "I'm afraid you're right, Eddie," Truman replied, "and it scares the hell out of me."[586]

Chapter Eighteen

FRANKLIN ROOSEVELT AND KING SAUD

JANUARY 20, 1945—WASHINGTON, DC

President Roosevelt's unprecedented fourth inaugural took place just before the Yalta Conference and his meeting with Ibn Saud. In a break with precedent, and at President Roosevelt's insistence, the inauguration ceremony was not held at the Capitol but on the South Portico of the White House on a bitterly cold January day. According to tradition, Henry Wallace administered the vice-presidential oath to Harry S. Truman, who wore a wool coat and scarf.

Just inside the French doors that led inside the White House, President Roosevelt arrived in a wheelchair, pushed by his son James. The president looked exhausted. His face was pale, with dark circles under his eyes. Out on the portico, James Roosevelt and a Secret Service man lifted the president to his feet, and he took hold of the speaker's lectern. He turned and shook hands with the new vice president, then turned back to take his oath.[587] Chief Justice Harlan Stone administered the oath of office to FDR, who refused to wear a hat or coat. His inaugural address to the relatively small crowd gathered on the slush-covered lawn lasted only five minutes. At its conclusion, Roosevelt flashed his famous grin at Truman and shook his hand again.

The president waved to the crowd, then returned inside the White House and quickly hid away in the Oval Office. Harry and Bess Truman joined Eleanor Roosevelt in greeting the 1,800 visitors at an official White House luncheon. During a break in the handshaking, Eleanor leaned over and whispered to Truman, "I can't get my husband to eat. He just won't eat."

After the reception, Bess and Margaret returned home. Vice President Truman bummed a ride back to the Capitol, where he telephoned his mother from his old Senate office. "Did you hear it on the radio?" he asked.

"Yes, I heard it all," she said. "Now you behave yourself up there, Harry!"

"I will, Mamma," he promised, hanging up the phone with a satisfied grin. [588]

Truman had been vice president for only six days when he received news that Tom Pendergast had died on January 26. Ignoring his political advisers, he commandeered an army bomber and went to Kansas City for the funeral.

"I'm as sorry as I can be," he told reporters. "He was always my friend, and I have always been his."[589] Truman's presence meant a great deal to Pendergast's family, which was all Harry cared about.

Returning to Washington, Truman's main job was presiding over the Senate. Anticipating struggles between the legislative and executive branches after the war, he did what he could to set the stage for smooth postwar governance. Truman lamented to a friend, "I am trying to make a job out of the vice presidency and it's quite a chore. The Vice President is a political eunuch."

He presided over the Senate, writing letters home during the long debates, then dropping by for a late afternoon drink with his old friends in Congress. He seemed wholly unaffected by his new title. "Homespun as ever," one senator remarked.

A few weeks after the inauguration, Truman joined the president at the head table for the annual dinner of the White House Correspondents Association. Like everyone else, Harry was shocked by how haggard Roosevelt appeared, and even more alarmed by his dazed, vacant manner.

JANUARY 1944—GREAT BITTER LAKE, EGYPT

By January 1944, the Zionists' campaign to have a resolution introduced in Congress supporting the establishment of a Jewish state in Palestine was finally gaining traction. But their hopes were dashed when the resolution, which had substantial support in both the House and Senate, was opposed by Secretary of State Cordell Hull, Secretary of War Henry L. Stimson, and FDR, who argued its passage would hurt the war effort.

The war had not been won, they said, and passage of the resolution by Congress might cause difficulties for Allied operations in the Middle East, a major supplier of oil for the European theater. Both the War Department and the State Department said Arab nations would be alienated by such a resolution, and their support was needed for victory in the war against the Nazis.[590]

Roosevelt's position on the Jews—as on so many other issues—was complicated. FDR wrote to his friend, New York's leading Democrat Senator Robert Wagner Jr., about his fear for the future of the Jews.

"There were about half a million Jews in Palestine," he wrote the senator, and on the other side were "seventy million Mohammedans who want to cut their throats the day they land."[591] His main goal, therefore, was to avoid a massacre. He hoped the situation could be resolved through negotiations. Any action toward a Jewish state, Roosevelt implied, would only "add fuel to the flames." American hopes were one thing. "If we talk about them too much," he cautioned Wagner, "we will hurt fulfillment. Better to keep discussions on the matter under the radar."[592]

The new Secretary of State, Edward Stettinius, wrote in his diary that the president was "confident" that he "will be able to iron out the whole Arab-Jewish issue on the ground where he can have a talk." FDR told Stettinius that "Palestine should be for the Jews and no Arabs should be in it, and he has definite ideas on the subject. It should be exclusive Jewish territory."[593]

The president told Judge Samuel Rosenman the issue of Palestine could be settled by "letting the Jews in to the limit that the country will support them—with a barbed-wire fence around the Holy Land." Rosenman thought it might work "if the fence was a two-way one to keep the Jews in and the Arabs out."[594]

This concept came to Roosevelt in part from a report made by assistant chief of the Soil Conservation Service, Walter Clay Lowdermilk. He argued that engineering marvels like the Tennessee Valley Authority dam projects had proven "modern engineers can harness wild waters to produce cheap power for industry and scientific agriculture to make over waste lands into fields, orchards and gardens, to support populous and thriving communities."

In 1938, Lowdermilk had been sent by the US Department of Agriculture to survey land use in Europe, North Africa, and the Middle East to help understand the factors that had led to the devastating Dust Bowl in the 1930s. Lowdermilk's special interest was how different populations throughout the centuries had used land and what the results of those practices had been.[595]

In addition to being a scientist, Lowdermilk was a Gentile Zionist who sincerely believed in the restoration of the Jews in the Land of Israel according to Bible prophecy. His trip to Palestine in 1939 was "a dream come true … because the Bible presents the most authentic and longest-written record of any nation except China."[596]

When he arrived in Palestine, he was dismayed to find that because of the "poor stewardship of the land," the once fertile Holy Land had been replaced by "denuded slopes" and "sandy wadis." During many centuries of abuse, he estimated more than three feet of soil had been swept away.[597]

Conversely, Lowdermilk was greatly impressed by what the Jews "who fled to Palestine from the hatreds and persecutions of Europe" had accomplished since the late nineteenth century. He was astonished to find 300 colonies "defying great hardships and applying the principles of co-operation and soil conservation." They have "demonstrated the finest reclamation of old lands that I have seen in three continents. They have done this by the application of science, industry and devotion to the problems of reclaiming lands, draining swamps, improving agriculture and livestock and creating new industries."

All this was done against "great odds and with sacrificial devotion to the ideal of redeeming the Promised Land."[598]

According to Lowdermilk, the Tennessee Valley Authority had demonstrated that waters could be harnessed to enable an area to support a much larger population. "The Holy Land can be reclaimed from the desolation of long neglect and wastage and provide farms, industry and security for possibly five million Jewish refugees from the persecutions and hatreds of Europe in addition to the 1,800,000 Arabs and Jews already in Palestine and Trans-Jordan."

Lowdermilk was quite optimistic about the absorptive capacity of the region. Settling millions of Jewish refugees in Palestine, he concluded, "would erect an eternal memorial to our victory in this world struggle for democracy and world freedom."

"Some place must be found to re-instate the Jews long without a country among the peoples of the earth." Lowdermilk proclaimed that this place could only be Palestine. "They have nowhere else to go."[599]

Lowdermilk returned home and presented his report to Vice President Wallace, who was amazed that the Methodist Lowdermilk "had become the most complete Zionist convert anyone could ask for."[600] In 1944, Lowdermilk published a book based on his research titled *Palestine: Land of Promise*, which became a best seller. The book had a significant impact on the debate in America over the creation of a Jewish state in Palestine.

On March 28, 1944, Senator Bennett Clark of Missouri, a member of the Foreign Relations Committee, gave an impassioned speech denouncing FDR and his administration for opposing the resolution for a Jewish homeland in Palestine. Clark told his Senate colleagues that for the past few nights he had been up reading Dr. Lowdermilk's book, *Palestine: Land of Promise*, and he urged them all to do the same. In Palestine, Clark told them, the soil was being reclaimed, and "an ancient land is being returned to the fruitfulness which the Creator intended."[601]

THE STATE DEPARTMENT AND THE MIDDLE EAST

As support for Zionism rapidly increased in America in reaction to Nazi atrocities, so did anger toward the United States by the Arabs. In May 1943, King Ibn Saud vented his rage in a memorandum to President Roosevelt. "Jews have no right to Palestine," Saud insisted, warning of a backlash against American interests in the Middle East if, "God forbid, ... the Allies should, at the end of their struggle, crown their victory by evicting the Arabs from their home."

Roosevelt's reply would become the mantra of the State Department for the next four years. He pledged the United States would take no position on Palestine without first consulting Saud and other leaders.[602]

Despite support for a Jewish homeland in Palestine by many in Congress and by millions across the country, the US State Department was diametrically opposed to it. Ignoring Britain's promises to the Jews in the Balfour Declaration and American support of it, the State Department viewed Palestine as an integral part of the Arab world.

The Department's Division of Near Eastern and African Affairs (NEA) recognized the existence of the Jewish Yishuv in Palestine and understood that the region was considered sacred by three of the world's major religions. But these non-Arab factors were considered "incidentals, hardly enough to change the Department's view that Palestine was, and must remain, an Arab area." They viewed Zionism in Palestine and the United States as an inherited nuisance that needed to be opposed. [603]

During the 1930s, American oil companies made significant investments in Saudi Arabia. In 1933, Saudi Arabia signed the historic Concession Agreement giving Standard Oil permission to explore its country. To support this effort, The Texas Company, later Texaco, acquired half of this agreement in 1936. In 1944, the enterprise was renamed the Arabian American Oil Company, or ARAMCO. [604] The State Department saw the region as a gold mine for American interests after World War Two.

Arab goodwill toward the United States was due to the weakness or preoccupation of other world powers with postwar problems. As far back as the Wilson administration, America had rejected imperialism in the region and pressured the European powers on behalf of emerging nations. These factors and others led to Ibn Saud's preference for American investment and friendship.

The State Department saw Zionism as jeopardizing this growing Arab-American relationship and the potential oil-fed bonanza. The greatest fear, which was touted consistently by the Washington oil lobby, was that governmental support for the Zionists in Palestine would turn Ibn Saud against ARAMCO and drive the Arabs into the Soviet camp. [605]

With these conflicting points of view in mind, President Roosevelt met with friend and adviser Rabbi Stephen Wise and asked for his opinion of Lowdermilk's optimistic projections. Wise admitted that some had called it impractical but said David Lilienthal, one of the directors at the Tennessee Valley Authority, saw it as "extremely practical and desirable."

The president was also concerned about Arab fears that the Jews would "seek to infiltrate the surrounding Arab countries." In truth, Wise responded, the reverse was taking place. The Arabs were migrating to Palestine to take advantage of its rapid development and rising standard of living. Most important, Wise assured FDR, "the Jews have not the slightest desire or intention to colonize the Arab lands outside Palestine." Jews living in Arab countries would undoubtedly leave for Palestine. He knew Jews currently in Iraq, Syria, and Yemen were ready to go at a moment's notice.

As for the president's fear of the Soviets opposing a Jewish state, Wise informed Roosevelt that President Edvard Benes of Czechoslovakia, a "Zionist of long standing," was told by Joseph Stalin that if Britain and the US had no objections to the creation of a Jewish commonwealth in Palestine, neither would Russia.[606]

But the State Department still dug in its heels. William Eddy, the US minister to Saudi Arabia, reported to FDR a message from King Saud: "... If America should choose in favor of the Jews, who are accursed in the Koran as enemies of the Muslims until the end of the world, it will indicate to us that America has repudiated her friendship with us."[607]

Secretary of State Stettinius, who had recently replaced Cordell Hull, reminded the president that Ibn Saud "regards himself as a champion of the Arabs of Palestine and would himself feel it an honor to die in battle in their cause."[608]

The State Department offered Roosevelt its own proposal. "Palestine should become an international territory under trusteeship of the British, with a charter granted it by the new United Nations. This arrangement would supersede all previous agreements on Palestine, including those in the Balfour Declaration."[609]

The president was ambivalent, giving assurances to both the Arabs and the Jews about future possibilities. In an election year, pacifying a key component of the coalition that had given him electoral victory was an important mission. In March 1944, FDR had reiterated his good intentions regarding the Jews in Palestine to both Wise and Rabbi Abba Silver. Emerging from a White House meeting, the two rabbis told the press FDR assured them the US government had not approved the British

White Paper of 1939. The president was happy, they reported, "that the doors of Palestine are today open to Jewish refugees, and that when future decisions are reached, full justice will be given to those who seek a Jewish national home."[610]

These Jewish leaders were unaware, however, that almost immediately, then-Secretary of State Cordell Hull sent a reply to his Arab colleagues throughout the Middle East. In FDR's comments to the rabbis, Hull stressed, "the president pointed out that the statement mentioned only a Jewish National Home, not a Jewish Commonwealth. He added that although the United States had never approved of the White Paper, it had never disapproved of it either."

FDR believed his personal charm and powers of persuasion could tip the scales in favor of a Jewish home in Palestine. He was convinced if he sat down with King Saud, whom he considered to be the leader of the Arabs, he could iron out a deal. He told his cabinet after the wartime meeting of the United States, Britain, and the Soviet Union at Yalta, he would meet with Ibn Saud and "try to settle the Palestine situation."[611]

In the midst of the war, Roosevelt had the convenient excuse of defeating the Nazis as the reason to postpone any action on the Jews in Palestine. "The mills of the gods grind slowly," he told his Zionist friends, "but they grind exceedingly small."[612] But since the Holocaust had become common knowledge, Jewish leaders and a growing number of American supporters of Zionism were becoming impatient with the president.

In the aftermath of six million murdered Jews, gradualism in both the government and in the Zionist movement was considered outdated— and even cowardly. Change was in the wind.[613]

YALTA AND THE FUTURE OF PALESTINE

Two days after the inauguration, on January 22, 1945, President Roosevelt departed for the Yalta Conference. During the negotiations, the Big Three agreed to dismantle Germany and to reestablish the border between Poland and the Soviet Union. Most important, Stalin and Roosevelt agreed to free elections in Poland and Eastern Europe. They discussed the structure of the United Nations as well as the question of reparations and war crimes.[614]

Many burning issues were discussed at Yalta, but the situation of the Jews was pushed aside.[615] However, Roosevelt did try to discover where Stalin stood on Zionism. After dinner on February 10, Roosevelt asked Stalin if he supported the Zionist program. Stalin answered warily, "Yes, in principle," but he recognized the difficulty of solving the Jewish problem. Roosevelt came away from the conversation pleased that Stalin did not seem opposed to Zionist aims in Palestine.

Roosevelt stunned both Churchill and Stalin by informing them of his plans to meet with King Saud. FDR was particularly interested in Palestine, and he announced his sympathies were entirely with the Jews.[616]

Palestine was not the only subject on the agenda. Roosevelt was fully informed about the importance of the Saudi oil reserves. The president's advisers made it clear that these oil fields were essential to American security due to both increased demand for oil in the West, along with dwindling domestic reserves. Securing Middle-Eastern oil was a key necessity of American foreign policy.[617]

IBN SAUD ON THE GREAT BITTER LAKE

After the strenuous eight-day meeting with Stalin and Churchill at Yalta, the ailing FDR took a five-and-a-half hour flight to Egypt and boarded a US Navy cruiser, the *Quincy*. Steaming down the Suez Canal, they dropped anchor in the Great Bitter Lake. Known as *Mara*, or "bitter," in biblical times, it was an ironic location for Roosevelt's debate with Ibn Saud over the fate of Jewish refugees.

Roosevelt had been informed that Moses had stopped on the shores of this great body of water as he led the Israelites on their flight from Egypt toward the Promised Land.[618]

The president's staff went all out to impress Saud. *The New York Times* reported in a banner headline that the warship had been made into an "Arab Court in Miniature." The display was "without precedent in American naval annals." The ship's crew had spread dozens of thick Oriental carpets on the deck and set up a royal tent in front of the forward gun turret, complete with silk cushions and gilded chairs. The president, understanding the high stakes, turned on the full power of the Roosevelt charm.

King Saud, who was nearly as ill as FDR, arrived from Jidda aboard the USS *Murphy*, but he could not make it across the gangplank. He was winched onto the *Quincy* in a lifeboat. Following him was an entourage of sixty men, including his sword-wielding Nubian bodyguards, described by one sailor as "lean and dark with murderous black eyes," who "looked as if they would get great enjoyment out of carving their initials on unfriendly anatomies."

Roosevelt greeted Saud with a full honor guard and a splendid display of flags snapping in the wind. In respect for his guest, FDR refrained from smoking while, in a traditional display of hospitality, the king served the president coffee.

FDR was "in top form," William Eddy wrote, "as a charming host, witty conversationalist, with the spark and light in his eyes and that gracious smile which always won people over whenever he talked with them as a friend. With Ibn Saud he was at his very best."[619]

Roosevelt opened the discussion with an animated review of America's vision of bringing modern technology and trade to the Middle East—transforming Arabia's deserts into luxuriant gardens. Saud graciously reminded the president he was a warrior, not a farmer, and had no interest in altering the Arabs' age-old ways of life.[620]

Roosevelt then introduced the problem of the Jewish refugees' plight. He prefaced his comments by stating he had "a serious problem in which he desired Saud's advice and help," namely the rescue and settlement of the remnant of European Jewry. "What would the King suggest?" FDR asked.

Saud told the president that, in his opinion, the Jews should return to live in the lands from which they were driven. If that was impossible because their homes were destroyed, the answer was to give them "living space in the Axis countries which oppressed them."

Roosevelt made plain his support for the Jewish survivors of what was not yet called the Holocaust. He also expressed his admiration for the Jews who fought against the Nazis and who had developed Palestine, and asked Saud to support his idea of establishing in Palestine a free and democratic Jewish commonwealth.[621]

The king brusquely replied no.

Saud would have none of it, arguing it was the Arabs and not the Jews who had fought against the Germans, and it was the British and not the Jews who made the deserts bloom.[622] He was not impressed with FDR's claim that Jewish farmers had developed land in Palestine. That had been accomplished with millions of dollars and pounds in American and British capital, he claimed, and only the Jews would gain from the prosperity.[623]

The king adamantly opposed allowing more Jews into Palestine or establishing their own state, suggesting they be given the "choicest" German homes instead. "Make the enemy and the oppressor pay; that is how we Arabs wage war," he insisted. "Amends should be made by the criminal, not the innocent bystander."[624]

When Roosevelt said three million Jews had been slaughtered in Poland alone, Saud replied there must now be room there for three million more.

FDR was shocked by the vehemence of the king's reaction. He should not have been, given Saud's previous uncompromising statements, including his remark on the eve of the Yalta Conference that Palestine would be drenched in blood and that the United States must choose between the Zionists and the Arabs.[625]

Roosevelt argued that Palestine was such a small part of the Middle East the Arabs would not be harmed by the creation of a Jewish state. He was prepared to guarantee "the Jews would not move into adjacent parts of the Near East from Palestine."[626]

The truth was, Saud continued, that Arabs and Jews "could never cooperate, neither in Palestine, nor in any other country." Arabs would rather die "than yield their land to the Jews."[627]

In the face of Saud's defiant rejection of Roosevelt's proposal of cooperation with the Jews, the president abruptly abandoned his advocacy of the Zionists. He decided it was best to assure Saud he would get precisely the support he expected from the United States. He would never, he assured the concerned monarch, help the Jews at the expense of the Arabs. America would come to Saudi Arabia's defense, if necessary, and would do everything "short of war" to strengthen Syrian and Lebanese independence. King Saud immediately seemed relieved.

The president conceded that the American people were "misinformed" about the Middle East. He then explained to Saud he was talking as the chief executive, but it was impossible for him to prevent speeches made on behalf of the Zionist project or to stop resolutions in favor of a Jewish homeland passed by Congress. The king should not confuse these outbursts, FDR emphasized, with US policy. His own future policy, he assured Saud, would be one friendly to the interests of the Saudi monarchy.[628]

Roosevelt once again promised the king the United States would not take any position on Palestine without first consulting him and other Arab leaders and would not do anything for the Jews at their expense.[629]

In a show of friendship, the king presented Roosevelt with a set of Arabian robes and a diamond-studded sword. The king returned to Jidda with a state-of-the-art wheelchair, which he pronounced "my most precious possession—the gift of my great friend, President Roosevelt, on whom Allah has had mercy."[630]

When the president's chief adviser, Harry Hopkins, received the news of the meeting, he was furious. On the *Quincy*, Hopkins had remained in his cabin, too sick to attend the talks. When he heard the outcome, Hopkins thought the president's ill health had led him to be "overly impressed" with Ibn Saud and had caused him to abandon his earlier pro-Zionist position far too easily.

Arab leaders rejoiced over the meeting, calling it their most significant achievement in Palestine since the 1939 White Paper. Arab League Secretary-General Abdul Rhaman Azzam often quoted Saud's vow to Roosevelt: "I will never rest until I and all my sons have been killed in the defense of Palestine."

Conversely, the Zionists were devastated by the talks and insulted by the Roosevelt administration's attempts to downplay the importance of its promises to the Jewish community. This "commitment" seemed to be merely lip service.[631]

CHURCHILL AND PALESTINE

Roosevelt's visit with Saud didn't concern Stalin, but it left Winston Churchill anxious about American designs on the Middle East, which he considered strategic to the future of the British Empire.[632] Churchill had his own plans for Palestine after the war. In 1943, he told Chaim Weizmann he wanted Britain to offer Saud the leadership of a Middle Eastern Arab Federation under British oversight, for which he would be paid £20 million a year. In exchange, the king would have to give his support for a Jewish state in Palestine.[633]

Churchill proclaimed the 1939 White Paper a "gross breach of faith" and told Weizmann that after victory he would see to it that Jewish refugees were free to immigrate to Palestine. The promise of a Jewish homeland, Churchill said, was "an inheritance left to him by Lord Balfour and he was not going to change his attitude."

After Hitler's defeat, he added, "the Allies will have to establish the Jews in the position where they belong." The Jews and the Zionists should not worry, the prime minister assured Weizmann, because they had a "wonderful case." He hadn't changed his views, and he promised that "he would bite deep into the problem and it is going to be the biggest plum of the war."[634]

But Churchill fared no better with King Saud when they met than Roosevelt had. He began the meeting by reminding the Saudi monarch how Great Britain had "supported and subsidized" him for twenty years and made his reign possible "by fending off potential enemies." As a result, Britain was entitled to ask for Saud's help "in the problem of Palestine, where a strong Arab leader can restrain fanatical Arab elements, insist on moderation in Arab councils, and affect a realistic compromise with Zionism." Both sides must make concessions, and Churchill expected the Saudi monarch to do his part.[635]

What Churchill suggested, Saud answered, would not help the Allies or Britain "but [was] an act of treachery to the Prophet and all believing Muslims which would wipe out my honor and destroy my soul … The British and their Allies would be making their own choice between 1. a friendly and peaceful Arab world, and 2. a struggle to the death between Arab and Jew if unreasonable immigration of Jews to Palestine is renewed. In any case, the formula must be one arrived at by and with Arab consent."[636]

Rabbi Stephen Wise told Chaim Weizmann that, like Roosevelt, Churchill was unable to make an impression on King Saud. "It may have been his own fault," Wise wrote to Weizmann, "because he set out to browbeat the old man for two hours, after which he changed his tack and was sweet as honey with him, but nothing availed."[637]

The Last Speech to Congress

After returning home, Roosevelt sent a letter to the king repeating the views he had expressed during their meeting. Again he reassured Saud the United States would take no measures that "might prove hostile to the Arab people."[638]

When the president arrived in Washington, his wasted appearance left Vice President Truman even further shaken. He realized Roosevelt might not have much time left.

As vice president, Truman was given a limousine with a chauffeur. One day when the driver came to take him to the Capitol, another man sat in the front seat beside him. Truman assumed he was a friend of the driver getting a free ride into town. This unknown visitor continued to occupy the front passenger seat in the coming days, and so one day Truman asked the chauffeur if the man were his friend. "He's no friend of mine," the driver responded. "He's a Secret Service man."

The Secret Service had never protected the vice president before, but, convinced Roosevelt was failing, the director assigned a special agent to guard Truman.[639]

In a solemn joint session of Congress, Vice President Truman sat on the dais behind the president as Roosevelt reported on the Yalta Conference. The representatives gathered in the House Chambers could see the toll the trip had taken on FDR. Despite his polio, Roosevelt had always given his speeches standing up. He delivered this one sitting down, apologizing for his "unusual posture."

"I know you will realize it makes it a lot easier for me in not having to carry about ten pounds of steel around the bottom of my legs, and also because I have just completed a 14,000 mile trip."[640]

His voice was hollow, lacking the famous Roosevelt fire. His left hand trembled noticeably as he turned the pages. He tripped through the presentation as though he hadn't prepared properly. The cadence and structure of the message were further marred by FDR's frequent ad-libs.[641] At times, his voice seemed to give out, and his hand shook again as he reached for a glass of water. "It has been a long journey," Roosevelt continued. "I hope you will also agree it has been so far, a fruitful one."[642]

Then in the midst of the speech, FDR made a comment that shocked the Zionists and their supporters. "I learned more about the whole problem of Arabia—the Moslems—the Jewish problem—by talking to Ibn Saud for five minutes than I could have learned in the exchange of two or three dozen letters." He was undoubtedly referring to the negative— some would say fanatical—response of the king on the subject of a Jewish homeland in Palestine.[643]

The Jewish community was horrified.

Roosevelt soon realized the harm his comments had caused, and he moved to minimize the damage. Once again, he turned to the Zionist leader he most trusted, Rabbi Stephen Wise.

"I have had a failure," Roosevelt mournfully acknowledged, "...with Ibn Saud." The president felt especially bad about this, he told Wise, because he had "arranged the whole meeting with him for the sake of your cause."

"I tried to approach the Jewish question a number of times," FDR explained. "Every time I mentioned the Jews he would shrink and give me some such answer as this: 'I am too old to understand new ideas!'"

When Roosevelt told him about what had been done for Palestine through irrigation and the planting of trees, Ibn Saud said, "My people don't like trees; they are desert dwellers. And we have water enough without irrigation."

The president added, "I have never so completely failed to make an impact upon a man's mind as in his case."[644]

The rabbi accepted FDR's explanation, telling Chaim Weizmann that Roosevelt had seen Ibn Saud "for our sake" but had come out of the meeting fearful that if the king united the Arab armies, he could easily defeat all the Jews of Palestine.

The president did give Wise some good news. "Stalin is all right and he is with us." As far as Churchill went, there had been no change "with regard to Zionist plans." Moreover, he assured Wise, Churchill was equally concerned with the plight of European Jewish refugees who sought entry to Palestine.

Finally, the president told Wise he was seeking another way to deal with the Saudi ruler. "He is seventy-five years old," the president commented, "and has swollen ankles, so that perhaps we had better wait until he goes!" Given the pressing situation of the European Jews, Wise countered that he had to act quickly and in a firm manner.

FDR thought perhaps there was "another way of dealing with the problem. Since we cannot move I.S., and since the other Arab chiefs will go along with him, I have been thinking about the plan of our putting the case up to the first meeting of the Council of the United Nations, whenever it meets."

"The President is dead in earnest about this," Wise concluded. "If we were to agree with him, he would feel that he and Churchill must put it up to their associates and urge the imposition of a Jewish State on I.S. and his associates by the Council of the United Nations."

"The President," Wise told Weizmann, "remains our friend as much as ever."[645]

Bombarded by the Zionists on the one hand and opponents in the State Department and Arab leaders on the other, FDR felt increasingly gloomy about the prospects for any kind of Middle East settlement. At a luncheon he held with the First Lady and Colonel Harold Hoskins, he reiterated sadly how opposed Saud was to Jewish concerns, even with a proposal floated by the president to settle Jews in Libya.

As usual, Eleanor was more sympathetic to the plight of the dispossessed Jews and tried to lift her husband's gloom. She noted the "wonderful work that had been done by the Zionists in certain parts of Palestine." Her comments did not impress the president. Except along the coastal plain, he replied, "Palestine looked extremely rocky and barren to him as he flew over it." But the First Lady believed the Zionists were stronger and "were perhaps willing to risk a fight with the Arabs at Palestine."

That prospect was exactly what upset FDR. "There were many more Arabs than Jews in and around Palestine," the president noted. In the long run, he thought these numbers would win out.

Hoskins said he had been attacked by American Zionists in 1943 when he had said the only way to establish a Jewish state in Palestine would be by force. Now the colonel asked the president if he agreed with this conclusion. Roosevelt replied that he did. The answer, Hoskins still maintained, lay in State's plan for a trusteeship and the establishment of Palestine as an international territory sacred to Muslims, Christians, and Jews. FDR concurred, saying he thought such a plan might well be given to the newly created United Nations.[646]

Eleanor Roosevelt, who supported the Zionist cause, wrote to her friend Joseph Lash telling him the president was frustrated that he did not convince the king to change his uncompromising position on Palestine.[647]

A solution to the Palestine problem seemed to lie far in the future. In the meantime, Roosevelt sought both to contain the damage from his spontaneous comment about Ibn Saud and to assure American Zionists his true sympathies lay with their cause. In his heart, Roosevelt may well have thought he had done what he could on their behalf.

The president's meeting with Wise and Silver on March 9 allowed the two to claim at a press conference that FDR's promises to them "appeared to affirm the President's support of the Zionist position." And when FDR wrote Senator Wagner of New York explaining that he supported the Democratic Party's Palestine plank—one sympathetic to Zionist aims—it further raised doubts for the Arabs about the veracity of Roosevelt's pledges to them.[648]

The last meeting the president held in the White House before departing for Warm Springs, Georgia—where he hoped to get some much-needed rest—was with American Jewish Committee leaders Jacob Blaustein and Joseph Proskauer. The president told them that he had previously warned Rabbi Wise "he gravely feared a continuation of the agitation for a Jewish state," because it might cause a world war as well as strife in Palestine. What he did not tell Wise, but did tell Proskauer and Blaustein, was that after talking with Ibn Saud, he had been "frightened" and wanted them "to talk to the Zionist leaders about it."[649]

FDR told Blaustein and Proskauer of his "belief that the project of a Jewish state in Palestine was, under present conditions, impossible of accomplishment" and the Jews' objective should be to secure liberal immigration into Palestine and work for the rights of Jews in all nations through the auspices of the new United Nations.

Admitting his new view was "somewhat at variance with his public utterances," Roosevelt explained he had "learned a great deal at Yalta" and hence supported the American Jewish Committee's attempts to "moderate the sharpness of the propaganda of the extreme Zionists."[650]

After Roosevelt's return from Yalta, Truman saw him only twice at the White House—and they did not discuss anything significant. The president made no effort to bring Truman into the inner circle of the administration.[651] "I could never shake the feeling that the Roosevelt White House considered me small potatoes."[652]

The last time Harry Truman saw Roosevelt was immediately after his speech before Congress. "Plainly, he was a very weary man," Truman wrote to a friend.[653] The president asked Truman to excuse his lackluster performance in his address to Congress. "As soon as I can, I will go to Warm Springs for a rest," Roosevelt explained. "I can be in trim again if I can stay there for two or three weeks."

On March 30, FDR left for his retreat in Georgia. "He seemed a spent man," Truman told a friend. "I had a hollow feeling within me."[654]

By the time FDR arrived in Warm Springs, there could be no recuperation. The same day the president departed for Georgia, FDR's correspondence secretary, William D. Hassett, spoke with heart specialist Dr. Howard Bruenn about the president's health.

"He is slipping away from us and no earthly power can keep him here," Hassett told the doctor.

"Why do you think so?" Dr. Bruenn asked contentiously.

"I know you don't want to make the admission, and I have talked this way with no one else save one," Hassett replied. "To all the staff, to the family, and with the Boss himself I have maintained the bluff; but I am convinced that there is no help for him."[655]

Chapter Nineteen

THE MOON, STARS, AND ALL THE PLANETS FALL

The vice president walked over to Sam Rayburn's "Board of Education," a hideaway quarters on the first floor of the Capitol's southern end. It was a dark room with a frayed rug, a fireplace, several black leather chairs, and a sofa. The ingredients to "strike a blow for liberty" were always ready—giving the legislators a chance for a relaxing drink after a long day.[656]

Entering the room, Truman was greeted by the Speaker, along with Lew Deschler, the parliamentarian of the House of Representatives, and James M. Barnes, a White House legislative assistant. As Rayburn mixed the bourbon with the right amount of water, he remembered White House Press Secretary Steve Early had called and asked that the vice president call right away. Truman immediately picked up the phone and called the White House.

"Please come right over as quickly and as quietly as you can," Early said in a strained voice. "And come in through the main Pennsylvania Avenue entrance. Come directly to the family quarters on the second floor."

The other men watched Truman turn pale and his jaw set hard. He hung up the phone. "Holy General Jackson! Steve Early wants me at the White House immediately." He paused, then said solemnly, "Boys, this is in the room. Something must have happened."[657]

As soon as Truman left Rayburn's office, he took off in a run, not even stopping to look for his Secret Service escort. He ran the length of the Capitol basement and through the underground tunnel to his room in the Senate Office Building. Grabbing his hat, he ordered Tom Rorty, his chauffeur, to get his car and meet him outside. "I'll either telephone you within an hour," he told Harry Vaughan, "or be back by that time."[658]

"I thought I was going down there to meet the President," he later said. "I didn't allow myself to think anything else." Yet many would question him later—why did he run?

It was 5:25 p.m. when he arrived at the White House. Two ushers escorted him to the elevator, which rose to the second floor, where he walked down the corridor and entered Mrs. Roosevelt's study. There he found Eleanor; her daughter, Anna; Anna's husband, Colonel John Boettiger; and Steve Early.[659]

Mrs. Roosevelt rose and walked toward him. She put her arm around his shoulder and said gently, "Harry, the President is dead."[660]

For more than an hour, Harry Truman had been the president without knowing it. He found out later that Roosevelt had died of a cerebral hemorrhage at the "Little White House" in Warm Springs at 4:35 p.m.[661]

Tears filled Truman's eyes. "Is there anything I can do for you?"

Eleanor Roosevelt shook her head. "Is there anything we can do for you?" she responded. "For you are the one in trouble now."[662]

Harry told Mrs. Roosevelt and Anna that anything necessary to be done for their help and convenience would be done. The First Lady said she wanted to fly to Warm Springs that evening and asked permission to use a government plane. Harry told her that as soon as he was sworn in he would order that all the facilities of the government should be at her command until the funeral was over.

Soon Secretary of State Stettinius entered the room, also wiping tears from his eyes. Stettinius thought a cabinet meeting should be called at once. Truman authorized him to notify all the members of the cabinet to report to their meeting room at 6:15.

Harry excused himself and made his way to the West Wing, where, in spite of his grief, he took charge as a national leader. From the president's office, he instructed the attorney general, Mr. Biddle, to call the chief justice of the Supreme Court to come at once and administer the oath of office. He called Sam Rayburn and asked him to bring key congressional leaders. He called Harry Vaughan with instructions to come to the White House along with his aide, Matt Connelly.

Word of Roosevelt's death was broadcast on the radio. Across Pennsylvania Avenue, in the twilight of the late afternoon, thousands of people gathered in silence in Lafayette Square.[663]

Bess and Margaret visited briefly with Mrs. Roosevelt in her private quarters, offering their condolences before joining Truman in the Cabinet Room. When Bess came in, Harry crossed the room and took her hand. Bess dabbed her eyes repeatedly as they waited for the ceremony to begin.

The members of FDR's cabinet arrived and crowded with Truman's family and congressional leaders into the Cabinet Room. The room was also filled with White House officials and reporters.[664] Chief Justice Harlan Stone stood at the end of the long table, and Truman stood under the portrait of Woodrow Wilson, one of his presidential heroes. Truman picked up the Bible in his left hand and raised his right hand in the air.

The chief justice began, "I, Harry Shipp Truman …"

"I, Harry S. Truman," he corrected him.

When the oath was completed, the chief justice added, "So help you God," a phrase not in the constitutional oath but used spontaneously by George Washington when he took his first oath of office. "So help me God," repeated the president, then solemnly raised the Bible to his lips—something George Washington had also done.[665] The clock under the Woodrow Wilson portrait stood at 7:09 p.m.

Harry S. Truman was the thirty-third president of the United States.

Afterward, Truman met with the cabinet. He spoke solemnly to the gathered members—some of them he knew well, and others hardly at all. Truman quoted Eleanor Roosevelt as saying that her husband had "died like a soldier."[666] He assured them he would carry out the policies of President Roosevelt and asked them to remain in their posts. But he also made it clear he would be "president in my own right." He told them he wanted their advice, and they should not hesitate to differ with him whenever they felt it was necessary. But he was going to make the final decisions.[667]

Stettinius observed that Secretary of Labor Frances Perkins was quietly praying. Each of the cabinet officers delivered brief pledges of support.

Secretary of War Henry Stimson, the senior member, said it was time to close ranks.

When the meeting ended, Stimson lingered behind. A matter of utmost urgency needed to be discussed. After everyone had left the room, he informed Truman, in a hushed tone, that the United States had developed a weapon of enormous explosive power they were about to test. Stimson said he would brief the president on the details as soon as possible.

"He wanted me to know about an immense project," Truman wrote later, "to develop a new explosive of almost unbelievable destructive power. That was all he felt free to say at the time, and his statement left me puzzled." Harry Truman was president, and he knew nothing of the atomic bomb.[668]

Although the White House reporters clamored for a meeting with the new president, Truman felt the time was not yet right for a press conference. Surrounded by Secret Service, he walked out to his car and drove home to his apartment. He would give the Roosevelt family all the time they needed to grieve.

Truman arrived at his Connecticut Avenue apartment at 9:30 p.m., completely famished. He hadn't eaten since lunch. Bess, Margaret, and Mrs. Wallace were still in shock and had wandered over to the apartment of their next-door neighbors, General and Mrs. Jeff Davis. President Truman joined them, and Mrs. Davis served him a large turkey sandwich and a glass of milk.[669] He wolfed down the sandwich, thanked them for their hospitality, and announced he was going to bed.

The president went next door to his small apartment and called his mother in Grandview, Missouri, who had heard the news. With the help of her other son, Vivian, she had been deflecting a barrage of phone calls from reporters. Truman assured her he was all right, but he would be very busy for the next few days. It might be a while before she received a letter from him. Then he got into bed and immediately fell asleep.

A Load of Hay

Truman was up at 6:30 a.m., and he soon left for the White House surrounded by a small army of Secret Service men. He asked the driver to stop so he could invite his friend Tony Vacarro, an Associated Press reporter who was waiting for the new president, to ride with him. "There have been few men in all history the equal of the man into whose shoes I am stepping," Truman told Vacarro as they headed downtown. "I pray God I can measure up to the task."

When they arrived at the White House, Truman went to the Oval Office. Everything was as Roosevelt left it—only the desk had been cleared of its pictures and knickknacks by an aide. Truman later wrote he felt the presence of Roosevelt acutely.[670]

Soon Harry's longtime friend Eddie McKim entered with Matt Connelly. After shaking hands, McKim remained standing in front of the big oak desk, completely at a loss for words—which was uncharacteristic for him. "Well, Mr. President, it doesn't count what's gone on before. What counts is what happens now."

After Truman returned to his seat, McKim stood quite erect, looking very uncomfortable. After a long, awkward moment of the two staring at each other, Truman finally blurted out, "Do you have to stand there?"

"Well, I suddenly find myself in the presence of the President of the United States, and I don't know how to act."

For the first time, Truman grasped the tremendous awe with which people view the presidency. "Come on over here and sit down," he said warmly to his old friend. Eddie sat in a nearby chair. "Do you have to go home?" Truman asked.

"Well, I was leaving this afternoon for Omaha."

"I need you," Truman responded. "Stick around a while. I need some help."[671]

While the new president had the greatest respect for Roosevelt's cabinet and White House staff, he knew he needed people around him who would be personally loyal to him. He understood that many from the Roosevelt administration would eventually move on to other things, but he was counting on them to help him through the transition.

That morning, the new president met with Secretary of State Stettinius and the Joint Chiefs of Staff, the Secretaries of War and the Navy, and

Admiral William Leahy, who served as President Roosevelt's Chief of Staff. Truman requested a thorough report on the major foreign policy problems facing the United States. The Joint Chiefs said they expected the war with Germany to last another six months, and the war with Japan to go on for another eighteen months.

At noon, the new president traveled to Capitol Hill with full presidential entourage—limousines, police escort, and Secret Service—to have lunch with thirteen key senators and four representatives. Closing the door to reporters, Harry took a drink and insisted on informality. He wanted to tell them in person that he needed their help in a "terrible job." Soon the congressmen were calling him "Harry" again and laughing like it was the day before.[672]

"It shattered all tradition," Senator Arthur Vandenberg later wrote in his diary. "But it was both wise and smart. It means that the days of executive contempt for Congress are ended."[673]

When Truman emerged from the lunch, a crowd of reporters stood waiting for him. As flash bulbs popped, Truman's eyes suddenly filled with tears. "Isn't this nice." Many of the reporters before him were friends he had made in his years as a senator. "This is really nice," he repeated.

He then showed his humility and sincerity to a nation wondering who this new president really was. "Boys, if you ever pray, pray for me now. I don't know whether you fellows ever had a load of hay fall on you, but when they told me yesterday what had happened, I felt like the moon, the stars, and all the planets had fallen on me."

"For just a moment he had taken us into his confidence," wrote United Press correspondent Allen Drury, "and shown us frankly the frightening thing that had happened to him—shown us, who represented something, a free and easy camaraderie and naturalness to which he knew he could never, for the rest of his life, quite return."[674]

With the exception of Abraham Lincoln during the Civil War and Franklin Roosevelt during the Great Depression, no president took office in a period of greater crisis than did Harry S. Truman.

Returning to the White House, Truman met with his former rival for the vice presidency, James Byrnes, who had accompanied Roosevelt to Yalta and had taken extensive shorthand notes of the conference. It was important for the new president to know all the agreements—and almost as important, the nuances of the agreements—that Roosevelt had made at this crucial meeting of the Allied leaders.

Truman spent the rest of the afternoon speaking with Secretary of State Stettinius and Charles Bohlen of the State Department, who had acted as an interpreter at the Yalta meetings with Stalin. Stettinius told Truman the Russians had already violated their agreements at Yalta—particularly in Poland where they had agreed to allow for elections but had instead installed a Communist puppet government. Truman immediately cabled Prime Minister Churchill to confer with him on the growing crisis. They agreed to meet with Stalin for further talks as soon as it could be arranged.

At 10:30 on Saturday morning, President Roosevelt's funeral train arrived in Washington from Warm Springs. In a gesture of political unity, Truman invited former Vice President Henry Wallace and James Byrnes to accompany him to Union Station to mark the arrival of Roosevelt's train and join him in the funeral procession. Roosevelt's casket was placed on a horse-drawn caisson, pulled by six white horses and escorted by an honor guard, moving slowly from the station to the White House to the accompaniment of dirge and muffled drums.[675] The streets were lined with people, many openly weeping.

That afternoon, Harry attended the state funeral for Roosevelt in the East Room of the White House. Several hundred dignitaries had gathered—including the cabinet, Supreme Court, foreign diplomats, the Chiefs of Staff, Governor Thomas Dewey, and Mrs. Woodrow Wilson. That evening Harry, Bess, and Margaret boarded the funeral train for the trip to Hyde Park. The train had seventeen cars, and it was filled to capacity by practically every official of the United States government.

The following morning, Franklin Roosevelt was laid to rest in the rose garden of his Hyde Park estate.

On the return trip, Truman tried to work on his speech for the next day's joint session of Congress, but he was continuously interrupted. Every congressman and senator on the train seemed eager to see the new president. Despite the frustration of trying to complete his speech, he smiled and shook hands with each of them and asked them to come see him in the White House.[676] After the passenger greetings finally slowed, Truman closeted himself with George Allen, Byrnes, Early, and Snyder to work on the speech.[677]

THE FIRST SPEECH

The following day, Harry S. Truman traveled to the Capitol to address a joint session of the House and Senate for the first time as president of the United States. Millions of Americans listened by radio. The speech emphasized Truman's intention to carry on with Roosevelt's policies. He drew the most enthusiastic applause when he announced his commitment to the war policy of unconditional surrender.[678]

> With great humility, I call upon all Americans to help me keep our nation united in defense of those ideals which have been so eloquently proclaimed by Franklin Roosevelt. I want in turn to assure my fellow Americans and all those who love peace and liberty throughout the world that I will support and defend those ideals with all my strength and all my heart. That is my duty and I shall not shirk it.[679]

The president concluded his speech hearkening back to his thorough knowledge of the Bible:

> At this moment I have in my heart a prayer. As I have assumed my duties, I humbly pray Almighty God, in the words of King Solomon: "Give therefore Thy servant an understanding heart to judge Thy people, that I may discern between good and bad: for who is able to judge this Thy so great a people?" I ask only to be a good and faithful servant of my Lord and my people.

The Congress interrupted him seventeen times through the fifteen-minute speech with generous applause. Then they gave him a standing ovation at the conclusion.[680]

THE PROBLEM OF PALESTINE AND THE JEWS

Truman talked with everyone who had served under Roosevelt to learn as much as possible about what FDR had agreed to in his various meetings. Lacking foreign policy experience, Truman believed it would be best to stay the course. But soon events evolved in ways no one could have foreseen, and Truman was forced to make the tough decisions as president—including the difficult choices regarding the future of the Jews and Arabs in Palestine.

On the night Franklin Roosevelt died, three American generals—Eisenhower, Bradley, and Patton—received the news in a house at Marburg, Germany. They sat up much of the night talking about FDR and speculating on the sort of man Truman might be. All three were greatly depressed. "From a distance Truman did not appear at all qualified to fill Roosevelt's large shoes," General Omar Bradley later wrote.

It had been an unusually difficult day for the American command. Before receiving the news about Roosevelt, they had seen their first Nazi death camp—Ohrdruf-Nord, near Gotha. An aide remembered that as Eisenhower bid the others good-night, he looked deeply shaken. But the American commander soon learned they were just scraping the surface of the horrors of the Nazi genocide against the Jews.[681]

Chapter Twenty

DEATH CAMPS AND DISPLACED PERSONS

APRIL 1945—BUCHENWALD CONCENTRATION CAMP, WEIMAR, GERMANY

On April 5, 1945, units from the Fourth Armored Division of the Third Army were the first Americans to discover a death camp with prisoners and corpses. Ohrdruf was a Buchenwald sub-camp, and of the 10,000 male inmates, many had been sent on death marches or shot in pits. Their corpses were stacked in the woods and burned. The Americans stumbled on the camp by accident, finding the starved, frail bodies of hundreds of prisoners who had managed to survive.

In Nordhausen, on April 11, the Timberwolf Division found 3,000 corpses and 700 starving survivors, slaves from the V-2 rocket factories. Fred Bohm, an Austrian-born Jewish US soldier, was one of the men who helped to liberate Nordhausen. His fellow GIs had "no particular feeling for fighting the Germans. They also thought that any stories they had read in the paper, or that I had told them out of first-hand experience, were either not true or at least exaggerated. And it did not sink in, what this was all about, until we got into Nordhausen."[682]

The GIs found the dead by the thousands everywhere—in mass graves, stacked like cordwood, scattered about the grounds, and even sharing bunks with the living. While touring the camps, the Allies discovered the gas chambers, the rooms for medical experiments, and the crematories.

The first major camp, Majdanek, had been discovered by the advancing Soviets on July 23, 1944, so the Western soldiers had heard rumors of the atrocities. But they didn't believe the depth of the depravity until they saw it.

As the death camps were liberated, nearby civilians swore they had not known of the atrocities. But the camp's stench and the odor of the crematories had carried for miles over the countryside. There was no denying the scent of death that hung in the air.

"My first impression of it was the odor," remembered John Glustrom of the 333rd Engineers. "The stench of it was all over the place and there were a bunch of very bewildered, lost individuals who came to me pathetically at the door in their unkempt uniforms to see what we were doing and what was going to be done about them … This was the most shattering experience of my life."[683]

When Generals George Patton, Omar Bradley, and Dwight Eisenhower arrived in Ohrdruf, they found 3,200 naked, emaciated bodies in shallow graves. Eisenhower stumbled into a shed piled to the ceiling with bodies, various torture devices, and a butcher's block for smashing gold fillings from the mouths of the dead. Patton became physically ill and left the building. Eisenhower turned white at the scene inside the gates but insisted on seeing the entire camp. "We are told that the American soldier does not know what he was fighting for," he said. "Now, at least he will know what he is fighting against."[684]

"I visited every nook and cranny," Eisenhower reported. It was his duty, he felt, "to be in a position from then on to testify about these things in case there ever grew up at home the belief … that the stories of Nazi brutality were just propaganda."[685]

Eisenhower ordered all American units within the vicinity to visit the camp. He also issued a call to the American and international press. A group of prominent journalists, led by the dean of American publishers, Joseph Pulitzer, visited the concentration camps. Pulitzer initially had "a suspicious frame of mind," he wrote. He expected to find many of "the terrible reports" were "exaggerations and largely propaganda." But not only did these reports prove to be true—they were understatements.[686]

Within days, congressional delegations came to the concentration camps, accompanied by journalists and photographers. Even veteran, battle-scarred correspondents were overwhelmed.

In a legendary broadcast on April 15, Edward R. Murrow gave the American radio audience a stunning matter-of-fact description of Buchenwald, of the piles of dead bodies so emaciated that those shot through the head had barely bled, and of children who still lived, tattooed with numbers, whose ribs showed through their thin shirts.

"I pray you to believe what I have said about Buchenwald," Murrow asked listeners. "I have reported what I saw and heard, but only part of it; for most of it I have no words." He added, "If I have offended you by this rather mild account of Buchenwald, I am not in the least sorry."[687]

On April 18, the general public finally learned the full extent of Nazi Germany's war against the Jews. A dispatch informed readers of *The New York Times* what the reporter called "the horror, brutality and human indecency" of the Dachau and Buchenwald concentration camps.

German neighbors who had feigned ignorance of the camp's existence were confronted with the reality when they were taken to see the remaining twenty thousand Jewish prisoners, "many of them barely living." They saw the torture rooms, execution mechanisms, gas chambers, and medical facilities, where Nazi doctors had performed fiendish experiments on living human beings. It might have been a picture of hell: "the stench, filth and misery here," the reporter wrote, "defied description."[688]

Harry Truman read these gruesome reports along with the rest of America. He saw the horrific newsreel footage that brought the pictures home forever. The evidence of what had taken place gave him nightmares. "It was a horrible thing I saw," he told CBS News in 1964, "and I dream about it even to this day."[689]

TRUMAN AND THE PALESTINE QUESTION

In office for only days, Truman was still getting his bearings as the reports of the Holocaust flooded the White House. He was immediately confronted with Jewish leaders and millions of concerned American citizens advising that, in light of these Nazi atrocities, the just and decent thing to do was to give the Jewish people a home in Palestine.

But he also faced representatives of the Arab nations with their enormous oil reserves and tens of millions of people around the world telling him they didn't want a Jewish state in the Middle East.[690]

When the US Army polled the Jewish Holocaust survivors, the vast majority said they would not go back to their homes in Europe. Most of them wanted to go to Palestine.

This response shocked many career bureaucrats. On April 18, Truman received a letter from Secretary of State Stettinius explaining the views of the State Department regarding Palestine. "It is very likely that efforts will be made by some of the Zionist leaders" to obtain commitments in favor of "unlimited Jewish immigration into Palestine and the establishment there of a Jewish state." Declaring his own sympathy for Europe's persecuted Jews and acknowledging the opinion of the American public regarding the Holocaust, Stettinius warned the Palestine question was highly complex and emotionally charged, and its ramifications went far beyond the plight of the Jews.

He warned Truman not to make any public statements on the issue without asking the experts at the State Department for full and detailed information. The United States had vital interests in the region, he advised, and the subject must be handled with the greatest care.[691]

Two days later, the president had his first meeting with a group from the American Zionist Emergency Council (AZEC) led by Rabbi Wise. Truman opened the meeting by telling them "he welcomed the opportunity to discuss the matter because he was sympathetic to the Zionist cause." When he had more time, he wanted to meet again to hear more, but for the moment he wanted to assure them "that he would follow the policies laid down by the late President Roosevelt on the Palestine issue."[692]

Not fully aware of the new president's knowledge of Zionism, Wise said he didn't know if Truman understood why the Jewish people favored a national home in Palestine. But as a student of history, the human condition, and the Bible, President Truman was thoroughly knowledgeable on the subject of Palestine and the Jews. To prepare for this meeting with the Zionist leaders, he had reviewed FDR's public statements and record regarding Palestine. He reread the Balfour Declaration and familiarized himself with the history of demands for a Jewish homeland. He also reviewed the Arab and British views on the subject.

Truman was quite aware that after World War One, fifty-two foreign governments had endorsed the major goals of world Zionism.[693]

Writing about this meeting in his memoir, Truman noted he "was skeptical" as he looked over the record and came across "the views and attitudes assumed by the 'striped-pants boys'"—the term he used for the professional bureaucrats in the State Department. He felt State "didn't care enough about what happened to the thousands of displaced persons," and he could both "watch out for the long-range interests of our country while at the same time helping" the survivors of the Holocaust to find a home.[694]

In the meeting, Truman explained to Rabbi Wise and his colleagues that the State Department would not be calling the shots while he was president. "I'd see to it that I made policy," Truman assured them, and State's job "was to carry it out."[695]

But Truman soon learned that in "carrying out the policies of President Roosevelt" he was walking into a diplomatic quagmire. In the beginning of May, while Secretary of State Stettinius was in San Francisco at the conference organizing the United Nations, Acting Secretary of State Joseph Grew provided Truman with more information on Roosevelt's position regarding the Arabs and Jews in the Middle East. "Although President Roosevelt at times gave expression to views sympathetic to certain Zionist aims, he also gave certain assurances to the Arabs which they regard as definite commitments on our part."

Grew submitted a summary of Roosevelt's conversation with Ibn Saud, a copy of the April 5 letter to the Saudi king, and statements to Arab rulers promising that "there should be no decision altering the basic situation in Palestine without full consultation with both Arabs and Jews."

Truman quickly realized Roosevelt had left him bound by seemingly irreconcilable pledges to both the Arabs and the Zionists. The US government had no clear Palestine policy.[696] Truman realized he would have to develop his own path, once he found a way to free himself of Roosevelt's murky obligations.

At the same time, Chaim Weizmann delivered a memo to Churchill in London describing the desperate straits of the Holocaust survivors as well as Jews living in Arab lands. Joseph Linton, the Jewish Agency officer in London, demanded the agency assume the full power to decide Palestinian immigration policy. In the meantime, he asked the British high commissioner to grant 100,000 entry permits to Palestine immediately.[697]

The Americans were working desperately to alleviate the grim refugee situation in Europe. From May through September 1945, the military repatriated six million refugees—the majority being Jews. But another 1.5 million refused to or could not go back to their former homes. The military at first did not distinguish between civilian refugees who had been displaced as a result of bombing or fighting and the persecuted Jews who had survived the death camps. Instead, they were treated like any other group of displaced persons (DPs).

Sometimes they found themselves housed in the same barracks as Germans who had been displaced by the war and who had supported Hitler. German Jews released from Polish and Czech camps were not given ration cards on the grounds that they were part of the enemy.

Some Jewish refugees even found themselves in the nightmare where they were placed in the same barracks with their former camp guards, who now also claimed to be refugees. In some cases, Jewish DPs realized with horror that the Allies had assigned ex-Nazis to be in charge of the camps where the inmates were once again held as virtual prisoners.[698]

VICTORY IN EUROPE

On May 7, 1945, Germany surrendered to the Allies. The following day, Truman announced the end of the war in Europe via radio.

"This is a solemn but glorious hour," the president told the gathered press. "General Eisenhower informs me that the forces of Germany have surrendered to the United Nations. The flags of freedom fly all over Europe."

Truman smiled. "It's celebrating my birthday today, too."

"Happy birthday, Mr. President!" the reporters responded amidst laughter.

"For this victory," the president continued, "we join in offering our thanks to the Providence which has guided and sustained us through the dark days of adversity … We must work to finish the war. Our victory is only half over.

"The longer the war lasts, the greater will be the suffering and hardships which the people of Japan will undergo—all in vain. Our blows will not cease until the Japanese military and naval forces lay down their arms in unconditional surrender."[699]

THE POTSDAM CONFERENCE

Soon after the surrender of Germany, Truman attended the conference at Potsdam with Joseph Stalin and Winston Churchill—"Mr. Russia and Mr. Great Britain," he called them.[700] The summit was a follow-up to the Yalta Conference, the terms of which the Russians were already ignoring.

Arriving in Berlin, Truman was given a tour of the city. The motorcade drove down Wilhelmstrasse to the remains of the Reich Chancellery. They drove past the Tiergarten, the Reichstag, the Foreign Office, and dozens of other sites, which had been world-famous before the war. They had become mostly piles of rubble, destroyed by ferocious Allied bombing.

The president had never seen such destruction. "That's what happens when a man overreaches himself," Truman wrote.[701]

The United Kingdom's general election of 1945 was held on July 5. The result was an unexpected landslide victory for Clement Attlee's Labour Party, giving them a mandate to implement their postwar reforms.

To everyone's surprise and shock, Churchill was replaced at the Potsdam Conference by Attlee in the middle of the negotiations. As Attlee and his foreign minister, Ernest Bevin, took their chairs at the round table for the tenth meeting of the conference, Truman noted this as "a dramatic demonstration of the stable and peaceful way in which a democracy changes its government."

The new prime minister had been present at the conference from the beginning. "Attlee had a deep understanding of the world's problems," Truman observed, "and I knew there would be no interruption in our common efforts."[702]

In the spirit of Woodrow Wilson's Fourteen Points, Truman insisted the United States would not enter into any hidden postwar agreements. He stayed true to his word, and at Potsdam there were no secrets.

Among the achievements of the negotiations was an agreement to avoid the mistake of heavy reparation payments to keep Germany weak. "We intended to make it possible for Germany to develop into a decent nation," Truman explained, "and to take her place in the civilized world."[703]

The Bomb and Victory in Japan

While Truman was engaged in Potsdam, the *Enola Gay*, a specially modified B-29, was rehearsing maneuvers to drop an atomic bomb. A list of four target cities in Japan had been prepared. There was no question of whether or not Truman was going to use the bomb. The question was when and where.

When the president received a description of the atomic bomb test, he became fully aware of its awesome power for the first time. He was told that thirteen pounds of explosives had evaporated a steel tower sixty feet high, left a crater in the New Mexican desert more than two miles wide, knocked down men 10,000 yards away, and was visible for more than 200 miles.

"We have discovered the most terrible bomb in the history of the world," President Truman wrote in his diary. "It may be the fire destruction prophesied after Noah and his fabulous ark."

The day after Truman learned of the bomb's power, he confronted Stalin with new confidence. Churchill noticed that once Truman heard the news that the atomic bomb worked, he was a "changed man." It became clear to Truman that, as he later said, he had "an ace in the hole and an ace showing." The ace in the hole was the atomic bomb, while the ace showing was American economic and military power.

On July 24, Truman rose from his chair and walked slowly around the table to have a private word with the Soviet dictator. "I casually mentioned to Stalin that we had a new weapon of unusual destructive force," Truman later wrote. "All he said was he was glad to hear it, and hoped we would make good use of it against the Japanese."[704]

Two atomic bombs were nearly ready, and seven more were in production. On July 25, Truman gave control of the bombs to the military and ordered they be used as soon as the Potsdam Conference was over. The next day, the Japanese were given one last chance to surrender. "We call upon the government of Japan to proclaim now the unconditional surrender of all the Japanese armed forces," the ultimatum declared in what was called "The Potsdam Declaration." The alternative for Japan was prompt and utter destruction.

Two days later, the Japanese rejected the Allies' ultimatum.

By July 31, the atomic bomb was fully assembled and ready to be released. At the conclusion of the Potsdam Conference, Truman was finally heading home aboard the USS *Augusta*. On August 6, at 8:15 a.m., the bomb dropped clear of the *Enola Gay*. Forty-three seconds later, it exploded over Hiroshima.[705]

Harry Truman was eating lunch when he received the decoded message. "Results clear cut—successful in all respects. Visible effects greater than in any test."[706]

Truman reacted immediately. "This is the greatest thing in history." The crew burst into applause and cheering when he announced this would end the war. Most of the crewmen understood they would have been on their way to fight the Japanese, and they were suddenly filled with hope.

That afternoon, the White House issued a warning to the Japanese government, approved by President Truman before leaving for Germany. "It was to spare the Japanese people from utter destruction that the ultimatum of July 26 was issued at Potsdam. Their leaders promptly rejected that ultimatum. If they do not now accept our terms, they may expect a rain of ruin from the air the like of which has never been seen on this earth."

Two days later, Secretary of War Stimson showed the president aerial photographs of Hiroshima. Truman did not yet know that the atomic bomb had killed more than 80,000 men, women, and children, or that tens of thousands more would die of radiation sickness in the days and years to come.

"This places a terrible responsibility upon myself and upon the War Department," Truman declared.

Three days after the atomic bomb was dropped on Hiroshima, the Soviet Union declared war on Japan. But still there was no word of surrender.

On August 9, a second atomic bomb was dropped on the Japanese seaport of Nagasaki, and another 40,000 people were killed.

The day after Nagasaki was destroyed, Truman took the authority to use the atomic bomb back from the military and placed it once again in his own hands.[707]

At 7:00 p.m. on August 14, 1945, the White House correspondents gathered in the Oval Office with the president, Bess, most of the cabinet members, and one special guest—former Secretary of State Cordell Hull, now seriously ill, who had worked tirelessly to see this day.

Truman stood behind his desk and read the statement:

> I have received this afternoon a message from the Japanese Government in reply to the message forwarded to that Government by the Secretary of State on August eleventh. I deem this reply a full acceptance of the Potsdam Declaration which specifies the unconditional surrender of Japan. In the reply there is no qualification.
>
> Arrangements are now being made for the formal signing of the surrender terms at the earliest possible moment.[708]

The reporters shouted their congratulations as they rushed out the doors to flash the news to their papers and radio outlets. President Truman and Bess went out to the fountain on the north lawn to greet the large crowd gathered outside the gates. When Truman raised his right hand in a V sign similar to Churchill, a tremendous cheer went up from the people.

On September 2, aboard the USS *Missouri* in Tokyo Bay, representatives of Japan signed the instrument of surrender. World War Two had finally come to an end.

DISPLACED PERSONS

The world's attention now turned to rebuilding after the war. One of the most pressing problems was the plight of hundreds of thousands of displaced persons (DPs). The Jewish refugees, after learning how their families had been slaughtered and communities destroyed, could not or would not return to their hometowns and cities. That feeling only hardened after the pogrom in the Polish town of Kielce in July 1946, where forty-one returning Jews were massacred with police help.[709]

Many Jews smuggled themselves across borders to reach refugee camps in the Allied occupied zones. Once in the DP camps, the refugees waited for permits admitting them to Palestine—or into the United States, Canada, Australia, and a handful of countries willing to take in refugees. But with stringent immigration restrictions around the world, the DPs often languished.

When Truman returned from Potsdam, the State Department stepped in to try to discourage him from charting any course offensive to the Arabs. They advised that any pressure to increase Jewish immigration into Palestine would gravely injure American interests in the Middle East. The diplomats encouraged the president to let the United Nations deal with the problem.

But Truman was deluged with reports of the suffering among the Jewish survivors of the Holocaust. For many Jews, the situation had not improved since the arrival of US troops. In May and June 1945, 18,000 Jews died of disease in Bergen-Belsen. At Dachau, sixty to one hundred survivors of the Holocaust died each day.[710]

The president suspected the State Department was more concerned with Arab business relations than with the sufferings of the DPs. But being new to the presidency, Truman was not up to speed on the intricacies of the situation in Palestine, so he decided to stall for time. On June 22, he sent Earl Harrison, the dean of the University of Pennsylvania Law School, and a former US commissioner of immigration, on a fact-finding mission to the DP camps in Europe.[711]

Truman received Harrison's initial report on August 24. After thorough investigation, Harrison described "Jewish displaced persons ... living under guard behind barbed-wire fences in camps ... amid crowded, frequently unsanitary and generally grim conditions, in complete idleness, with no opportunity, except surreptitiously, to communicate with the outside world, waiting, hoping for some encouragement and action in their behalf ... The desire to leave Germany is an urgent one ... They want to be evacuated to Palestine now."[712]

"We appear to be treating the Jews as the Nazis treated them," Harrison exclaimed, "except that we do not exterminate them."[713]

Harrison pointed to the tragic irony as the White Paper's deadline for Jewish immigration was due to go into effect in August 1945. "To anyone who visited the concentration camps and who has talked with the despairing survivors, it is nothing short of calamitous to contemplate that the gates of Palestine should be soon closed."[714]

Some 1,500,000 European Jews had survived the war, and more than 250,000 of them were in DP camps. Hundreds more arrived every day. The Jewish Agency had recently submitted a memorandum to the British government calling for the immediate admission of 100,000 Jewish refugees to Palestine.

In response to the Harrison Report, a distressed President Truman chose to support the Jewish Agency's request. On August 31, he forwarded a copy of Harrison's report to Prime Minister Attlee along with a personal letter:

> It appears that the available certificates for immigration to Palestine will be exhausted in the near future. It is suggested that the granting of an additional one hundred thousand of such certificates would contribute greatly to a sound solution for the future of Jews still in Germany and Austria, and for other Jewish refugees who do not wish to remain where they are or who for understandable reasons do not desire to return to their countries of origin.[715]

The British replied that any abrupt change in immigration in the face of Arab opposition "would probably cause serious disturbances throughout the Middle East, involving a large military commitment, and would arouse widespread anxiety in India."

In his own play for time, Attlee proposed a study by an Anglo-American Committee of Inquiry. Hopeful for any action to relieve the suffering of the displaced persons, Truman agreed to the proposal.[716]

On August 16, a member of the press asked Truman, "What is the American position on Palestine?"

The president's answer was straightforward: "We want to let as many of the Jews into Palestine as is possible ... Then the matter will have to be worked out diplomatically with the British and the Arabs so that if a State can be set up there, they may be able to set it up on a peaceful basis. I have no desire to send 500,000 American soldiers there to make peace in Palestine."[717]

Truman had good reason for concern about US troops in Palestine. After Yalta, King Saud told President Roosevelt his country would go to war to prevent large Jewish immigration. In March 1945, Saudi Arabia joined Egypt, Syria, and Lebanon in signing a pledge to take united action to protect the Arab position in Palestine and Trans-Jordan.[718]

Truman had publicly embarked on the journey to develop his own Palestine policy. Although he wanted Britain to jettison the White Paper and let the Jewish refugees go to Palestine, he was not going to take responsibility for creating a Jewish state. That would be the responsibility of the Jews, the British, and the Arabs—and ultimately, the United Nations.

Despite these pressures from Truman, the Jewish refugees in the British Zone were given only 6,000 immigration certificates, and other zones received only 1,460. Illegal immigration became the only option for most refugees. The stage was set for the inevitable confrontation.

Chapter Twenty-One

BRITISH OPPRESSION AND JEWISH RESISTANCE

1945—PALESTINE

As far back as 1943, Winston Churchill's government attempted to nullify the 1939 White Paper. Then on December 20, 1943, a cabinet committee recommended the partition of Palestine using the 1937 Peel Report as the guideline. Churchill saw this as the most expedient way forward. "Some form of partition is the only solution," he declared.[719]

The Zionists had held out for all of Palestine west of the Jordan River, which the British originally promised in the Balfour Declaration and also in the League of Nations' Mandate. But most Zionists understood that, in the current political climate, partition of the land west of the Jordan was likely the best deal they could get, even though it was only 10 percent of what was originally promised.

To have the British abrogate the White Paper and give their blessing to a separate Jewish state within Palestine toward the end of World War Two not only would have been a tremendous political triumph, but it also would have flung the doors open for Holocaust survivors.

"There is no doubt that this is probably the greatest and most horrible crime ever committed in the whole history of the world," Churchill wrote in 1944. "I cannot conceive why this martyred race, scattered about the world, and suffering as no other race has done at this juncture, should be denied the satisfaction of having a flag."[720]

Just as it appeared Churchill and Weizmann were close to convincing the government to approve partition, on November 6, 1944, a Jewish terrorist—insisting on all of Palestine, including Trans-Jordan, for the Jews or nothing—assassinated Churchill's friend, Lord Moyne, the British Minister Resident in Cairo. All plans for partition came to an immediate stop, and Churchill, a lifelong friend of the Jewish people, grew cold to the idea of helping the Zionists.

Mourning the tragedy in an address to the House of Commons, Churchill declared:

> If our dreams for Zionism should be dissolved in the smoke of the revolvers of assassins and if our efforts for its future should provoke a new wave of banditry worthy of the Nazi Germans, many persons like myself will have to reconsider the position that we have taken so firmly for such a long time.[721]

In response, the Zionist leadership announced a policy of full cooperation with the British authorities against the terrorist splinter groups. During this time, Haganah soldiers helped the British round up members of the Irgun and the Stern Gang. It appeared civil war would break out within the Yishuv, but the leader of the Irgun, Menachem Begin, declared a policy of non-retaliation against Jews.

As World War Two came to a close, British Foreign Secretary Eden pushed to maintain the status quo in Palestine. "If we lose Arab goodwill, the Americans and the Russians will be on hand to profit from our mistakes," he advised.[722] The British government decided to maintain the White Paper, slamming shut the doors of Palestine to Holocaust survivors.

The Jewish response was instant and nearly unanimous. Most Jews in the Yishuv considered Britain an enemy. All cooperation with the Jewish agency and Haganah ground to a halt.

Reacting to the British announcement, Eliezer Kaplan, treasurer of the Jewish Agency in Palestine, held a press conference to report that the situation of the Jewish people in Europe was becoming unbearable. "They are afraid to stay in Hungary, Romania and Poland," he told the press. Even though some European nations had quickly passed new laws guaranteeing equality, European Jews knew such legislation often meant nothing.

"A whole generation has been raised on anti-Semitism," Kaplan explained. Holocaust survivors "did not want to stay in the countries where their mothers, brothers and sisters were killed." Kaplan argued the new United Nations had "the responsibility to enable all parentless Jewish children to gain entry into Palestine."[723]

Greatly troubled by the British decision, Truman wrote to Winston Churchill on July 24, 1945. "There is great interest in America in the Palestine problem." British policy continued to "provoke passionate protest from Americans. They fervently urge the lifting of those restrictions which deny to Jews, who have been so cruelly uprooted by ruthless Nazi persecution, entrance into the land which represents for so many of them their only hope of survival."[724]

Two days after Truman sent this memo to Churchill, the British electorate voted overwhelmingly for the Labour Party, throwing the wartime unity coalition government and its leader out of office. Churchill was to be replaced by Clement Attlee.

Zionist leaders were overjoyed. The Labour Party had a long history of commitment to Zionism.

Attlee found Truman's memo to Churchill waiting on his desk. To Truman's surprise, Attlee's formal response was rather abrupt. He would not give the president his views until his government had time to consider the issue, to which he promised careful consideration.[725]

BEN-GURION IN AMERICA

David Ben-Gurion understood the time was ripe for action on Palestine. The great centers of Jewish population in Eastern Europe no longer existed. The Jewish communities of Western Europe were decimated. After years of hiding or living in concentration camps, the Jews who had survived the Nazi massacre were demoralized and displaced. The survivors wanted to go to Palestine.

Ben-Gurion understood that the Yishuv needed them, and no other country wanted them.

It was time to face the reality of the situation—inevitably, Britain would have to leave Palestine. When that happened, the Arab nations, despite their differences, would unite to invade Eretz Israel with the goal of destroying the Yishuv.

This time, however, the Jews would fight to defend themselves.

Ben-Gurion's observation in 1933 turned out to be all too true: "We have sinned in their land, in all other lands, we have sinned for two thousand years, the sin of weakness. We are weak—that is our crime."

Ben-Gurion did not plan to make that mistake again.

He finally understood that the survivors of Hitler's genocide had to be brought to Palestine by the Zionist movement—using its own ships. Once there, the sick would be cared for, and the young men and women would be trained to fight the Arabs in the inevitable invasion.[726]

Relations between the Yishuv and the British became even more strained after the new prime minister, Clement Attlee, rejected President Truman's request to allow 100,000 Jewish displaced persons into Palestine.

The Labour government had always said it favored lifting the White Paper restrictions. But now that they were in power, they abruptly changed their position, as Ben-Gurion predicted.

"One must remember," Attlee wrote in response to Truman's request, "that within these camps were people from almost every race in Europe and there appears to have been very little difference in the amount of torture and treatment they had to undergo. Now if our offices had placed the Jews in a special racial category at the head of the queue, my strong view is that the effect of this would have been disastrous for the Jews."[727]

Facing the prospect of a possible war with the Soviets, and thus needing Arab oil, the British decided to maintain the status quo at the expense of the Holocaust survivors.

One major flaw with this policy was that President Truman, and much of America, didn't support it.

Truman's commitment to the immediate immigration of 100,000 Jewish DPs turned up the heat on the crisis. With a sympathetic president in the White House, the Yishuv had a powerful ally with the military and economic might to form international policy.

Truman was annoyed by Attlee's response, and he called in his assistant on minority issues, David Niles, to confer on the matter. The president was familiar with the pro-Zionist statements Labour Party leaders had made over the years, and he had assumed they expressed the official position of the party. Harrison had quoted Labour leader Hugh Dalton's statement from May 1945 in his report on the DP camps, stating it "is morally wrong and politically indefensible to impose obstacles to the entry into Palestine now of any Jews who desire to go there."

At Truman's request, Niles gathered the pro-Zionist statements of Labour leaders, including Attlee and Foreign Minister Bevin, from over the years. Reading these, Truman expressed his frustration to Niles. "How can we trust the Labour people in London when they do not respect their pledges? Today they are cheating the Jews, and where is the assurance that they won't cheat us tomorrow?"[728]

Truman felt Attlee's response seemed devoid of "all human and moral considerations." Niles later said he believed British intransigence on immigration helped Truman to conclude that the Jews, without sovereignty, were helpless to control their destiny, and therefore he determined to rectify all that had been taken away from them.[729]

THE RISE OF JEWISH RESISTANCE

The Jews had comforted themselves with the hope that at the war's end they would see their aspirations for a nation in Palestine realized. During the war, Chaim Weizmann had urged the Jews of the world to "follow a policy of moderation and not to expect a solution … along Zionist lines before the end of the war in Europe."[730]

After the war, he warned that if something was not done soon to alleviate the suffering of the Holocaust survivors, more militant Jewish leaders would arise to replace the moderate ones.

The State Department knew Weizmann was right. Active in Palestine were members of militant groups of Zionists organized into terrorist organizations like the Irgun and the Stern Gang. These groups advocated the use of terror against both the British and the Arabs.

"Anything might happen," president of the Zionist Organization of America Sol Goldman cautioned. Thousands of young men had been trained by the British and were ready to fight for their homeland. "Unless something favorable was done for the Jews," he explained, "control of the Zionist movement might pass to those not averse to violence."[731]

Ben-Gurion, accompanied by Nahum Goldmann and Eliezer Kaplan of the American branch of the Jewish Agency, paid a visit to the State Department to update them on their current perspective. After tracing the situation from Balfour to the White Paper, Ben-Gurion told Evan Wilson and Loy Henderson, "This intolerable [British] regime had to be dealt with." If it were not, "the Jews could not continue indefinitely to put up with the breach by the administration of its obligations to the Jewish people."

The Yishuv had to be allowed to make its own decisions without consideration of the demands of Arabs in Egypt, Iraq, or elsewhere. Ben-Gurion understood that Arabs in Palestine needed different consideration since they had a legitimate interest in the future. "Jews and Arabs had lived there in amity for many years and there was no reason why they should not continue to do so."

He again stressed that the Jews had supported the Allied military effort and expected the Allies to honor their promises to address the Yishuv's needs after the war ended. "The world," he emphasized, "must not underestimate the strength of the Jews' feeling on this point." They did not seek a battle with the British government but would fight if necessary to defend their rights. The "consequences would be on Great Britain's head if the Jews were provoked into some action."

What if the British listened to them? Henderson asked. How would they deal with the Arabs? "I know the Arabs well," Ben-Gurion responded. "They would not really put up any kind of a fight." The leaders of the Arab states would have little luck in rallying their people on behalf of the official Arab position.

"Is not your immediate objective," Henderson asked, "to increase Jewish immigration into Palestine?"

"Of course," Ben-Gurion replied, "that is imperative. But it is not enough. The time has come to grant this and the Jews' other demands, including the immediate establishment of a Jewish state."[732]

The previous month, Ben-Gurion had issued a public warning: "I wish to tell the British Labour Party, if for some reason or another, it maintains the White Paper for an unlimited period ... we in Palestine will not draw back in the face of England's great power and we shall fight against her."[733]

On October 1, Ben-Gurion set the fight in motion. He sent a coded telegram to Haganah headquarters instructing the military leaders to unleash an armed uprising against Britain. Haganah immediately reestablished relations with Irgun and Lehi and set out on a mission of sabotage and military action. On the night of October 31, the Palestine railway system was blown up in 153 places.[734]

These Jewish freedom fighters had one goal: to make the governance of Palestine so miserable the British would want to leave.[735]

THE STRUGGLE INTENSIFIES

In the summer of 1946, British authorities decided to disband the Jewish Brigade. These trained soldiers returned to Palestine just as the news of the British maintaining the White Paper was released. They brought the training and experience they received during the war to the struggle for Eretz Israel. Together, these groups carried out strategic military action, including the destruction of communication facilities and of road and railway bridges linking Palestine with neighboring states.

As the situation in Palestine deteriorated, Foreign Minister Ernest Bevin began applying severe repressive measures against the Yishuv. June 29, 1946, became known as Black Saturday, as the British government arrested scores of Jews, including members of the Jewish Agency Executive, exiling many to Cyprus. The British conducted searches for Haganah, Irgun, and Stern members, along with arms and ammunition.

At the same time, they intensified the policy against what they called illegal immigration.

Defying what they considered to be an immoral policy, the Jewish militia helped illegal immigrants into the country. They engaged in various forms of sabotage against mainly military installations, and as Ben-Gurion himself declared, engineered "an armed uprising against Britain."[736]

The Yishuv put their public-relations machine into full gear. They began daily broadcasts throughout Palestine from the illegal "Voice of Israel" radio station. Around the world, Jews conducted massive propaganda campaigns to raise sympathy for the plight of the oppressed Jews.

The British faced the possibility of alienating their ally, the United States, when they were in desperate need of her financial assistance to recover from the war. In an effort to gain political cover, Attlee proposed the twelve-man Anglo-American Committee of Inquiry to examine the problem, both in Europe and in Palestine.

But the world got a glimpse of British political thought when Bevin held a press conference to announce the joint inquiry. When asked about the goals of the study, Bevin publicly repeated the warning Attlee had given privately to Truman: "Jews must not try to get to the head of the queue."[737]

After the diabolical murder of six million Jewish men, women, and children at the hands of the Nazis, Bevin's statement infuriated Jews, both in Palestine and in the United States.

Most Jews, and many Americans, considered the British attitude toward the Yishuv as anti-Semitic. For refusing to remove limits on Jewish immigration to Palestine, Bevin earned the hatred of Zionists.

Rather than impose a Jewish state on the Arabs, he desired to broker some kind of settlement between Jews and Arabs. These views went counter to the publicly held position of the Labour Party for years. But in Bevin's view, the world had changed, and with the outbreak of the Cold War, the Labour Party's Palestine policy also had to change.

In response to President Truman's request for the 100,000 refugees, Bevin sealed his fate as the enemy in the eyes of most Jews around the world with his response: "There has been agitation in the United States, and particularly in New York, for 100,000 Jews to be put in Palestine. I hope I will not be misunderstood in America If I say that this was proposed by the purest of motives. They did not want too many Jews in New York."

Unwittingly, Bevin's callous remarks built sympathy for the Jews from people around the world who questioned the way Britain was carrying out its Mandate in Palestine—and especially its attitude toward Holocaust survivors.

The State of the State Department

But not everyone was so moved. Career State Department bureaucrat Loy Henderson was convinced Palestine could not absorb the European Jewish refugees who wanted to go there. He believed American support for the Zionist program would harm US interests in the Islamic and Arab world. Like the British, the State Department convinced themselves that a favorable policy toward Zionism might interfere with the flow of oil and push the Arabs into the arms of the Soviets.

As for the refugees, Henderson believed they should be sent to other "civilized" Western nations. In Palestine, he later wrote, "they would not find the happy, quiet Jewish National Home which they were looking for." It was "the Zionist juggernaut," as he called it, responsible for the idea that Jews had no place but Palestine to go to. But where else, he could not say.

The Zionists, on the other hand, believed such an opportunity might not come "in another thousand years"; therefore, "the time for the Jews to be assembled again in their old homeland" had come.[738]

The only significant effort by Arab states to put pressure on the United States came in October 1946, after President Truman made another public effort to secure admission of the 100,000 refugees. For the first time, he endorsed the establishment of a "viable Jewish State in Palestine."[739] In response, Iraq declared it would not discuss air agreements with the US State Department. Then Syria refused to grant transit rights to ARAMCO for the pipeline, which was going to terminate in Lebanon, bypassing Palestine.

But the two governments quickly reversed their decisions when Pan American Airways announced it would overfly Syria and Iraq, and the Trans-Arabian Pipeline Company announced it would shift the terminus back to Palestine. Having far too much to lose, Ibn Saud backpedaled on sanctions; instead, he wrote a letter of protest to President Truman. Within a short time, the king received a polite but unmoved reply from the American president, and that was the end of the Arab protest.[740]

The American Response

Senator Robert Wagner of New York told Eliahu Epstein that as a good Christian he felt it was his duty to do all he could to assist the return of the Jews to their homeland. Because the war was no longer an issue, Wagner was adamant that Jewish goals finally be realized. Palestine, he believed, was not only indispensable to the rehabilitation of the few European Jewish survivors but equally essential "to the health of Europe." The Christian world that allowed the Holocaust to happen "has Palestine on its conscience," he told Epstein, and "if it would regain its moral self-respect, it must promptly do justice to Palestine."[741]

In a press conference the previous week, Truman had denied "that President Roosevelt had made any commitment to King Ibn Saud not to support Jewish claims if and when they arise. There was no record of any conference between the King of Arabia and President Roosevelt" in which FDR had made any such statement.

This statement refuted the assertion of the secretary-general of the Arab League that FDR had shaken hands with Ibn Saud and pledged that the United States would "never support the Zionists' fight for Palestine against the Arabs." Even if Roosevelt had done that, Truman added, "he would not feel bound by any such understanding."[742]

In response, the letters exchanged between Roosevelt and Ibn Saud were published on October 19. Saud wrote erroneously that the Arabs had been in Palestine since 3,000 BC, while the "Jews were merely aliens" who had come there in intervals and been turned out in 2,000 BC. To allow Jews entry, Saud argued, would be to allow them to enter a land "already occupied" and would then "do away with the original inhabitants." The Jews' ambition was not only to occupy Palestine, he continued, but to "take hostile action against neighboring Arab countries."

Secretary of State James Byrnes included a statement reiterating Roosevelt's stated policy was that the United States would not adopt any proposals that would change the basic situation in Palestine without "full consideration of Jewish and Arab leaders." President Truman, he said, agreed with this policy. Byrnes added the United States would "continue to explore every possible means of relieving the situation of the displaced Jews of Europe."

The letters shocked Zionists and Jews around the world. Rabbi Silver said the worst aspect of FDR's response "was his failure to reject the false and slanderous utterances" by Ibn Saud regarding Jewish history in Palestine. The leaders of AZEC composed a nine-page memorandum to be delivered by Rabbis Silver and Wise to Secretary of State Byrnes and President Truman.

They declared that US policy was "clear and unmistakable" in favor of a Jewish commonwealth in Palestine. FDR's letter and Byrnes' statement did not recognize past policy announcements by Roosevelt. It was "deeply disturbing that it should not have been found necessary to make affirmatively clear that American policy on Palestine has already been established by the public pronouncements of the Presidents of the United States—a policy predicated upon the right of the Jewish people to rebuild their National Home."[743]

One of the most upsetting elements of FDR's letter was his failure to answer Saud's "vilifications of the Jewish people." These slanders, they declared, should not "have been allowed to stand unchallenged by one who knew how false those statements are." They conceded that the Arabs had conquered Palestine more than 1,300 years before, but their rule was intermittent. In addition, Palestine also had been ruled by Byzantines, the Christians during the Crusades, and also the Turks.

"In the eroded, poverty-stricken and disease-ridden country which within the last few decades the Jewish people set out to reclaim," the leaders pointed out, "it was difficult to recognize the land of milk and honey described in the Bible. In the twenty years between the two World Wars the Jews have done much to repair the ravages of the previous 1,300."

The American Zionist Emergency Committee (AZEC) leaders reminded President Truman and Secretary of State Byrnes that 75 percent of the Arabic-speaking people then in Palestine were recent immigrants or the descendants of people who came in "comparatively recent times."

"If Palestine exists as a separate concept, it is because of its immemorial association with the Jews and Jewish history. At no time was there a Palestine Arab State. The Pan-Arab claim to Palestine is an attempt to add yet another to the immense, but for the most part thinly populated and underdeveloped territories of the independent Arab states."[744]

Despite the Zionists' anger and frustration at the release of the letters, Supreme Court Justice Felix Frankfurter cautioned them "not to make tactical mistakes which might harm the cause with President Truman." They must not forget, he advised, that "he is the man who is to decide what shall be done." Some of the Zionists leaders heeded Frankfurter's advice, and some did not, which almost brought disaster as the debate reached a fever pitch in the months to come.

Attlee and Bevin could see they were headed for disaster and decided the only way to resolve the standoff was to involve the Americans in finding a solution. On October 19, Great Britain announced it would postpone its plan to take the Palestine situation before the United Nations and would instead seek a joint solution with the United States. The Anglo-American Committee would study the issue and hopefully find a solution that both nations—and the inhabitants of Palestine—could embrace.

THE ANGLO-AMERICAN COMMITTEE

The committee would be charged with visiting both British and American-occupied European zones to assess the current status of the refugees. Britain's ambassador to the United States, Lord Halifax, told Byrnes the British government refused to accept the view that the present living conditions of the Jews were any worse than those of the other Nazi victims. Furthermore, the British government believed the Zionists were using intimidation to stop Jews in Palestine from moving back to Europe.

After hearing these things from Byrnes, Truman sought advice from Judge Rosenman. "I think it is a complete run-out on the mandate," Rosenman responded. He saw it as "temporizing, appeasing and seeking to delay the settlement of the issue." The only valid purpose for such an investigation, he believed, would be to "determine just how many people could be absorbed into Palestine per month."

On Rosenman's advice, Byrnes told Halifax that from America's viewpoint, the terms of reference proposed by the British government needed to mention Palestine as one possible destination for the refugees. In fact, Byrnes argued, it seemed meant to "divert the mind of the committee from Palestine" to finding other countries that might take the European Jewish remnant. If the proposal did not specifically discuss Palestine as part of the solution to the homeless refugees, "the Jews are going to say this is just another trick and nothing will be done." Therefore, Byrnes demanded the committee address how many Jews would actually be absorbed into Palestine.[745]

President Truman decided to give Byrnes the go-ahead to accept US participation in the Anglo-American Committee, but he insisted they have a limit of 120 days to complete the work. The committee would first look at "conditions in Palestine as they bear upon the problem of Jewish immigration" as well as carrying out estimates "of those [Jews] who wish, or who will be impelled by their conditions to migrate to Palestine."

In his statement to the British, Byrnes clarified that the president's agreement did not mean he had changed his mind on the immediate immigration to Palestine of 100,000 Jewish refugees.

WEIZMANN AND TRUMAN MEET

In December 1945, Ambassador Halifax brought Chaim Weizmann to meet President Truman at the White House. Thanking him for his position on the 100,000 refugees, Weizmann then shared his misgivings on the Anglo-American Committee. "The whole ground had been repeatedly worked over during the last twenty years," he explained.

Interrupting Weizmann, Truman said he thought the Jewish problem should not be viewed simply through the prism of Palestine, and he said he favored the term "Palestinian state" rather than "Jewish state." Truman explained that "there were many Jews in America, representatives of whom he had been receiving before he had seen Weizmann, who were not at all keen of the Zionist solution."[746]

Weizmann was so disturbed by his discussion with Truman that he wrote him a nine-page single-spaced typed letter to counter the position of the anti-Zionist Jewish leaders. Then he delved into the vital issue of the absorptive capacity of Palestine. The one useful question the committee could look at was how to develop Palestine through irrigation. Agricultural studies had proven large stretches of land that had never been touched could be cultivated with proper irrigation. If this were accomplished in Palestine, Weizmann declared, the land would be able to absorb three to four million additional people.

The Arabs and British would not undertake such development, Weizmann advised, since for them it would not be a matter of sheer existence.

The truth was "only Jews are capable of initiating and executing such development schemes" in the Holy Land. The Jews would have to develop such water projects if they were to be able to bring in hundreds of thousands who would become citizens of the Jewish homeland—which not only included the survivors of the European Holocaust but also oppressed Jews from the Orient and Arab states.[747]

Weizmann challenged Ernest Bevin's claim that the Balfour Declaration did not promise a Jewish state in Palestine. Its intent, Weizmann charged, had been to create a home not for individual Jews "but a home for the Jewish people."

Refuting those who were trying to convince Truman that Israel could not be democratic, Weizmann countered that the Zionists had never intended the new national home to "become a 'religious' or theocratic state." Palestine would be a "modern and progressive" nation, with "no stress on the religion of the individuals who would form the majority of its inhabitants." He assured Truman it would be "a secular state based on sound democratic foundations."

The Jews living in Palestine had worked diligently to set up a governmental structure with state functions in place, Weizmann explained, yet without recognition and executive powers to enforce its decisions. The work of several generations of the Yishuv had not been for the purpose of setting up another Jewish "ghetto" minority society.

Regarding the Arabs, Weizmann suggested President Truman could give a speech reminding them the Allied armies had saved them from Fascist enslavement, and therefore the Western powers had earned the right to ask them not to hinder the settlement of the homeless Jewish people into Palestine—"a small notch in the vast under-populated Arab Peninsula." The Jews would treat any Arab minority in the new state with dignity, he assured the president, and they would be assured guarantees of civil and religious rights by the United Nations.[748]

THE ANGLO-AMERICAN HEARINGS

Before the hearings began in Washington on January 7, 1946, the American delegation met with Truman at the White House. Nothing concerned him more deeply than the fate of the DPs. It was the obligation of the "democratic world to give these people who had wronged no one a chance to rebuild their lives." He pledged that he and the American government would do all in its power to find a solution.[749]

The committee held hearings in Washington and London, and then dispersed to visit DP camps in Germany, Austria, Poland, and Czechoslovakia. British member Richard Crossman, who had earlier been against opening Palestine to the Jews, referred to Attlee's and Bevin's comments that Jews should not push to the head of the queue: "That might go down in Britain; in Belsen it sounded like the mouthing of a sadistic anti-Semite."[750]

Near Frankfurt, the group was given a result of a poll taken of the 18,311 Jewish DPs. Only thirteen wanted to stay in Europe. Everyone else wanted to go to Palestine.

James McDonald was with the group that toured DP camps in France, Austria, and Switzerland. They also met with a unanimous desire among the Jewish refugees to leave Europe for Palestine. After visiting a boys' camp in Lugano, Switzerland, McDonald wrote, "Nearly every one of them had lost all his relatives in concentration camps and had known little but terror and death. They had built a new world for themselves of dreams and hopes and would tolerate no questioning of their realization," which was to reach Palestine. "Their earnestness tempted one to weep."[751]

The committee reconvened for hearings in Cairo, Jerusalem, Damascus, Beirut, Baghdad, Riyadh, and Amman.

In Jerusalem, the committee stayed in the King David Hotel and held hearings at the YMCA across the street. Weizmann was the first to give testimony. "Here is a people who have lost all the attributes of a nation, but still have maintained their existence as a ghost nation, stalking the arena of history, maintained for thousands of years. It is a belief in a mystical force, our conviction of a return to the Land of Israel, which has kept us alive."

Weizmann's honesty impressed the committee when he admitted that "the issue is not between right and wrong but between the greater and less injustice." It was unavoidable, he candidly declared. They would have to decide "whether it is better to be unjust to the Arabs of Palestine or the Jews."[752]

The committee also heard from Jamal Husseini, a representative of the Arab Higher Committee and a relative of the Grand Mufti, Haj Amin al-Husseini. The Americans, who were aware of the Mufti's activities in Nazi Germany during the war, wanted to know what would happen if Palestine became an entirely Arab state. Would the Grand Mufti be proclaimed head of a new Arab Palestine government?

If they succeeded, Jamal Husseini responded, at least 30 percent of the Jews in Palestine would leave, and the rest would accept life under Arab rule.

As for the Mufti, he might well become head of the new Palestinian Arab state. Husseini argued the Mufti only had the interest of the Arabs at heart when he went to live in Berlin and that his collaboration with Hitler was intended to "get something out of them in case they were victorious."[753]

Finally, the committee received a written statement from the Jewish resistance movement, the combined forces of the Haganah with the Irgun and others. Since the group now functioned underground, its leaders could not testify in public—and the press was not given the memo. "We consider it our duty to warn you against any attempt to impose an anti-Zionist political solution and mask it with a token increase of immigration permits." No minority status for Jews in Palestine would be acceptable. The committee had to be courageous, they exhorted, and most important, "decisive."[754]

The Anglo-American Committee Report

All the committee members said they had been particularly moved by their experiences in Europe. Sir Frederick Leggett had been hostile to the Jewish position initially. But he had become emotionally exhausted by the trip and resolved to do something to help those who had survived. "Unless we can do something and do it soon, we shall be guilty of having finished the job Hitler started; the spiritual and moral destruction of the tiny remnant of European Jewry."[755]

Things became even more difficult for the British Labour government when the committee released its report in May 1946, calling for a binational Palestinian state with a UN-appointed trustee to oversee its creation. They also unanimously recommended the end to the White Paper restrictions and the immediate admission of 100,000 Jews into Palestine to alleviate some of the suffering in Europe.

Truman called on Britain to act on the recommendation immediately, but Attlee dug in his heels. He announced the British government would not allow more Jews to immigrate to Palestine "until disarmament of the Jews had taken place."[756]

In a statement to the House of Commons, Attlee said Britain would not implement the recommendation unless "the United States would be prepared to share the … additional military and financial responsibilities"—which was international-speak for a rejection of the recommendations.[757]

On June 16, the Haganah stepped up their attacks, blowing up eight bridges on the Palestine frontier, which hindered communication and transportation with neighboring territories. At the same time, the Irgun kidnapped five British officers and held them hostage. The Jewish military groups were sending the Arabs, and the world, a clear message: if attacked, the Jews of the Yishuv would fight as a disciplined, effective, modern military force.[758]

In July 1946, the Irgun blew up the south wing of the King David Hotel in Jerusalem, the seat of the Mandate government and the British army in Jerusalem, killing ninety-one British, Jewish, and Arab civil servants and wounding seventy others. The terrorist group had called in advance to warn everyone to leave the hotel, but the British authorities did not take the threat seriously.

The Irgun immediately took responsibility for their action on their clandestine radio station. "This is the voice of fighting Zion, the underground radio of the Irgun. Today our soldiers, in defense of their country, attacked the enemy's police headquarters in Jerusalem. This is the voice of fighting Zion, broadcasting for the freedom of Eretz Israel."[759]

Britain was facing the growing possibility of a war in Palestine. "Palestine is a British armed camp," one reporter wrote. "Arab and British sentiment was completely against the Palestinian Jews, while the Jewish sentiment for moderation was evaporating, and the moderate Jews who used to back up Weizmann are diminishing" and moving over to the militant leadership of Ben-Gurion.

Writing in *The Nation* magazine, Freda Kirchwey reported Palestine's population was living under "massive rolls of barbed wire." The British

Mandate authorities had instituted severe censorship. Political prisoners were held in armed camps. "Palestine is an occupied country from end to end," Kirchwey wrote. "The Jews and Arabs alike live under military rule while civilian officials take shelter behind sandbags and armed guards ... Arrests are frequently made under similar emergency decrees."[760]

A few days after Kirchwey's article appeared, the crisis reached the boiling point. On the morning of June 29, explosions and gunfire erupted on the streets of Tel Aviv. Over the radio, British High Commissioner Sir Alan Cunningham announced a major military operation against the Yishuv, the Jewish Agency, and the Haganah. Thousands of Jews were arrested, including members of the Agency Executive. David Ben-Gurion narrowly escaped arrest, having been out of the country at the time. The Yishuv found itself subjected to a military siege with intensive searches carried out in the primary Jewish population centers.[761]

But the British military operation was anemic, demonstrating the extreme weakness of Britain's position in the postwar world. Desperately needing a large loan from the United States, the British were forced to suspend the unsuccessful crackdown against the Yishuv under pressure from the American Congress and public.

The Jews of the world were shocked and enraged by the British policies in Palestine. The idea of being disarmed while surrounded by hostile Arab nations and an increasingly anti-Semitic British Mandatory government sounded like an invitation to a new kind of death camp. The British Royal Navy continued its attempt to stop all Jewish immigration, turning back any ships that reached Palestine's coastal harbors. At the same time, British officers trained and equipped the soldiers and militias of the Arab League in an attempt to empower Arab suppression of mounting Jewish claims for independence.

England had made herself an enemy of the Jews. And the Jews were determined to drive the British from what they considered to be their rightful homeland.

Chapter Twenty-Two

DAVID AND GOLIATH

1945—WASHINGTON, DC

As the struggle for Palestine between Britain and the United States intensified, a fierce political battle also heated up inside the Truman White House. The pro-Jewish faction was led primarily by an unknown "David"—a bureaucrat named David Niles. The pro-Arab faction was led by a "Goliath" of the world stage—General George C. Marshall.

Among those retained by Truman from FDR's staff were two Jewish men who became instrumental in dealing with the Palestine issue—Judge Samuel Rosenman and David Niles.[762] Rosenman had been a speechwriter for Roosevelt when he was governor in New York. In 1943, he became special counsel to the president. He worked on every Roosevelt campaign, drafted the majority of his speeches, and even coined the term *New Deal*. Rosenman became an important adviser to Truman on Jewish matters.[763]

Niles had served FDR as an adviser on patronage and minority-group issues. He was also a liaison with the Jews as they pressed the White House for action. Roosevelt depended on Niles to advise him on which Jewish leaders he was obligated to see and which ones he could avoid without harming his political standing.

Niles later explained his role to one of Truman's aides: "I envision my chief job to protect the President" from those who might "create some political damage."[764] According to acquaintances, he was a lonely bachelor whose "whole life was the President," whether Roosevelt or Truman. He rented a room in the Carlton Hotel and returned to his hometown of Boston almost every weekend to stay with his sister.[765]

Abraham Feinberg said Niles became truly devoted to Truman, perhaps because of the momentous events for the Jewish people they walked through together.[766]

Matthew Connelly urged Truman to retain this valuable ally, explaining that if he lost Niles, "he would lose somebody who would be completely loyal to him." Niles had backed Truman for nomination as vice president in 1944. Connelly said that Niles "was a very bright political analyst. He was quiet, he was receptive, he was never out in front." In FDR's days, the staff called him the "back stair boy at the White House."[767]

Truman took Connelly's advice and put Niles in charge of information coming to the White House on Jewish issues, including Palestine. Niles was deeply sympathetic to the establishment of a Jewish state in Eretz Israel, and he became an important ally in providing access to the White House for American Zionists. Niles was said to be capable of bending the president's ear to Zionist arguments.

His feelings on Zionism were influenced by Rabbi Stephen Wise with whom he shared a strong dedication to the Democratic Party. He also shared Wise's dislike of Rabbi Silver and his resentment of Silver's attacks on the Truman administration.[768]

Truman's legal counsel, Clark Clifford, respected Niles for his role in formulating and promoting policies regarding the plight of the displaced Jews of Europe. This was an area the State Department had long neglected. Niles filled the gap by becoming a key author of directives regarding President Truman's policy.

More than any other administration official, Niles kept after Truman to further the Zionist cause.

Because of Niles' strategic position, Jewish leaders kept him abreast of developments. Keenly aware of the controversy associated with his position in the White House, Niles developed a passion for anonymity. He almost never brought an assistant when he spoke with the president and seldom attended staff meetings. He communicated primarily over the telephone, writing as little as possible on paper. Every January, he celebrated the New Year by "stripping" his files down to the bare minimum.

This covert style enabled Niles to cut through the red tape of White House bureaucrats and cabinet officers—at times, completely avoiding involvement of other government departments to get things done.

Truman grew to trust Niles and began to confide in him.

Loy Henderson regarded Niles as "the most powerful and diligent advocate of the Zionist cause ..." Henderson believed the wily Niles was hiding in the corridors of the White House to ambush every move the State Department made.[769]

THE MORRISON-GRADY PLAN

The British raid on the Yishuv and the arrests of Jewish Agency leaders on June 29, 1946, elicited outrage from Jews around the world. In a display of unity, Rabbis Silver and Wise called the British crackdown "nothing less than an act of war against the Jewish people." They charged the purpose had not been to stop terrorism but "to liquidate the Jewish national home." The two leaders joined with Sol Goldman from the Jewish Agency and Zionist leader Louis Lipsky for a meeting with President Truman at the White House. Asking the president to intervene, they explained their fear of the British trying to "destroy generations of labor and achievement of the Jewish pioneers."

According to Goldman, Truman immediately phoned Prime Minister Attlee and "talked very bluntly" to him about the situation in the Holy Land. The prime minister responded immediately, giving orders for the army to cease its military action in Palestine.[770]

Despite Truman's action on the Jews' behalf, he was not happy with the aggressive tactics of Rabbi Silver. After the group left the White House, Truman's friend Abe Feinberg came to see him in the Oval Office. Feinberg found the president "red in the face." "Was anything wrong," Feinberg asked. "Yes," Truman responded. "The presidency is something to be respected, and that clown had the nerve to shake his finger in front of me ... I told him he'd never be welcome here again."[771]

In frustration, Truman organized a cabinet committee, headed by former Assistant Secretary of State Henry Grady and charged with the task of reconciling American and British differences on the Anglo-American

Committee's recommendations.[772] On July 12, the committee representatives flew to London in the president's official plane. Truman assured the Jewish Agency he had expressed to the committee the urgency of moving the refugees out of the camps.

Grady began the negotiations with a plea for the immediate admission of the 100,000 DPs to Palestine, but the British had another agenda. They presented the committee with a plan to divide Palestine into two partially self-governing Arab and Jewish provinces with a British-controlled central government. They proposed Jerusalem and the Negev be under the direct jurisdiction of the British Mandatory power. The British would have power over defense, foreign affairs, taxation, and immigration. The British capped their proposal with the caveat that the admission of the 100,000 European Jews was dependent on acceptance of the plan.[773]

Grady believed the Jews would be pleased with this proposal as the plan, in his view, gave them the "best land in Palestine, practically all citrus and industry, most of the coast line and Haifa port." With the exception of Jerusalem and the Negev, he thought the plan included all that was needed to build a national home. If it was unfair to anyone, Grady believed, it was to the Arabs.

In reality, *The New York Times* reported, the Jews would only receive 1,500 square miles under restrictive federal oversight. This was less than the British Peel Report had proposed in 1936 when that commission recommended 2,600 square miles. It was much less than the 45,000 square miles originally promised to the Jews for a national home. The proposed power in the hands of the British government was greater than in India, and the British would retain control over Jewish immigration.[774]

After hearing details of the proposal, New York Senators Robert Wagner and James Mead visited Truman in the White House, bringing with them James McDonald of the Anglo-American Committee. McDonald brought a long memorandum explaining how the Morrison-Grady Plan was completely at odds with the Anglo-American Committee report Truman had endorsed. The plan, he said, "would establish in Palestine a Jewish ghetto wholly unacceptable to Jews throughout the world and to the conscience of mankind." The Jews would never agree to it since it was a "whittling down of the territory of the Jewish National Home" and a surrender of everything Balfour had promised them.

The Jews were so opposed to it, McDonald argued, they would rather not have 100,000 Jewish refugees go to Palestine than agree to Morrison-Grady. If we get the 100,000 at the price of this, you will go down in history as anathema."

Hearing this, Truman exploded and insisted he was not underwriting anything as a price for getting the 100,000 into Palestine.

McDonald refused to back down. If you accept this plan, he told the president, you "will be responsible for scrapping the Jewish interests in Palestine."

The pressure on Truman regarding the Jews and Palestine was wearing on him. "Hell, you can't satisfy these people," Truman retorted. "The Jews aren't going to write the history of the United States, or my history."

"You must refuse to be a party to it," McDonald boldly responded. Wagner and Mead were shocked. They had never seen anyone who was not a politician speak so frankly to the president. "I have an obligation to come and tell you what I feel about Morrison-Grady," he told the president, reminding him that almost 98 percent of American Jews agreed with him. Had Truman sent the American members of the Anglo-American Committee to London instead of the novice Grady, they would have refused to go along with any such plan.

Truman complained about "how ungrateful everybody was" and kept looking at the clock. McDonald thought it was time for the group to leave.[775]

After Truman calmed down and thought about the conversation, he wrote McDonald a note. "I hope I wasn't too hard on you. It has been a most difficult problem and I have about come to the conclusion that there is no solution, but we will keep trying."[776]

As predicted, the Zionists and their supporters voiced severe disapproval of the plan. Senators Wagner and Taft both blasted it on the Senate floor. Its adoption would cause "deep despair for the million and one-half surviving Jews in Europe," Taft declared.

New York Representative Emanuel Celler led nine House members to the White House to protest the proposal. The plan "would be approving a ghetto in Palestine," Celler stated, adding neither the Arabs nor the Jews would ever accept it.[777]

Once again, Truman lost his cool and told the congressmen he already knew everything about the subject. He said he was working on a broader plan to gain admission for the DPs in South America or another British possession. He proceeded to insult his guests by telling them he understood the visit was political, as they were all up for reelection in the fall.

Political pressure on Truman from all sides was relentless, and he was losing patience. But this irritation was not new to the presidency. According to Judge Rosenman, Roosevelt also resented similar pressures and became reluctant to receive certain abrasive people.[778]

David Niles was concerned not only with the terms of the Morrison-Grady Plan but also with how Truman would be perceived if he endorsed it. Agreeing with McDonald, he told Truman if he accepted it, he would be accused of giving up everything for the 100,000 DPs. Niles suggested Truman stay neutral until he could convene a meeting of both the Grady team and the American members of the Anglo-American Committee to try to reconcile their positions before making a statement.

Taking the opposite opinion, Secretary of State Byrnes drew up a statement for the president to issue accepting the Morrison-Grady Plan as the basis for future negotiations.

Truman had to decide where exactly he stood on the question.

The next day, the entire cabinet meeting was devoted to the question of Palestine. Dean Acheson and Secretary of the Navy James Forrestal wanted Truman to accept the British plan. Secretary of Commerce Henry Wallace and Secretary of the Treasury John Snyder were opposed to it. After a heated debate, Truman decided to wire Byrnes to tell him not to go along with Attlee.[779]

In his frustration, Truman took out his anger at the Jews for sinking the plan. "Jesus Christ couldn't please them when he was here on earth," Truman exclaimed, "so how could anyone expect that I would have any luck?"

American Jews all had relatives in Europe, Wallace responded, and most of them had been killed by Hitler's extermination. "No other people have suffered that way," he concluded.[780] Forrestal disagreed, stating the "Poles had suffered more than the Jews" and again stressed the need for Saudi oil should another war break out with the Soviets.

Truman had heard enough. He didn't want to handle this from the standpoint of oil "but from the standpoint of what is right."[781]

Truman's anger was stoked by public attacks against him by the Zionist lobby—primarily from Rabbi Silver. But this did not lead to any break in friendship with his Jewish pro-Zionist advisers inside the White House— David Niles, Max Lowenthal, or Samuel Rosenman. Truman drew a clear distinction between the militants or "extremists," such as Silver, and the "moderates" such as Chaim Weizmann, Rabbi Wise, and Nahum Goldmann.

Judge Rosenman believed the Zionist leadership had bothered the president too much and should have limited their appeals to only the most critical issues. Rosenman understood Truman was especially sensitive to criticism he considered unwarranted. In response to what he believed were unfair attacks, Truman withdrew, closing the White House for long periods to the Zionists. Members of the State Department recognized this and took full advantage of it. During these times, advisers such as Clark Clifford and David Niles who truly understood and supported Truman's position on Palestine, were extra vigilant in watching over Zionist affairs.[782]

A NEW PATH FORWARD

Concerned over Truman's growing frustration and anger, Niles placed an urgent call to Jewish Agency leader, Nahum Goldmann. Truman was fed up with both the British and the American Zionists, he told him, and was "threatening to wash his hands of the whole matter."[783] The only thing to stop him was if the Jewish Agency came up with an alternative but realistic proposal to take the place of Morrison-Grady.

Goldmann and other members of the Jewish Agency executive had been considering distancing themselves from the Zionists' Biltmore Declaration of 1942, which called for a Jewish state in the entire area of Palestine, and instead adopting the goal of partition. In light of Morrison-Grady, they would rather have a smaller state where they controlled their own destiny than be a minority in an Arab or British-controlled country.

After a few days of deliberation, the Jewish Agency Executive adopted a resolution stating it was "prepared to discuss a proposal for the establishment of a viable Jewish state in an adequate area of Palestine." They insisted this state should have full autonomy, including control over immigration. They sent Goldmann out to gain support from various representatives of the American Jewish community and also from key government officials.

On August 6, Goldmann arrived in Washington and met the next day with Acting Secretary of State Dean Acheson, who was also the senior State Department official dealing with Palestine. Goldmann reported Acheson had been "sold" on partition, provided he could also convince Niles and Secretaries Snyder and Patterson from the president's cabinet committee on Palestine.[784]

Goldmann first met with the influential but prickly leader of the Zionist Organization of America, Rabbi Silver. Although he supported the Biltmore Program, Silver agreed to go along with the majority resolution for partition and not to interfere.

Next, Goldmann met with David Niles at the Washington hotel where he kept a room. He knew Niles had the ear of President Truman and had been one of the moderate Zionists' "best and most loyal friends in Washington." After a two-hour talk, Niles became convinced the agency's new resolution was the only way out of the impasse.[785]

Goldmann then had to persuade the other members of the cabinet committee—Secretaries Snyder and Patterson. Snyder quickly acquiesced, but Goldmann could not secure a meeting with Secretary of War Patterson. Goldmann learned Patterson's close friend, Judge Joseph Proskauer, the president of the non-Zionist American Jewish Committee, was available for a meeting. Goldmann told Proskauer the problem with the DPs of Europe had become so urgent the Jewish Agency was ready to consider partition. Proskauer was persuaded, and together they met with the Secretary of War at the Pentagon.

Goldmann explained the Jewish Agency position, then left Proskauer and Patterson alone. Secretary Patterson reacted sympathetically to the proposition. "Joe, it makes sense. I don't know what to do with these poor people any more. MacDonald's White Paper keeps them out of Israel [Palestine]. I can't get them into America because of our terrible immigration laws. I'm for it, but you've got to clear it with the State Department."[786]

In a second meeting with Acheson, Goldmann informed him that Secretaries Patterson and Snyder agreed to partition. It was time to take the case to the president. Niles and Acheson would present the partition plan to Truman with their endorsement.

On the evening of August 9, with tears in his eyes, Niles later told Goldmann "that the President had accepted the plan without reservation and had instructed Dean Acheson to inform the British government."[787]

Goldmann traveled to London to share the partition proposal with Foreign Minister Bevin, who belligerently rejected the idea. Bevin brought up the issue of Jewish terrorism, citing the recent bombing of the King David Hotel. He warned Goldmann the Jews were "creating a situation in which they were likely to lose the one great friend they always had in the world." Goldmann countered that the British had not been communicating with the Jewish Agency.

It is very difficult "to cooperate with people who were … having talks with us on the one hand and arming their people on the other," Bevin shot back.

Goldmann asked if the British government could at least allow entry of 10,000 extra immigrants. Bevin adamantly refused, stating "we are committed to the White Paper," and the British had already inflamed the Arabs by agreeing to let more refugees in. "Not a word of appreciation had ever been received from the Jews for this."

As he ended the meeting, Goldmann pleaded with Bevin that Britain not "drive the Jews again into desperation."[788]

Next, the Jewish Agency sent the chief of its Arab Department to Cairo to talk with responsible Arab leaders who favored secret preliminary meetings with all sides to consider Morrison-Grady and also partition. At the same time, Attlee announced the British would go ahead with the planned London conference.

The Jewish Agency announced it would not participate since the British insisted on using the Morrison-Grady Plan as the basis for discussion.

Attlee opened the conference with a surprisingly candid speech directed at the Arab delegation, telling them they would have to agree to a
separation of the two communities. Furthermore, they could no longer
continue to block further Jewish immigration into Palestine, which was
essential to the well-being of the Jewish DPs in Europe. Any solution
would have to consider the political rights of the 600,000 Palestinian
Jews, agreement to Jewish immigration into Palestine, and the establishment of institutions that would enable both the Arabs and the Jews to
govern themselves.

The Arabs were aghast. They immediately submitted a list of counter-
proposals. They demanded that the Mandate be ended and that a unitary
Arab state in Palestine governed by an elected constituent assembly be
established. The Jews would be limited to one third of the total membership. They would have all rights consistent with those usually granted to
minorities. They demanded that Jewish immigration end. They called for
a treaty of alliance with Britain, along with guarantees for the sanctity of
all holy places.

Zionist spokesmen rejected the Arab proposals, condemning them as a
refusal to acknowledge the existence of two actual nationalities existing
in Palestine. The Haganah issued a statement from their underground
headquarters declaring, "We will not allow Arab effendis [men of high
standing in Arab culture] to decide the number of Jewish immigrants for
Palestine. We will continue to fight to bring our brothers here.[789]

THE YOM KIPPUR STATEMENT

Even though the British rejected it, the partition plan marked a major
turning point in President Truman's view of the Palestine crisis.

Abe Feinberg, Truman's friend and political adviser, had been horrified by
the Holocaust and strongly believed the Jews should be given a nation in
order to defend themselves in the future. Traveling to Europe, he toured
the Jewish DP camps, where he saw the survivors of Hitler's genocide
held in almost unbearable conditions. Nearly everyone he spoke to wanted only to go to Palestine.

Feinberg immediately purchased and outfitted ships to take the refugees
from France and Italy to Palestine. He was actually in the Holy Land when

the British crackdown occurred. Feinberg was arrested and charged with smuggling out British military information to give to the Haganah. His personal relationship with President Truman ultimately persuaded the British military authorities to release him.

When he returned to the United States, he gave an eyewitness account to Truman and David Niles of the repressive measures the British used against the Jews. Informed of Truman's support of partition, Feinberg advised the president to make his position known to the Jewish people "just before the holiest day in the Jewish year, Yom Kippur. Even unobservant Jews, such as myself tend to go to the synagogues on the night before, which is the most somber night." The services include a liturgy, and "the rabbis use their most dramatic efforts in the sermons. If you will make the announcement before that night, every single Rabbi in every single synagogue will broadcast what you say."[790]

With the assistance of Niles, Truman prepared a statement to be issued on Yom Kippur, October 4, 1946. Niles asked Eliahu Epstein and Judge Rosenman to draft a statement expressing American support for partition. Niles gave the draft to Truman, who passed it on to Acheson for his input.[791]

Truman began his statement by reminding Americans of his many attempts to gain admission to Palestine for the 100,000 Jewish DPs, recommended to him by Earl Harrison's investigation of the DPs and the unanimous report of the Anglo-American Committee:

> Meanwhile, the Jewish Agency proposed a solution of the Palestine problem by means of the creation of a viable Jewish state in control of a part of Palestine instead of the whole. It proposed furthermore the immediate issuance of certificates for 100,000 Jewish immigrants. This proposal received widespread attention in the United States ... From the discussion which ensued it is my belief that a solution along these lines would command the support of public opinion in the United States. I cannot believe that the gap between the proposals which have been put forward is too great to be bridged by men of reason and goodwill. To such a solution our Government could give its support.[792]

For the first time, a president of the United States had publicly endorsed the creation of a "viable" Jewish state in Palestine.

The Yom Kippur statement was universally viewed as an expression of Truman's support for the Zionist position. Eliahu Epstein reported to the Jewish Agency: "… All the headlines carried by the papers read 'Truman's support of a Jewish State.'"[793]

After Attlee expressed anger over the president's statement, *Time* magazine said the usually mild-mannered prime minister was in a "towering rage."

It had been more than a year since Truman had brought the Harrison Report to the attention of the British government. In that time, there had been no action regarding the plight of the DPs. Even after the recommendation of the Anglo-American Committee, nothing had been accomplished. He had tried to be restrained, he explained, not doing anything to interfere with British attempts to carry on negotiations on the issue. But he had no alternative but to "express regret at this outcome."

The feeling of despair and hopelessness faced by the Jewish DPs was intensified with the approach of Yom Kippur, and Truman said he was certain "you will agree that it would be most unfair to these unfortunate persons to let them enter upon still another winter" without being allowed to proceed to Palestine, "where so many of them wish ardently to go."

He realized Britain alone had the Mandatory responsibility for Palestine, but he reminded Attlee that the original intent and purpose of "the Mandate was to foster the development of the Jewish National Home," a step in which the United States maintained "a deep and abiding interest."[794]

After reading Truman's declaration, Ibn Saud wrote an irate letter in protest. The Saudi monarch reminded the president his position had not changed since he had written to FDR claiming the Arabs' "natural rights" to Palestine. He said the Jews were "only aggressors, seeking to perpetrate a monstrous injustice … in the name of humanitarianism," who would later try to get their way by "force and violence." He reiterated his contention that their demands included not only Palestine but all the Arab lands, including their holy cities. Because of this, he had been astonished to read Truman's statement, which, if put into policy, would "alter the basic situation in Palestine in contradiction to previous promises." He could not understand how the American people could support "Zionist aggression against a friendly Arab country."[795]

Truman's representative to the Vatican, Myron Taylor, warned of Ibn Saud's reaction to developments. "I am inclined to think that 100,000 Jews would be of great assistance in that area as the Jews of Palestine were during the second World War," Niles reminded the president. "The Allies got no help from the Arabs at all, but considerable help from the Jews of Palestine."[796]

Truman responded to Ibn Saud with all the appropriate diplomatic courtesy, but he expressed his views, saying the Jews of Europe "represent the pitiful remains of millions who were deliberately selected by the Nazi leaders for annihilation," and many of them "look to Palestine as a haven," where they could assist "in the further development of the Jewish National Home." It had always been American policy, Truman explained, to support such an objective and therefore was only natural the United States would favor the entry of Jewish DPs into Palestine.

"I am at a loss to understand why Your Majesty seems to feel that this statement was in contradiction to previous promises or statements made by this Government," Truman said. It did not in any sense represent a contradiction to previous promises made by the United States, nor was it "an action hostile to the Arab people."[797]

THE TWENTY-SECOND ZIONIST CONGRESS

While the Arabs protested Truman's position on partition, the Zionists met in Basel in December 1946 for their first congress since the Holocaust. Since their last meeting, the world's Jewish population had been reduced by more than one-third. The majority of delegates were from Palestine and America because the Nazis had murdered most of the European delegates who had previously filled the seats. With almost half of the world membership, the United States had replaced Poland as the chief Zionist center.

Despite Truman's support of partition, the Basel Congress once again endorsed the Biltmore Program, with its explicit commitment to establishing a Jewish state in all of Palestine. The overall attitude of the delegates was militant. After losing six million of their brethren to Nazi genocide, they saw Britain's actions to stop refugees from immigrating to Palestine as inhumane and illegal.

Britain's Mandate from the League of Nations was to facilitate the building of the Jewish national home, not to create a permanent British colonial bastion in Palestine. They were also responding to intelligence from the Haganah, which indicated the British army was preparing for a war against the Yishuv and its leadership.

The highlight of the Twenty-Second Congress was Chaim Weizmann's address on December 16. An old man and almost completely blind, Weizmann spoke with the same familiar strong voice. His remarks were a direct attack against the terrorists in Palestine and also their American sympathizers.

Jewish terrorists in Palestine were employing road bombs, explosives, kidnapping, and even hanging of captured British troops—inviting harsh reprisals from the Mandatory government. Weizmann acknowledged the absence of "faith, or even hope, in the British Government" which led Palestine's Jewish leaders to "rely on methods never known or encouraged among Zionists before the war."[798]

Abba Eban described it as "the most remarkable of his oratorical feats at any Congress." Weizmann continued,

> Masada for all its heroism was a disaster in our history. It is not our purpose or our right to plunge to destruction in order to bequeath a legend of martyrdom to posterity. Zionism was to mark the end of our glorious deaths and the beginning of a new path, leading to life.

Eban then described a confrontation that erupted from the floor: As he delivered his attack against vicarious "activism" by those who intended to stay away from the gunpowder, a delegate called out "Demagogy." He stopped his discourse, took off his glasses, and stood in stunned silence. Never had this happened to him. His age, infirmity, patient toil, and sacrifice had been violated in a moment of dreadful rancor. The Assembly sat in horrified tension as he pondered his reply:

> Somebody has called me a demagogue. I do not know who. I hope that I never learn the man's name. I—a demagogue! I

who have borne all the ills and travails of this movement (*loud applause*). The person who flung that word in my face ought to know that in every house and stable in Nahalal, in every little workshop in Tel-Aviv or Haifa, there is a drop of my blood. (*Tempestuous applause. The delegates all rise to their feet except the Revisionists and Mizrachi*) … If you think of bringing the redemption nearer by un-Jewish methods, if you lose faith in hard work and better days, then you commit idolatry (*avodah zarah*) and endanger what we have built. Would that I had a tongue of flame, the strength of prophets, to warn you against the paths of Babylon and Egypt. "Zion shall be redeemed in Judgment"—and not by any other means. [799]

Weizmann made a great emotional impact on the Congress, yet in the end, he was rejected politically. The Yishuv had tried unsuccessfully to pressure the British authorities into repealing the White Paper. The delegates were still upset over the Morrison-Grady proposal. Beloved as Chaim Weizmann was, his continued appeal for moderation was wearing thin.

Weizmann, still president of the World Zionist Organization, called on the delegates to approve the political platform of the Zionist movement as passed at conferences at the Biltmore Hotel in New York during May 1942, and then again in London in 1945. The central passage of this program: "Palestine be established as a Jewish Commonwealth integrated in the structure of the democratic world."

Weizmann favored Zionist participation in the resumed London Conference the next month. But a majority of the delegates rejected this idea—and Weizmann's leadership—as being too "pro-British." After this rejection of his position, Weizmann withdrew his name for reelection to the presidency of the organization. The office was left unfilled, out of respect for the great old man. [800]

Instead, a dual leadership emerged, reflecting the new reality of the Zionist movement. Ben-Gurion became the executive chairman in relation to Yishuv affairs, and the activist Rabbi Silver became executive chairman in relation to America. The two leaders were unified in their belief that the Mandate must end.

Britain had to go.

GOLIATH TAKES OFFICE

A major shake-up occurred in the Truman cabinet when Secretary of State James Byrnes resigned, citing his doctor's recommendation that he retire to protect his health. In his private diary, Truman noted: "Byrnes is going to quit on the tenth and I shall make Marshall Secretary of State … Marshall is the ablest man in the whole gallery."[801] Truman thought the general was "the greatest man of World War Two."

Marshall was confirmed with the unanimous consent of the Senate.

Alluding to all the troubles he had with State up to that point, Truman added, "We'll have a real State Department now."[802]

Marshall was truly a giant on the world stage. But his ascendance meant a confrontation was looming for Truman. Marshall, the State Department, and a majority of diplomats at the UN saw a direct UN trusteeship in Palestine, succeeding the British Mandate, as the only solution to halt the bloodshed. Otherwise, they knew, neighboring Arab states would send military units across the border the day the British withdrew.

The acrimony between the State Department—and particularly Loy Henderson—and certain White House aides only increased after Marshall took office. That same month, Niles warned the Zionist representative in Washington, Eliahu Epstein, that the Jewish Agency had to maintain relations with the State Department. They must not underestimate Henderson and the Near Eastern Affairs Office.[803]

As Marshall settled into his new role, the Jewish Agency and the British government conducted private negotiations to see if they could form a basis for more formal talks. But when the Zionists sat down at the Colonial Office, Bevin declared he was against partition, seeing it as unfair to the Arabs.

On February 7, Bevin made his last suggestion for a solution—a division of Palestine into Arab and Jewish provinces with local self-government. The British would remain as the Mandatory government for five years. Immigration would be permitted for the first two years at the rate of 4,000 a month. The Arabs would have to be consulted about any further immigration, but the final decision would remain with the high commissioner and the Trusteeship Council of the United Nations. The Arabs and the Jews both rejected the plan.[804]

After the failure of the London talks, Churchill rose in Parliament. "If we cannot fulfill our promises to the Zionists we should, without delay, place our Mandate for Palestine at the feet of the United Nations, and give due notice of our impending evacuation from that country."[805]

The Attlee government finally agreed.

On February 15, 1947, Bevin held a press conference. "I have been instructed by His Majesty's government to announce with all solemnity, that they have consequently decided that in the absence of a settlement, they must plan for an early withdrawal of British forces and of the British administration from Palestine."[806]

The question would go before the UN, setting up an ultimate showdown between Truman's David and his Goliath.

Chapter Twenty-Three

LAKE SUCCESS

1947—LAKE SUCCESS, NEW YORK

In reality, the British government didn't believe the United Nations—
meeting temporarily at Lake Success, New York—would hammer out a
solution on Palestine. That would leave Britain still holding the Mandate
and free to continue building a strategic colonial outpost in the Middle
East, while governing the Arabs and Jews in some sort of trusteeship.

But the British strategy backfired.

During a special UN session to consider the Palestine question, Soviet
Deputy Foreign Minister Andrei Gromyko stood and attacked the "bankruptcy of the mandatory system of Palestine." Then, quite unexpectedly,
he endorsed "the aspirations of the Jews to establish their own State." The
whole assembly was shocked by this about-face in Soviet foreign policy.
Gromyko declared the Soviet government would prefer some form of binational solution, but if that was unavailable, then it favored "the partition
of Palestine into two independent states, one Jewish and one Arab."[807]

UNSCOP

Acting on Britain's proposal, the UN leadership established the United
Nations Special Committee on Palestine (UNSCOP), made up of representatives from eleven nations, to investigate the situation and offer
recommendations to the General Assembly.[808]

Despite the British action to place the matter before the UN, their representative said they would not carry out any decision of which they disapproved and "could not reconcile with our conscience." Furthermore, the
British government would not enforce any solution in Palestine that was
not acceptable to both the Arabs and the Jews.[809]

The Arab states attending the meeting made their objections to the whole affair abundantly clear. They entered a motion calling for the immediate "termination of the Mandate over Palestine and the declaration of its independence." If adopted, Palestine would become an Arab state.[810] The United States opposed the measure, declaring it premature to consider such a proposition before UNSCOP conducted its study and made its recommendations.

The UNSCOP delegates arrived in Palestine on June 15, 1947.[811] While the Jewish Agency and the Jewish National Council cooperated with UNSCOP in its deliberations, the Arab Higher Committee charged UNSCOP with being pro-Zionist and boycotted every aspect of the investigation. Arab opposition figures were threatened with death if they spoke to UNSCOP.[812]

The head of UNSCOP, Swedish Chief Justice Emile Sandstrom, went on the radio to plead with the Arab Higher Committee to cooperate with the UN group. "I cannot put it too strongly that this Committee has come to Palestine with a completely open mind … We have reached no conclusions."[813]

Jamal Husseini, vice-chairman of the Arab Higher Committee, informed the UN secretary-general that any decision not granting the Arabs an independent state in Palestine would have immediate repercussions. Fifty million Arabs were ready to support their Palestinian brothers with armed force, he declared. Partition would not work since "Palestine is too small," and if the United Nations failed them, they would attack.[814]

The Jewish Agency, on the other hand, worked diligently to make UNSCOP members comfortable. In Tel Aviv, they were deluged with a "staggering volume of information." Crowds clapped and sang for the delegates and pressed around their cars to shake their hands."[815]

David Horowitz later noted, "The warm reception by the Yishuv, in contrast with the cold malevolence shown by the Arabs, did not pass unnoticed by UNSCOP."[816]

The committee embarked on a tour of Palestine, visiting Jerusalem, Haifa, the Dead Sea, Hebron, Beersheba, Gaza, Jaffa, the Galilee, Tel Aviv, Acre, Nablus, Beit Dajan, Tulkarm, and Rehovot. They visited both Arab and Jewish settlements in the Negev, and several Jewish agricultural communities.[817]

Horowitz escorted Canada's chief justice, Ivan Rand, to Ramallah and then to Haifa. Rand asked Horowitz his opinion on the possible solutions to the seeming impasse in Palestine. He was especially interested in the question of partition. Under existing conditions, partition offered the "sole possibility of extricating the country from its political dilemma," Horowitz answered.

In the late afternoon, as evening approached, Horowitz and Rand went to the top of Mount Carmel to view the Haifa harbor below. Horowitz pointed to the rusting hulks of the Jewish "refugee fleet" lying at anchor in the harbor and described the "epic drama of the fight for free immigration, its grandeur and suffering, its anguish and heroism." The judge stood quietly, Horowitz later wrote, "his blue eyes gazing out over the vista of the harbor and rickety vessels illumined by the glow of the setting sun."

Rand witnessed the Arabs' attitude toward the Jews and the Jewish refugees' plight as they fought their way to their haven. Horowitz believed Rand's reservations about the Zionists slowly disappeared and sympathy emerged as he learned about the "broad panorama of the Jewish struggle." As they parted, Rand turned to Horowitz and said, "I fully appreciate that you're fighting with your backs to the wall."[818]

THE UNSCOP HEARINGS

The committee held twelve public hearings in the ornate Jerusalem YMCA auditorium in front of eighty journalists and 125 spectators. During this time, thirty-one representatives from twelve Jewish organizations gave testimony.[819]

Ben-Gurion described Palestine as "the supreme test of the United Nations." Despite all attempts to crush the Jewish people's identity, it had been preserved through the ages.

Speaking on how Arabs would fare in a Jewish state, Ben-Gurion pledged they would remain safe, whereas a Jewish minority in an Arab Palestine "would mean the final extinction of hope for the entire Jewish people." Hitler had been able to implement his policy of extermination, Ben-Gurion declared, because the Jews were the only people without a state of their own, which had left them "unable to protect, to intervene, to save and to fight."[820]

Once again, Weizmann shined in his testimony. As soon as a Jew came into contact with Palestine, the diplomat explained, he began "to feel as if he has returned. The country releases energies … in the Jewish people which are not released anywhere else." Everything that UNSCOP had seen—from the drained marshes to the homes and plants to the great institutions such as Hebrew University—were "the work of Jewish planning, of Jewish genius, of Jewish hands and muscles."

He read to them a letter he had recently received from Jan Smuts, the South Africa premier who had been among those who had drafted the Balfour Declaration. "I see now," Smuts wrote, "at this sad stage, no escape except by way of partition."[821]

When the Jewish portion of the testimony was completed, the UNSCOP delegates once again invited the Arab Higher Committee to give their point of view. Once again, the Arabs refused to cooperate.[822]

EXODUS 1947

As the committee neared the end of the testimony phase of their deliberations, their attention was captured by the unfolding drama of a ship called the *Exodus 1947*, a former Chesapeake Bay excursion steamer used as a troopship in the Allied landing in Normandy. Purchased after the war by the Friends of Haganah, it was refitted as a transport ship for the Jewish immigrants.[823] It left America in late March, boarding Jewish DPs at the French port of Sett, near Marseilles. The ship sailed from France on July 11, 1947, with 4,515 immigrants, including 655 children.

As soon as it left the territorial waters of France, British destroyers intercepted it. On July 18, near the coast of Palestine but outside territorial waters, the British rammed the ship and boarded it, while the immigrants put up a desperate defense.[824] Two immigrants and a crewman were killed in the battle, and thirty were wounded. The ship was towed to Haifa, where the British planned to force the immigrants onto deportation ships bound for France.[825]

An American journalist, Ruth Gruber, was reporting on UNSCOP for the *Herald Tribune*. Driving to Haifa to cover the story, Gruber listened on the radio as an American Methodist minister gave his eyewitness account of how the ship had been attacked by the British seventeen miles from the shore of Palestine. The British "immediately opened fire, threw gas bombs, and rammed our ship from three directions. On our deck there are one dead, five dying, and one hundred and twenty wounded."

When Gruber arrived at the Haifa docks, the scene looked like a war zone "with coils of rusted barbed wire, British army tanks and trucks and some five hundred troops …" As the damaged ship limped into the harbor, "one whole deck had been blasted open," Gruber noted. "I could see plumbing, broken staircases, and children running, their faces tormented with fear. Thousands of people crowded on the uppermost deck." They were singing "Hatikvah."

As the refugees disembarked, "their tattered bags and bundles were taken away." They were told they would get everything back in Cyprus. In a scene reminiscent of a typical Nazi "selection," the men were separated from the women as they stepped onto the docks. Some started screaming, as the concentration camp separation had meant death. Then they were all frisked and sprayed with DDT.[826]

As if God ordained that the eyes of the world be focused on this scene, UNSCOP Chairman Judge Emile Sandstrom and committee member Vladimir Simic of Yugoslavia happened to be in Haifa that day with Aubrey Eban. They witnessed the entire tragic event, which became a public-relations disaster for Great Britain.

"I had a feeling that the British Mandate died that day," Eban later said. "A regime that could maintain itself only by such … squalid acts was clearly on its way out. What they were doing was against the whole temperament and structure of the British character. It was both cruel and ridiculous … I was sure that seeing with their own eyes this British behavior, the committee members would realize that the British simply had to go."[827]

After watching the torrid scene, Sandstrom announced aloud, "Britain must no longer have the mandate over Palestine."[828]

In her nationally syndicated newspaper column, Eleanor Roosevelt wrote, "The thought of what it must mean to those poor human beings seems almost unbearable. They have gone through so much hardship and had thought themselves free forever from Germany, the country they associate with concentration camps and crematories. Now they are back there again. Somehow it is too horrible for any of us in this country to understand."[829]

On August 22, the ship left for the port of Hamburg, then in the British occupation zone. The immigrants were forcibly taken off and transported to two camps near Lubeck. Journalists who covered the dramatic struggle described the heartlessness and cruelty of the British. People around the world were outraged. After this, the British changed their policy. Illegal immigrants were not sent back to Europe; they were instead transported to detention camps in Cyprus.[830]

The UNSCOP delegates proceeded to Lebanon to meet with representatives from the Arab states. They were invited to a cocktail party hosted by the Ministry of Foreign Affairs where Granados spoke with the chief Lebanese delegate to the United Nations, Camille Chamoun. The two had met at Lake Success, and Granados considered Chamoun a "cultured and cultivated man." But when Granados asked his opinion on partition as a possible solution, Chamoun's demeanor changed. "It will be very difficult to reach an understanding," he declared. "… the Arabs will never accept it. They will fight it."

"Let the other countries of the world … accept their share" of the Jews, Chamoun argued. "The Arabs will never accept any further Jews."

The committee then met with the heads of the Arab states, including Hamid Frangieh, the foreign minister of Lebanon, Emir Adel Arslan of Syria, and Fouad Hamza of Saudi Arabia. Granados described a colorful meeting with "the Saudi-Arabians in their white and brown robes, and white, gold-braided headdress; the Yemenites in their picturesque garb carrying curved daggers in their belts; the others wearing Western clothes, their only concession to the East being the bright red tarbooshes they wore instead of hats." These Arab leaders agreed completely with Chamoun of Lebanon—Palestine must be an Arab state where the Jews could only live as a minority.[831]

The Lebanese foreign minister said all the Jews who had come to Palestine since Balfour in November 1917 were, as far as they were concerned, illegal immigrants. The leaders refuted the notion that the Arab Higher Committee was led by Nazi supporters. "The only reason the Mufti had taken refuge in Nazi Germany was because it too was fighting against the Jews."

Sandstrom tried to reason with them about the necessity of some kind of compromise, reviewing the various proposals—a binational state, a federal state, or partition—but the Arabs refused to consider any of them.

Later, the representatives met with the only group that was sympathetic to the idea of a Jewish state, the Lebanese Maronites—one of the oldest Christian communities in the world. Pro-Western and European, the Maronites desired an independent Lebanese state and did not want to be forced into an Arab federation. They believed the Jews were also justified in asking for their state, feeling they would be a positive force in the region.[832]

From Lebanon, the UNSCOP delegates traveled to Geneva where they were given offices in the *Palais des Nations*, the home of the defunct League of Nations. After a vote, it was decided a subcommittee would visit the refugee camps in Germany and Austria.[833] Those who visited the refugee camps heard similar stories and received the same feedback given to members of the Anglo-American Committee. Almost every refugee expressed a passionate desire to go to Eretz Israel.

THE END OF THE MANDATE

After much deliberation and debate in the halls and offices of the old League of Nations, the delegates finally came to agreement on eleven points— including an end to the British Mandate, independence granted to Palestine under the United Nations, protection of the holy places, international agreements for Jewish DPs in Europe, and an economic union established between the many groups of Palestine.

The Report of the UNSCOP Committee, released to the public in September 1947, contained a majority proposal for a Plan of Partition into two independent states—one Jewish and one Arab—with economic union. Jerusalem would be established as an international zone. The minority report called for a federal state to be created within three years, of which the Arab and Jewish states would become provinces with a common capital in Jerusalem.[834]

The Arab Higher Committee attacked both the majority and minority proposals as "absurd, impractical and unjust." The Arabs, its representative exclaimed, "would never allow a Jewish state to be established in one inch of Palestine," and he warned that attempts "to impose any solution contrary to the Arabs' birthright will only lead to trouble and bloodshed and probably to a third World War."[835]

Samir Rifai, the minister for foreign affairs for Trans-Jordan, sent a letter to Bevin and to other British representatives in Arab countries. In their eyes, he wrote, once the League of Nations was dissolved, everything the Great Powers had accepted, including the Balfour Declaration, was null and void. If the UNSCOP majority report were implemented, he threatened, "the whole of the Middle East [would] flare up in disastrous and widespread disturbances."[836]

Golda Meir, head of the Political Department of the Jewish Agency, was the only authorized Zionist spokesperson left in Palestine while the others were with the UN at Lake Success. She told the press the Jewish Agency was skeptical because there had been so many commissions and nothing had come of them. They were also troubled by the proposed internationalization of Jerusalem, the exclusion of western Galilee from the proposed Jewish state, and the indefiniteness of the transition period. "The words Palestine and Jerusalem were almost synonymous to Jews," she explained. "We can hardly imagine a Jewish state without Jerusalem."[837]

Despite some dissenting voices, the majority of the Yishuv supported the UNSCOP partition plan. They believed the success or failure of the UN-SCOP majority plan would depend on the position taken by the US government. As a result, the Jewish Agency launched a massive campaign in the United States to convince the delegation to vote in favor of partition.[838]

THE BATTLE AT THE UN

When the UNSCOP report was made public, Secretary of State Marshall said America needed to support the establishment of a Jewish state as a matter of principle. But his State Department deputies disagreed and told him he was wrong. According to Eleanor Roosevelt, they told Marshall that "to stand by his support of the UNSCOP recommendations [would be] to go against the advice of all the qualified experts in the Department."[839]

On October 3, the American delegates were called to meet with Secretary of State Marshall in Washington. Although the US position in principle was to support the UNSCOP majority report, Marshall said he now favored "certain modifications" to be proposed as amendments. He then said candidly these were "modifications ... of a pro-Arab nature."

He predicted the majority report would probably not receive the two-thirds majority of the General Assembly, and "some form of Trusteeship for Palestine might be desirable." Although the United States was committed to Jewish immigration into Palestine, Marshall declared, it was "not committed to support the creation of a Sovereign Jewish State." The United States "should not attempt to persuade members of the General Assembly to vote for the majority plan," he concluded.[840]

As word leaked out on the position of Marshall and the State Department, pressure started to mount for Truman to make his position on partition clear to the public. Jewish leaders approached Eddie Jacobson, the president's lifelong friend, to encourage him to make an appeal on behalf of the Yishuv. Jacobson had never been a Zionist, but like many American Jews, after six million of his brothers and sisters were murdered by the Nazis, he concluded his people needed a nation of their own to protect themselves against future attacks.

Eddie wrote to his old friend in the White House:

> Again I am appealing to you on behalf of my People. The future of one and one-half million Jews in Europe depends on what happens at the present meeting of the United Nations. With winter coming on with its attendant hardships, time is short for action by this meeting to alleviate further suffering by these helpless people. How they will be able to survive another winter in concentration camps and the hell holes in which they live is beyond my imagination. In all this World, there is only one place where they can go—and that is Palestine. You and I know only too well this is the only answer.

I have read Secretary Marshall's recent statement that the US would give great weight to UNSOP's [*sic*] recommendation; that was a great deal to be thankful for. Now, if it were possible for you, as leader and spokesman for our country, to express your support of this action, I think we can accomplish our aims before the United Nations Assembly.

Jacobson said he trusted "to God that he give you strength and guidance to act immediately." Then he added:

I think I am one of a few who actually knows and realizes what terrible heavy burdens you are carrying on your shoulders during these hectic days. I should, therefore, be the last man to add to them; but I feel you will forgive me for doing so, because tens of thousands of lives depend on words from your mouth and heart. Harry, my people need help and I am appealing to you to help them.[841]

Harry responded to his friend, asking that he not be quoted. As the matter stood before the UN General Assembly, "I don't think it would be right or proper for me to interfere at this stage, particularly as it requires a two-thirds vote to accomplish the purpose sought. Marshall was handling the issue, I think, as it should be and I hope it will work out all right."[842]

Despite his wish for the Palestine issue to be "handled," it was becoming clear Truman would have to decide whether the United States would support partition. The Arabs' unyielding position helped Truman make that decision.

On October 9, Clifton Daniel of *The New York Times* reported the Grand Mufti had arrived in Lebanon for a meeting of the Arab League to discuss military measures should partition be attempted. The League announced they intended to occupy Palestine if the British forces withdrew and to resist by force any effort to create a Jewish state.[843]

When Truman read the report, he called the Arab League's move "belligerent and defiant." From that moment, he instructed the State Department to support the partition plan.

The next day, Herschel Johnson, US representative on the Ad Hoc Committee on Palestine, rose to publicly endorse partition, calling on the United Nations to establish a volunteer police force to help keep the peace in the Holy Land if needed. *The New York Times* called the statement "clear and explicit" and observed it gave "considerably stronger support to partition than had been expected."[844]

VOTE FOR PARTITION

As the official vote neared, the British became increasingly uncooperative. Sir Alexander Cadogan, the British representative to the UN, announced troops would not be available to enforce any settlement. Britain planned to evacuate the last of its forces by August 1948.[845] This did not mean Britain would continue to maintain a civil administration in Palestine until that date. It intended to lay down its Mandate any time it wanted after the General Assembly took a position not accepted by both Arabs and Jews.[846]

Angered by developments, Henderson wrote a memo to Undersecretary Lovett pointing out that in light of the British statement, the US partition plan would leave only local law enforcement organizations to preserve the peace in Palestine. He warned there would be wide-scale violence on all sides. As he saw it, the United States was fostering a plan that would draw American, Soviet, and possibly other troops into Palestine.[847]

Lovett brought Henderson's memo to Truman and read it at their daily meeting. "I explained to him, that the Department thought the situation was serious and that he should know of the probable attempts to get us committed militarily." Lovett also questioned the president on what role the US delegates should play in ensuring that partition passed the General Assembly. Should the delegates actively lobby other nations?

"The President did not wish the United States Delegation to use threats or improper pressure of any kind on other Delegations to vote for the majority report favoring partition of Palestine," Lovett reported. "We were willing to vote for that report ourselves because it was a majority report but we were in no sense of the word to coerce other Delegations to follow our lead."[848]

But as the vote loomed, some key nations announced their opposition to partition, despite their good relations with the United States. With a two-thirds vote required for passage, it suddenly appeared that the vote might be lost by a margin of only a few renegade nations. Truman's hands-off policy was giving the impression to other delegations that the creation of the Jewish state was not especially important to the US government. Countries like the Philippines, Haiti, Greece, Liberia, and Ethiopia either announced their opposition to partition, or the possibility of voting against the UNSCOP majority recommendation. The fate of partition rested in the hands of these countries.[849]

The Jewish Agency called all hands on deck and rallied their forces to persuade these nations to vote for partition. "Cablegrams sped to all parts of the world," David Horowitz remembered. "People were dragged from their beds at midnight and sent on peculiar errands … not an influential Jew, Zionist, or non-Zionist refused to give us his assistance."[850]

Although Truman never admitted it publicly, officials later claimed the administration played a part in persuading the rogue nations to come in line. "By direct order of the White House every form of pressure, indirect and direct, was brought to bear by American officials upon those countries outside of the Moslem world that were known to be uncertain or opposed to partition," Undersecretary of State Sumner Welles claimed.[851]

The Jewish Agency encouraged people to flood the White House with support. With this avalanche of positive backing, Truman threw his personal weight behind the effort to get a decision. "It was only in the last 48 hours," wrote one Jewish official, "that we really got the full backing of the United States."[852]

When Loy Henderson heard reports of pressure being applied by the US delegates, he called Herschel Johnson at the United Nations. "What's going on up there?" he bellowed. "We are being told here in Washington that the Americans at the United Nations are engaging in a lot of arm-twisting in order to get votes for the Majority Plan."

"Dave Niles called us up here a couple of days ago," Johnson answered, "and said that the president had instructed him to tell us that, by God, he wanted us to get busy and get all the votes that we possibly could; that there would be hell if the voting went the wrong way. We are working, therefore, under terrific strain trying to carry out the President's orders."[853]

Johnson asked Niles what to do about the State Department. "Never mind the State Department," Niles answered. "This is an order from the President!" Johnson and Eleanor Roosevelt went from delegation to delegation, telling them they had been instructed by Truman to seek their support for partition.

When the British recognized the new proactive American position, they became even more defiant. On November 28, Bevin handed Marshall a summary of a revised British plan for withdrawal from Palestine. The plan called for an end of their civilian administration and Mandatory responsibilities for Palestine on May 15, 1948. If partition was voted in, they would not allow anyone from the UN commission to arrive in Palestine before May 1, arguing it would not fit in with their withdrawal plans. Of course, this would leave only a two-week window for the transition of power.[854]

On November 29, 1947, people around the world listened to their radios as the UN voted on the question of partition. A small number of votes would decide the future of Palestine. When the French delegate voted yes, cheers broke out in the Assembly Hall from the audience packed into every seat—as that was the tipping point in favor of partition. The UN delegates voted to establish both Jewish and Arab states in Palestine, by a vote of thirty-three to thirteen with ten abstentions.

The British had abstained. Attlee and Bevin's strategy blew up in their faces. "Mr. Bevin is our sworn enemy," Weizmann later wrote. "He has twice tried to break us: first through the Anglo-American Committee, which produced a verdict quite contrary to his expectations; and a second time by handing us over to the UN, which he hoped might bring about the liquidation of the whole affair. But in fact it has done just the opposite."[855]

As the votes were tallied, suddenly a shiver went down the spine of Emanuel Neumann, and he felt the spirit of Theodor Herzl haunting the assembly. In 1897, Herzl, the father of modern Zionism, had made the audacious prediction that a Jewish state would be founded within fifty years. As the scale tipped in favor of partition, Neumann marveled that it was fifty years since Herzl wrote those prophetic words.[856]

As the Arab delegates realized partition had been adopted, they stood and stormed out of the hall. Standing in the doorway, Azzam Bey shouted in Arabic-accented English, "Any line of partition drawn in Palestine will be a line of fire and blood."[857]

Around the world, though, Jews danced in the streets late into the night. The following day, war erupted in Palestine.

Chapter Twenty-Four

PALESTINE ON FIRE

NOVEMBER 1947—ERETZ ISRAEL

With the vote for partition, leaders of the surrounding Arab nations vowed to destroy the Jewish state, even before it was born. In Haifa, where 70,000 Arabs lived alongside 70,000 Jews, an Arab gathering took place. Sheikh Sabri Abdeen stood and announced: "If the Jews want to take Palestine from us, we swear that we will throw them into the sea." He pointed to the Mediterranean, a few hundred meters from where they had gathered.[858]

Despite these public threats, the British did not allow the Jews to arm themselves. So the Yishuv continued the feverish construction of clandestine weapons in homes or hidden factories. At the same time, Jewish agents searched for weapons dealers around the world who would sell to them.

"On the night of the 29th of November we all danced in the streets," said one Palestinian Jew. "And we were still dancing when the first news came that some people were killed on the roads."

The conflict was summed up for people around the world in a 1947 Movie News reel:

> To the Jews, Palestine is their traditional and spiritual home—
> the Promised Land. But the majority of the inhabitants of Palestine are Arabs. They too regard Palestine as their rightful home.
> But with the end of the war, into Palestine ports came ship after
> ship crammed with illegal immigrants—refugees of recent persecution from Germany, Austria, Poland, Belsen, and Dachau.
> The Arabs, fearful of becoming a minority, persuaded the British
> to limit Jewish immigration. Jewish extremists attacked British

troops; wrecked government buildings; blew up trains and ships. And so Palestine remains a place of martial law where all go their way under watch—where the innocent must suffer with the guilty.[859]

THE WAR BEFORE THE WAR

The euphoric dream of Jewish statehood in the Land of Israel was punctured by the harsh reality of gunfire between Arabs and Jews. Three days after the vote, Arab snipers attacked a civilian bus on the Mediterranean coast, killing five Jews. Arabs stormed the Jewish commercial center in Jerusalem outside the Jaffa gate, causing havoc and destruction—and nearly burning it to the ground.[860]

There had been violence between Jews and Arabs before the partition plan, but it quickly escalated after the vote. Within a week, an undeclared civil war had erupted. The British, counting the days until they could leave, were stuck in the middle.

Short of weapons, the biggest advantage the Haganah had over the Palestinian Arabs was leadership that had spent years preparing for this moment. "We were better organized because Ben-Gurion, with a very far-sighted look, he knew that we were going to come to a conflict," Israeli fighter Asher Levy recalled.[861]

Ben-Gurion envisioned a democratic Jewish state, and his strategy for winning that state—putting in place the necessary mechanisms for nationhood—shaped the Jews' fight against their enemies.[862]

THE HUNT FOR ARMS

In an effort to appear neutral in the conflict and to not ruffle the feathers of the British, President Truman gave in to pressure from the State and Defense Departments and approved the suspension of American arms sales to the Middle East. While the US embargo had little effect on the Arabs, who were thoroughly equipped with European weapons and had access to weapons dealers in other nations, it deprived the Jewish forces of a key arms supplier.

The Zionists immediately dispatched agents around the globe to find military-grade weapons. With the possibility of actual Arab armies attacking in the coming months, the Haganah took stock of its supplies. The leadership reported to Ben-Gurion they had only a handful of artillery units and tanks and not a single warplane.[863]

Although Britain never explained its reason for choosing to remain in Palestine for five months after the vote on partition, the effect of its decision was clear to the Jews. During this period, the British could hamper the Yishuv's efforts to increase its weapons supply, while the Arabs could vastly increase theirs—with British cooperation. Many observers saw the British actions as a means to bolster the Arabs so a friendly Palestinian state would emerge in their favor.

For the British, maintenance of their empire was paramount.

The Fight for Jerusalem

Fearing an outbreak of civil war in Palestine could frighten the UN into rethinking its vote on partition, Ben-Gurion directed the Haganah to maintain restraint. But the strategy backfired when the Arabs attacked, laid siege to Jewish settlements, and blocked the mountainous road to Jerusalem.[864] The British were not scheduled to pull out of Palestine until May 1948, but the war between the Jews and the Arabs was already under way. The new year began with the bombing of Arab headquarters in the Semiramis Hotel by the Jews on January 5, 1948.

Although living in exile in Egypt, Haj Amin al-Husseini responded through his Palestinian militia. He appointed his cousin, Abdel Khader al-Husseini to lead his forces, the Holy War Army. Neither side could imagine a future that didn't include being in control of Jerusalem.

So once again in its bloody history, Jerusalem was engulfed in war.

With the outbreak of hostilities, the Arabs were determined to separate Jerusalem from the rest of the Yishuv. Soon, the Jewish community of 100,000 persons inside the city of Jerusalem was under siege. They quickly ran low on water and food. There were not enough soldiers, ammunition, or weapons to hold Jerusalem for long.[865]

With the population on the verge of starvation, supply vehicles began traveling the road in convoys accompanied by armored guards. The Haganah's crack Harel Brigade of the Palmach Division was given the job of taking back and holding the road to Jerusalem. The Haganah constructed improvised armored vehicles known as sandwiches—buses and trucks covered with steel plates surrounding wooden boards. Their slow ascent to Jerusalem made them an easy target.

"We fought our way to Jerusalem, and the convoys were almost suicidal operations," remembered Haganah soldier Amos Horev. "The situation was such that we didn't want to fall alive in the hands of the Arabs. So we used to have high explosives inside the truck, so that if worse comes to worst, and you see that there is no hope, we prefer to die than to fall alive into their hands."

On February 22, a major explosion on Ben Yehuda Street killed fifty-two Jews and injured 130 innocent bystanders. The Jews suspected deserters from the British army helping Arabs to plant the bombs.[866]

The Jerusalem commander, Dov Joseph, reported a convoy was "wiped out" on March 27. Two days later, a sixty-vehicle convoy came under attack at Hulda and was forced to turn back. Five Arabs and seventeen Jews were killed. A food convoy escorted by the Harel Brigade reached the city on April 6 without casualties, despite being ambushed by a force of 150 Arabs.[867]

The sixteen-mile trip from Bab el Wad to Jerusalem averaged three hours. The Haganah equipped trucks with bulldozer blades to push away roadblocks. Arabs, in turn, mined the roadblocks to disable the besieged trucks. The Arabs then poured down fire from the hillside through the thin metal of the truck roofs. As the weeks passed, the road became littered with burned-out vehicles.[868]

THE STRATEGIES OF WAR

Ben-Gurion was determined to hold Jerusalem, even though the city was far from the coastal plain, subject to Arab siege, and extraordinarily difficult to defend. He was also determined, against military advice, to defend every Jewish settlement.[869]

Watching from Washington, a minority faction within the State Department started to feel the arms embargo was a grave injustice to the embattled Palestinian Jews, who appeared to be in danger of defeat. The

Arabs commanded strategic positions overlooking the highway from Tel Aviv to Jerusalem. The British were "maintaining order" by giving guns to the Arabs and arresting the Jewish defenders. Within the State Department, bureaucrats argued in favor of legalizing the shipment of arms to the Haganah, but they were overruled by the leadership.

Soon, the White House mailroom overflowed with protests from American citizens calling for arms for the Zionists. In the first quarter of 1948, the volume of mail coming into the White House was three times higher than it had ever been.[870]

In March 1948, the Jews went on the offensive after a shipment of arms finally arrived from Communist-controlled Czechoslovakia.[871] The priority for Ben-Gurion and the Haganah was opening the road to Jerusalem. As the Arab militias didn't coordinate with each other, Jewish forces picked off villages one by one. The houses were usually blown up to keep the villagers from coming back to occupy the area. If the residents hadn't already left, they were most often expelled.

The Jews suffered a blow on March 11, 1948, when the official limousine of the American consul general, flying the Stars and Stripes and driven by the usual chauffeur, was admitted to the courtyard of the Jewish Agency compound in Jerusalem. Although the Haganah general staff had received a warning of an assault on the Jewish Agency, there was no inkling the attacker would be a US citizen, much less a past collaborator with Zionist intelligence. But the consul general's Armenian-American driver, Anton Da'ud Kamilyo, was actually a Palestinian double agent. Hidden in the trunk of the green Ford were 220 pounds of TNT—more than enough to wipe out the entire general staff of the Haganah. Kamilyo parked the consulate car in front of the Agency headquarters and fled in a taxi.

A security official became suspicious of wires dangling from the trunk, and he pushed the car away from the building. As he set the brake, the charge exploded. Part of the wing collapsed as flames engulfed the building. The chairman of the Jewish National Fund, Leib Yaffe, and six colleagues were killed. Almost 100 were injured.[872]

THE CRUEL MONTH

By April 1, 1948, Jerusalem had run out of water, and the population was reduced to eating plants. Haganah troops stationed in the hills around Jerusalem planned an attack to free the corridor so food and other supplies could be brought in to the city. Each village around Jerusalem was crucial to the control of the city.

In an attempt to open the blocked road to Jerusalem, the Haganah launched an attack on the strategic and historic Castel. The view from this ancient fortress stretched from Judea down to the Mediterranean Sea. Due to its location, the ruins of what had once been a Roman fort, and later a Crusader stronghold, remained. Arab control of the Castel commanded the road below. On April 3, Jewish forces attacked and captured the hill.

When word of the Castel's fall reached Arab leaders, they ordered revered commander Abdul Khader Husseini to take it back.[873] Thousands answered Husseini's call to arms. Equipped with knives, clubs, rifles, guns, and explosives, they ascended the hill. After a continuous six-day battle, the Jewish defenders ran out of food and ammunition, and reinforcements failed to arrive.[874]

"The one who sits on the Castel controls all the area," remembered Menachem Urman, one of the Jewish platoon leaders. "Husseini sent everybody he could—thousands of them. In the last attack we let them come in to the fence because we had been short of bullets … but then we pushed them back."

A half hour later, a jeep with the United Nations insignia pulled up to the compound. The UN staffer asked to see the Jewish commander. "You don't know who you killed?" he asked. "Abdul Khader Husseini is dead here on the road."

Furious over the death of Husseini, scores of Arabs rushed to the slopes of the Castel and opened fire on three fronts. Many Jewish fighters were killed and the Castel was recaptured.

The next day, Jewish commandos returned at dawn and found only a few people left on the hill. The Arabs had recovered al-Husseini's body, and they organized a massive funeral for him in Jerusalem at *Haram al-Sherif* (the Temple Mount).

Husseini's death sowed disillusionment and discouragement among the Arab ranks.[875]

DEIR YASSIN

One of the Arab villages on the Haganah's list to be cleared was Deir Yassin. Situated on a hill, about 2,600 feet high, it commanded a wide view and was located less than a mile from Jerusalem. On the same day as Husseini's funeral, a combined force of radical Lehi and Irgun fighters attacked Deir Yassin. "In every house they entered, they killed the people inside," said Mohammad Salah, a Deir Yassin eyewitness.

"The conquest of the village was carried out with great brutality," wrote Itzak Levi, a commander of the Haganah intelligence service. "Whole families—women, old people, children—were killed and piles of corpses accumulated. Some of the prisoners taken to places of detention, including women and children, were brutally murdered by their guards. Among the prisoners was [sic] a young mother and baby. The guards killed the baby in front of his mother and after she fainted, also murdered her."[876]

The New York Times' description of the battle reported more than 200 Arabs were killed, forty captured, and seventy women and children were released. A study by Bir Zeit University, based on discussions with each family from the village, arrived at a figure of 107 Arab civilians dead and twelve wounded, in addition to thirteen armed fighters—evidence that the number of dead was smaller than claimed and that the village did have troops based there.[877]

Arab leaders called it a massacre and reported exaggerated claims of murder and rape on the radio. Hazem Nuseibeh, who worked for the Palestine Broadcasting Service in 1948, admitted being told by Hussein al-Khalidi, a Palestinian Arab leader, to fabricate the atrocity claims. Abu Mahmud, a Deir Yassin resident in 1948, told Khalidi "there was no rape." But Khalidi replied, "We have to say this, so the Arab armies will come to liberate Palestine from the Jews."[878]

"This was our biggest mistake," Nuseibeh explained. "We did not realize how our people would react. As soon as they heard that women had been raped at Deir Yassin, Palestinians fled in terror."[879] The publicity for the purpose of attracting sympathy actually created a flight of demoralized non-combatant Arabs.

Menachem Begin, the Irgun's leader, denied the attack was a massacre but said the "legend of terror" was worth half a dozen battalions because Arabs were seized with panic when they heard the Irgun were coming.

After Deir Yassin, King Abdullah of Trans-Jordan and other Arab leaders came under strong domestic pressure to intervene in Palestine. To try to keep peace with his moderate Arab neighbor, Ben-Gurion sent Abdullah an apology. The king of Jordan rejected this gesture from the Jewish Agency.[880]

Mount Scopus Ambush

Four days later, the Arabs retaliated against the Jews for Deir Yassin. The Hadassah Hospital on Mount Scopus, situated next to the Hebrew University, was connected to the rest of Jewish Jerusalem by a narrow road through an Arab quarter. Hadassah was Jerusalem's main Jewish hospital, serving both Jews and Arabs.[881]

On April 14, a large group of professors, doctors, researchers, and scholars crowded into buses and ambulances headed for the hospital. Many in these vehicles had fled the Nazi persecutions in Europe.

The prestigious director of Hadassah Hospital, the world-renowned ophthalmologist Chaim Yassky, sat exposed to danger in the front passenger seat in the first ambulance. Without warning, the Arabs ambushed the convoy when a tailor named Mohammed Neggar detonated a mine. Neggar had been given the time of the convoy's passage by a British officer, who also promised if the Arabs attacked the convoy, they would not be molested as long as they did not fire on British patrols.[882]

The convoy ground to a halt, and Arab gunmen opened fire. Seventy-eight Jewish doctors, nurses, students, patients, faculty members, and Haganah fighters—along with one British soldier—were killed in the attack. Many unidentified bodies, burned beyond recognition, were later buried in a mass grave in the Sanhedria Cemetery.

The massacre occurred within two hundred yards of a British military post, but the soldiers made no attempt to intervene, even though the attacks continued over seven hours. British commentator Christopher Sykes—whose father, Mark Sykes, was a friend of the Zionists—wrote of the incident: "This most hideous achievement of the 'crass kind' was perhaps the worst blemish on the tarnished British military record of that time."[883]

PREPARED TO DECLARE

The British Mandate would officially end on May 15, 1948. For Ben-Gurion, the time had come to declare a Jewish state. Others around him weren't so sure. Everyone understood once the Jews declared an independent state all the Arab countries surrounding the infant nation would invade. US Secretary of State George Marshall and Secretary of Defense Forrestal warned the Israelis that America would not support them if they did.[884]

Ben-Gurion called a meeting with his top military leaders. "We are going to declare the State of Israel," he announced. "I need from you the list of what weapons you will need because we are going to have a war." He gave them a couple of hours, and they came back with their lists, which included rifles, machine guns, pistols, and grenades. He threw the piece of paper back at them. "Gentlemen, we are going to war," he shouted. "I need a list of how many tanks you need; how many battle ships; how many planes; how many cannons."[885]

"We were, of course, totally unprepared for war," said Golda Meir. "We needed weapons, urgently—if we could find anyone willing to sell them to us. But before we could buy anything we needed money—millions of dollars. And there was only one group of people in the whole world that we had any chance of getting these dollars from—the Jews of America."[886]

Most of the council members thought Ben-Gurion should go to America to raise funds. But Meir disagreed. "I will go," she insisted. "I know how to speak to Americans. We can't spare Ben-Gurion right now. He is needed here. I can do it." She was fluent in the two languages the Americans understood—Yiddish and English."[887]

The Jewish treasurer told Ben-Gurion he could expect they wouldn't be able to raise more than $7 or 8 million. But after just six weeks of fund-raising, Golda Meir returned from the States with more than $50 million. This money paid for the heavy weapons Israel bought from Czechoslovakia, which helped turn the tide of the war raging with the Palestinian Arabs. And it helped them to prepare for the larger war yet to come.

By the time Britain withdrew from Palestine, the Haganah had carved out for the Yishuv a state roughly equivalent to what was approved by the United Nations in November 1947.[888]

Golda Meir and King Abdullah

Facing opposition on all sides, Ben-Gurion made one last plea for diplomacy. The only possibility for stopping the onslaught was to persuade the king of Trans-Jordan, Abdullah, to remove himself from the coalition of Arab armies. Impressed by her successful fund raising in America, Ben-Gurion designated Golda Meir his secret emissary.[889]

Israel's only chance for peace with the Arabs rested on a former schoolteacher from Wisconsin—a woman Ben-Gurion later called "the best man in my cabinet."[890]

On May 11, Golda Meir left Tel Aviv disguised in Arab costume and accompanied by Ezra Danin, an expert on the Middle East and a friend of the king. They were smuggled secretly at night through Trans-Jordan to the king's palace. Through her veil, Meir witnessed columns of the Arab Legion and their armored vehicles moving toward Eretz Israel.[891]

When the king entered the room, Meir rose and gave the familiar Jewish greeting, "*Shalom*." Smiling, Abdullah responded with the cousin-word with the same meaning: "*Salam*"—peace.

"Have you broken your promise to me, after all?" Meir began.

"When I made that promise, I thought I was in control of my own destiny," the king responded. "But since then I have learned otherwise. I was alone then. Now I am one of five and I have discovered I cannot make any decisions alone."[892]

The king said there would be no war if the Jews agreed to not declare a state and if they halted all future Jewish immigration.[893] Meir made it clear this was no longer a possibility. She urged him not to join the other Arab countries in attacking the Jews. King Abdullah was the commander of the Arab Legion, the strongest Arab army involved in the war with 10,000 soldiers, trained and commanded by British officers.

Danin tactfully reminded the king the Jews were his only real friends in the region. "I know that," he said sadly. "I have no illusions. I believe with all my heart that Divine Providence has brought you back here, restoring you, a Semitic people who were exiled in Europe, and have shared in its progress to the Semitic East which needs your knowledge and initiative. But, conditions are difficult."[894]

He offered the Jews the status of a protected minority in an enlarged Jordanian state. "Why don't you wait a few years? Drop your demands for free immigration. I will take over the whole country and you will be represented in my parliament. I will treat you very well and there will be no war."

"We've been waiting for 2,000 years," Meir replied. "Is that hurrying?" Unsurprisingly, she rejected the king's offer as unacceptable. One and one-half million survivors of the Holocaust waited in squalid European DP camps to enter Palestine. There could be no more waiting. "If His Majesty wants war," she told the king, "there will be war. Perhaps we will meet again soon after the establishment of the state."

"I am sorry," he responded. "I deplore the coming bloodshed and destruction. Let us hope we shall meet again and not sever our relations." The trio shook hands and parted ways. The last sight Meir and Danin had of the king was him standing on the stairs in his royal white robe and headgear—"slowly, sadly, waving goodbye."[895]

Chapter Twenty-Five

EDDIE JACOBSON'S HERO

MARCH 13, 1948—WASHINGTON, DC

In the spring of 1948, pressure on Truman from all sides became almost unbearable. In Damascus, angry mobs vandalized the US embassy, and Islamic radical terrorists bombed the American consulate in Jerusalem. With an undeclared war raging in Palestine, experts at the State Department, the Defense Department, the newly formed Central Intelligence Agency, along with the Joint Chiefs of Staff pointed to the chaos as proof that partition was a mistake. With an uncooperative British government, the biggest fear looked like it could become a reality—order in Palestine could only be restored by the introduction of American and Soviet troops.

Truman's faith in partition wavered. Many of his advisers believed the partition plan should be abandoned.

The issue was oil.

In mid-February, the Arab League announced American oil companies would not be permitted to lay pipelines across the territory of any member country until the United States changed its views on partition. Syria voided a signed contract for a pipeline through her territory. King Ibn Saud was pressured to take punitive measures against ARAMCO.[896]

At the same time, Truman was absolutely fed up with the tactics of the radical Zionists—and especially Rabbi Silver. These heavy-handed maneuvers only alienated Truman from the Zionists. The president shut the doors to the White House to all Jewish leaders.[897]

"As the pressure mounted, I found it necessary to give instructions that I did not want to be approached by any more spokesmen for the Zionist cause," Truman later wrote.[898]

Hundreds of thousands of letters and postcards flooded the White House in support of partition. Thirty-three state legislatures passed resolutions favoring a Jewish state in Palestine. Forty governors and more than half the Congress signed petitions to the president. Ed Flynn, Truman's trusted political adviser, told the president he must either "give in" on Palestine or expect New York's opposition to his renomination in July.[899]

As the man who followed FDR into the presidency, Truman sometimes believed people did not take him seriously enough. This led to a build-up of anger that erupted every once in a while with particularly vivid consequences in the presidency.[900] He didn't like to be pushed around, and as the lobbying from the Zionists and their supporters became more intense, he shut down.

In this mounting crisis, the Jewish Agency Executive turned once again for help to their elder statesman, Chaim Weizmann, who was bombarded with phone calls and telegrams urging him to exert his personal influence at the White House. Weizmann cancelled his plans to travel to Palestine and instead booked passage on the *Queen Mary* for New York.[901]

David Niles was asked to secure an interview between Weizmann and the president. But Niles did not think the president would be willing to receive him.[902]

Weizmann wrote to Truman, pleading for "a few minutes of your precious time" in the interest of preventing a "catastrophe not only for my people, but for Palestine and indeed the United Nations." An official reply advised brusquely that an appointment had become "out of the question." Weizmann checked into the Waldorf Astoria in New York City and waited.[903]

Ambassador Austin would soon have to give a statement at the UN on America's position. Truman had written to Marshall: "I want to make it clear that nothing should be presented to the Security Council that could be interpreted as a recession on our part from the position we took in the General Assembly [for partition]. Send final draft of Austin's remarks for my consideration."[904]

Despite these instructions, on February 24, with Truman's approval, Austin delivered an ambiguous speech to the UN that seemed to indicate the United States was backing away from its commitment to partition.[905] The State Department, in league with the British government, made a concerted effort to stall, and possibly to kill, the plan for partition, arguing that it could not be achieved without an international police force.

Jewish leaders were in a state of near panic. They needed American support—and Truman's door had been slammed shut.

On March 8, Eliahu Epstein wrote to one of Truman's trusted advisers, Judge Samuel Rosenman. "It is clear now that only the President can countermand this obstruction of the implementation of the General Assembly recommendation. I am aware of how important a factor you have been, in the past, in influencing the President to a right attitude on the Palestine issue. There has never been so great a need for persuasion as now."

What made matters worse for the Zionists was that David Niles was ill and unavailable for his regular meetings with President Truman. The one man inside the White House who might have secured Weizmann an audience was absent.[906]

Weizmann confided his fears to Dewey Stone, who then told his friend Frank Goldman, the national president of the Jewish service organization, *B'nai B'rith*. "I just spent the day with Chaim Weizmann," Stone told Goldman. "He thinks he can convince Truman to turn around on partition. But he can't get into the White House."

Goldman had an idea. The previous year he had been introduced to Truman's old friend and business partner, Eddie Jacobson, one of the few people with an open door to the White House. After hearing about Jacobson, Goldman put in a call to a Kansas City attorney named A. J. Granoff. "Do you know a man by the name of Jacobstein ... who is supposed to be a very close friend of President Truman?"

"You mean Eddie Jacobson," said Granoff. "Sure, I ought to! I'm his friend and lawyer."[907]

Goldman called Eddie after midnight on February 20, 1948. "You've got to go and talk to the president—the situation is dire. You must help us, Eddie."[908]

Jacobson sent a wire to his old friend, who was on vacation:

> Mr. President I know that you have very excellent reasons for not wanting to see Dr. Chaim Weizmann. No one realizes more than I the amount of pressure that is being thrown on you during these critical days, but as you once told me this gentlemen is the greatest statesman and finest leader that my people have. He is very old and heartbroken that he could not get to see you. Mr. President I have asked you for very little in the way of favors during all our years of friendship, but am begging of you to see Dr. Weizmann as soon as possible. I can assure you I would not plead to you for any other of our leaders.[909]

Six days later, Truman replied to Jacobson by letter from his retreat at the US submarine base at Key West. "There wasn't anything he [Weizmann] could say to me that I didn't already know, anyway. The situation has been a headache to me for two and a half years. The Jews are so emotional, and the Arabs are so difficult to talk with that it is almost impossible to get anything done. The British, of course, have been exceedingly non-cooperative in arriving at a conclusion. The Zionists, of course, have expected a big stick approach on our part, and naturally have been disappointed when we can't do that."[910]

"Knowing the President as I did," Jacobson later explained, "the letter gave me a feeling that he would not change his mind. I decided that the best thing to do was to wait until the President returned to the White House."

"My anxiety increased during these intervening days," Jacobson remembered, "because I briefed myself in preparing to see the President. I soon realized that the British were hoping for an Arab victory which would drive the Jews into the sea. It also seemed that, when the British would withdraw from Palestine on May 15, the settlements in the Negev and other spots might be wiped out by the Arabs and also expose Haifa to danger. The situation facing my people in Palestine was extremely dangerous even to my inexperienced eye, and so I determined to do all that I could as soon as possible."

On Saturday, March 13, soon after Truman's return to Washington, Jacobson presented himself at the White House. "As usual, I do not think I made an appointment, but took my chances. I was greeted by Mr. Matt Connelly…"

"Does the boss have any time to talk to me for a while?" Eddie asked.

Connelly advised, urged, and begged Eddie not to discuss Palestine with the president.

"I quickly told Matt that that's what I came to Washington for, and that I was determined to discuss this very subject with the President."

When he entered the Oval Office, Eddie noticed with pleasure that Truman looked well, as his trip to Florida did him much good. "For a few minutes we discussed our families and my business in which he has always shown a brother's interest, and other personal things." Then Jacobson became quiet as he searched for the words to say to his old friend.

"He stood around and didn't say very much," Truman later said. "He was as quiet as he could be. I finally said, 'Eddie, what in the world is the matter with you? Have you at last come to get something? Because you have never asked me for anything since I've been in the White House—or even since we've been friends.'"[911]

"I then brought up the Palestine subject," Jacobson recalled. "The President immediately became tense in appearance, abrupt in speech, and very bitter in the words he was throwing my way. In all these years of our friendship, he never talked to me in this manner, or in any way even approaching it." Truman said he was satisfied to let these subjects take their course through the United Nations.

For the first time, Truman was freezing his friend Eddie with a display of official dignity.[912]

"I then actually argued with him," Eddie explained, "and I am now surprised at myself that I had the nerve to do that. I argued with him from every possible angle, reminding him of his feelings for Dr. Weizmann, which he often expressed to me, telling him that I could not understand why he wouldn't see him."

Eddie then added, "Dr. Weizmann is an old and a sick man, and he has had made a long journey to the United States especially to see you."

This response touched off an explosion. Truman bellowed that the "Eastern Jews" had "slandered and libeled" him since the moment he became president.[913] He said sharply he didn't want to discuss Palestine, or the Jews, or the Arabs, or the British.

Tears suddenly rolled down Eddie's face, which he quickly wiped away with his handkerchief. He was surprised and saddened by the president's brash tone with him.[914] "I suddenly found myself thinking that my dear friend, the President of the United States, was at that moment as close to being an anti-Semite as a man could possibly be."

Jacobson was equally shocked that some Jewish leaders would be responsible for Truman's attitude. "I could not think of any arguments to give him in order to soften his anger, because, after all, he had been slandered and libeled by some of the leaders of my people whom he had tried to help …"

Then Jacobson's eye caught a replica of the courthouse statue in Jackson County, Missouri, that Truman had worked so hard to build.

> I happened to rest my eyes on a beautiful model of a statue of Andrew Jackson mounted on a horse which I had noted the many previous times I had been to the White House. I then found myself saying this to the President …
>
> Harry, all your life you have had a hero. You are probably the best read man in America on the life of Andrew Jackson. I remember when we had our store together and you were always reading books and papers and pamphlets on this great American. When you built the new Jackson County Court House in Kansas City, you put this very statue, lifesize, on the lawn right in front of the new Court House, where it still stands. Well, Harry, I too have a hero, a man I never met, but who is, I think, the greatest Jew who ever lived. I too have studied his past and I agree with you, as you have often told me, that he is a gentleman and a great statesman as well.
>
> I am talking about Chaim Weizmann. He is a very sick man, almost broken in health, but he travelled thousands and thousands of miles just to see you and plead the cause of my people. Now

you refuse to see him because you were insulted by some of our American Jewish leaders, even though you know that Weizmann had absolutely nothing to do with these insults and would be the last man to be a party to them.

It doesn't sound like you, Harry, because I thought that you could take this stuff they have been handing out to you. I wouldn't be here if I didn't know that, if you will see him, you will be properly and accurately informed on the situation that exists in Palestine, and yet you refuse to see him.[915]

As he finished, Jacobson noticed Truman was drumming on his desk with his fingers. The president abruptly swiveled his chair and gazed out the window. Deep in thought, he stared at the South Grounds. Eddie held his breath, but he thought, *I got him!*[916]

"I knew that he was changing his mind. I don't know how many seconds passed in silence, but it seemed like centuries. All of a sudden he swiveled himself around again, facing his desk, looked me straight in the eyes and then said the most endearing words I had ever heard from his lips. "You win, you baldheaded _____ ___ _ _____. I will see him."[917]

Jacobson stood to say good-bye, and Harry pressed the button for Matt Connelly and told him he would see Dr. Weizmann. He asked him to make the proper arrangements for the meeting, which was to be off the record and on condition that the press and public would know absolutely nothing about it.

When Jacobson left the White House, he was both excited and nervous:

I started for my hotel where Frank Goldman and Maurice Bisgyer were waiting for the President's verdict. I walked to the hotel, because it was only a few blocks away. I was still nervous and excited when I reached the Statler, and before I knew it, I found myself at the bar and drank two double Bourbons alone, something I never did before in my life. But even then I didn't go up to my room, but went outdoors and walked for another ten minutes and then went up to the room. I remember that as I entered Maurice Bisgyer was sitting on a chair and Frank Goldman was pacing the floor. When I told them the good news that the President would see Dr. Weizmann, Frank Goldman ran over and kissed me, and Maurice Bisgyer was absolutely speechless—for Maurice to be speechless under any circumstances was to me quite a miracle!

A Meeting with Weizmann

When the excitement died down, the trio made arrangements to leave for New York to see Dr. Weizmann at the Waldorf. They arrived the next morning, and Jacobson met Chaim Weizmann for the first time.

"The dear Doctor was in bed when I was introduced to him," Jacobson remembered. "When I told him of the success of my mission, he gave me the sweetest smile I have ever seen. He replied that he was ready to go at any time."

Jacobson was also introduced to Dr. Weizmann's wife, Vera. "A very lovable and gracious lady," he recalled. "She was also very appreciative of what I had done and assured me that she would have the Doctor in good shape to make his important trip."

Jacobson called Matt Connelly from New York, who told him the meeting between the president and Dr. Weizmann was set for Thursday, March 18, with the strict understanding it would be off the record. To ensure Dr. Weizmann would not be seen by representatives of the press, he was instructed to enter the White House through the East gate rather than the Northwest gate.[918]

Later, Truman wrote that during their White House meeting Weizmann "talked about the possibilities of development in Palestine, about the scientific work that he and his assistants had done that would someday be translated into industrial activity in the Jewish state that he envisaged. He spoke of the need for land if the future immigrants were to be cared for, and he impressed on me the importance of the Negev area in the south to any future Jewish state."

"I told him, as plainly as I could, why I had at first put off seeing him. He understood. I explained to him what the basis of my interest in the Jewish problem was and that my primary concern was to see justice done without bloodshed."[919]

Then it was Weizmann's turn. He looked Truman in the eye and laid down the hammer. "No one will remember you if you reject the Zionists and a State for the Jews. If you support it, you will be remembered."[920]

His cordial but frank discussion with the president lasted almost three-quarters of an hour. "And when he left my office," Truman wrote in his memoirs, "I felt that he had reached a full understanding of my policy and that I knew what it was he wanted."[921] Truman pledged to "press forward with partition."

Worried about leaks, the president did not even tell Secretary of State Marshall about Weizmann's visit.[922]

STATE DOUBLE CROSS

The next day, the US ambassador to the United Nations, Warren Austin, made a speech to the Security Council that shook Zionists around the world.

The recent UN report gave "clear evidence," Austin began, that the Jews, Arabs, and British could not agree to implement the partition plan. If the British vacated Palestine as scheduled, it would lead to chaos, fighting, and loss of life. The Security Council could not permit this to happen and had the responsibility to protect international peace.

Austin called for the General Assembly to establish a "temporary trusteeship for Palestine." In the meantime, he declared, "we believe that the Security Council should instruct the Palestine Commission to suspend its efforts to implement the proposed partition plan."[923]

Eddie Jacobson was shocked and sickened when he heard the news of the reversal. "About 5:30 in the afternoon of that day—Black Friday, it will always remain—my lawyer, A. J. Granoff called me on the telephone and told me of our country's reversal of position at the United Nations as announced that afternoon by Ambassador Warren Austin … I was as dazed as a man could be."

Almost immediately, calls and wires started coming in to Jacobson from all over America—all telling him what a terrible traitor his friend Harry S. Truman turned out to be, how he had betrayed the Jewish people, and how he had violated his promises. This bombardment continued throughout the weekend.

"There wasn't one human being in Kansas City or elsewhere during those terrible days who expressed faith and confidence in the word of the President of the United States," Jacobson remembered. "No one would listen to me, and all blamed Truman for Austin's statement, made scarcely twenty-four hours after Dr. Weizmann walked out of the Oval Room. I told them all that I had explicit faith in my friend and that faith would remain unshaken until he, himself, told me differently with his own lips. I kept on telling all who would listen that I would not and could not believe that President Truman knew or had any reason whatever to believe on Thursday what Mr. Warren Austin was going to say on Friday."[924]

Feeling "physically sick," Jacobson collapsed into bed for two days.[925]

Unfolding his Saturday morning newspapers, Truman was outraged to read about his administration's "badly bungled" about-face on partition.

"The State Dept. pulled the rug from under me today," he wrote in his diary. "This morning I find that the State Dept. has reversed my Palestine policy. The first I know about it is what I see in the papers! Isn't that hell? I'm now in the position of a liar and a double-crosser. I've never felt so in my life." Truman ranted against the "people on the 3rd and 4th levels of the State Dept. who have always wanted to cut my throat."

At 7:30 that morning, the president called his special counsel, Clark Clifford, asking him to come to the White House. "There's a story in the papers on Palestine and I don't understand what has happened." When Clifford arrived, he found an angry and frustrated Harry Truman, as disturbed as he had ever seen him. "How could this have happened?" Truman fumed. "I assured Chaim Weizmann that we were for partition and would stick to it. He must think I am a plain liar."

Clifford called Secretary of State Marshall, at that time in San Francisco, and Undersecretary Lovett, who was in Florida—both were as amazed by the trusteeship proposal as Truman. After some investigation, a State Department memorandum was discovered stating if partition proved unworkable, trusteeship should be put forth as an alternative to a political vacuum. Marshall had initialed the memo, and State Department middlemen, who were opposed to partition, took advantage of Marshall's absence and instructed Ambassador Austin to make the proposal in his speech.[926]

The New York Times reported Zionist representatives were "stunned, some near tears," while Arab delegates "indicated openly that they thought partition was dead and the victory theirs."

The UN secretary-general, Trygve Lie, agreed. He met with Austin the following day to share his "sense of shock and of almost personal grievance." He called the reversal "an attack on the sincerity of your devotion to the United Nations cause, as well as mine." Lie suggested both men resign "as a measure of protest … and as a means of arousing popular opinion."[927]

On March 21, *The New York Times* condemned the change in policy with both guns blazing. "It comes as a climax to a series of moves which has seldom been matched for ineptness, in the handling of an international issue by an American administration … Somewhere along the line there has been a shocking lack of liaison and of common purpose between the American State Department and the American delegation in the United Nations, with the White House apparently utterly at sea … We have played a shabby trick on the Jewish community in Palestine, which put its faith in our promise."[928]

Eleanor Roosevelt was so upset by the reversal she asked to resign as an American UN delegate in order to be free to speak out against it. According to the *Chicago Sun*, both Truman and Secretary of State Marshall told her she could criticize the decision as much as she cared to, but need not resign.[929]

Truman immediately sent word through Samuel Rosenman to Weizmann that "there was not and would not be any change in the long policy he and I had talked about." Weizmann accepted this pledge, and he alone among Jewish leaders took no part in the denunciation of Truman.

On Monday, Jacobson received a call from Dr. Weizmann. "This telephone call I shall never forget as long as I live, because it not only proved Dr. Weizmann to be a great statesman, but as it turned out, he was the only human being outside of myself who expressed the utmost faith in the word of President Truman."

Weizmann said, "Mr. Jacobson, don't be disappointed and do not feel badly. I do not believe that President Truman knew what was going to happen in the United Nations on Friday when he talked to me the day before. I am seventy-two years old, and all my life I have had one disappointment after another. This is just another letdown for me. Don't forget for a single moment that Harry S. Truman is the most powerful single man in the world. You have a job to do; so keep the White House doors open."

"[Weizmann] recognized the need for retaining and maintaining my relationship to the White House, because the lives of hundreds of thousands of men, women, and children depended upon it," Jacobson recalled. "You cannot imagine how this encouraged me to go on with the work which fate put on my shoulders."[930]

As for trusteeship, Weizmann thought it could never work. From his room in the Waldorf-Astoria, he composed a lengthy letter to Truman explaining why he felt trusteeship was not the answer.

> The only choice for the Jewish people is between Statehood and extermination. History and providence have placed this issue in your hands, and I am confident that you will yet decide it in the spirit of the moral law.[931]

For Truman's part, he could not repudiate his own UN ambassador's declaration without exposing the chaotic state of his relationship with the State Department. On March 20, Secretary of State Marshall hurriedly called a press conference in California to announce the new policy had been adopted when it "appeared to me after most careful consideration to be the wisest course to follow, and after President Truman approved my recommendation." Trying to create some wiggle room, he insisted it didn't necessarily mean permanent shelving of the idea of partition.

Fixing the Mess

At his regular press conference, Truman said it "had become clear that the partition plan cannot be carried out at this time by peaceful means. We could not undertake to impose this solution on the people of Palestine by the use of American troops, both on Charter grounds and as a matter of national policy ... Trusteeship is not proposed as a substitution for the partition plan but as an effort to fill the vacuum soon to be created by the termination of the mandate on May 15."

"You are still in favor of partition at some future date?" a reporter asked. Truman replied that he was trying to say that as plainly as he could.[932]

The move on the part of the State Department so infuriated Truman he planted himself firmly in the Zionist camp.

He felt he had been undermined, betrayed, deceived, and mocked by members of his own government. In addition to feelings of personal betrayal, Truman also felt the office of the president—which he believed should be treated with the utmost respect—had been maligned by the State Department. From that time forward, he paid no heed to those who sought to appease the Arabs. He did not share the State and Defense Department's worries over oil. His legendary temper had been aroused, and he was determined to have his revenge on the career men who had tried to dictate policy behind his back.[933]

By then, Truman had decided the "striped-pants boys" at the State Department who put Jews "in the same category as Chinamen and Negroes" were trying to "put it over on me about Palestine." He told his brother in a letter that he would "do what I think is right and let them all go to hell."[934]

Harry S. Truman determined the Jews would have their state, with the official blessing of the United States of America.

Chapter Twenty-Six

SHOWDOWN WITH MARSHALL

MAY 1948—WASHINGTON, DC

Truman made it clear to his cabinet and advisers that his long-term goal was partition, but as a result of Austin's trusteeship proposal, he had to allow the proposal to work its way through the United Nations. The president wanted to avoid a violent conflict in Palestine, and he opposed sending US troops to the region. He spoke his true mind when he said that partition could not currently be implemented without armed conflict, so he had no choice but to watch and wait.

When the State Department presented its proposal for trusteeship, the UN members immediately rejected it—not only the Jews and the Arabs but also the Soviet Union, which adamantly defended partition.[935]

At the same time, the Yishuv moved forward aggressively to set up a provisional Jewish government in accordance with the timetable set up by the November 29 UN resolution. They had agreed to a provisional council of government and had submitted it to the UN Palestine Commission ahead of the April 1 deadline. Dana Adams Schmidt, *The New York Times* correspondent in Jerusalem, reported "the problem of a Jewish state is no longer really one of being born but of getting a birth certificate." The Jewish state already exists—"certified or uncertified."[936]

The Arabs could not accept this reality. Dean Rusk of the US State Department told Prince Faisal of Saudi Arabia that Truman leaned toward partition. "I would not be frank," he explained, "if I did not say that the President considers partition a fair and equitable solution for Palestine." Faisal was equally frank in his response. The Arab states, he declared, "could not ever accept a Jewish State," which would be nothing less than an "abscess to the political body of the Arabs."[937]

Anticipating the British exit from Palestine, the Arabs maneuvered to take control over the area they considered exclusively their domain.

The Yishuv leadership had hoped it could work out an agreement where Abdullah would take over control of the Palestine areas designated for the Arab state by the UN partition vote. But after meeting with Golda Meir, Abdullah refused. "I have advised the Jews before to content themselves and live as citizens in an Arab state, and my army is an Arab army. I shall do as I please."[938]

At the same time, Jamal Husseini, the nephew of the Grand Mufti and the vice-chairman of the Arab Higher Committee, announced the Arabs would immediately set up their own state when the British pulled out on May 15. They intended to create "a single democratic state" for all Palestine. But when the United Nations searched for someone from the Arab Higher Committee in Palestine to negotiate a possible truce proposal, it could not find anyone available to talk to.[939]

While the Jews and Arabs made their plans, President Truman and his staff made their own preparations. David Niles wrote an announcement for the president on recognition of a Jewish state. He proposed Truman say he rejected trusteeship and that "Secretary Marshall and I have concluded that we should recognize the practical reality, since it conforms to the resolution of the U.N., to the security interests of the U.S., and to the announced and oft repeated objective of the U.S. Government."[940] The president would then announce the intention of the United States "to accord formal recognition to the Jewish Government in Palestine when it was established."

Truman didn't think the time was right for such a statement and chose to wait until he could meet with Marshall one last time. "Marshall was the American that Harry Truman admired more than any other," historian David McCullough observed. "Now for Truman to go against George Marshall was, for him, one of the most difficult moments in his entire presidency."

The two men were on a collision course regarding the US policy in Palestine. Marshall staunchly opposed American recognition of the new Jewish state. State Department officials had done everything in their power to prevent or delay the president's Palestine policy. Truman was forced to choose between the advice of George Marshall and his sympathies for the Jewish people.[941]

On May 7, one week before the end of the British Mandate, President Truman held his customary day-end Oval Office chat with his Chief Counsel, Clark Clifford. At one point, Clifford handed him a draft of a public statement he had prepared regarding the Jewish state in Palestine. Clifford suggested that Truman announce his intention to recognize the Jewish state during his next press conference on May 13, the day before the British Mandate would end.

"The President was sympathetic to the proposal," Clifford later wrote. "Keenly aware of Secretary Marshall's strong feelings, though, he picked up the telephone to get his views. As I sat listening to the President's end of the conversation, I could tell that Marshall objected strongly to the proposed statement. The President listened politely, then told Marshall he wanted to have a meeting on the subject."

"Clark, I am impressed with General Marshall's argument that we should not recognize the new state so fast," Truman said after hanging up the phone. "He does not want to recognize it at all, at least not now. I've asked him and Lovett to come in next week to discuss this business. I think Marshall is going to continue to take a very strong position. When he does, I would like you to make the case in favor of recognition of the new state."

Truman paused and looked intently at Clifford for a moment. "You know how I feel. I want you to present it just as though you were making an argument before the Supreme Court. Consider it carefully, Clark. Organize it logically. I want you to be as persuasive as you possibly can be."[942]

> "I felt that I knew what the President wanted," Clifford wrote of the preparations, "and, more important, how he felt ... From his youth, he had detested intolerance and discrimination. He had been deeply moved by the plight of the millions of homeless, the Jews had no homeland of their own to which they could return. He was, of course, horrified by the Holocaust and he denounced it vehemently, as, in the aftermath of the war, its full dimensions became clear.

"Also, he believed that the Balfour Declaration, issued by British Foreign Secretary Arthur Balfour in 1917, committed Great Britain, and by implication, the United States, which now shared a certain global responsibility with the British, to the creation of the Jewish state in Palestine.

"And finally, he was a student and believer in the Bible since his youth. From his reading of the Old Testament he felt the Jews derived a legitimate historical right to Palestine, and he sometimes cited such biblical lines as Deuteronomy 1:8: 'Behold, I have given up the land before you; go in and take possession of the land which the Lord hath sworn unto your fathers, to Abraham, to Isaac, and to Jacob.'"[943]

On May 9, Max Lowenthal suggested Clifford approach the meeting with Marshall with the argument that the Jews had already made partition a reality through their actions over the decades since the Balfour Declaration. Not only did they control the Jewish part of Palestine through their military, but they also had built all the mechanisms of government, from elected officials to postal carriers. Partition was already a reality.

The bottom line, Lowenthal argued, was that "it is unrealistic to believe that the Jews of Palestine could be persuaded to relinquish the state which they achieved largely through their own efforts."

Lowenthal advised Truman to make a statement announcing he intended to recognize the Jewish state as soon as it came into being. That act alone "would retrieve the prestige which has been lost on this issue during the past few months." It might also make the Arabs accept the reality of the situation in Palestine and accept the Jewish presence in their ancient homeland.

Lowenthal believed if Truman didn't move quickly on recognition, the Soviet Union would fill the vacuum, and then any similar action by the United States would "seem begrudging—no matter how well-intentioned" and would amount to a "diplomatic defeat."[944]

CONFRONTATION IN THE OVAL OFFICE

On May 12, the advisers gathered in the Oval Office. President Truman sat at his desk, his back to the large window overlooking the lawn. In the seat to his left sat Marshall, with his deputy, Robert Lovett. Behind Lovett were two State Department officials, Robert McClintock and Fraser Wilkins. David Niles, Appointments Secretary Matthew Connelly, and Counsel Clark Clifford sat in chairs to the right.

The meeting began in a deceptively calm manner. President Truman did not raise the issue of recognition at first. He wanted Clifford to make his arguments, but only after Marshall and Lovett had spoken, so he could assess Marshall's opposition before showing his own hand.

Marshall was concerned the Zionists did not have the manpower or weapons to wage a successful war, and that the demobilization of the US military following World War Two made the United States incapable of providing Israel immediate support.

Lovett criticized what he termed signs of growing "assertiveness" by the Jewish Agency. "On the basis of some recent military successes and the prospect of a 'behind the barn' deal with King Abdullah," Lovett said, "the Jews seem confident that they can establish their sovereign state without any necessity for a truce with the Arabs of Palestine."

Marshall interrupted Lovett, saying he was strongly opposed to the Jewish Agency's behavior. He had warned them it was "dangerous to base long-range policy on temporary military success." If the Jews got into trouble and "came running to us for help," Marshall said he had told them, "they were clearly on notice that there was no warrant to expect help from the United States."[945]

The United States, Marshall said, should continue supporting UN trusteeship resolutions and defer any decision on recognition.[946]

Truman then turned to Clifford.

"Even though I disagreed with many of Marshall's and Lovett's statements," Clifford later wrote, "I had waited without saying a word until the President called on me—in order to establish that I was speaking at his request, not on my own initiative."

Clifford attacked the State Department's proposal of trusteeship, which he argued, presupposed a single Palestine. "Partition into Jewish and Arab sectors has already happened. Jews and Arabs are already fighting each other from territory each side presently controls."

Clifford knew it was time to turn on the heat. "Mr. President, I strongly urge you to give prompt recognition to the Jewish state immediately after the termination of the British Mandate on May 14. This would have the distinct value of restoring the President's firm position in support of the partition of Palestine. Such a move should be taken quickly, before the Soviet Union or any other nation recognizes the Jewish state."

Clifford later wrote, "I knew my comment would displease Marshall and Lovett, since I was implying that State had embarrassed the President by reversing the American position in the UN two months earlier. But I strongly believed this, and I saw no reason not to bring it up."

His final point referred to the integrity of the Balfour Declaration. "Jewish people the world over have been waiting for thirty years for the promise of a homeland to be fulfilled. There is no reason to wait one day longer. Trusteeship will postpone that promise indefinitely … The United States has a great moral obligation to oppose discrimination such as that inflicted on the Jewish people."[947]

Clifford then quoted directly from a speech Truman had given as a senator in 1943. "There must be a safe haven for these people."[948]

> "Here is an opportunity to try to bring these ancient injustices to an end," Clifford continued. "The Jews could have their own homeland. They could be lifted to the status of other peoples who have their own country. And perhaps these steps would help atone, in some small way, for the atrocities, so vast as to stupefy the human mind, that occurred during the Holocaust.
>
> "I fully understand and agree that vital national interests are involved," he concluded. "In an area as unstable as the Middle East, where there is not now and never has been any tradition of democratic government, it is important for the long-range security of our country, and indeed the world, that a nation committed to the democratic system be established there, one on which we can rely."[949]

Throughout his presentation, Clifford noticed Marshall's face was reddening with suppressed anger. When Clifford finished, the secretary of state exploded: "Mr. President, I thought this meeting was called to consider an important and complicated problem in foreign policy. I don't even know why Clifford is here. He is a domestic adviser, and this is a foreign policy matter."

President Truman responded in a calm, characteristically simple way. "Well, General, he's here because I asked him to be here."

Marshall no longer attempted to conceal his anger. "These considerations have nothing to do with the issue. I fear that the only reason Clifford is here is that he is pressing a political consideration with regard to this issue. I don't think politics should play any part in this."[950]

At that point, Lovett joined in the attack. "... Such a move would be injurious to the prestige of the President. It is obviously designed to win the Jewish vote, but in my opinion, it would lose more votes than it would gain."

Lovett had finally brought to the surface the root cause of Marshall's fury—his view that the position Clifford presented was dictated by a quest for Jewish votes in a presidential election year.[951]

When Lovett concluded, Marshall spoke again. "If you follow Clifford's advice and if I were to vote in the election, I would vote against you."

"Everyone in the room was stunned," Clifford remembered. "Here was the indispensable symbol of continuity whom President Truman revered and needed, making a threat that, if it became public, could virtually seal the dissolution of the Truman Administration."

Lovett and Clifford knew this was a dangerous situation for everyone, and they stepped into the ensuing silence with words of conciliation. "We both knew how important it was to get this dreadful meeting over with quickly, before Marshall said something even more irretrievable," Clifford later wrote. "Lovett said that State's Legal Adviser, Ernest Gross, had prepared a paper on the legal aspects of recognition, and he would send it to us immediately."

President Truman also understood he had to end the meeting. Understanding Marshall's agitation, he rose and turned to him. "I understand your position, General, and I'm inclined to side with you in this matter."[952]

With this statement of conciliation, the meeting concluded. As soon as the State Department men had all exited the room, the president looked over at Clark Clifford and declared, "Well, that was rough as a cob … But you did your best … I never saw the General so furious. Suppose we let the dust settle a little—then you can get into it again and see if we can get this thing turned around. I still want to do it. But be careful. I can't afford to lose General Marshall."[953]

As the meeting concluded, less than fifty hours remained before the new Jewish nation, still without a name, would be born.

DAY OF DESTINY

Arriving at his office on May 14, 1948, Clifford immediately called Lovett. Both men were looking for ways to calm things between the president and the secretary of state. As they talked, Lovett searched for the minimum that would satisfy the president.

Then Clifford had an idea. "Look, Bob, the President understands General Marshall is not going to support him on this. Let's forget Wednesday. We're not seeking a formal retraction of what the General said. The President doesn't care whether he supports this now or never. If you can get him simply to say that he will not oppose this, that's all the President would need."

There was a brief pause at the other end of the line. "Let me see what I can do," Lovett replied.[954] At last, this was a hopeful sign.

By this time, Harry S. Truman had made up his mind on the question of partition. As president of the United States, he needed to allow the process to unfold. In the meantime, he waited for the right time to announce his decision to the world.

On April 12, Eddie Jacobson eluded reporters by entering the White House through the East Gate—"something I had never done before." Briefed in advance by Weizmann, he informed Truman that a Jewish state would be declared as soon as the British left Palestine. It was vital for the United States to recognize it. Truman "agreed with a whole heart," saying that "Henderson or a thousand Henderson's [sic] won't stop me." But he asked his friend not to mention this private pledge to anyone else.[955]

Jacobson later said he was relieved to hear "from my friend's own lips" what had really happened after Truman's meeting with Weizmann. According to Jacobson, the president "reaffirmed, very strongly, the promises he had made to Dr. Weizmann and me; and he gave me permission to tell Dr. Weizmann so."[956]

On April 23, Truman sent another message to Weizmann through Judge Rosenman. "I have Dr. Weizmann on my conscience," the president told him. Truman wanted Weizmann to know that "he would recognize the Jewish State as soon as it was proclaimed," but he asked Weizmann to keep it secret.

When he heard this news, Weizmann finally allowed himself to believe the creation of a Jewish state was imminent. Rosenman asked Weizmann to write a letter to President Truman officially requesting he recognize the new state a few days before the end of the Mandate.

Soon, Bartley Crum confirmed Truman's intentions to Weizmann and his wife, Vera. He had seen Truman on May 7 and told the Weizmanns the president intended to recognize the Jewish state on May 14. Crum advised them not to be too optimistic, however, because "one never knows what influence will be brought to bear on the president by the British, the State Department, and anti-Zionists."

"It was almost zero hour," Vera Weizmann wrote in her diary. She hoped Truman would carry out his plan on schedule because "the President will have no credit in the Jewish State's birth if his recognition comes too late."[957]

Weizmann honored Truman's request and only sent a strong encouragement to Abba Eban and the Jewish Agency delegates at the United Nations that they could not afford to lose the fight against the US trusteeship proposal. Truman would be able to act on his pledge only if trusteeship were abandoned as an option.

Eban stepped up to the challenge. Addressing the General Assembly, he declared the Jewish state was a reality in everything but name. "More force would now be needed to prevent Jewish statehood than to let it take its course ... How absurd it would be to ask a nation that had advanced to the threshold of independence to retreat back to tutelage ...

The flight from partition would be a blatant acceptance of illicit force as the arbiter of international policy."

Impressed with his performance, Trygve Lie invited Eban to lunch with other Agency leaders and UN delegates at his apartment later that day. At one point, Andrei Gromyko approached Eban. "Congratulations. You have killed American trusteeship."[958]

President Truman kept his word about not issuing a statement about his intention to recognize the Jewish state in advance. At a press conference on May 13, he was asked whether or not the United States would recognize a Jewish state. "I will cross that bridge when I get to it."[959]

Chapter Twenty-Seven

REBIRTH OF A NATION

MAY 15, 1948—TEL AVIV

On the morning of May 12, 1948, the day after Golda Meir met with King Abdullah, she received an urgent message to attend a meeting of the Jewish National Council. She sat at the conference table next to David Ben-Gurion, scribbled a note, and slid it over to him. "It didn't work. There will be war."[960]

Within two days, the Yishuv leadership had to make a final decision on independence. Meeting in the small Tel-Aviv library where he did much of his thinking, Ben-Gurion pondered the upcoming events. He called a meeting of the Council of Thirteen, a group he created to eventually serve as a provisional government.[961] Word had reached them of the presence of the Arab armies gathered at every border. As the council deliberated, members started to favor the US State Department's truce proposal.

Ben-Gurion was bound to the decision of the council. He knew the vote would be close, so he dispatched a Piper Cub to Jerusalem to fly in an Orthodox rabbi who would vote in favor of the proclamation.[962]

Ben-Gurion was in complete agreement with Weizmann's statement to the council: "Proclaim the State, no matter what happens."[963]

If the Jewish people had hesitated at this crucial hour, it could have proven fatal. Whether the council proclaimed a state or not, he believed the Arabs would invade. Declaring themselves a nation would bolster the spirit of the Jews of Palestine to fight. It would give them the mechanisms of statehood to help the Yishuv survive. With a state, they could buy arms openly on the market, just as the Arabs had done. They would also finally have the authority to open the doors of immigration to the hundreds of thousands of persecuted Jews yearning to enter the Promised Land.[964]

At the council's request, Yigal Yadin presented the Haganah's assessment of their chances.

"We have 35,000 trained fighters," the commander responded. "But less than 20,000 of them are fully armed. And as of right now, the tanks and planes that we purchased have still not arrived."

"And the Arabs?" Ben-Gurion asked.

"If Abdullah added his army, they could be 100,000."

"And all of them armed and trained by the British," Ben-Gurion declared. "Your assessment?"

"We can only be sure of two things," the commander replied. "On May 15th the British will pull out, and the Arabs will invade."

"And then?" Ben-Gurion questioned.

"The best thing I can tell you is that we have a 50-50 chance. We're as likely to win as to lose."

"On that bright note," Meir later wrote, "it was decided on a vote of 6 to 4 on Friday, May 14th, 1948, the Jewish state would be declared. Israel would be born with 5 Arab armies surrounding it, poised for attack."[965]

The Jewish National Council had just twenty-four hours to prepare for a day anticipated by Jews around the world for 2,000 years.

"I fear for our morale," David Ben-Gurion declared. Moving to bolster the council's wavering confidence, he opened a file containing two reports. Thanks to the fundraising of Golda Meir and the work of their military agents, the Yishuv possessed arms that could alter the situation on the battlefield.[966] Avriel, he slowly explained, had purchased 25,000 rifles, 5,000 machine guns, fifty-eight million rounds of ammunition, 175 howitzers, and thirty airplanes. He had also secured ten tanks, thirty-five antiaircraft guns, twelve 120-millimeter mortars, fifty 65-millimeter cannons, 5,000 rifles, 200 heavy machine guns, 97,000 artillery and mortar shells of assorted calibers, and nine million rounds of small arms ammunition.

The Arab armies would probably march into Palestine before these arms could arrive in any significant quantity. The Yishuv would have to prepare itself for a difficult fight with heavy losses. But with these new weapons en route, he nearly shouted, "I dare believe in victory. We shall triumph!"[967]

The group then took up the question of the name for the infant nation. Two names were presented—Zion and Israel. On Ben-Gurion's urging, the council chose Israel.

Three hundred and fifty invitations were sent to Jewish leaders, rabbis, and members of the Haganah. The time and place of the ceremony was to be kept secret. The council decided to hold the ceremony in the Tel Aviv art museum, which was small enough to be easily guarded, and partly below ground level in case of an air raid.

The council looked over the wording of the Declaration, written by a group of lawyers. Religious leaders refused to sign the document unless it contained a mention of God. Others refused to sign anything that did mention God. Ben-Gurion came up with a compromise. To the final line of the Declaration he added, "With trust in the Rock of Israel," a phrase that satisfied both sides.[968]

In Jerusalem, the bell tower of the Church of the Holy Sepulcher chimed another sunset. At the same time, the muezzin's call to prayer echoed down the stone streets of the Old City. The few British soldiers and civil servants remaining in Jerusalem heard those familiar sounds for the last time. The next morning, the last British soldiers would leave Palestine thirty years, five months, and four days after General Sir Edmund Allenby's arrival at the Jaffa Gate.[969]

A British Intelligence officer, Mike Scott, was engaged to a young Jewish woman and planned to move from his native army to service in the Haganah. When he asked his new superior if there was anything he could bring along with him, the answer was "a cannon."

On the afternoon of May 13, accompanied by a crane, a truck, and three British soldiers, Major Scott drove into the British army's main weapons park in Haifa. The Jerusalem command, he told the general, had just lost a twenty-five-pound gun in a road accident outside Ramallah and wanted an immediate replacement in case of trouble during the withdrawal. "Help yourself," said the general.

And so, only minutes later, in a garage on Mount Carmel, Scott delivered the Haganah's first piece of field artillery.[970]

Final Good-byes

That evening Sir Alan Cunningham bid his guests good-night just before nine o'clock and was escorted in a black Rolls Royce, flanked by two armored cars, to the studios of the Palestine Broadcasting System. The Arab station manager escorted the high commissioner to Studio A, a tiny broadcasting booth equipped with a microphone, a chair, and a table.

At exactly nine o'clock, the station manager cut in to announce "an important declaration by his Excellency the High Commissioner." The technician flipped the switch on Sir Alan's microphone and pointed his finger to indicate Cunningham was now on the air. In a brief but poignant speech, the high commissioner said his final farewell to the people of Palestine. The station manager asked Sir Alan if he wanted him to add a few phrases in Arabic before resuming the regular broadcast.

"No," the high commissioner quietly replied, "just play 'God Save the King,' please. It's perhaps the last occasion you'll have to play it."[971]

On the morning of Friday, May 14, 1948, the skeleton crew running British administration announced Cunningham would not wait for the end of the Mandate at midnight. At nine in the morning, Cunningham's bulletproof car drove out of the capital, taking him to Haifa for the homeward voyage.[972]

British soldiers who had been caught in the middle trying to keep the peace between the Jews and the Arabs deserted to one side or the other. Three soldiers in civilian clothes and carrying their weapons and ammunition walked into the home of Antoine Sabella, an Arab leader, and offered their services.

In the Jewish Quarter of the Old City, a British army private named Albert seized a Bren gun and crossed over to the Haganah—bringing not only the valuable weapon but also vital information. The British army would evacuate in only an hour. When the bagpiper began to march the British out of the Old City, the Haganah needed to be ready.[973]

The withdrawal had been under way for weeks. As soon as the British walked out of a building, the Haganah and other Jewish officials walked in. There was no formal transfer of authority from the British to their successors—they simply left, making no provision for the orderly continuation of governmental functions.

One of the few exceptions occurred on May 13, 1948, as the British army left Jerusalem. A major from the Suffolk Regiment in Jerusalem presented the key to Jerusalem's Zion Gate to Rabbi Mordechai Weingarten, the mukhtar of the Jewish Quarter.

"Not since 70 AD has the key to Jerusalem been in the hands of the Jews," the major declared. "This is the first time in 1,900 years that your people have been allowed this privilege. This is the key to the Gate of Zion. Our relationship has never been easy, but I hope we part as friends. Goodbye. Shalom."[974]

Thanks to the information from Albert, the Haganah was ready, slipping into each British post as soon as it was cleared. By nightfall, Operation *Shfifon*, or "Serpent," had achieved all its objectives in Jerusalem.[975]

THE JEWISH STATE PROCLAIMED

The Tel Aviv Museum of Art had originally been the home of Meir Dizengoff, the city's first mayor.[976] Ironically, but appropriately, the dignitaries sat in the midst of the museum's galleries containing pottery shards, stone relics, and religious artifacts of a long-slumbering Jewish civilization—one that was about to be reawakened.

At the entrance, Haganah military police carefully checked the credentials of the two hundred guests privileged to witness the rebirth of a nation after nearly 2,000 years. These dignitaries were amazingly representative of the Jewish Diaspora that had returned to Eretz Israel over the previous seventy years. Some were pioneers who, like Ben-Gurion, had cleared rocks and stumps from the fields and drained the malarial swamps. Some had miraculously survived the death camps of Nazi Germany. Others drifted back to their ancient homeland from the United States, Canada, England, South Africa, Iraq, and Egypt. They migrated from cities in the north like Minsk, Cracow, and Cologne. But for each one, Zionism was the common bond that united them and had drawn them back.[977]

Despite instructions for secrecy, news had leaked out, and a large crowd gathered outside the museum. Jewish leaders were racing the sunset to finish the ceremony before the Sabbath began at five o'clock. At precisely 4:00 p.m., David Ben-Gurion called the meeting to order. The crowd rose and sang "Hatikvah." Then Ben-Gurion lifted up a scroll of white parchment. The Tel Aviv artist commissioned to prepare the scroll did not have time to finish the job, so the text of the Declaration had been typed on a separate piece of paper and stapled to the parchment.[978] He read aloud:

> The Land of Israel was the birthplace of the Jewish people. Here their spiritual, religious and political identity was shaped. Here they first attained to statehood, created cultural values of national and universal significance and gave to the world the eternal Book of Books.
>
> After being forcibly exiled from their land, the people kept faith with it throughout their Dispersion and never ceased to pray and hope for their return to it and for the restoration in it of their political freedom.
>
> Impelled by this historic and traditional attachment, Jews strove in every successive generation to re-establish themselves in their ancient homeland. In recent decades they returned in their masses. Pioneers, defiant returnees, and defenders, they made deserts bloom, revived the Hebrew language, built villages and towns, and created a thriving community controlling its own economy and culture, loving peace but knowing how to defend itself, bringing the blessings of progress to all the country's inhabitants, and aspiring towards independent nationhood.
>
> In the year 5657 (1897), at the summons of the spiritual father of the Jewish State, Theodor Herzl, the First Zionist Congress convened and proclaimed the right of the Jewish people to national rebirth in its own country.
>
> This right was recognized in the Balfour Declaration of the 2nd November, 1917, and re-affirmed in the Mandate of the League of Nations which, in particular, gave international sanction to the historic connection between the Jewish people and Eretz-Israel and to the right of the Jewish people to rebuild its National Home.

The catastrophe which recently befell the Jewish people—the massacre of millions of Jews in Europe—was another clear demonstration of the urgency of solving the problem of its homelessness by re-establishing in Eretz-Israel the Jewish State, which would open the gates of the homeland wide to every Jew and confer upon the Jewish people the status of a fully privileged member of the community of nations.

On the 29th November, 1947, the United Nations General Assembly passed a resolution calling for the establishment of a Jewish State in Eretz-Israel; the General Assembly required the inhabitants of Eretz-Israel to take such steps as were necessary on their part for the implementation of that resolution. This recognition by the United Nations of the right of the Jewish people to establish their State is irrevocable.

This right is the natural right of the Jewish people to be masters of their own fate, like all other nations, in their own sovereign State.

Accordingly we, members of the People's Council, representatives of the Jewish Community of Eretz-Israel and of the Zionist Movement, are here assembled on the day of the termination of the British Mandate over Eretz-Israel and, by virtue of our natural and historic right and on the strength of the resolution of the United Nations General Assembly, hereby declare the establishment of a Jewish State in Eretz-Israel, to be known as the State of Israel.

Out of faith in the Rock of Israel we hereby sign by our hands our signatures as testament to this Declaration, in the session of the temporary State Council, on the soil of the homeland, in the city of Tel Aviv, on this day, Sabbath eve, Hey [5th] in Eiyar 5608, 14th of May 1948.[979]

Ben-Gurion later wrote of his feelings on the historic occasion, that there "was no joy in my heart. I was thinking of only one thing, the war we were going to have to fight."[980]

After each member of the new government had signed the proclamation, the orchestra played "Hatikvah" once again. As the music died down, Ben-Gurion declared, "The State of Israel is established. This meeting is adjourned." It had taken just thirty-two minutes to bring independence to a people who had been without a country for 2,000 years.[981]

Outside the museum, hundreds of people danced, while others wept. The news shot around the world in a flash.[982]

Final Preparations for War

Ben-Gurion wrote a simple entry in his diary that night. "Throughout the country profound joy and jubilation. And once again, as on 29th November, I feel like the bereaved among the rejoicers."[983]

Throughout Eretz Israel, Haganah officers and soldiers had the same sober reaction to the Proclamation: "…There was no time for celebrating. There were wounded and killed." These soldiers understood the state would be under attack from the Arab armies within hours.[984]

At Haifa harbor, Sir Alan Cunningham trudged up the gangway of the cruiser *Euralysus*.[985] As Cunningham stood atop a large wooden platform on the deck, the ship moved slowly into the channel, where an aircraft carrier and half a dozen destroyers of the British Mediterranean Squadron were lined up to escort her back to England. On their decks, the various crews, donning their dress whites, snapped to a salute. Coming alongside the aircraft carrier, a band on the quarterdeck played "God Save the King."

Listening to his nation's anthem fill the night air, Cunningham thought, *It's the end of the show*. As the ship gained speed and entered the open Mediterranean, the high commissioner's gaze was fixed on the outline of Mount Carmel, towering over the harbor. Then to honor Cunningham's Scottish lineage, the band played "The Highland Lament." As the cruiser finally reached the three-mile limit, she slowed to observe the act that would officially mark the end of Great Britain's Palestine Mandate. In an instant, the night sky lit up with an enormous display of fireworks of orange, red, and yellow. When the last explosion of sparks dropped quietly into the sea, Cunningham thought, *That's the end. It's all over*.

But when he looked at his watch, Sir Alan gasped—it was only eleven o'clock. The Mandate would not end for another hour. The ship's captain had forgotten to take into account the difference between British summer time and Palestine time. The British Mandate would not end in fireworks, but instead in the darkness of oncoming war.[986]

Ben-Gurion's predictions were soon proven correct. In the Declaration of Independence, he had offered the Arabs an equal place in the new state. But that night his olive branch was answered by the roar of Egyptian warplanes. At one minute past midnight, they bombed the city of Tel Aviv.[987]

ISRAEL REQUESTS US RECOGNITION

Meanwhile, in Washington, at 10:00 a.m., Clark Clifford called the Jewish Agency representative. "We would like you to send an official letter to President Truman before twelve o'clock today formally requesting the United States to recognize the new Jewish state. Please also send a copy of the letter to Secretary Marshall."

"It was particularly important," Clifford continued, "that the new state claim nothing beyond the boundaries outlined in the UN resolution of November 29th, 1947, because those boundaries were the only ones which had been agreed to by everyone, including the Arabs, in any international forum."

Epstein and his team drafted the recognition request: "My dear Mr. President, I have the honor to notify you that the state of …"

Here Epstein and Clifford had a problem, as they had not been informed of the official name of the new state. After some discussion, Epstein simply typed in "the Jewish State" and finished the letter.

Epstein handed the letter to his press aide, Harry Zinder, and told him to take it to Clifford's office immediately. As the letter was en route, Epstein got word on his shortwave radio that the new state would be called "Israel." He immediately sent a second aide after Zinder to change the letter. Two blocks from the White House, Zinder, sitting in the car Epstein had provided, crossed out with a pen the words "Jewish State" and inserted the word "Israel."

When they received Epstein's letter, Niles and Clifford began drafting the official White House reply, but there was still no word from Lovett or Marshall. In the late morning, unable to contain his concern, Clifford called Lovett and suggested they resolve the differences between Truman and Marshall. Lovett suggested they meet for lunch at the private F Street Club, not far from the White House.

Clifford brought Epstein's request for recognition, the proposed reply, and a draft of a presidential statement. In a friendly but firm manner, Lovett continued to argue against recognition. "Delay," he said, "is essential."

"Delay," Clifford responded, "is the equivalent of non-recognition in the explosive conditions that exist at this moment in the Mideast. The President was impressed, as I was, by your argument, but at 6 p.m. tonight, without action by us, there will be no internationally recognized government or authority in Palestine ... The President wishes to take action on recognition."

"Speed is essential to preempt the Russians," Clifford added. He reminded Lovett that the Soviet Union might take advantage of indecision to gain a toehold in the area. "And a one-day delay will become two days, three days, and so on."

Finally, Lovett recognized President Truman's position was absolutely firm. If the State Department did not change its attitude, the feared explosion between the president and General Marshall could not be averted.

"If Lovett wanted me to play the heavy in this minuet, by allowing me to reject their arguments one by one, partly in the name of the President, I was more than willing," Clifford later wrote. "And if he was trying to get himself and State off the hook by saying the decision was dictated by domestic politics, I thought that was an acceptable price for us at the White House to pay to get the job done."[988]

MIRACLE AT THE STATE DEPARTMENT

Around 4:00 p.m., Lovett made an unexpected telephone call to Clifford. "Clark, I think we have something we can work with. I have talked to the General. He cannot support the President's position, but he has agreed that he will not oppose it."

"God, that's good news," Clifford responded and thanked Lovett for his efforts. He asked if Marshall could call the president directly with the news. Lovett said he would try.

Marshall never did make the call himself, but Lovett confirmed Marshall's position directly with the president a few minutes later. As Lovett called the president, Clifford called Epstein at the Jewish Agency and told him the good news, swearing him to secrecy.

At 5:45 p.m., Clifford called Dean Rusk to ask him to inform Ambassador Warren Austin, the head of the UN delegation, that the White House would announce recognition of Israel right after 6:00 p.m.—the moment Israel would become a nation. Rusk had not talked to Lovett yet, and he was shocked. "This cuts directly across what our delegation had been trying to accomplish in the General Assembly—and we have a large majority for it," he responded angrily.

"Nevertheless, Dean, this is what the President wishes you to do," Clifford replied.

Still bewildered by the call from Clifford, Rusk called Austin off the floor of the General Assembly and told him what was about to happen. Stunned at the news, Austin decided not to return to the floor to signal the other delegates that he had not known in advance of the president's decision. Instead, he got into his car and went home. Still not aware of the president's decision and thinking Austin had simply gone to the washroom, his colleagues in the American delegation continued to round up votes for trusteeship.

Just after 6:00 p.m., Clifford walked to the office of Charlie Ross, the president's press secretary. Handing Ross a piece of paper, he asked him to gather the press as quickly as possible. At 6:11 p.m., Ross read the president's statement aloud to them.[989]

Simultaneously, at the UN in New York, acting ambassador of the United States, Francis Sayre, received the official news of President Truman's decision to recognize Israel. Because Warren Austin had left the building, Sayre had to make the announcement to the General Assembly—adding that he had known nothing about Truman's decision on recognition.

> This government has been informed that a Jewish state has been proclaimed in Palestine, and recognition has been requested by the provisional government thereof. The United States recognizes the provisional government as the de facto authority of the new State of Israel.

As Rusk put it, the entire General Assembly was in a "state of Pandemonium." Then in the midst of the hullabaloo, another surprise was sprung on the General Assembly.

"Scarcely had the United States pronounced these words of recognition," remembered Abba Eban, one of the Jewish representatives, "and almost unnoticed by our own delegation, which was still celebrating our American victory, Andrei Gromyko rose and said that the Soviet Union, which unlike the western powers that had abandoned the Jewish people to its dark and fearful fate, the Soviet Union recognizes the State of Israel."

"The issue of Israel's recognition was solved almost miraculously within a few hours of our independence declaration," Eban declared.

Truman weighed personal, political, and strategic concerns, then he made his own decision on what he considered best for America and for the world. The American statement recognizing the new State of Israel bears Truman's last-minute handwritten changes. American recognition came shortly after midnight in Palestine, just eleven minutes after the British Mandate officially ended. [990]

After the announcement was released to the public, Truman turned to one of his aides and said—referring to Chaim Weizmann—"the old Doctor will believe me now." [991]

He then called David Niles to let him know that he had just announced recognition. "You're the first person I called, because I knew how much this would mean to you." [992]

THE WAR BEGINS

The next day, the armies of Egypt, Syria, Jordan, and Lebanon, along with a contingent from Iraq, attacked the new State of Israel.

The war began in earnest, and the situation in Jerusalem became even more desperate for the Jews. Ben-Gurion was determined to hold the city. But Jerusalem was still cut off from the coast, and food was scarce. When a convoy did get through with precious food and ammunition, it was a joyous event. It was not certain that the Israelis could defend the new city, much less the Jewish Quarter of the Old City.[993]

Entirely cut off from the rest of Jewish Jerusalem and surrounded by hostile Arab troops, the Jewish Quarter was effectively indefensible. The soldiers assigned to this sliver of the Old City were severely undermanned and undersupplied. Like the rest of Jewish Jerusalem, they were dependent for food and other necessities on the occasional convoy coming up from Tel Aviv.

One of the fighters helping to defend the Jewish Quarter was a young girl named Esther Cailingold, originally from Great Britain. Esther had arrived in Palestine on December 1, 1946, to serve as a teacher. With the coming of hostilities, she had been assigned to guard duty in the Old City of Jerusalem. When the war erupted, she became a runner, supplying arms, ammunition, food, and drink to the various outposts throughout the quarter. She often used exposed rooftops as her means of access between posts.

On May 16, during the first sustained attack on the Quarter, Esther was slightly wounded. She quickly returned to her duties after receiving a field dressing from the medic. On May 19, a small Palmach unit broke through the Zion Gate and reached the beleaguered garrison. Esther was there to receive them. For a moment, it seemed their fortunes might have turned, but the force swiftly withdrew under heavy fire.

On that same day, King Abdullah's Arab Legion arrived at the Mount of Olives and began shelling the Jewish Quarter. As Arab ground troops advanced, it became a house-to-house battle. Esther joined one of the defending groups as a Sten gunner.

On May 26, she was seriously injured when the building she entered exploded, shattering her spine. She was carried to the Quarter's hospital, but little medical treatment was available. When the hospital came under shellfire the next day, Esther and the other wounded were moved again. She remained conscious and able to talk, reading her Bible and reciting prayers. But when the Arabs destroyed the Hurva synagogue, the Jewish Quarter soldiers surrendered on May 28 with less than forty defenders still holding out.

The Arab Legion freed the women and children and allowed them to proceed to West Jerusalem. They held the men as prisoners of war. Jordanian soldiers brought Esther, wounded but still alive, to the nearby Armenian Monastery.

Suffering with a high fever and terrible pain, Esther lay dying that Sabbath eve. There was no morphine left for her pain, but one of the orderlies leaned over and offered the only sedative he had—a cigarette. She lifted her hand and started to take it. Then she pulled her hand back. "No," she whispered weakly. "*Shabbat*." It was the Sabbath and smoking was forbidden. They were her last words.[994]

Under her pillow was a letter she had written to her parents five days earlier, anticipating the possibility she would not survive the battle of Old Jerusalem:

> Dear Mummy, Daddy and everyone:
>
> I am writing to beg of you that, whatever might have happened to me, you will make the effort to take it in the spirit that I want and to understand that for myself I have no regrets. We have had a bitter fight, I have tasted of hell—but it has been worthwhile because I am convinced that the end will see a Jewish State and the realization of all our longings.
>
> I shall only be one of many who fell [in] sacrifice, and I was urged to write this letter because one in particular was killed today who meant a great deal to me. Because of the sorrow I felt, I want you to take it otherwise—to remember that we were soldiers and had the greatest and noblest cause to fight for.
>
> Please, please do not be sadder than you can help. I have lived my life fully if briefly, and I think that is the best way— "short and sweet," very sweet it has been here in our own land … I am thinking of you all, every single one of you in the family, and am full of pleasure at the thought that you will one day, very soon I

hope, come and enjoy the fruits of that for which we are fighting. Much, much love, and remember me only in happiness. Shalom and Lehitraot [Good-bye for now],

Your loving Esther[995]

Esther soon fell into a coma and did not regain consciousness. She died at 5:00 a.m. on May 29. But she had lived to see the rebirth of the nation of Israel.[996]

Epilogue

BORN FOR SUCH A TIME

THE BEGINNING OF PEACE

After five months of intense fighting with many killed on both sides, the Israeli cabinet decided to cut their losses in Jerusalem and discontinued the war with Jordan.[997] This decision allowed the newly renamed Israeli Defense Forces (IDF) to pull troops from around Jerusalem to send against the Egyptians in the Negev.

Because Israel could redirect troops, the IDF suddenly had a clear military advantage. On October 15, the Jews launched Operation *Yoav*, or the "Ten Plagues," against Egypt with much success.

On December 11, the United Nations passed Resolution 194, calling for a cessation of hostilities and the return of refugees who wished to live in peace. Ignoring the provisions of the truce, the Egyptians denied Jewish convoys passage through the Hatta-Karatiya gap in their line. The convoys had been offered by the Jews as "bait," and the Egyptians sprung the trap, which enabled the IDF to keep fighting.[998]

The Egyptians were dug in to well-fortified positions. IDF commanders Yadin and Allon knew the Egyptians were expecting an attack against their northern lines. The Israeli leaders agreed to thrust southward, driving toward al-Auja, the anchor of the Egyptian position in the Negev Desert. If al-Auja fell, the Jews could then sweep up behind the Egyptians in a surprise maneuver.

The main road from Bir Asluj to al-Auja was well protected by Egyptian tank and artillery units. A direct assault would be suicide. Yadin grappled with this problem for nearly a week. Then he stumbled on a possible solution in his archaeological guide to Greco-Roman Palestine. There, in the classicist's map, was an ancient Roman road located just south of al-Auja. Allon ordered his scouts to determine whether the road existed. They discovered it in the dunes above Bir Asluj. The experts determined that with effort it could be made useable for the army.

During the next three nights, engineers laid boards and Bailey-bridge remnants on the damaged sections of this ancient roadway. The work was carried out as quietly as possible so that the Egyptian outpost, less than two miles away, would not be alerted to the Israeli strategy.

It worked.

On the night of December 22, Allon sent an armored column toward Gaza. He ordered another brigade of infantrymen, covered by strafing aircraft, along the main highway between Bir Asluj and al-Auja—diversions to keep the Egyptians from suspecting the main attack in their rear. As the Egyptians cautiously watched these demonstrations, a powerful Israeli column of half-tracks and troop carriers crept along the Roman road.

At dawn on December 26, the Jews came within firing range of al-Auja. As the muzzles of the Egyptian artillery faced north, expecting an attack from the main highway, the Israeli army descended on them from the rear. Despite the surprise attack, the Egyptians fought back courageously. But after a full day and night of intense fighting, they finally surrendered to the Israelis.

Allon pushed forward into Egyptian territory, quickly overrunning Abu Ageila, ten miles inside the border. He then drove his columns toward the central Egyptian base at al-Arish, cutting off the Egyptian army escape.

In a panic, the Egyptian government begged for help from the other Arab states. No one responded to the pleas. The Syrians and Iraqis were exhausted, and Abdullah considered his part of the war over. In a series of meetings between Moshe Dayan and Trans-Jordanian Colonel Abdullah al-Tel, the Legion commander in Jerusalem, the Israelis and Trans-Jordanians hammered out an agreement for a "sincere cease-fire."

Humiliated by the defeat of their army, Egyptians rioted in the streets of the major cities, largely instigated by the Muslim Brotherhood. The prime minister, Nuqrashi Pasha, reacted by outlawing the Brotherhood and ordering the confiscation of its property. In response, a member of the Brotherhood assassinated the prime minister on December 28.

With Egypt on the edge of civil war, the UN Security Council ordered an immediate cease-fire in Palestine. The British issued a stern warning against the Israelis. Unless Israel obeyed the Security Council resolution and withdrew from Egypt, the British would send its forces back into the region in accordance with a 1936 treaty of mutual defense with Egypt.

Despite their recent successes, Ben-Gurion dared not risk a confrontation with a great power. Yadin agreed the Israeli armed forces had won too much to gamble with their victory. On January 2, 1949, Allon was ordered to withdraw his men from Sinai.

On January 12, the Egyptians announced that no armistice negotiations would begin unless the Jews first evacuated the Rafah Heights, allowing the army to return across the border into the Sinai. Ben-Gurion understood that refusal of Egyptian terms would bring with it a continuation of the war on Egyptian soil and the possibility, then, of British intervention.

As he pondered his decision, he recognized that the fledgling Jewish state had, in the midst of the war, carved out an additional 600 square miles of territory. The other Arab nations had signaled their willingness to follow Egypt to the armistice table. The wise course was to allow the Egyptians the opportunity of saving face. In the second week of January, the Jews withdrew their troops from the Rafah Heights. Two weeks later, following the opening of armistice negotiations, the battered Egyptian troops crossed back into their country.[999]

THE INK FLAG

In March 1949, the IDF Alexandroni Brigade launched Operation Uvda, with naval support, taking control of part of the Dead Sea, Ein Gedi, Masada, and the potash works in the eastern Negev with no opposition from the Trans-Jordan Legion. Then the IDF completed the conquest of the Negev, capturing Eilat with no resistance.

During the capture of Eilat, the troops famously raised an improvised flag drawn in ink. The raising of this flag and the singing of "Hatikvah" by the Negev brigade soldiers in Eilat was the ceremonial conclusion of the war.[1000]

The armistice agreements determined the borders of Israel for the next nineteen years. The Arab countries never recognized those "green line" borders until after the Six-Day War when Israel had conquered additional territory.[1001]

The dream had become reality. After nearly 2,000 years, the Jews finally had a home—a nation—to call their own in their ancient homeland of Eretz Israel.

ERETZ ISRAEL, 1949

As the army drove the Arabs out of Eretz Israel, the Israeli people were going to the polls to elect their national leaders for the first time. To no one's surprise, David Ben-Gurion was elected the first prime minister of Israel. And to honor a life of service given to establish the Jewish state, Chaim Weizmann was elected by the *Knesset*—Israel's parliament—as the first president.[1002]

De jure recognition was announced by the United States on January 31, 1949, after the Israeli election. Voter turnout was 86.9 percent.[1003] The Truman administration also arranged for a $100 million loan in response to a request from Weizmann.[1004]

Israel controlled 78 percent of Mandatory Palestine—approximately 50 percent more than it had been allocated in the partition plan. The remaining 22 percent was split between Jordan in the West Bank and East Jerusalem, and Egypt in the Gaza Strip. An independent Arab state in western Palestine was never established. Not one of the Arab states recognized Israel's existence.[1005]

The United Nations made no serious attempt to enforce the internationalization of Jerusalem, which was now divided between Jordan and Israel—separated by barbed-wire fences and stretches of no man's land.

But the Yishuv paid a dear price for their victory. More than 6,000 Israelis were killed in the war—1 percent of the population—including more than 1,000 civilians. Some of these casualties were refugees and Holocaust survivors, newly arrived in the country from the DP camps in Europe.[1006]

Palestinian Arabs suffered a similar number of casualties. Egyptians officially admitted to 1,400 dead, the Jordanians and Syrians lost several hundred, and the Lebanese several dozen.[1007]

Approximately 726,000 Arabs fled or were driven out of Israel and became refugees in neighboring Arab countries. Some fled due to fear, such as those who left their homes after the Deir Yasin attack. Some fled because they believed the propaganda of the Arab national leaders who promised that the war would be short and that they would be able to return to their homes in only weeks. Others were forced out by the IDF because they cooperated with the invaders against the Jews, because they were seen as a security threat, or because they were known terrorists.

While Israel's Plan *Daled* called for temporary evacuation of strategically placed towns that could not be held, the majority of Palestinian Arabs who fled did so voluntarily. In Haifa, for example, Jewish leaders pleaded with the Arab inhabitants to stay. The same was true in Tiberias, and in many of the villages of the north that had been occupied by the Arab Liberation Army. In Beersheba and Safed, all the Arabs left before Jewish forces entered the towns. In Isdood and Majdal, most of them left when the Egyptian army departed. Towns and villages that did not resist the Israelis, or those that cooperated with them, including Abu Gosh, Nazareth, and the Druze villages of the Galilee, remained intact—and most of the people later became Israeli citizens.

The Trans-Jordanians and Egyptians, conversely, practiced systematic ethnic cleansing, expelling all Jews from territories conquered by Arab forces and refusing to allow them to return to those territories after the war. This was true in Gush Etzion, East Jerusalem, and in all the villages conquered in Gaza.

Although hostilities ceased and the armistice was signed between Israel and the individual Arab nations, the refugee problem on both sides was never solved. Negotiations broke down because Israel refused to readmit more than 100,000 refugees on the one hand, and the Arabs refused to recognize the Jewish state on the other.[1008]

In addition, beginning in 1947, the Arab League launched systematic persecution and expulsion of Jews in most Arab countries. These measures included punitive levies, confiscation of property, and abridgement of civil rights, resulting in mass migrations of Jews from Arab lands. As a result, approximately 467,000 Jews fled from Arab countries.[1009]

At the same time, thousands of Arab refugees from Palestine were forced by their Arab hosts to live in squalid refugee camps, sometimes for decades—used as propaganda props in an absurd international political theater. Jewish refugees from Arab lands, on the other hand, were immediately embraced by their fellow Jews and quickly integrated into society.[1010]

The Palestinian Arab exodus had begun in earnest after the UN partition vote and the British announcement of their withdrawal from Palestine. Many Arabs announced they would not live under Jewish rule and the exit of communal officials, village mayors, judges, and fellahin commenced. The departure of mukhtars, judges, and cadis from places like Haifa, Jerusalem, Jaffa, Safed, and elsewhere brought crippling ramifications to the Arab population. A collapse of the Palestine Arab political structure ensued after the flight of the Arab leadership—at the very moment this leadership was most needed.

Not all these people left Palestine. Approximately 240,000 Arabs crossed over into the Legion-occupied eastern sector of the country. There were 180,000 refugees who fled to Egyptian-controlled Gaza. Nearly 100,000 Arabs sought refuge in Lebanon and another 70,000 in Syria, with smaller groups traveling to Iraq, Egypt, and the Persian Gulf sheikhdoms.[1011]

Israel Established

In May 1949, exactly one year after Ben-Gurion proclaimed the modern state, the nation of Israel received full membership in the United Nations.[1012] As the Israeli flag was ceremoniously hoisted at the General Assembly building, Moshe Shertok, Abba Eban, and other Israeli participants wondered whether it could be true that only four years had passed since the Star of David had been a seal of doom for concentration camp inmates.[1013]

The newly elected Knesset immediately declared Jerusalem the capital of Israel. The borderlines were redrawn with Trans-Jordan occupying half of Jerusalem and sections of the West Bank. The Law of Return was enacted by the Knesset on July 5, 1950, declaring, "Every Jew has the right to come to this country as an *oleh* [or aliyah]." The law granted every Jew from anywhere in the world the right to become an Israeli citizen.[1014]

Within three years of Israel's rebirth, nearly 700,000 Jews returned to the Holy Land. Many of these immigrants were Holocaust survivors. One third of the Jews from Romania fled to Israel. The European Jews were joined by nearly all the Jews in Libya, Yemen, Iraq, Morocco, and Tunisia. In the ensuing years, as Détente eased tensions in the Soviet Union, thousands of Russian Jews also streamed into Israel—more than 700,000 by 1996.

CHAIM WEIZMANN

In his first official act as president of Israel, Weizmann met with President Truman on May 24, 1948, to ask for a loan that would help build the new country and settle the immigrants. It was the first time in 2,000 years that a Jewish spokesman with the rank of head of state was recognized by a sovereign power.

"The Jews have a fine tradition for repaying their debts," Truman joked. "I know it from my good friend Eddie."

In gratitude for the president's recognition of Israel, Weizmann gave Truman a Torah scroll and a blue velvet mantle embellished with the Star of David. "I take the first opportunity to express my heartfelt thanks to the President of the United States and to the government of this country for all they've done in making out of Israel, a reality."

"Well thanks, Cham," Truman responded with his trademark grin. "I've always wanted one of these."[1015]

Truman later reflected on that meeting. "Dr. Weizmann's first name was 'C-h-a-i-m', and I didn't know how to pronounce it. So I called him 'Cham'—I called him that to his face and he liked it.[1016] He was a wonderful man; one of the wisest people I think I've ever met."[1017]

"We had a long, long conversation and he explained the situation from his viewpoint, and I listened to him very carefully. At the same time, I sent for Eddie Jacobson and they both talked to me for a long, long time. When we were through, I said, 'All right. You two Jews have put it over on me, and I'm glad you have.'"[1018]

Chaim Weizmann died of a heart attack at the age of seventy-seven on November 9, 1952, leaving behind a legacy as Israel's first great diplomat.[1019]

DAVID BEN-GURION

In addition to prime minister, David Ben-Gurion was also named the first Minister of Defense—holding the two offices for fourteen years. He was later named one of *Time* magazine's 100 most important people of the twentieth century.[1020]

In 1961, a decade after Truman left office, Ben-Gurion met him in New York City. "I told [Truman] that … his helpfulness to us, his constant sympathy with our aims in Israel, his courageous decision to recognize our new State so quickly and his steadfast support since then had given him an immortal place in Jewish history." After hearing these words, Truman's eyes filled with tears.

He held Truman back for a few moments until he regained his composure, so the press waiting outside the hotel suite where they were meeting wouldn't notice. "A little later, I too had to go out, and a correspondent came up to me to ask, 'Why was President Truman in tears when he left you?'"[1021]

"I had rarely seen anyone so moved," Ben-Gurion later wrote.

When Ben-Gurion retired from political life, he moved to a kibbutz in the Negev Desert where he spent his final years writing a history of Israel. In November 1973, Ben-Gurion suffered a cerebral hemorrhage that took his life two weeks later.

GOLDA MEIR

"I never realized what John Hancock meant until I signed Golda Meir on the Declaration of Independence—me, little Golda Meir signing the Declaration of Independence."[1022]

Two days after Israel declared independence, Golda Meir traveled again to America to raise more funds for the new Israeli army. For this trip, she received the first Israeli passport ever issued. "The day when history is written," Ben-Gurion told her, "it will be recorded that it was thanks to a Jewish woman that the Jewish state was born."[1023]

After the sudden death of Prime Minister Levi Eshkol in 1969, the seventy-one-year-old Meir became the fourth prime minister of Israel—the first woman to hold the title.[1024] During her tenure, she gained economic and military aid from US President Richard Nixon, which helped her open peace talks with the Arabs.

One of the key events of her premiership was the Yom Kippur War. Syrian forces attacked from the north and Egypt from the west. After three weeks, Israel was victorious and had gained more Arab land.

Meir resigned on April 10, 1974, exhausted and willing to let others lead. On December 8, 1978, Meir died of leukemia at the age of eighty and was buried at Mount Herzl in Jerusalem.[1025]

THEODOR HERZL

Herzl boldly wrote in 1897 that he had founded the Jewish state and in fifty years everyone would know it. Remarkably, fifty years later, in November 1947, the United Nations voted to establish the Jewish state—just as Herzl had foreseen.

David Ben-Gurion wrote of Herzl: "While the Jewish state was the product of many complex historic forces, including two world wars and the labors of Herzl's many followers, it was he who organized the political force of Jewry that was able to take advantage of the accidents of history."

In accordance with his wish, Herzl's remains were removed to Jerusalem in 1949 after the creation of the Jewish state and entombed on a hill west of the city now known as Mount Herzl.

ARTHUR BALFOUR

The biblical, evangelical faith of Arthur Balfour influenced his attitudes, actions, and political decisions. This Christian heritage—which was shared by Prime Minister Lloyd George—is often overlooked by historians seeking motives for the Balfour Declaration. As a boy, he was brought up by his mother with daily Bible classes, which gave Balfour a remarkable knowledge of the geography of Palestine.

His niece, Blanche Dugdale, wrote, "Balfour's interest in the Jews and their history was lifelong, originating in the Old Testament training of his mother, and his Scottish upbringing." He regarded history as "an instrument to carrying out divine purpose."

But this religious orientation was undergirded by strategic territorial interests protecting British imperialism in the Middle East. In 1917, Palestine was the key missing link that could form a continuous chain from the Atlantic to the middle of the Pacific. These factors came together in the signing of the Balfour Declaration when Lloyd George became prime minister.

Given an earldom in 1922, Balfour's first speech in the House of Lords was to defend the British Mandate. [1026]

Soon after receiving a visit from his friend Chaim Weizmann, Balfour died on March 19, 1930.

Winston Churchill

Nine months after the British pulled out of Palestine and Ben-Gurion announced the birth of Israel, the British still had not recognized the new nation. Winston Churchill, now leader of the opposition, delivered a scathing speech in the House of Commons, railing against what he called the government's gross and glaring treatment of the Israelis and urging Britain to send an ambassador to Tel Aviv. The speech was a great success, and Britain formally recognized the State of Israel nine days later.

Churchill's old friend Chaim Weizmann, who had become Israel's first president, sent him a telegram of thanks. Churchill's brief reply was "I look back with much pleasure on our association." Then he added in his own handwriting, "the light grows." [1027]

"The Zionist ideal," he declared in 1921, "is a very great ideal, and I confess, for myself, it is one that claims my keen personal sympathy."

Together with the chief rabbis, Churchill had planted a tree on Mount Scopus to dedicate the sight of the future Hebrew University. Then he told the crowd, "I believe that the establishment of a Jewish national home in Palestine will be a blessing to the whole world … The hope of your race for so many centuries will be gradually realized here, not only for your own good, but for the good of all the world." [1028]

As colonial secretary, his 1922 White Paper led to the immigration of 300,000 Jews over fourteen years. They were in Palestine "of right and not on sufferance, and that, with due weight given to the economic absorptive capacity of Palestine, they could build up their self-governing institutions there until they were a majority, at which point they would achieve statehood."

Churchill died at the age of ninety on January 24, 1965. Both the prime minister and the president of Israel attended his funeral in London.

King Abdullah of Trans-Jordan

As the famous discussion concluded between King Abdullah and Golda Meir just before the War of Independence, their mutual friend, Ezra Danin, turned to Abdullah with concern. "Your Majesty," he cautioned, "beware when you go to the mosque to worship and let people rush up to kiss your robe. Someday a man will shoot you like that."

"*Habibi*, dear friend," the king replied, "I was born a free man and a Bedouin. I cannot leave the ways of my father to become a prisoner of my guards."[1029]

On July 16, 1951, the former prime minister of Lebanon was assassinated in Amman, amidst rumors that Lebanon and Jordan were discussing a joint separate peace with Israel. The following week, Abdullah was in Jerusalem to give a eulogy at the funeral at the Al-Aqsa Mosque when he was shot dead by a Palestinian from the Husseini clan—almost exactly as Danin predicted.

Abdullah's grandson, Prince Hussein, was at his side and was hit too, but a medal that had been pinned to Hussein's chest at his grandfather's insistence deflected the bullet and saved his life. Two years later, he succeeded his father and grandfather to become king of Jordan at the age of seventeen, ruling for the next forty-five years. In 1994, King Hussein signed a treaty with his Semitic cousins, securing peace between Israel and Jordan.[1030]

Haj Amin al-Husseini

Some evidence suggests that al-Husseini was part of the plot to assassinate King Abdullah, a significant rival to the Mufti in his quest for power in Palestine. In their discussion before the outbreak of the Israeli War of Independence, Abdullah and Gold Meir agreed, "We both have a common enemy—the Mufti."[1031]

When he learned that Yugoslavia and Hungary wanted to indict him for crimes against humanity, al-Husseini fled again from Paris to Cairo, one step ahead of the Nuremberg tribunal. There he remained as a guest of Egypt's King Farouk and later his protégé, General Gamel Abdel Nasser. From Cairo, he devoted his energies to the destruction of the State of Israel.

In 1947, the Arab League rejected the leadership of al-Husseini, who continued to insist on the total annihilation of Israel. The league instead voted in favor of the more moderate King Abdullah of Trans-Jordan, who sought peace with the Jewish state. When his cousin Abd al-Qadir al-Husseini was not appointed as commander of the Arab League forces according to the Mufti's wishes, al-Husseini formed his own militia. His nephew Mohammed Yasser Abdel Rahman Abdel Raouf Arafat al-Qudwa al-Husseini—known later to the world as Yasir Arafat—was placed in charge of arms procurement. Arafat, who became al-Husseini's protégé, said he considered it an honor to walk in Husseini's footsteps.[1032]

In 1962, al-Husseini was appointed to lead the World Islamic Congress, which was his last public office. The congress drew up resolutions to cleanse the entire Arab world of Jews. Ancient and indigenous Jewish communities throughout the Arab world were driven from their homes. As a result, few Jews remain in the Arab world today.

At the conclusion of the World Islamic Congress, al-Husseini retired from public life, spending his remaining years in Beirut, where he died in July 1974.[1033]

David Niles

Over the years of working together, President Truman and David Niles became close friends. Niles was truly devoted to Truman, and the president appreciated Niles' many contributions to both domestic and international political initiatives.

To express his appreciation, President Truman awarded him the Medal for Merit in 1947. The citation, read by the president, lauded Niles for "exceptionally meritorious conduct in the performance of outstanding service to the United States" as adviser on labor problems to the War Production Board.

In May 1951, Niles submitted his resignation, claiming fatigue after fifteen years of government service. Truman reluctantly accepted it and wrote to thank Niles for his service. "You have been a tower of strength to me during the past six years and I can't tell you how very much I appreciate it."

In retirement, David Niles wanted to travel, especially to Israel, but his health quickly declined. He lost his battle with cancer on September 28, 1952. He never made it to the Holy Land.[1034]

Eddie Jacobson

The challenges in the midst of the recognition and founding of Israel had strained their relationship at times, but in the end, it brought Harry Truman and his friend Eddie Jacobson closer together. Although he never aspired to being anything more than a haberdasher, in the strife-filled time before recognition, Jacobson found himself acting as an important mediator between the Zionist movement and the president.

"After the recognition and the State of Israel came into being, Daddy's role became even more important because there was no Ambassador yet," Jacobson's daughter Eleanor remembered. "Every bit of business that was done between Israel and the United States came through Eddie Jacobson. It came through our living room."[1035]

In December 1952, Vera Weizmann, the wife of the president of Israel, wrote a letter to Eddie Jacobson. "Only the most intimate friends knew the extraordinary role that was played by you in swinging the scale in our favour when the future looked so precarious and ambiguous … One day the world will know the part you played in helping my husband to achieve his goal … [He] was forever grateful to you."

Truman later cited as decisive in his decision to recognize the Jewish state the advice of his old business partner, Eddie Jacobson, a nonreligious Jew whom Truman absolutely trusted.[1036]

After Truman left the White House in 1953, he and Jacobson were often seen lunching together in Kansas City. In 1955, they began planning the trip of a lifetime. Truman wrote to Jacobson with the itinerary. They would leave by ship from New York for England, where Truman was to receive an honorary degree from Oxford. Then they would spend time with Winston Churchill and Queen Elizabeth. From there they would cross over the channel to Holland, where they would meet the royal family, then on to Paris to meet various political leaders. From there they would travel to Rome, where Truman and Jacobson would have an audience with the pope. Finally, to cap this adventure, they would travel to Israel by ship, arriving in the port of Haifa around mid-October.[1037]

Sadly, Jacobson died of a heart attack in October 1955. "Daddy was in the hospital for a short period of time and I went to call on him," Eleanor recalled. "I stood next to his bed and he said, 'You know, I spent all this money going to and from Washington with all this business I have to transact for the new little State. I won't have anything to leave you.' And I said, 'Daddy, you're leaving me the best thing of all! This is quite a heritage I have.'"

Truman canceled the trip and never visited Israel. After Jacobson's funeral, Truman went to the family's home to offer condolences. As tears clouded his eyes, he told Jacobson's daughters, Gloria and Eleanor, that their father was the "closest thing he had had to kinfolk."

After Jacobson's passing, Truman said of his friend and former business partner: "I don't think I have ever known a man that I thought more of outside my own family than I did of Eddie Jacobson. He was an honorable man … He was one of the finest men that ever walked on this earth … Eddie was one of those men that you read about in the Torah … if you read the articles in Genesis concerning two just men [Enoch and Noah] … you'll find those descriptions will fit Eddie Jacobson to the dot."[1038]

"Eddie was one of the best friends I had in this world," Truman told reporters. "He was absolutely trustworthy. I don't know how I'm going to get along without him."[1039]

President in His Own Right

On September 17, 1948, with most political pundits and journalists giving him little chance of winning election to the presidency, Harry Truman set out from Washington's Union Station on his first coast-to-coast whistle-stop trip of the campaign. At a rally arranged by the Democrats to send him off, vice president candidate Alben Barkley cried out, "Go out there and mow 'em down." Truman's reply became his epitaph: "I'll mow 'em down, Alben—and I'll give 'em hell."

The scrappy reply became the headline of the day. The use of the word *hell* was somewhat risqué at the time, and his daughter, Margaret, scolded him for using it. But the phrase caught on like wildfire across the country. Wherever Truman's train stopped along the campaign trail, people in the crowd would shout out, "Give 'em hell, Harry."[1040]

Truman crisscrossed the nation in the presidential railroad car, the Ferdinand Magellan. He traveled nearly 31,700 miles, averaging ten speeches every day for thirty-five days.

After weeks of speechmaking, handshaking, and traveling the rails day and night, Truman returned to his hometown of Independence, Missouri, on October 31.

On Election Day, Truman asked the Secret Service to drive him to a little resort across the Missouri River in Excelsior Springs called the Elms Hotel. Truman had left home without his luggage, so he borrowed a robe and some slippers from the hotel manager and went for a steam bath and massage. At 6:30 p.m., he returned to his room for a ham-and-cheese sandwich and a glass of buttermilk. As he ate dinner, he switched on the radio next to his bed to listen to the returns. By eight o'clock Missouri time, Dewey had pulled ahead in the important states of New York and Pennsylvania, but Truman led in the nationwide popular vote.

Around nine o'clock, Truman called Secret Service agent Jim Rowley into his room to tell him he was going to get some sleep, but Rowley was to wake him if anything important happened.

The head of the Secret Service, James J. Maloney, had traveled to New York after deciding Governor Dewey would likely be the next president. He and five agents stationed themselves outside the upper-floor suite of the Roosevelt Hotel where Dewey and his friends were waiting to go down to the packed ballroom to announce his victory.

But as the evening wore on, the mood in Dewey's suite began to sour, while the excitement in Independence, Missouri, began to build. By 11:00 p.m., Truman was still ahead in the popular vote. Well-wishers in front of the Truman house on 219 North Delaware Street had filled the sidewalks on both sides of the street and much of the front lawn. As word of Truman's lead filtered through the crowd, the people sang "For He's a Jolly Good Fellow." Suddenly, the porch light went on, and Margaret Truman came out grinning with her famous smile. Waving her arms to quiet the crowd, she announced, "Dad isn't here."

The reporters had been camped outside the house all day waiting for Truman to make a statement. Disappointed, the crowd slowly drifted away. But the lights inside the Truman house remained on as the family anxiously listened to the returns. By midnight, Truman was ahead in the popular count by more than one million votes.

And all the while, Harry Truman was sleeping.

He awoke around midnight and switched on the radio, tuning in to the NBC station and veteran broadcaster H. V. Kaltenborn. The president was ahead by 1,200,000 votes, Kaltenborn reported, but he was still "undoubtedly beaten." Truman turned off the radio and went back to sleep.[1041]

The Secret Service agents stayed awake listening to the radio through the wee hours of the night. Then at about four in the morning, Rowley received a call from the Truman headquarters at the Muehlebach Hotel in Kansas City to say Illinois had gone for Truman. The message was confirmed on NBC radio. "All of a sudden, about four in the morning comes this thing that the tide has changed," Rowley explained. "And so I figured, 'This is important!' And so I went in and told him, 'We've won!'"[1042]

"That's it," Truman exclaimed. He turned on his radio and heard Kaltenborn report he now led by two million votes, but he still did not see how Truman could possibly be elected, since in key states like Ohio the "rural vote," the Dewey vote, had yet to be tallied. "We've got 'em beat," Truman snapped, ordering his men to get his car. "We're going to Kansas City."[1043]

At the Muehlebach Hotel, Truman's childhood friend and current press secretary, Charlie Ross, was sprawled face down on a bed, completely exhausted. He remembered being awakened by someone shaking him at 6:30 a.m. "I looked up and there was the boss at my bedside—grinning. We all started talking at once."

After the commotion died down, Truman called Bess and Margaret on the telephone—both of them burst into tears at the sound of his voice.

The disheveled president then called for a barber to give him a shave and a trim. He changed into a fresh shirt and a double-breasted blue suit. Two states remained undecided at that point—California and Ohio. By 8:30 a.m., Ohio went for Truman, putting him over the top with 270 electoral votes. A celebration erupted in the presidential suite.

At 9:30 a.m., Truman was also declared the winner in California. A little after 10:00 a.m., Dewey conceded the election. A wild cheer went up on the seventeenth floor of the Muehlebach as friends, politicians, and reporters crowded into the suite.

"Thank you, thank you," Truman repeated as he shook hands with everyone in the room.[1044]

Earlier that morning, as Truman slept in Excelsior Springs, the first-edition deadline approached for the *Chicago Tribune*. With Truman leading in the popular vote but pundits still calling for a Dewey win when the rural vote came in, managing editor J. Loy "Pat" Maloney had to decide what the headline would be. Even though many East Coast polls had not yet reported, Maloney put his faith in the track record of Arthur Sears Henning, the paper's longtime Washington correspondent. Henning called the election for Dewey.

The ink was hardly dry on 150,000 copies of the paper when radio bulletins reported the race was surprisingly closer than expected. The headline was changed to DEMOCRATS MAKE SWEEP OF STATE OFFICES for the second edition. By morning, Truman was the winner in an election surprise.[1045]

On his return trip to Washington, DC, Truman stopped in St. Louis to greet a screaming crowd. He was joined by Treasury Secretary Snyder and campaign advance man Don Dawson, who handed the president an amazing historical artifact—the *Chicago Tribune* with the infamous headline, DEWEY DEFEATS TRUMAN.[1046] Holding up his least favorite newspaper with both hands, grinning from ear to ear, he shouted to the crowd, "That's one for the books!"

In Washington, the *Tribune's* political correspondent, Arthur Sears Henning, was informed that effective Inauguration Day, 1949, he would no longer be employed by the newspaper.[1047]

In 1945, Truman had taken the oath of office in a private ceremony several hours after Roosevelt's death, shaken and unsure of his ability to lead the country. In 1949, millions of Americans watched on their new TVs as he repeated the oath. Truman's left hand was on two Bibles—a large facsimile of the Gutenberg Bible given to him by the people of Independence and the Bible he had used when he took the oath in 1945.

He was now the president of the United States in his own right.

TRUMAN AND ISRAEL

A few days after partition was adopted by the United Nations, crowds overflowed a theater in New York City. Outside, more than five thousand people listened to the speeches broadcast over loudspeakers. Emanuel Neumann of the Zionist Organization of America gave credit to President Harry S. Truman. "If we now have this decision of the United Nations, it is due in very large measure, perhaps the largest measure, to the sustained interest and the unflagging efforts of President Truman."[1048]

"Palestine was," his daughter, Margaret, pointed out, "the most difficult dilemma of his entire administration."[1049]

Truman later spoke of his reasons for recognizing the State of Israel. "Hitler had been murdering Jews right and left. I saw it, and I dream about it even to this day. The Jews needed some place where they could go. It is my attitude that the American government couldn't stand idly by while the victims [of] Hitler's madness are not allowed to build new lives."[1050]

After Israel was created, Truman pondered his role in the return of the Jews to Eretz Israel and how this could possibly be connected to biblical prophecy. The president often had long talks with friend and counsel Clark Clifford about the Jews' return to Zion in the Old Testament. Clifford considered himself an amateur Bible student, and the two exchanged

Scripture verses on the subject. Truman was moved by the passages in Genesis that speak of the Promised Land as "an everlasting possession."

This was confirmed by Alfred Lilienthal, an Arabist State Department official and staunch opponent of partition and recognition. Lilienthal was a consultant to the US delegation to the United Nations during its founding conference. He observed that Truman "was a biblical fundamentalist who constantly pointed to these words of the Old Testament," citing the passage from Deuteronomy 1:8.[1051]

For Truman—after thoroughly considering all his political options and the information presented to him by the experts—these passages were confirmation from a higher authority that he was making the right decision regarding recognition of Israel.

In the spring of 1949, Eliahu Elath joined Israel's Chief Rabbi, Isaac Halevi Herzog, for a meeting with the president in the White House. Truman asked Rabbi Herzog if he knew what he had done for the refugees and to establish Israel. Herzog "reflected for a moment and replied that when the President was still in his mother's womb ... the Lord had bestowed upon him the mission of helping his Chosen People at a time of despair and aiding in the fulfillment of His promise of Return to the Holy Land."

In ancient times, Rabbi Herzog continued, "a similar mission had once been imposed on the head of another great country, King Cyrus of Persia, who had also been given the task of helping to redeem the Jews from their dispersion and restoring them to the land of their forefathers." Then the rabbi read aloud the words of Cyrus: "The Lord God of heaven hath ... charged me to build him a House at Jerusalem, which is in Judah."

As Truman listened to this biblical quote "he rose from his chair and with great emotion, tears glistening in his eyes ... turned to the Chief Rabbi and asked him if his actions for the sake of the Jewish people were indeed to be interpreted thus and the hand of the Almighty was in the matters." The rabbi answered that "he had been given the task once fulfilled by the mighty king of Persia, and that he too, like Cyrus, would occupy a place of honor in the annals of the Jewish people."[1052]

"God put you in your mother's womb," Herzog concluded, "so you would be the instrument to bring the rebirth of Israel after two thousand years."

"I thought he was overdoing things," remembered David Niles, "but when I looked over at the President, tears were running down his cheeks."[1053]

Despite their differences with Truman on some of his decisions as president, over time, most Israelis and Jews around the world came to understand the importance of Harry S. Truman's actions in the rebirth of Israel. The new state needed the recognition of the world's great powers for legitimacy to survive. Truman was the first to give them this vital recognition and then his steadfast support. David Niles, who worked closely with both FDR and Truman, concluded that if Roosevelt had lived and Truman had not been president, there probably would not have been an Israel.[1054]

"He was the one who helped the Jews rebuild the 3rd Jewish Commonwealth," said presidential historian Troy Gil. "And he was the one who history was fortunate enough to have in the right place at the right time. History was fortunate; the American people were fortunate; the Jewish people were fortunate. He was a true hero."[1055]

Truman never forgot the words of Rabbi Herzog. Soon after leaving the White House in 1953, he was invited to speak at the Jewish Theological Seminary in New York City. His friend Eddie Jacobson rose and said he was introducing the man who had helped create Israel. Truman stood amidst the applause and strode to the podium. When the applause finally subsided, he turned to his old friend and declared, "Helped create Israel? I am Cyrus. I am Cyrus!"[1056]

ENDNOTES

1. Garry K. Brantley, M.A., M.Div., "The Conquest of Canaan: How and When?," Compositebiblereflections.blogspot.com, 2018, http://compositebiblereflections.blogspot.com/2017/03/the-conquest-of-canaan-how-and-when-by.html.

2. "The Babylonian Exile," Jewish Virtual Library, American-Israeli Cooperative Enterprise (hereafter cited as AICE), 2018, https://www.jewishvirtuallibrary.org/the-babylonian-exile.

3. *The Hope*, CBN Documentaries, Virginia Beach, VA: The Christian Broadcasting Network (hereafter cited as CBN), 2015, DVD.

4. Alfred Steinberg, *The Man from Missouri: The Life and Times of Harry S. Truman* (New York: G. G. Putnam & Sons, 1962), 20.

5. Jewish Virtual Library, "The Babylonian Exile."

6. "After the Babylonian Exile," Jewish Virtual Library, AICE, 2018. https://www.jewishvirtuallibrary.org/after-the-babylonian-exile.

7. Nick McCarty, *Alexander the Great: The Real-Life Story of the World's Greatest Warrior King* (New York: Gramercy Books, 2004), 31.

8. Roger B. Beck, *World History: Patterns of Interaction* Reprinted (New York: McDougal Littell, 1999), 131. Page references are to the 1999 edition.

9. "The Maccabees/Hasmoneans," Jewish Virtual Library, AICE, 2018. https://www.jewishvirtuallibrary.org/the-maccabees-hasmoneans.

10. Jewish Virtual Library, "The Maccabees/Hasmoneans."

11. Beck, *World History,* 153.

12. "First Jewish-Roman War," Historynct, Historynet.com, 2018, http://www.historynet.com/first-jewish-roman-war.htm.

13. "Visual Timeline: The Story of the Jews with Simon Schama," pbs.org, Public Broadcasting System (hereafter cited as PBS), 2018, http://www.pbs.org/wnet/story-jews/explore-the-diaspora/visual-timeline/.

14. "The Bar-Kokhba Revolt 132–135 CE," Jewish Virtual Library, AICE, 2018, https://www.jewishvirtuallibrary.org/the-bar-kokhba-revolt-132-135-ce.

15. Jacqueline Schaalje, "Ancient Synagogues in Bar'am and Capernaum," *The Jewish Magazine*, June 2001, http://www.jewishmag.com/44mag/synagogues/synagogues.htm.

16 "Jewish Diaspora," Wikipedia, Wikimedia Foundation, https://en.wikipedia.org/wiki/Jewish_diaspora.

17 Robert Silverberg, *If I Forget Thee, O Jerusalem* (New York: Pyramid Communications, 1970), 9. Page references are to the 1972 Pyramid edition.

18 "Jewish History," Wikipedia, Wikimedia Foundation, https://en.wikipedia.org/wiki/Jewish_history.

19 "History of the Jews in the Roman Empire," Wikipedia, Wikimedia Foundation, https://en.wikipedia.org/wiki/History_of_the_Jews_in_the_Roman_Empire.

20 "Palestine under Persian, Byzantine and Arab Rule," My Jewish Learning, http://www.myjewishlearning.com/article/palestine-under-persian-byzantine-and-arab-rule/

21 John L. Espositio, *Islam: The Straight Path,* 1st ed. (New York/Oxford: Oxford University Press, 1988), 37–67. http://www-personal.umich.edu/~vika/TeachPort/islam00/esposito/chapt2.html.

22 "Dome of the Rock," Encyclopedia Brittanica, https://www.britannica.com/topic/Dome-of-the-Rock.

23 "Jerusalem Captured in First Crusade," History, http://www.history.com/this-day-in-history/jerusalem-captured-in-first-crusade.

24 PBS, "Visual Timeline." http://www.pbs.org/wnet/story-jews/explore-the-diaspora/visual-timeline/.

25 "Mamluk," The Columbia Encyclopedia, 6th ed., http://www.encyclopedia.com/history/asia-and-africa/egyptian-history/mamluk.

26 PBS, "Visual Timeline."

27 W. D. Rubinstein, *A History of the Jews in the English-Speaking World: Great Britain* (New York: Macmillan Press, 1996), 39.

28 Bernard Glassman, *Anti-Semitic Stereotypes without Jews: Images of the Jews in England 1290-1700* (Detroit: Wayne State University Press, 1975), 16.

29 "A Day in the Life of 13th-Century England," BBC, http://www.bbc.co.uk/radio4/history/sceptred_isle/page/27.shtml?question=27.

30 David Ross, "The Edict of Expulsion," Express.com, http://www.britainexpress.com/History/medieval/expulson-jews.htm.

31 PBS, "Visual Timeline."

32 Silverberg, *If I Forget Thee,* 58–59.

33 Chuck Morse, *The Nazi Connection to Islamic Terrorism: Adolf Hitler and Haj Amin Al-Husseini* (Washington, DC: WND Books, 2010), 15.

34 CBN Documentaries, *The Hope*, 2015.

35 James Fin, *Letter to the Earl of Clarendon, Jerusalem, September 15, 1857*, British Foreign Office, 78/1294 (Pol. No. 36), 249–52.

36 H. B. Tristram, *The Land of Israel: A Journal of Travels in Palestine* (London: 1865): 490, quoted in "Palestine, a land virtually laid waste with little population," EretzYisroel.Org, http://www.eretzyisroel.org/~peters/depopulated.html.

37 Mark Twain, *The Innocents Abroad* (New York: The Modern Library / Random House, 2003), 361.

38 Twain, *Innocents Abroad*, 386.

39 "Mark Twain Quotations on Judaism and Israel," Jewish Virtual Library, AICE, 2018, http://www.jewishvirtuallibrary.org/mark-twain-quotations-on-judaism-and-israel.

40 Twain, *Innocents Abroad*, 456.

41 "Moses Montefiore," Wikipedia, Wikimedia Foundation, https://en.wikipedia.org/wiki/Moses_Montefiore.

42 CBN Documentaries, *The Hope*, 2015.

43 CBN Documentaries, *The Hope*, 2015.

44 Wikipedia, "Moses Montefiore."

45 David Ben-Gurion, *Israel: A Personal History* (New York: Funk and Wagnalls, Inc., 1971), 16.

46 CBN Documentaries, *The Hope*, 2015.

47 Jack Fellman, "Hebrew: Eliezer Ben-Yehuda & the Revival of Hebrew," Jewish Virtual Library, AICE, 2018, http://www.jewishvirtuallibrary.org/eliezer-ben-yehuda-and-the-revival-of-hebrew.

48 CBN Documentaries, *The Hope*, 2015.

49 Benjamin Balint, "Confessions of a Polyglot," Haaretz, Haaretz Daily Newspaper, Ltd., www.haaretz.com/news/confessions-of-a-polyglot-1.258033.

50 CBN Documentaries, *The Hope*, 2015.

51 CBN Documentaries, *The Hope*, 2015.

52 Fellman, "Eliezer Ben-Yehuda."

53 Fellman, "Eliezer Ben-Yehuda."

54 Hatzvi, 1886, found in Fellman, "Eliezer Ben-Yehuda & the Revival of Hebrew," Jewish Virtual Library, AICE, 2018, www.jewishvirtuallibrary.org/jsource/biography/ben_yehuda.html.

55 Fellman, "Eliezer Ben-Yehuda."

56 Tom Ivy, dir. *Against All Odds: Israel Survives* (American Trademark Pictures, 2005), 6-disc DVD.

57 Howard M. Sachar, *A History of Israel: From the Rise of Zionism to Our Time* (New York: Knopf, 1976), 12.

58 "Pale of Settlement," The Yivo Encyclopedia of Jews in Eastern Europe, http://www.yivoencyclopedia.org/article.aspx/Pale_of_Settlement.

59 "Shtetl," Encyclopedia Judaica, http://www.jewishvirtuallibrary.org/shtetl.

60 PBS, "Visual Timeline."

61 "What Are the Origins of Zionism," ProCon.org, http://israelipalestinian. procon.org/view.answers.php?questionID=000347&print=true.

62 David Wollenberg, "The Myth of Jewish 'Colonialism': Demographics and Development in Palestine," *Harvard Israel Review*, http://www.hcs.harvard.edu/~hireview/content.php?type=article&issue=spring01/&name=myth.

63 "Petah Tikva," WikiVisually, Wikimedia Foundation, http://wikivisually.com/wiki/Petah_Tikva.

64 "Israel Belkind," Jewish Virtual Library, AICE, http://www.jewishvirtuallibrary.org/israel-belkind.

65 CBN Documentaries, *The Hope*, 2015.

66 David Ben-Gurion, *Memoirs* (Cleveland, OH: World Publishing, 1970), 32.

67 Chaim Weizmann, *Trial and Error: The Autobiography of Chaim Weizmann* (Philadelphia: The Jewish Publication Society of America, 1949), 11.

68 Ben-Gurion, *Memoirs*, 11.

69 CBN Documentaries, *The Hope*, 2015.

70 Alex Bein, *Theodore Herzl* (Philadelphia: The Jewish Publication Society of America, 1941), 10.

71 Bein, *Theodor Herzl*, 4–8.

72 Rabbi Deborah Bravo, "Theodor Herzl and the Dream," Rabbi Deborah Bravo, http://www.rabbibravo.com/theodore-herzl-and-the-dream.html

73 Bein, *Theodore Herzl*, 10.

74 Bein, *Theodore Herzl*, 11.

75 David Collier, "The Jewish State," Beyond the Great Divide, http://david-collier.com/the-jewish-state-theodor-herzl/.

76 Bein, *Theodore Herzl*, 13–14.

77 CBN Documentaries, *The Hope*, 2015.

78 Bein, *Theodore Herzl*, 19–20.

79 Bein, *Theodore Herzl*, 19–20.

80 Bein, *Theodore Herzl*, 21–22.

81 Bein, *Theodore Herzl*, 21–22.

82 Sachar, *History of Israel*, 37.

83 Bein, *Theodore Herzl*, 36–37.

84 Sachar, *History of Israel*, 37.

85 Bein, *Theodore Herzl*, 80–82.

86 CBN Documentaries, *The Hope*, 2015.

87 Sachar, *History of Israel*, 38.

88 Bein, *Theodore Herzl*, 94–95.

89 Bein, *Theodore Herzl*, 108.

90 Bein, *Theodore Herzl*, 109-111.

91 Sachar, *History of Israel*, 38.

92 CBN Documentaries, *The Hope*, 2015.

93 Silverberg, *If I Forget Thee*, 42.

94 Bein, *Theodore Herzl*, 115–116.

95 Ben-Gurion, *Memoirs*, 36.

96 CBN Documentaries, *The Hope*, 2015.

97 Sachar, *History of Israel*, 41.

98 Silverberg, *If I Forget Thee*, 44.

99 Theodor Herzl, "The Jewish State," 1896, *MidEast Web*, http://www.mideastweb. org/jewishstate.pdf.

100 Weizmann, *Trial and Error*, 43–44.

101 Sachar, *History of Israel*, 40.

102 David Ben-Gurion, *Recollections* (London: Macdonald Unit 75, 1970), 34–35.

103 Louis Lipsky, "Introduction to The Jewish State," Project Gutenburg, https://www.gutenberg.org/files/25282/25282-h/25282-h.htm

104 Bein, *Theodore Herzl*, 191.

105 Theodor Herzl, "The Complete Diaries of Theodor Herzl," Internet Archive, https://archive.org/stream/TheCompleteDiariesOfTheodorHerzl_201606/TheCompleteDiariesOfTheodorHerzlEngVolume1_OCR_djvu.txt.

106 CBN Documentaries, *The Hope*, 2015.

107 CBN Documentaries, *The Hope*, 2015.

108 Lipsky, "Introduction to The Jewish State."

109 Bein, *Theodore Herzl*, 193.

110 Bein, *Theodore Herzl*, 199–201.

111 Sachar, *History of Israel,* 44.

112 Sachar, *History of Israel,* 54.

113 Bein, *Theodore Herzl*, 214–215.

114 CBN Documentaries, *The Hope*, 2015.

115 Bein, *Theodore Herzl*, 229.

116 Sachar, *History of Israel,* 45.

117 CBN Documentaries, *The Hope*, 2015.

118 Bein, *Theodore Herzl*, 233.

119 Silverberg, *If I Forget Thee,* 44.

120 "The Balfour Declaration," Wikipedia, Wikimedia Foundation, http://en.wikipedia.org/wiki/The_Balfour_Declaration.

121 Bein, *Theodore Herzl*, 240.

122 Bein, *Theodore Herzl*, 241–241.

123 Bein, *Theodore Herzl*, 243.

124 Silverberg, *If I Forget Thee,* 46.

125 Sachar, *History of Israel,* 46.

126 Sachar, *History of Israel,* 49.

127 Bein, *Theodore Herzl*, 300.

128 Bein, *Theodore Herzl*, 307.

129 Lipsky, "Introduction to The Jewish State."

130 Sachar, *History of Israel,* 51.

131 Bein, *Theodore Herzl*, 355–356.

132 Bein, *Theodore Herzl*, 357–358.

133 Bein, *Theodore Herzl*, 372.

134 Bein, *Theodore Herzl*, 376.

135 Sachar, *History of Israel,* 53.

136 Silverberg, *If I Forget Thee,* 47–48.

137 CBN Documentaries, *The Hope*, 2015.

138 Sachar, *History of Israel,* 59.

139 CBN Documentaries, *The Hope*, 2015.

140 Sachar, *History of Israel,* 61.

141 Weizmann, *Trial and Error,* 83–84.

142 Silverberg, *If I Forget Thee,* 47–48.

143 Weizmann, *Trial and Error,* 85.

144 Weizmann, *Trial and Error,* 85–86.

145 Sachar, *History of Israel,* 61.

146 Weizmann, *Trial and Error,* 87–88.

147 Weizmann, *Trial and Error,* 88.

148 Sachar, *History of Israel,* 63.

149 Silverberg, *If I Forget Thee,* 48.

150 Melvin I. Urofsky, *American Zionism from Herzl to the Holocaust* (Lincoln: University of Nebraska Press, 1995), 132.

151 Weizmann, *Trial and Error,* 92.

152 CBN Documentaries, *The Hope*, 2015.

153 Weizmann, *Trial and Error,* 92.

154 Ben Halpern, *A Clash of Heroes: Brandeis, Weizmann, and American Zionism* (New York: Oxford University Press, 1987), 38.

155 Allis Radosh and Ronald Radosh, *A Safe Haven: Harry S. Truman and the Founding of Israel* (New York: Harper Perennial, 2009), 4.

156 Silverberg, *If I Forget Thee,* 49.

157 CBN Documentaries, *The Hope*, 2015.

158 Radosh and Radosh, *A Safe Haven*, 4.

159 Weizmann, *Trial and Error*, 74.

160 Weizmann, *Trial and Error,* 67–68.

161 Weizmann, *Trial and Error*, 93.

[162] Silverberg, *If I Forget Thee,* 49–50.

[163] Weizmann, *Trial and Error,* 95–96.

[164] Halpern, *Clash of Heroes,* 42.

[165] Weizmann, *Trial and Error,* 95.

[166] Weizmann, *Trial and Error,* 105–106.

[167] Halpern, *Clash of Heroes,* 47.

[168] CBN Documentaries, *The Hope*, 2015.

[169] Silverberg, *If I Forget Thee,* 50.

[170] Silverberg, *If I Forget Thee,* 50.

[171] Weizmann, *Trial and Error,* 110.

[172] Weizmann, *Trial and Error,* 110–111.

[173] CBN Documentaries, *The Hope*, 2015.

[174] Silverberg, *If I Forget Thee,* 51.

[175] CBN Documentaries, *The Hope*, 2015.

[176] Martin Gilbert, *Churchill and the Jews: A Lifelong Friendship* (New York: Henry Holt and Company, 2007), 4.

[177] CBN Documentaries, *The Hope*, 2015.

[178] Gilbert, *Churchill and the Jews,* 10–11.

[179] Gilbert, Martin, *Churchill and the Jews*, xv.

[180] CBN Documentaries, *The Hope*, 2015.

[181] Silverberg, *If I Forget Thee,* 52.

[182] CBN Documentaries, *The Hope*, 2015.

[183] "Chaim Weizmann," Wikipedia, Wikimedia Foundation, http://en.wikipedia.org/wiki/Chaim_Weizmann

[184] CBN Documentaries, *The Hope*, 2015.

[185] CBN Documentaries, *The Hope*, 2015.

[186] Ivy, *Against All Odds*, 2005.

[187] CBN Documentaries, *The Hope*, 2015.

[188] Weizmann, *Trial and Error,* 125–127.

[189] Weizmann, *Trial and Error,* 130.

[190] Silverberg, *If I Forget Thee,* 53.

[191] Silverberg, *If I Forget Thee,* 53.

[192] CBN Documentaries, *The Hope*, 2015.

[193] Silverberg, *If I Forget Thee,* 53.

[194] Silverberg, *If I Forget Thee,* 82.

[195] T. R. Fyvel, "Weizmann and the Balfour Declaration" in *Chaim Weizmann: A Biography by Several Hands*, ed. Meyer W. Weisggal and Joel Carmichael, (London: Weidenfeld and Nicolson, 1962), 148.

[196] Fyvel, "Weizmann," in Weisggal and Carmichael, *Chaim Weizmann*, 148.

[197] Weizmann, *Trial and Error,* 157.

[198] Weizmann, *Trial and Error,* 148.

[199] Silverberg, *If I Forget Thee,* 85.

[200] Simon Sebag Montefiore, *Jerusalem: The Biography* (New York: Knopf, 2011), 429.

[201] CBN Documentaries, *The Hope*, 2015.

[202] David Fromkin, *A Peace to End All Peace: The Fall of the Ottoman Empire and the Creation of the Modern Middle East* (New York: Henry Holt and Company, 1989), 285.

[203] Fyvel, "Weizmann," in Weisggal and Carmichael, *Chaim Weizmann*, 149.

[204] Fyvel, "Weizmann," in Weisggal and Carmichael, *Chaim Weizmann*, 150.

[205] Sachar, *History of Israel,* 100.

[206] Fyvel, "Weizmann," in Weisggal and Carmichael, *Chaim Weizmann*, 151–152.

[207] Silverberg, *If I Forget Thee,* 85–87.

[208] Fromkin, *Peace to End All Peace,* 287.

[209] Silverberg, *If I Forget Thee,* 87.

[210] Fromkin, *Peace to End All Peace,* 287.

[211] Silverberg, *If I Forget Thee,* 88–89.

[212] Silverberg, *If I Forget Thee,* 89–90.

[213] Silverberg, *If I Forget Thee,* 89–90.

[214] Fyvel, "Weizmann," in Weisggal and Carmichael, *Chaim Weizmann*, 157.

[215] Sachar, *History of Israel,* 107.

[216] Fromkin, *Peace to End All Peace,* 293.

[217] "Behind the Balfour Declaration: Britain's Great War Pledge to Lord Rothschild," Robert John, Institute for Historical Review, http://www.ihr.org/jhr/v06/v06p389_john.html.

218 Silverberg, *If I Forget Thee,* 93.

219 Fromkin, *Peace to End All Peace,* 268.

220 Fromkin, *Peace to End All Peace,* 267.

221 Sachar, *History of Israel,* 99.

222 Barbara W. Tuchman, *Bible and Sword: England and Palestine from the Bronze Age to Balfour* (New York: Ballantine Books / Random House, 1984), chap. 7.

223 Michael B. Oren, *Power, Faith, and Fantasy: America in the Middle East 1776 to Present* (New York: W. W. Norton & Company, 2007), 221.

224 Fromkin, *Peace to End All Peace,* 269.

225 Fromkin, *Peace to End All Peace,* 269.

226 Silverberg, *If I Forget Thee,* 92–93.

227 Weizmann, *Trial and Error,* 207.

228 Sachar, *History of Israel,* 108.

229 Urofsky, *American Zionism,* 220.

230 Radosh and Radosh, *Safe Haven,* 4.

231 Weizmann, *Trial and Error,* 157.

232 Silverberg, *If I Forget Thee,* 94–95.

233 Sachar, *History of Israel,* 109.

234 Weizmann, *Trial and Error,* 211.

235 Sachar, *History of Israel,* 111.

236 Fromkin, *Peace to End All Peace,* 298.

237 Sachar, *History of Israel,* 116.

238 Sachar, *History of Israel,* 110.

239 Sachar, *History of Israel*, 110.

240 "Edmund Allenby," Wikipedia, Wikimedia Foundation, https://en.wikipedia.org/wiki/Edmund_Allenby,_1st_Viscount_Allenby.

241 Major Vivian Gilbert, "The Romance of the Last Crusade," 1923, 183–186, Internet Archive, https://ia601700.us.archive.org/16/items/romanceoflastcru00vivi/romanceoflastcru00vivi.pdf.

242 Ivy, *Against All Odds*, 2005.

243 Weizmann, *Trial and Error,* 213.

244 Weizmann, *Trial and Error,* 214.

245 Silverberg, *If I Forget Thee,* 103.

246 Weizmann, *Trial and Error,* 218.

247 Weizmann, *Trial and Error,* 219.

248 Weizmann, *Trial and Error*, 219.

249 Silverberg, *If I Forget Thee,* 103.

250 Weizmann, *Trial and Error,* 221.

251 "The Protocols of the Elders of Zion," Jewish Virtual Library, AICE, 2018, http://www.jewishvirtuallibrary.org/the-ldquo-protocols-of-the-elders-of-zion-rdquo.

252 Weizmann, *Trial and Error,* 217–218.

253 O'Brien, *The Siege*, 160.

254 Weizmann, *Trial and Error,* 223.

255 O'Brien, *The Siege,* 144.

256 Weizmann, *Trial and Error,* 224.

257 Ivy, *Against All Odds*, 2005.

258 Silverberg, *If I Forget Thee,* 103.

259 Weizmann, *Trial and Error,* 232.

260 Silverberg, *If I Forget Thee,* 103–104.

261 Weizmann, *Trial and Error,* 233–234.

262 O'Brien, *The Siege,* 144.

263 Silverberg, *If I Forget Thee,* 104.

264 Sachar, *History of Israel,* 120.

265 Sachar, *History of Israel,* 121.

266 Silverberg, *If I Forget Thee,* 104.

267 Sachar, *History of Israel,* 120.

268 Weizmann, *Trial and Error,* 236.

269 Isaiah Berlin, "The Biographical Facts," in *Chaim Weizmann: A Biography by Several Hands*, ed. Meyer W. Weisggal and Joel Carmichael, (London: Weidenfeld and Nicolson, 1962), 38.

270 Robert Silverberg, *If I Forget Thee,* 105.

271 Chaim Weizmann, *Trial and Error,* 237.

272 Aharon Katzir-Katchalsky, "Vision Versus Fantasy," in *Chaim Weizmann: A Biography by Several Hands*, ed. Meyer W. Weisggal and Joel Carmichael, (London: Weidenfeld and Nicolson, 1962), 135.

273 Weizmann, *Trial and Error,* 236–237.

274 Oren, *Power, Faith, and Fantasy*, 391.

275 Oren, *Power, Faith, and Fantasy*, 380.

276 Weizmann, *Trial and Error,* 194.

277 Oren, *Power, Faith, and Fantasy*, 391.

278 Oren, *Power, Faith, and Fantasy*, 382.

279 Silverberg, *If I Forget Thee,* 113.

280 Chris Mitchell, *Dateline Jerusalem* (Nashville: Thomas Nelson. 2013), 120.

281 CBN Documentaries, *The Hope*, 2015.

282 "The San Remo Conference," Jewish Virtual Library, https://www.jewish-virtuallibrary.org/the-san-remo-conference

283 Mitchell, *Dateline Jerusalem*, 118.

284 "The San Remo Conference," Jewish Virtual Library, https://www.jewish-virtuallibrary.org/the-san-remo-conference

285 Oren, *Power, Faith, and Fantasy*, 383.

286 Emir Faisal, "Jews and Arabs in Syria: The Emir Feisul Looks To A Bright Future," *The Times*, Thursday, December 12, 1918, page 7; Issue 41971; column B, quoted in https://en.wikipedia.org/wiki/Faisal-Weizmann_Agreement

287 Weizmann, *Trial and Error,* 246.

288 "Faisal-Weizmann Agreement," Wikipedia, Wikimedia Foundation, https://en.wikipedia.org/wiki/Faisal-Weizmann_Agreement.

289 A. L. Tibawi, *A Modern History of Syria Including Lebanon and Palestine* (Macmillan St. Martin's Press, 1969), 318, quoted in Ayse Tekdal Fildis, *The Troubles in Syria: Spawned by French Divide and Rule*, Middle East Policy Council, XVIII, no. 4 (Winter 2011), http://www.mepc.org/journal/middle-east-policy-archives/troubles-syria-spawned-french-divide-and-rule.

290 Eliezer Tauber, *The Formation of Modern Syria and Iraq* (Frank Cass and Co. Ltd., Portland, OR, 1995), quoted in "Arab Kingdom of Syria," Wikipedia, Wikimedia Foundation, https://en.wikipedia.org/wiki/Arab_Kingdom_of_Syria.

291 Elie Kedourie, *England and the Middle East: The Destruction of the Ottoman Empire 1914–1921* (London: Mansell Publishing Limited, 1987) quoted in "Arab Kingdom of Syria," Wikipedia, Wikimedia Foundation, https://en.wikipedia.org/wiki/Arab_Kingdom_of_Syria.

292   Curzon to Allenby, March 8 and 13, 1920, XIII, nos. 215, 220, Foreign Office: Documents on British Foreign Policy (hereafter DBFP), 19191939, ed. R. Butler et al. First series, vols. I–XXIX. London, 1947–74, quoted in Fildis, *Troubles in Syria*.

293   Curzon to Derby, November 7, 1919, IV, No.54, DBFP, quoted in Fildis, *Troubles in Syria*.

294   Jan Karl Tanenbaum, "France and the Arab Middle East, 1914–1920," *Transactions of the American Philosophical Society*, New Series 68, no. 7 (1978): 44 quoted in Fildis, *Troubles in Syria*.

295   Christopher M. Andrew and A. S. Kanya-Forstner, *The Climax of French Imperial Expansion: 1914-1924* (Stanford University Press, 1981), 204, quoted in Fildis, *Troubles in Syria*.

296   Eliezer Tauber, *Formation of Modern Syria and Iraq*, quoted in "Arab Kingdom of Syria," Wikipedia.

297   D. K. Fieldhouse, *Western Imperialism in the Middle East 1914–1958* (Oxford University Press, 2006), 253, quoted in Fildis, *Troubles in Syria*.

298   Eliezer Tauber, *Formation of Modern Syria and Iraq*, quoted in "Arab Kingdom of Syria," Wikipedia.

299   Aron S. Klieman, *Foundation of British Policy in the Arab World: The Cairo Conference of 1921* (The Johns Hopkins University Press, 1970), 51, quoted in Fildis, *Troubles in Syria*.

300   Eliezer Tauber, *Formation of Modern Syria and Iraq*, quoted in "Arab Kingdom of Syria," Wikipedia.

301   Radosh and Radosh, *Safe Haven*, 5.

302   O'Brien, *The Siege,* 148.

303   O'Brien, *The Siege,* 148–149.

304   Oren, *Power, Faith, and Fantasy*, 396.

305   Robert H. Ferrell, *Harry S. Truman: A Life* (Columbia, MO: University of Missouri Press, 1994), 70.

306   Steinberg, *Man from Missouri,* 51.

307   Steinberg, *Man from Missouri,* 52.

308   David McCullough, *Truman* (New York: Simon & Schuster, 1992), 142–143.

309   Steinberg, *Man from Missouri,* 53–54.

310   Hamby, *Man of the People: A Life of Harry S. Truman.* (Oxford: Oxford University Press. 1995), 95–96.

[311] McCullough, *Truman*, 147.

[312] Hamby, *Man of the People* 95–96.

[313] Steinberg, *Man from Missouri,* 53–54.

[314] PBS, *Truman: The American Experience*, 1997.

[315] Frank J. Adler, "From Dream to Reality: Truman, Jacobson, and Israel," *Roots in a Moving Stream: The Centennial History of Congregation B'nai Jehudah of Kansas City, 1870-1970* (Kansas City: The Temple, Congregation B'nai Jehudah, 1972), 198–225.

[316] PBS, *Truman: The American Experience*, 1997.

[317] Steinberg, *Man from Missouri,* 55.

[318] McCullough, *Truman*, 149.

[319] Steinberg, *Man from Missouri,* 55–56.

[320] McCullough, *Truman*, 148–149.

[321] Steinberg, *Man from Missouri,* 54–57.

[322] Hamby, *Man of the People*, 97.

[323] Adler, "Dream to Reality," 198–225.

[324] Steinberg, *Man from Missouri,* 54–57.

[325] Hamby, *Man of the People*, 99–100.

[326] McCullough, *Truman*, 151.

[327] PBS, *Truman: The American Experience*, 1997.

[328] PBS, *Truman: The American Experience*, 1997.

[329] Steinberg, *Man from Missouri,* 59–62.

[330] Margaret Truman, *Harry S. Truman* (New York: William Morrow & Company, 1973), 64.

[331] McCullough, *Truman*, 160–161.

[332] PBS, *Truman: The American Experience*, 1997.

[333] McCullough, *Truman*, 161.

[334] PBS, *Truman: The American Experience*, 1997.

[335] Margaret Truman, *Harry S. Truman*, 65.

[336] PBS, *Truman: The American Experience*, 1997.

[337] Hamby, *Man of the People*, 114.

[338] Radosh and Radosh, *Safe Haven*, 122.

339   Radosh and Radosh, *Safe Haven*, 5.

340   Silverberg, *If I Forget Thee,* 110.

341   Silverberg, *If I Forget Thee,* 115–116.

342   O'Brien, *The Siege,* 156–157.

343   O'Brien, *The Siege,* 159.

344   Silverberg, *If I Forget Thee,* 118–121.

345   O'Brien, *The Siege,* 158.

346   Silverberg, *If I Forget Thee,* 121–122.

347   Silverberg, *If I Forget Thee,* 130–133.

348   Silverberg, *If I Forget Thee,* 134.

349   O'Brien, *The Siege,* 166.

350   O'Brien, *The Siege,* 189.

351   Silverberg, *If I Forget Thee,* 138–139.

352   Silverberg, *If I Forget Thee,* 140–141.

353   O'Brien, *The Siege,* 170.

354   Weizmann, *Trial and Error,* 316–317.

355   Weizmann, *Trial and Error,* 318–319.

356   Weizmann, *Trial and Error,* 320.

357   Weizmann, *Trial and Error,* 323.

358   O'Brien, *The Siege,* 180–181.

359   O'Brien, *The Siege,* 180–181.

360   O'Brien, *The Siege,* 186.

361   Ben-Gurion, *Memoirs*, 34.

362   CBN Documentaries, *The Hope*, 2015.

363   Ben-Gurion, *Memoirs*, 41–43.

364   CBN Documentaries, *The Hope*, 2015.

365   Ben-Gurion, *Memoirs*, 48.

366   Ben-Gurion, *Memoirs*, 50–53.

367   Ben-Gurion, *Memoirs*, 54.

368   Ben-Gurion, *Memoirs*, 54–55.

369   Ben-Gurion, *Memoirs*, 56–57, 60.

370   Ben-Gurion, *Memoirs*, 191.

371   CBN Documentaries, *The Hope*, 2015.

372   Ben-Gurion, *Memoirs*, 65.

373   "Haganah," Zionism & Israel, http://www.zionism-israel.com/Haganah. htm.

374   "Jewish Defense Organizations: The Haganah," Jewish Virtual Library, The Pedagogic Center, The Department for Jewish Zionist Education, The Jewish Agency for Israel, 2000, http://www.jewishvirtuallibrary.org/jsource/ History/haganah.html.

375   "Haganah," Zionism & Israel.

376   O'Brien, *The Siege,* 188–189.

377   O'Brien, *The Siege,* 189–190.

378   Sachar, *History of Israel,* 177.

379   O'Brien, *The Siege,* 191.

380   "Irgun," Wikipedia, Wikimedia Foundation, http://en.wikipedia.org/ wiki/Irgun.

381   Silverberg, *If I Forget Thee,* 148–149.

382   O'Brien, *The Siege,* 203.

383   Lucy Dawidowicz, *The War Against the Jews: 1933–1945,* Tenth Anniversary Edition (New York: Holt, Rinehart and Winston/Bantam Books, 1986), 3.

384   David J. Hogan, *The War Against the Jews: 1939,* The Holocaust Chronicle, 21, http://www.holocaustchronicle.org/staticpages/149.html.

385   Dawidowicz, *War Against the Jews*, 5.

386   Adolf Hitler, *Mein Kampf*, 294, Internet Archive, https://archive.org/ stream/Mein_Kampf_Facsimilie/MK_djvu.txt.

387   Hitler, *Mein Kampf*, 324.

388   Hitler, *Mein Kampf*, 306.

389   "Mein Kampf Work by Hitler," Encyclopedia Britannica, https://www.britannica.com/topic/Mein-Kampf.

390   Hogan, *War Against the Jews,* 49–50.

391   Dawidowicz, *War Against the Jews*, 47.

392   Hogan, *War Against the Jews,* 51.

393   Hogan, *War Against the Jews*, 51.

394 Hogan, *War Against the Jews,* 75.

395 Hogan, *War Against the Jews,* 86–87.

396 "SS Police State," US Holocaust Museum, https://www.ushmm.org/outreach/en/article.php?ModuleId=10007675.

397 US Holocaust Museum, "SS Police State."

398 Hogan, *War Against the Jews,* 113, 116.

399 Hogan, *War Against the Jews,* 122–123, 144.

400 Dawidowicz, *War Against the Jews*, xxxviii.

401 Hogan, *War Against the Jews*, 149.

402 Hogan, *War Against the Jews,* 149–151.

403 Hogan, *War Against the Jews*, 151.

404 CBN Documentaries, *The Hope*, 2015.

405 Ben-Gurion, *Personal History*, 48.

406 O'Brien, *The Siege,* 212.

407 O'Brien, *The Siege,* 214–215.

408 O'Brien, *The Siege,* 219.

409 Peel Commission Minutes: Weizmann, quoted in O'Brien, *The Siege,* 225.

410 Peel Commission Minutes: Testimony of David Ben-Gurion, 1937, https://worldpeace365.wordpress.com/2018/05/28/ben-gurion-testimony-to-peel-commission-1937/.

411 Peel Commission Minutes: Mufti, quoted in O'Brien, *The Siege,* 226.

412 Peel Commission Report, Ch. XX, 370–375.

413 Peel Commission Report, Vol. V, 2.

414 Ben-Gurion, *Memoirs*, 194.

415 O'Brien, *The Siege,* 227.

416 O'Brien, *The Siege,* 227.

417 Sachar, *History of Israel,* 215–216.

418 O'Brien, *The Siege,* 232.

419 O'Brien, *The Siege,* 237.

420 Sachar, *History of Israel,* 221–222.

421 Radosh and Radosh, *Safe Haven*, 6.

422 Ben-Gurion, *Personal History*, 53.

[423] Sachar, *History of Israel,* 224.

[424] O'Brien, *The Siege,* 238–239.

[425] O'Brien, *The Siege,* 238.

[426] Ivy, *Against All Odds*, 2005.

[427] O'Brien, *The Siege,* 221.

[428] O'Brien, *The Siege,* 223.

[429] Sachar, *History of Israel,* 214.

[430] O'Brien, *The Siege,* 242.

[431] Ben-Gurion, *Personal History*, 55.

[432] O'Brien, *The Siege,* 223.

[433] O'Brien, *The Siege,* 239.

[434] Ben-Gurion, *Personal History*, 53–54.

[435] O'Brien, *The Siege,* 242.

[436] "Invasion of Poland," John Radzilowski, World War II Database, http://ww2db.com/battle_spec.php?battle_id=28.

[437] "Winston Churchill," McGill School of Computer Science, McGill University, https://www.cs.mcgill.ca/~rwest/link-suggestion/wpcd_2008-09_augmented/wp/w/Winston_Churchill.htm.

[438] Ben Gale, Letter to Martin Gilbert, February 20, 1996, quoted in Gilbert, *Churchill and the Jews,* 171.

[439] Gilbert, *Churchill and the Jews,* 163.

[440] War Cabinet Minutes, 12 February 1940: Cabinet papers, 65/5 quoted in Gilbert, *Churchill and the Jews,* 170.

[441] "Weizmann Papers Notes of Meeting," December 17, 1939, quoted in Gilbert, *Churchill and the Jews,* 164.

[442] Sachar, *History of Israel,* 231.

[443] Winston Churchill, "Telegram to Israel Rokach," September 15, 1940, Churchill papers, 20/14 quoted in Gilbert, *Churchill and the Jews,* 177.

[444] Sachar, *History of Israel,* 240.

[445] "*Patria* Disaster," Wikipedia, Wikimedia Foundation, https://en.wikipedia.org/wiki/Patria_disaster.

[446] Sachar, *History of Israel,* 237.

447 Winston Churchill, Telegram of December 2, 1940: Premier papers, 4/51/2, quoted in Gilbert, *Churchill and the Jews,* 179.

448 Winston Churchill, handwritten note, November 14, 1940: Premier papers, 4/51/1, quoted in Gilbert, *Churchill and the Jews,* 179.

449 Winston Churchill, Telegram, December 24, 1940: Premier papers, 4/51/1, quoted in Gilbert, *Churchill and the Jews,* 180.

450 Winston Churchill, Letter of May 10, 1941: Churchill papers, 20/36, quoted in Gilbert, *Churchill and the Jews,* 183.

451 Winston Churchill, Cabinet memorandum, May 19, 1941: Cabinet papers, 120/10, quoted in Gilbert, *Churchill and the Jews,* 183.

452 "Joint Declaration by the President and the Prime Minister,"August 12, 1941: Premier papers, 3/485/7, quoted in Gilbert, *Churchill and the Jews,* 184.

453 Winston Churchill, Prime Minister's Personal Minutes, August 20, 1941: Churchill papers, 20/36, quoted in Gilbert, *Churchill and the Jews,* 183.

454 Winston Churchill, War Cabinet Minutes, October 2, 1941: Cabinet papers, 65/19, quoted in Gilbert, *Churchill and the Jews,* 185.

455 Gilbert, *Churchill and the Jews,* 186.

456 *Jewish Chronicle*, November 14, 1941, quoted in Gilbert, *Churchill and the Jews,* 187.

457 Sachar, *History of Israel,* 243.

458 Ayhan Ozer, "The *Struma* Tragedy," *The Turkish Times*, February 1992, Republished in TurkishJews.com, http://turkishjews.com/struma/.

459 Sachar, *History of Israel,* 237.

460 Ivy, *Against All Odds,* 2005.

461 Ozer, "The *Struma* Tragedy."

462 "Ben Hecht," Holocaust Encyclopedia, *New York Times*, February 16, 1943, 1, https://www.ushmm.org/wlc/en/article.php?ModuleId=10007040.

463 Steinberg, *Man from Missouri,* 130.

464 Margaret Truman, *Harry S. Truman,* 90–91.

465 Steinberg, *Man from Missouri,* 130.

466 PBS, *Truman: The American Experience*, 1997.

467 Steinberg, *Man from Missouri,* 130–131.

468 Ferrell, *Harry S. Truman,* 135.

469 Steinberg, *Man from Missouri,* 131–132.

470 Michael Joseph Cohen, *Truman and Israel* (Oakland: University of California Press, 1990), 25.

471 PBS, *Truman: The American Experience*, 1997.

472 Cohen, *Truman and Israel*, 25.

473 Steinberg, *Man from Missouri,* 167.

474 Cohen, *Truman and Israel*, 25.

475 Robert H. Ferrell, *Dear Bess* (New York: W. W. Norton & Co., 1983), 446.

476 Steinberg, *Man from Missouri,* 169–170.

477 Steinberg, *Man from Missouri,* 171.

478 Steinberg, *Man from Missouri,* 172–173.

479 Steinberg, *Man from Missouri,* 178.

480 Steinberg, *Man from Missouri,* 179.

481 McCullough, *Truman*, 254–255.

482 Hamby, *Man of the People*, 248.

483 McCullough, *Truman*, 256.

484 Hamby, *Man of the People*, 249.

485 McCullough, *Truman*, 258.

486 McCullough, *Truman*, 259.

487 McCullough, *Truman*, 261.

488 McCullough, *Truman*, 263.

489 McCullough, *Truman*, 264–265.

490 Hamby, *Man of the People*, 260.

491 "The 10 Most Useful Officials in Washington," *Look*, May 16, 1944, 26–27, quoted in Hamby, *Man of the People*, 260.

492 William E. Leuchtenburg, "The Conversion of Harry Truman," *American Heritage Magazine* 42, no. 7 (November 1991), http://www.americanheritage.com/content/conversion-harry-truman?page=show.

493 Cohen, *Truman and Israel*, 44–45.

494 Emanuel Neumann, *In the Arena*, 154, quoted in Radosh and Radosh, *Safe Haven*, 49.

495 "68 Senators Back Palestine Refuge," *New York Times*, April 20, 1941, 28, http://www.nytimes.com/1941/04/20/archives/68-senators-back-palestine-refuge-sign-declaration-for-wagner-group.html.

496 Cohen, *Truman and Israel*, 35–36.

497 Cohen, *Truman and Israel*, 36–37.

498 Michael T. Benson, *Harry S. Truman and the Founding of Israel* (Westport, CT: Greenwood Publishing Group, 1997), 57.

499 Morse, *Nazi Connection,* xiv.

500 Ben Sales, "Who Was Haj Amin al-Husseini, the Grand Mufti of Jerusalem?" *Haaretz,* Haaretz Daily Newspaper, Ltd., http://www.haaretz.com/israel-news/1.681935.

501 Morse, *Nazi Connection,* 28.

502 "Al-Haj Amin al-Husayni," Encyclopedia of World Biography, 2004, http://www.encyclopedia.com/history/encyclopedias-almanacs-transcripts-and-maps/al-hajj-amin-al-husayni.

503 Andrew G. Bostom, "A Salient Example of Hajj Amin el-Husseini's Canonical Islamic Jew-Hatred," Center for Security Policy, 2013, 5, https://www.centerforsecuritypolicy.org/wp-content/uploads/2013/10/CSP_A_Salient_Example_of_Hajj_Amin_el-Husseinis.pdf.

504 Bostom, "Salient Example," 3.

505 Morse, *Nazi Connection,* 6.

506 "The Muslim Period," American University, http://www1.american.edu/TED/hpages/jeruselum/muslim.htm.

507 Morse, *Nazi Connection,* 31.

508 "Al-Haj Amin al-Husayni," Encyclopedia of World Biography.

509 Bostom, "Salient Example" 3.

510 Morse, *Nazi Connection,* 36.

511 Joel Fishman, "The Historical Problem of Haj Amin al-Husseini, 'Grand Mufti' of Jerusalem," Jerusalem Center for Public Affairs, 2016, http://jcpa.org/article/historical-problem-hajj-amin-al-husseini-grand-mufti-jerusalem/.

512 Morse, *Nazi Connection,* 9.

513 Encyclopedia of World Biography, "Al-Haj Amin al-Husayni," Encyclopedia of World Biography.

514 Morse, *Nazi Connection,* 58.

515 Morse, *Nazi Connection,* xiv.

516 Morse, *Nazi Connection,* 60–61.

[517] David Patterson, "Anti-Semitism Prevents Peace," Middle East Quarterly (Summer 2011): 73–83, http://www.meforum.org/3022/anti-semitism-prevents-peace.

[518] Morse, *Nazi Connection,* 64.

[519] Morse, *Nazi Connection,* 64.

[520] Bostom, "Salient Example," 4.

[521] Morse, *Nazi Connection,* 65.

[522] "The Iraq Coup Attempt of 1941, the Mufti, and the Farhud," MidEast Web, http://www.mideastweb.org/iraqaxiscoup.htm.

[523] Morse, *Nazi Connection,* 9–10.

[524] MidEast Web, "The Iraq Coup Attempt of 1941."

[525] Gerhard Falk, *The Restoration of Israel: Christian Zionism in Religion, Literature, and Politics* (Frankfurt: Peter Lang, 2006), 136.

[526] "Undeniable Historical Links," *The Washington Times*, February 8, 2006, http://www.washingtontimes.com/news/2006/feb/8/20060208-093102-5258r/.

[527] Morse, *Nazi Connection,* 53.

[528] Morse, *Nazi Connection,* 56–67.

[529] Bostom, "Salient Example," 5.

[530] Morse, *Nazi Connection,* 2–3.

[531] "Full Official Record: What the Mufti Said to Hitler," *Times of Israel*, October 21, 2015, http://www.timesofisrael.com/full-official-record-what-the-mufti-said-to-hitler/.

[532] *Times of Israel*, "What the Mufti Said to Hitler."

[533] Morse, *Nazi Connection,* 10.

[534] Carl K. Savich, "The Holocaust in Bosnia-Hercegovina, 1941-1945," http://www.serbianna.com/columns/savich/006.shtml.

[535] Bostom, "Salient Example," 4.

[536] Morse, *Nazi Connection,* xv.

[537] Elpeleg and Himelstein, *Grand Mufti,* 69.

[538] Yasser Dasmabebi, "Peace in Our Time: Quotations from Palestinians Who Yearn for a Jew-Free Country," FrontPage Mag, November 14, 2011, http://www.frontpagemag.com/fpm/112021/peace-our-time-dr-yasser-dasmabebi.

539 "Haj Amin al-Husseini and Nazi Racial Policies in the Arab World," Children of Jewish Holocaust Survivors, December 8, 2014, https://cjhsla.org/2014/12/08/haj-amin-al-husseini-and-nazi-racial-policies-in-the-arab-world/.

540 Morse, *Nazi Connection,* 81.

541 Morse, *Nazi Connection,* xii.

542 Hamby, *Man of the People*, 279.

543 Ferrell, *Truman: A Life*, 162.

544 Margaret Truman, *Harry S. Truman*, 168.

545 Steinberg, *Man from Missouri,* 201.

546 Margaret Truman, *Harry S. Truman*, 168.

547 Robert Dallek, *Harry S. Truman* (New York: Times Books / Henry Holt and Co., 2008), 15.

548 McCullough, *Truman*, 295.

549 "D-Day and the Battle of Normandy," D-Day Museum, http://www.dday-museum.co.uk/d-day/d-day-and-the-battle-of-normandy-your-questions-answered.

550 Margaret Truman, *Harry S. Truman*, 170.

551 McCullough, *Truman*, 297.

552 McCullough, *Truman*, 297–298.

553 Steinberg, *Man from Missouri,* 204.

554 McCullough, *Truman*, 300–301.

555 Margaret Truman, *Harry S. Truman*, 170.

556 Ferrell, *Truman: A Life*, 165.

557 PBS, *Truman: The American Experience*, 1997.

558 McCullough, *Truman*, 302–303.

559 Steinberg, *Man from Missouri,* 207–208.

560 McCullough, *Truman*, 300–305.

561 McCullough, *Truman*, 298–299.

562 McCullough, *Truman*, 306.

563 McCullough, *Truman*, 306.

564 Margaret Truman, *Harry S. Truman*, 174.

565 Steinberg, *Man from Missouri,* 211.

566   Steinberg, *Man from Missouri,* 208.

567   McCullough, *Truman*, 311–312.

568   Margaret Truman, *Harry S. Truman*, 175.

569   Steinberg, *Man from Missouri,* 213.

570   McCullough, *Truman*, 311–312.

571   Margaret Truman, *Harry S. Truman*, 176.

572   McCullough, *Truman*, 315–316.

573   Margaret Truman, *Harry S. Truman*, 177.

574   McCullough, *Truman*, 314.

575   McCullough, *Truman,* 315–316.

576   McCullough, *Truman*, 323–324.

577   Margaret Truman, *Harry S. Truman*, 181.

578   McCullough, *Truman*, 319–320.

579   Margaret Truman, *Harry S. Truman*, 183.

580   PBS, *Truman: The American Experience*, 1997.

581   David M. Jordan, *FDR, Dewey, and the Election of 1944* (Bloomingon: Indiana University Press, Sep 2, 2011), 202.

582   McCullough, *Truman*, 321.

583   Margaret Truman, *Harry S. Truman*, 186.

584   McCullough, *Truman*, 328.

585   Margaret Truman, *Harry S. Truman*, 190.

586   McCullough, *Truman*, 327.

587   Margaret Truman, *Harry S. Truman*, 195.

588   Steinberg, *Man from Missouri,* 228.

589   Steinberg, *Man from Missouri,* 229.

590   Radosh and Radosh, *Safe Haven*, 10–11.

591   Monty Noam Penkower, *Franklin D. Roosevelt and the Palestine Imbroglio* (New Hampton, NY: AB Books, 1996), 18, http://www.bjpa.org/Publications/downloadFile.cfm?FileID=19654.

592   Radosh and Radosh, *Safe Haven*, 18.

593   Peter Grose, "The President vs the Diplomats," 37, Harvard University, http://isites.harvard.edu/fs/docs/icb.topic1238553.files/peter%20grose%20the%20president%20vs%20the%20diplomats.pdf.

594 William D. Hassett, *Off the Record with F.D.R, 1942–1945*, 209, quoted in Radosh and Radosh, *Safe Haven*, 20.

595 Allis Radosh and Ronald Radosh, "Lowdermilk Makes the Case," http://www.jbooks.com/interviews/index/IP_Radosh.htm.

596 Rory Miller, "Bible and Soil: Walter Clay Lowdermilk, the Jordan Valley Project and the Palestine Debate," HighBeam Research, 2003, https://www.highbeam.com/doc/1G1-102554752.html.

597 Radosh and Radosh, "Lowdermilk Makes the Case."

598 Radosh and Radosh, "Lowdermilk Makes the Case."

599 W. C. Lowdermilk, "TVA Reclamation Project for the Jordan Valley and a Post-war Solution for the Jewish Refugee Problem," Aug. 10, 1942, Ben Cohen Papers, Box 12, Folder 1, Library of Congress, Washington, DC, quoted in Radosh and Radosh, *Safe Haven*, 22.

600 Radosh and Radosh, "Lowdermilk Makes the Case."

601 Radosh and Radosh, "Lowdermilk Makes the Case."

602 Oren, *Power, Faith, and Fantasy*, 469.

603 Cohen, *Truman and Israel*, 87–88.

604 "Who We Are," ARAMCO, http://www.aramcoservices.com/Who-We-Are/Our-History.aspx.

605 Cohen, *Truman and Israel*, 88–89.

606 "Wise to FDR," Central Zionist Archives, Jerusalem, Israel, Jan. 24, 1945, quoted in Radosh and Radosh, *Safe Haven*, 23.

607 William Eddy, "The Minister in Saudi Arabia (Eddy) to the Secretary of State," Office of the Historian, Department of State, Foreign Relations of the United States, 867N.01/2-145: Telegram, https://history.state.gov/historicaldocuments/frus1945v08/d669.

608 Martin Jones, *Failure in Palestine: British and United States Policy after the Second World War* (London: Bloomsbury Publishing, 2016), 20, https://books.google.com/books?isbn=1474291287.

609 "Memo from the State Department," FRUS, Jan. 30, 1945, vol. 8, 684–687.

610 Nancy MacLennan, "Roosevelt Backs Palestinian Plan as Homeland for Refugee Jews," *The New York Times*, March 10, 1944, 1.

611 Radosh and Radosh, *Safe Haven*, 19.

612 Oren, *Power, Faith, and Fantasy*, 467.

613 Oren, *Power, Faith, and Fantasy*, 468.

614 "Yalta Conference," Encyclopedia Britannica, 2014, https://www.britanni-ca.com/event/Yalta-Conference.

615 Radosh and Radosh, *Safe Haven*, 24.

616 Oren, *Power, Faith, and Fantasy*, 467.

617 Radosh and Radosh, *Safe Haven*, 25.

618 Radosh and Radosh, *Safe Haven*, 27.

619 Oren, *Power, Faith, and Fantasy*, 470.

620 Cynthia Koch, "FDR's Last Personal Diplomacy: Ibn Saud and the Quest for a Jewish Homeland," The Franklin Delano Roosevelt Foundation at Adams House, Harvard College, October 28, 2016, http://fdrfoundation.org/tag/ibn-saud/.

621 Radosh and Radosh, *Safe Haven*, 27.

622 "Roosevelt Meets King Saud at Bitter Lake," Jewish Virtual Library, AICE, http://www.jewishvirtuallibrary.org/president-roosevelt-meets-king-saud-at-bitter-lake-february-1945#_edn7.

623 Radosh and Radosh, *Safe Haven*, 27.

624 Oren, *Power, Faith, and Fantasy*, 471.

625 Jewish Virtual Library, "Roosevelt Meets King Saud."

626 Koch, "FDR's Last Personal Diplomacy."

627 Radosh and Radosh, *Safe Haven*, 27.

628 Radosh and Radosh, *Safe Haven*, 27–28.

629 Herbert Parzen, "The Roosevelt Palestine Policy, 1943–1945: An Exercise in Dual Diplomacy," The Jacob Rader Marcus Center of the American Jewish Archives, 54, http://americanjewisharchives.org/publications/journal/PDF/1974_26_01_00_parzen.pdf.

630 William A. Eddy, "F.D.R. Meets Ibn Saud American-Mideast Education-al and Training Service," Saudi-US Relations Information Service, 1954, 27, http://susris.com/wp-content/uploads/2014/02/100222-fdr-ab-dulaziz-eddy.pdf.

631 Oren, *Power, Faith, and Fantasy*, 472.

632 Oren, *Power, Faith, and Fantasy*, 467.

633 Gilbert, *Churchill and the Jews,* 202.

634 Chaim Weizmann, "Summary of Reports Sent by Dr. Weizmann," Jan. 17, 1944; sent to Judge Samuel Rosenman, David Niles manuscripts, Harry S. Truman Presidential Library & Museum (hereafter cited as Truman Library).

635 Radosh and Radosh, *Safe Haven*, 29.

636 William A. Eddy, "Letter to Edward Stettinius," Feb. 22, 1945, in FRUS, vol. 8, 689-90, quoted in Radosh and Radosh, *Safe Haven*, 29.

637 Rabbi Steven Wise to Chaim Weizmann, March 21, 1945, Chaim Weizmann Archives, Rehovoth, Israel, no. 2575, quoted in Radosh and Radosh, *Safe Haven*, 29-30.

638 Radosh and Radosh, *Safe Haven*, 30.

639 Steinberg, *Man from Missouri,* 232.

640 Radosh and Radosh, *Safe Haven*, 291.

641 Hamby, *Man of the People*, 289.

642 McCullough, *Truman*, 337.

643 Radosh and Radosh, *Safe Haven*, 30.

644 Radosh and Radosh, *Safe Haven*, 31–32.

645 Rabbi Steven Wise to Chaim Weizmann, March 21, 1945, Chaim Weizmann Archives.

646 Lieutenant Colonel Harold B. Hoskins, "Letter to the Deputy Director of the Office of Near Eastern and African Affairs (Alling), March 5, 1945, in FRUS, vol. 8, 690-91, quoted in Radosh and Radosh, *Safe Haven*, 33.

647 Jewish Virtual Library, "Roosevelt Meets King Saud."

648 Radosh and Radosh, *Safe Haven*, 34.

649 Joseph M. Proskauer, *A Segment of My Times*, 69–70, quoted in Radosh and Radosh, *A Safe Haven*, 34.

650 Joseph Proskauer, "Memorandum to the leadership of the American Jewish Committee," April 1945, American Jewish Committee files, YIVO Instituted for Jewish Research; American Jewish Historical Society, New York City, quoted in Radosh and Radosh, *Safe Haven*, 34.

651 Margaret Truman, *Harry S. Truman*, 203.

652 PBS, *Truman: American Experience*, 1997.

653 McCullough, *Truman*, 337.

654 Steinberg, *Man from Missouri,* 232.

655 Margaret Truman, *Harry S. Truman*, 206.

656 Ferrell, *Truman: A Life*, 176.

657 Ferrell, *Truman: A Life*, 176.

658 Steinberg, *Man from Missouri,* 234.

659 Steinberg, *Man from Missouri,* 234.

660 McCullough, *Truman*, 342.

661 Margaret Truman, *Harry S. Truman*, 208–209.

662 McCullough, *Truman*, 342.

663 McCullough, *Truman*, 346.

664 Hamby, *Man of the People*, 294.

665 Margaret Truman, *Harry S. Truman*, 212

666 Hamby, *Man of the People*, 293.

667 Margaret Truman, *Harry S. Truman*, 213.

668 PBS, *Truman: American Experience*, 1997.

669 Margaret Truman, *Harry S. Truman*, 214.

670 McCullough, *Truman*, 352.

671 Margaret Truman, *Harry S. Truman*, 215.

672 McCullough, *Truman*, 353.

673 Hamby, *Man of the People*, 295.

674 McCullough, *Truman*, 353.

675 Hamby, *Man of the People*, 295.

676 Margaret Truman, *Harry S. Truman*, 224.

677 Hamby, *Man of the People*, 296.

678 Hamby, *Man of the People*, 297.

679 McCullough, *Truman*, 359.

680 Margaret Truman, *Harry S. Truman*, 224.

681 McCullough, *Truman*, 432.

682 "U.S. Army & the Holocaust," Jewish Virtual Library, AICE, http://www.jewishvirtuallibrary.org/u-s-army-and-the-holocaust.

683 "Oh, No, It Can't Be," Holocaust Teacher Resource Center, http://www.holocaust-trc.org/the-holocaust-education-program-resource-guide/oh-no-it-cant-be/.

684 "Holocaust," Georgia Tech, Ohrdruf, http://www.library.gatech.edu/holocaust/ohrdrufdes.htm.

685 Douglas E. Clark, *Eisenhower in Command at Columbia* (Lanham, MD: Lexington Books, 2013), 34.

686 Jewish Virtual Library, "U.S. Army & the Holocaust."

687 A. M. Sperber, *Murrow, His Life and Times* (New York: Fordham University Press, 1998), 252.

688 Gene Currivan, "Nazi Death Factory Shocks Germans on a Forced Tour," *The New York Times*, April 18, 1945, 1.

689 "The Conflicts of Harry S. Truman: At War with the Experts," CBS TV, 1964, Film Collection, Truman Library.

690 CBN Documentaries, *The Hope, 2015*.

691 Radosh and Radosh, *Safe Haven*, 57–58.

692 Memo for the AZEC reporting on the meeting, American Zionist Emergency Council (AZEC), April 23, 1945, CZA Z5/1206.

693 Samuel Halperin, *The Political World of American Zionism*, 9, quoted in Radosh and Radosh, *Safe Haven*, 5.

694 Harry S. Truman, *Memoirs*, 69.

695 Merle Miller, *Plain Speaking: An Oral Biography of Harry. S. Truman* (New York: Berkley Publishing Corporation, 1973), 216–217.

696 Silverberg, *If I Forget Thee,* 284.

697 Eliahu Elath, "Zionism at the UN: A Diary of the First Days," Scribd, Scribd Inc, 294, https://www.scribd.com/document/86772234/Zionism-at-the-Un.

698 Leonard Dinnerstein, *America and the Survivors of the Holocaust,* 24–36, quoted in Radosh and Radosh, *Safe Haven*, 72–73.

699 Harry S. Truman, "The President's News Conference on V-E Day: May 8, 1945," The American Presidency Project, University of California, Santa Barbara, http://www.presidency.ucsb.edu/ws/?pid=12248.

700 McCullough, *Truman*, 499.

701 Harry S. Truman, *Memoirs: Year of Decisions* (New York: Doubleday and Company, 1955), 341.

702 Harry S. Truman, *Year of Decisions*, 394.

703 Harry S. Truman, *Year of Decisions*, 411.

704 PBS, *Truman: American Experience*, 1997.

705 PBS, *Truman: American Experience*, 1997.

706 Harry S. Truman, *Year of Decisions*, 421.

707 PBS, *Truman: American Experience*, 1997.

[708] Harry S. Truman, *Year of Decisions*, 436–437.

[709] "The Kielce Pogrom: A Blood Libel Massacre of Holocaust Survivors," United States Holocaust Memorial Museum, https://www.ushmm.org/wlc/en/article.php?ModuleId=10007941.

[710] Melvin I. Urofsky, *We Are One!*, 105, quoted in Radosh and Radosh, *Safe Haven*, 73.

[711] Silverberg, *If I Forget Thee,* 289.

[712] Silverberg, *If I Forget Thee,* 292.

[713] Eric Lichtblau, "Surviving the Nazis, Only to Be Jailed by America," *The New York Times*, February 7, 2015, https://www.nytimes.com/2015/02/08/sunday-review/surviving-the-nazis-only-to-be-jailed-by-america.html?_r=0.

[714] Silverberg, *If I Forget Thee,* 292.

[715] Silverberg, *If I Forget Thee,* 292.

[716] Robert J. Donovan, *Conflict and Crisis: The Presidency of Harry S. Truman, 1945-1948* (New York: W. W. Norton and Company, 1977), 314.

[717] Harry S. Truman, *Personal Papers of the Presidents of the United States: Harry S. Truman*, 1945, 228, quoted in Donovan, *Conflict and Crisis,* 313.

[718] Donovan, *Conflict and Crisis*, 313.

[719] O'Brien, *The Siege,* 257.

[720] Michael Makovsky, *Churchill's Promised Land: Zionism and Statecraft* (New Haven: Yale University Press, 2007), 180.

[721] John Bowyer Bell, *Terror Out of Zion* (Livingston, NJ: Transaction Publishers, 1976), 127.

[722] J. C. Hurewitz, *The Middle East and North Africa in World Politics* (New Haven: Yale University Press, 1979), 782.

[723] "Shift of 100,000 to Palestine Set," *The New York Times*, April 13, 1945, 30, https://www.nytimes.com/1945/04/13/archives/shift-of-1000000-to-palestine-set-jewish-agency-has-postwar-plans.html.

[724] Harry S. Truman, "Memorandum by President Truman to the British Prime Minister," July 24, 1945, in *FRUS*, VOL. 8, 716–17, Digital Collections of the University of Wisconsin-Madison Libraries, http://digicoll.library.wisc.edu/cgi-bin/FRUS/FRUS-idx?type=turn&entity=FRUS.FRUS1945v08.p0728&id=FRUS.FRUS1945v08&isize=M.

[725] Clement Attlee, "Attlee to Truman, July 31, 1945," in *FRUS,* vol. 8, 719, Digital Collections of the University of Wisconsin-Madison Libraries, http://digicoll.library.wisc.edu/cgi-bin/FRUS/FRUS-idx?type=turn&entity=-

FRUS.FRUS1945v08.p0731&id=FRUS.FRUS1945v08&isize=M.

726 Makovsky, *Churchill's Promised Land,* 144.

727 O'Brien, *The Siege,* 261.

728 Benson, *Founding of Israel,* 69.

729 Eliahu Elath, *Harry S. Truman,* 29–31, quoted in Radosh and Radosh, *Safe Haven,* 101.

730 Rafael Medoff, *Militant Zionism in America: The Rise and Impact of the Jabotinsky Movement* (Tuscaloosa: University of Alabama Press, 2002), 135.

731 Radosh and Radosh, *Safe Haven,* 75.

732 Evan M. Wilson, "Memorandum of Conversation, June 27, 1945, in FRUS, vol. 8, 713-715, Digital Collections of the University of Wisconsin-Madison Libraries, http://digicoll.library.wisc.edu/cgi-bin/FRUS/FRUS-idx?type=turn&entity=FRUS.FRUS1945v08.p0725&id=FRUS.FRUS1945v08&isize=M.

733 O'Brien, *The Siege,* 261.

734 Martin Sicker, *Pangs of the Messiah: The Troubled Birth of the Jewish State* (Westport, CT: Greenwood Publishing Group, 2000), 184–185.

735 "The Role of Jewish Defense Organizations in Palestine (1903–1948)," Jewish Virtual Library, AICE, http://www.jewishvirtuallibrary.org/the-role-of-jewish-defense-organizations-in-palestine-1903-1948.

736 O'Brien, *The Siege,* 267.

737 Abraham Malamat, *A History of the Jewish People* (Boston: Harvard University Press, 1976), 1048.

738 Loy W. Henderson, "Oral History Interview, June 14, 1973, and July 5, 1973," Truman Library.

739 O'Brien, *The Siege,* 269.

740 O'Brien, *The Siege,* 269.

741 Robert F. Wagner, "Palestine—A World Responsibility," *The Nation,* Sept. 15, 1945, 247–49, quoted in Radosh and Radosh, *Safe Haven,* 82.

742 "Palestine 'Pledge' Denied by Truman," *The New York Times,* Sept. 27, 1945, 14, https://www.nytimes.com/1945/09/27/archives/palestine-pledge-denied-by-truman-says-roosevelt-made-no-us.html.

743 Radosh and Radosh, *Safe Haven,* 108–109.

744 Radosh and Radosh, *Safe Haven,* 109–110.

745 Radosh and Radosh, *Safe Haven,* 113–114.

746 Radosh and Radosh, *Safe Haven*, 119.

747 Radosh and Radosh, *Safe Haven*, 119–120.

748 Radosh and Radosh, *Safe Haven*, 120–121.

749 Radosh and Radosh, *Safe Haven*, 125.

750 Colin Shindler, *Israel and the European Left: Between Solidarity and Delegitimization* (New York: Bloomsbury Publishing USA, 2011), 127.

751 Norman J. W. Goda, *Surviving Survival: James G. McDonald and the Fate of Holocaust Survivors*, US Holocaust Memorial Museum, 8–9, https://www.ushmm.org/m/pdfs/20150904-Goda-OP.pdf.

752 "Does Not Demand State Now, Wants Peace With Arabs, Dr. Weizmann Declares in Testimony Before Inquiry Body," *The Jewish Post*, March 15, 1946, Jewish Telegraphic Agency, Indianapolis, IN, 4, https://newspapers.library.in.gov/cgi-bin/indiana?a=d&d=JPOST19460315-01.1.4.

753 Radosh and Radosh, *Safe Haven*, 138–139.

754 Radosh and Radosh, *Safe Haven*, 139–140.

755 Radosh and Radosh, *Safe Haven*, 141.

756 O'Brien, *The Siege,* 263.

757 O'Brien, *The Siege,* 267.

758 "The Jewish Resistance Movement," Jewish Virtual Library, AICE, http://www.jewishvirtuallibrary.org/the-jewish-resistance-movement-in-pre-state-israel.

759 BBC, *Israel: Birth of a Nation*, 2008.

760 Freda Kirchwey, "Palestine in Crisis," *The Nation Associates*, 3, Internet Archive, https://archive.org/stream/ldpd_11217260_000/ldpd_11217260_000_djvu.txt.

761 Radosh and Radosh, *Safe Haven*, 167–168.

762 Jeffrey Gurock, *American Zionism: Missions and Politics: American Jewish History* (Oxfordshire, UK: Routledge, 2014), 251.

763 Radosh and Radosh, *Safe Haven*, 43.

764 Radosh and Radosh, *Safe Haven*, 44.

765 Michael Berkowitz, *The Crime of My Very Existence: Nazism and the Myth of Jewish Criminality* (Oakland: University of California Press, 2007), 286.

766 Abraham Feinberg, Interview, August 23, 1973, 7–9, Oral History Collection, Truman Library, https://www.trumanlibrary.org/oralhist/feinberg.htm.

767 Radosh and Radosh, *Safe Haven*, 44.

768 Cohen, *Truman and Israel*, 75.

769 Cohen, *Truman and Israel*, 77.

770 Radosh and Radosh, *Safe Haven*, 168–169.

771 Michael J. Devine, *Harry S. Truman, the State of Israel, and the Quest for Peace in the Middle East* (Kirkman, MO: Truman State University Press, 2009), 98.

772 "Creation of Israel, 1948," US Department of State, https://history.state.gov/milestones/1945-1952/creation-israel.

773 Radosh and Radosh, *Safe Haven*, 171–173.

774 Michael L. Hoffman, "Divided Palestine is Urged by Anglo–U.S. Cabinet Body," *The New York Times*, July 26, 1946.

775 Radosh and Radosh, *Safe Haven*, 174–175.

776 Harry S. Truman, "Truman to McDonald," July 31, 1946, L35/121 CZA.

777 Cohen, *Truman and Israel*, 130.

778 Donovan, *Conflict and Crisis*, 318.

779 Radosh and Radosh, *Safe Haven*, 177.

780 Donovan, *Conflict and Crisis*, 319.

781 Radosh and Radosh, *Safe Haven*, 177–178.

782 Cohen, *Truman and Israel*, 66–67.

783 Cohen, *Truman and Israel*, 138.

784 Cohen, *Truman and Israel*, 138.

785 Radosh and Radosh, *Safe Haven*, 181–182.

786 Cohen, *Truman and Israel*, 139–140.

787 Radosh and Radosh, *Safe Haven*, 181–182.

788 Radosh and Radosh, *Safe Haven*, 182–183.

789 Clifton Daniels, "Arabs Ask Parley by World on Jews," *The New York Times*, October 4, 1946, 8.

790 Abraham Feinberg, "Oral interview, Aug. 31, 1973," by Richard D. McKinzie, Truman Library.

791 Cohen, *Truman and Israel*, 144.

792 "Statement by the President," *The New York Times*, 46, 2.

793 "Epstein to Goldmann," October 9, 1946, WA, quoted in Cohen, *Truman and Israel*, 145.

[794] Radosh and Radosh, *Safe Haven*, 190–191.

[795] Ibn Saud, "Letter to Truman," transmitted to Acting Secretary of State on Oct. 15, 1946; FRUS, vol. 7, 708-9; OF, Box 771, Truman Library.

[796] Donovan, *Conflict and Crisis*, 316.

[797] Radosh and Radosh, *Safe Haven*, 193–194.

[798] Radosh and Radosh, *Safe Haven*, 199.

[799] Radosh and Radosh, *Safe Haven*, 200.

[800] O'Brien, *The Siege,* 269–270.

[801] Harry S. Truman, "Diary Entry," Jan. 3, 1947, Truman Library, https://www.trumanlibrary.org/diary/transcript.htm.

[802] Harry S. Truman, "Diary Entry," Jan. 8, 1947, Truman Library, https://www.trumanlibrary.org/diary/transcript.htm.

[803] Cohen, *Truman and Israel*, 91.

[804] Radosh and Radosh, *Safe Haven*, 202–203.

[805] Nick Reynold, *Britain's Unfulfilled Mandate for Palestine* (Lanham, MD: Lexington Books, 2014), 249.

[806] Ivy, *Against All Odds.*

[807] O'Brien, *The Siege,* 274.

[808] "The Plan of Partition and the End of the British Mandate," United Nations, http://www.un.org/Depts/dpi/palestine/ch2.pdf.

[809] Evan M. Wilson, *A Calculated Risk: The U.S. Decision to Recognize Israel* (Covington, KY: Clerisy Press, 2009), 212.

[810] "Marshall the United Nations and Palestine," The George C. Marshall Foundation, Ch. 20, 348, http://marshallfoundation.org/library/digital-archive/statesman-chapter-20-marshall-the-united-nations-and-palestine/.

[811] "Background Story on Palestine Report," UN Department of Public Information, August 31, 1947, https://unispal.un.org/DPA/DPR/unispal.nsf/0/2D17B10E29EBCB4B85256A76006DD2DA.

[812] "UNSCOP Summary of the Seventh Meeting," United Nations, June 23, 1947, https://unispal.un.org/DPA/DPR/unispal.nsf/0/7651F1007D-32B88E852575AD0068CE3C.

[813] "Foreign Relations of the United States, 1947, The Near East and Africa," Office of the Historian, US Department of State, Volume V, 501, BB Palestine/6–2347, https://history.state.gov/historicaldocuments/frus1947v05/d778.

814 Radosh and Radosh, *Safe Haven*, 223–224.

815 "Foreign Relations of the United States, 1947, The Near East and Africa," Office of the Historian, US Department of State, https://history.state.gov/historicaldocuments/frus1947v05/d780.

816 Radosh and Radosh, *Safe Haven*, 227.

817 "Background Story on Palestine Report," UN Department of Public Information, August 31, 1947, https://unispal.un.org/DPA/DPR/unispal.nsf/0/2D17B10E29EBCB4B85256A76006DD2DA.

818 Horowitz, *State in the Making,* 166–171.

819 Radosh and Radosh, *Safe Haven*, 223–224.

820 "Record of the Sixteenth Meeting, Jerusalem, Palestine," United Nations, July 4, 1947, https://unispal.un.org/DPA/DPR/unispal.nsf/0/7735B-7DC144807B985256E8B006F4A71.

821 "Weizmann Asks United Nations for Partition As Only Feasible Solution for Palestine," Jewish Telegraphic Agency, July 9, 1947, http://www.jta.org/1947/07/09/archive/weizmann-asks-united-nations-for-partition-as-only-feasible-solution-for-palestine.

822 "UNSCOP Report to the General Assembly," United Nations, Lake Success, NY, 1947, https://unispal.un.org/DPA/DPR/unispal.nsf/0/07175DE-9FA2DE563852568D3006E10F3.

823 "*Exodus 1947*," US Holocaust Memorial Museum, https://www.ushmm.org/wlc/en/article.php?ModuleId=10005419.

824 Radosh and Radosh, *Safe Haven*, 233.

825 "Exodus 1947," US Holocaust Memorial Museum.

826 Ruth Gruber, *Inside of Time: My Journey from Alaska to Israel*, 272–289, quoted in Radosh and Radosh, *Safe Haven*, 232–233.

827 Robert St. John, *Abba Eban*, 168, quoted in Radosh and Radosh, *Safe Haven*, 234.

828 Ruth Gruber, *Inside of Time,* 272–289, quoted in Radosh and Radosh, *Safe Haven*, 234.

829 Eleanor Roosevelt, "My Day," August 23, 1947, George Washington University, https://www2.gwu.edu/~erpapers/myday/displaydoc.cfm?_y=1947&_f=md000739.

830 "*Exodus 1947*: Illegal Immigration Ship," Jewish Virtual Library, AICE, http://www.jewishvirtuallibrary.org/quot-exodus-1947-quot-illegal-immigration-ship.

831 Granados, *Birth of Israel*, 183–188, quoted in Radosh and Radosh, *Safe Haven*, 238.

832 Granados, *Birth of Israel*, 200, quoted in Radosh and Radosh, *Safe Haven*, 239.

833 Granados, *Birth of Israel*, 200, quoted in Radosh and Radosh, *Safe Haven*, 239.

834 "UNSCOP Report to the General Assembly," United Nations, Lake Success, NY, September 3, 1947, https://unispal.un.org/DPA/DPR/unispal.nsf/0/07175DE9FA2DE563852568D3006E10F3.

835 Joshua Muravchik, *Making David into Goliath: How the World Turned Against Israel* (New York: Encounter Books, 2015), 8.

836 "Simir Rifai to Bevin," Sept. 22, 1947, FO 371 61880/E9354, PRO, quoted in Radosh and Radosh, *Safe Haven*, 245.

837 Clifton Daniel, "Zionists Ask U.N. to Pass New Plan," *The New York Times*, September 2, 1947, 1.

838 Radosh and Radosh, *Safe Haven*, 246–247.

839 Joseph P. Lash, *Eleanor: The Years Alone*, 114–115, quoted in Radosh and Radosh, *Safe Haven*, 250.

840 "Memorandum to Herschel Johnson, Oct. 3, 1947," Gordon Knox, *FRUS*, vol. 5, 1173-1174.

841 Eddie Jacobson, "Letter to Harry S. Truman," Oct. 3, 1947, Eddie Jacobson Papers, Truman Library.

842 Harry S. Truman, "Letter to Eddie Jacobson," October 8, 1947, Eddie Jacobson Papers, Truman Library.

843 Clifton Daniel, "Arab States to Send Troops to the Borders of Palestine," *The New York Times*, Oct. 10, 1947, 1.

844 Thomas J. Hamilton, "Arabs Are Warned," *The New York Times*, Oct. 12, 1947, 1.

845 "Termination of the Mandate," The United Nations, January 9, 1948, https://unispal.un.org/DPA/DPR/unispal.nsf/0/B661E1F0862A7D8685256AF-1006BA2DF.

846 Radosh and Radosh, *Safe Haven*, 264–265.

847 Loy W. Henderson, "Henderson to Lovett," Nov. 24, 1947, *FRUS*, vol. 5, 1281–1282.

848 Loy W. Henderson, "Oral History Interview," 136, Truman Library, https://www.trumanlibrary.org/oralhist/hendrson.htm.

849 Peter Grose, "The Partition of Palestine 35 Years Ago," *The New York Times*, November 21, 1982, http://www.nytimes.com/1982/11/21/magazine/the-partition-of-palestine-35-years-ago.html?pagewanted=all.

850 Horowitz, *State in the Making,* 300.

851 "Question of Palestine," The United Nations, November 22, 1976, https://unispal.un.org/DPA/DPR/unispal.nsf/0/6BCDDCC682371CA-585256F7200694ADC.

852 Michael Comay, "Letter to B. Gering, Dec. 3, 1947," *Israel Documents, December 1947–May, 1948,*" 3–13, quoted in Radosh and Radosh, *Safe Haven*, 273.

853 Henderson, "Oral History Interview."

854 George Marshall, "Letter to Lovett," Nov. 28, 1947, *FRUS*, vol. 5, 1289–1290.

855 Chaim Weizmann, "Letter to Ginsburg," December, 1947, *The Letters and Papers of Chaim Weizmann*, vol. 23, Aug. 1947–June, 1952, 67, quoted in Radosh and Radosh, *Safe Haven*, 275.

856 Emanuel Neumann, *In the Arena*, 254, quoted in Radosh and Radosh, *Safe Haven*, 275.

857 Ruth Gruber, *Witness*, 158, quoted in Radosh and Radosh, *Safe Haven*, 275.

858 Dai Richards, dir., and David Ash, dir., *The 50 Years War: Israel and the Arabs*, 1998, A PBS/WGBH/BBC Film, PBS.

859 Richards and Ash, *The 50 Years War: Israel and the Arabs*, 1998, A PBS/WGBH/BBC Film.

860 *Israel: Birth of a Nation*, 1996, History Channel, A&E Television Networks,

861 BBC, *The Birth of Israel,* 2008.

862 History Channel, *Israel: Birth of a Nation*, 1996.

863 Oren, *Power, Faith, and Fantasy*, 493.

864 Oren, *Power, Faith, and Fantasy*, 493.

865 BBC, *The Birth of Israel,* 2008.

866 History Channel, *Israel: Birth of a Nation*, 1996.

867 "Battle for Jerusalem," Wikipedia, Wikimedia Foundation, https://en.wikipedia.org/wiki/Battle_for_Jerusalem.

868 Collins and Lapierre, *O Jerusalem* (Simon and Schuster / Pocket Books, 1973), 145–146.

869 Ronald W. Zweig, *David Ben-Gurion: Politics and Leadership in Israel* (London: Routledge, 2013), 174.

870 Silverberg, *If I Forget Thee,* 386.

871 Fred J. Khouri, *The Arab-Israeli Dilemma* (Syracuse, NY: Syracuse University Press, 1985), 69.

872 Collins and Lapierre, *O Jerusalem*, 223–225.

873 Collins and Lapierre, *O Jerusalem*, 288–289.

874 History Channel, *Israel: Birth of a Nation*, 1996.

875 History Channel, *Israel: Birth of a Nation*, 1996.

876 BBC, *The Birth of Israel,* 2008.

877 "The Capture of Deir Yassin (April 9, 1948)," Jewish Virtual Library, AICE, http://www.jewishvirtuallibrary.org/the-capture-of-deir-yassin.

878 *The 50 Years War: Israel and the Arabs*, "1947 British Newsreel," 1998, a PBS/WGBH/BBC Film.

879 "The Capture of Deir Yassin (April 9, 1948)," Jewish Virtual Library, AICE.

880 Benny Morris, "What Happened in the Village of Deir Yassin during the First Arab-Israeli War?" ProCon.org, 2008, http://israelipalestinian.procon.org/view.answers.php?questionID=000479.

881 History Channel, *Israel: Birth of a Nation*, 1996.

882 Collins and Lapierre, *O Jerusalem*, 319–320.

883 Christopher Sykes, *Crossroads to Israel*, 417, quoted in O'Brien, *The Siege*, 282.

884 CBN Documentaries, *The Hope,* 2015.

885 CBN Documentaries, *The Hope,* 2015.

886 CBN Documentaries, *The Hope,* 2015.

887 CBN Documentaries, *The Hope,* 2015.

888 Ian J. Bickerton and Carla L. Klausner, *A Concise History of the Arab-Israeli Conflict,* 3rd ed., (Upper Saddle River, New Jersey: Prentice-Hall / Simon & Schuster, 1998), 95.

889 History Channel, *Israel: Birth of a Nation*, 1996.

890 CBN Documetaries, *The Hope,* 2015.

891 Collins and Lapierre, *O Jerusalem*, 394–395.

892 Collins and Lapierre, *O Jerusalem*, 396.

893 History Channel, *Israel: Birth of a Nation*, 1996.

894 Collins and Lapierre, *O Jerusalem*, 396–397.

895 Collins and Lapierre, *O Jerusalem*, 396–398.

896 Silverberg, *If I Forget Thee,* 400.

897 Oren, *Power, Faith, and Fantasy*, 493.

898 Silverberg, *If I Forget Thee,* 388.

899 McCullough, *Truman*, 604.

900 PBS, *Truman: American Experience*, 1997.

901 Cohen, *Truman and Israel*, 182.

902 Cohen, *Truman and Israel*, 183.

903 Silverberg, *If I Forget Thee,* 400.

904 Donovan, *Conflict and Crisis*, 372.

905 Cohen, *Truman and Israel*, 180.

906 Cohen, *Truman and Israel*, 185.

907 CBN Documetaries, *The Hope,* 2015.

908 Michael Beschloss, "Book Excerpt: A Case of Courage," Newsweek, http://www.newsweek.com/book-excerpt-case-courage-101539.

909 Josef Cohn, *Two Presidents and a Haberdasher*, American Jewish Archives, April, 1968, http://americanjewisharchives.org/publications/journal/PDF/1968_20_01_00.pdf.

910 Silverberg, *If I Forget Thee,* 402–403.

911 Bob Cohen, "Bob Cohen Introduces the Truman-Jacobson Video," The American Israel Public Affairs Committee (AIPAC), https://www.youtube.com/watch?v=P7f5p42rorg.

912 Adler, "From Dream to Reality," 198–225.

913 Cohn, *Two Presidents and a Haberdasher*.

914 Beschloss, "A Case of Courage."

915 Cohn, *Two Presidents and a Haberdasher*.

916 Beschloss, "A Case of Courage."

917 Cohn, *Two Presidents and a Haberdasher*.

918 Cohn, *Two Presidents and a Haberdasher*.

919 Harry Truman, *Memoirs of Harry S. Truman: 1946–52, Years of Trial and Hope* (New York: Time, Inc., 1955), 161.

920 CBN Documentaries, *The Hope,* 2015.

921 CBN Documentaries, *The Hope,* 2015.

922 Beschloss, "A Case of Courage."

923 Silverberg, *If I Forget Thee,* 404–405.

924 Cohn, *Two Presidents and a Haberdasher.*

925 Beschloss, "A Case of Courage."

926 Silverberg, *If I Forget Thee,* 408.

927 Silverberg, *If I Forget Thee,* 405.

928 Silverberg, *If I Forget Thee,* 405–406.

929 Silverberg, *If I Forget Thee,* 406.

930 Cohn, *Two Presidents and a Haberdasher.*

931 Benson, *Founding of Israel,* 187.

932 Silverberg, *If I Forget Thee,* 409.

933 Silverberg, *If I Forget Thee,* 409–410.

934 Beschloss, "A Case of Courage."

935 Thomas J. Hamilton, "Soviet Charges U.S. Wrecks Partition for Oil and a Base," *The New York Times,* March 31, 1948, 1.

936 Radosh and Radosh, *Safe Haven,* 312.

937 Warren Austin, "Austin to Marshall, Enclosing Rusk to Lovett," May 3, 1948, *FRUS,* vol. 5, 886–889.

938 "Arab King Warns Palestine Invasion … Is Set," *The New York Times,* April 27, 1948, 1.

939 Radosh and Radosh, *Safe Haven,* 321.

940 John Snetsinger, *Truman, The Jewish Vote, and the Creation of Israel* (Stanford, CA: Hoover Press, 1974), 106.

941 PBS, *Truman: The American Experience,* 1997.

942 Clark Clifford and Richard Holbrooke, *Counsel to the President* (New York: Random House, 1991), 5–6.

943 Clifford and Holbrooke, *Counsel to the President,* 7–8.

944 "Max Lowenthal, May 9, 1948," Clark Clifford Papers, Box 13, Truman Library.

945 "Memorandum of Conversation, by Secretary of State," Office of the Historian, US Department of State, May 12, 1948, https://history.state.gov/historicaldocuments/frus1948v05p2/d252.

946 Clifford and Holbrooke, *Counsel to the President,* 10–11.

947 Clifford and Holbrooke, *Counsel to the President,* 11–12.

948 Gary Scott Smith, *Religion in the Oval Office: The Religious Lives of American Presidents* (Oxford: Oxford University Press, 2015), 250.

949 Clifford and Holbrooke, *Counsel to the President*, 12.

950 Clifford and Holbrooke, *Counsel to the President*, 12.

951 Richard Holbrooke, "President Truman's Decision to Recognize Israel," last modified May 1, 2008, http://jcpa.org/article/president-truman%E2%80%99s-decision-to-recognize-israel/.

952 Clifford and Holbrooke, *Counsel to the President*, 13.

953 Clifford and Holbrooke, *Counsel to the President*, 15.

954 Clifford and Holbrooke, *Counsel to the President*, 18–19.

955 Beschloss, "A Case of Courage."

956 Radosh and Radosh, *Safe Haven*, 318.

957 Vera Weizmann, *The Impossible Takes Longer*, 231–232, quoted in Radosh and Radosh, *Safe Haven*, 319.

958 Abba Eban, *Personal Witness*, 140–143, quoted in Radosh and Radosh, *Safe Haven*, 319–320.

959 Harry S. Truman, "Presidential Press Conference," May 13, 1948, Truman Library.

960 CBN Documentaries, *The Hope,* 2015.

961 "To Declare or Not to Declare," The Jewish Agency, http://www.jewishagency.org/ben-gurion/content/23435.

962 Collins and Lapierre, *O Jerusalem*, 403.

963 Sachar, *History of Israel,* 311.

964 Daniel J. Elazar, "Israel As a Jewish State," Jerusalem Center for Public Affairs, http://www.jcpa.org/dje/articles2/isrjewstate.htm.

965 CBN Documentaries, *The Hope,* 2015.

966 Letty Cottin Pogrebin, "Golda Meir: 1898–1978," Jewish Women's Archive, https://jwa.org/encyclopedia/article/meir-golda.

967 Collins and Lapierre, *O Jerusalem*, 409–410.

968 Peter Medding, *The Founding of Israeli Democracy, 1948-1967* (Oxford: Oxford University Press, 1990), 27.

969 Collins and Lapierre, *O Jerusalem*, 427.

970 Collins and Lapierre, *O Jerusalem*, 424–425.

971 Collins and Lapierre, *O Jerusalem*, 429–430.

972 Silverberg, *If I Forget Thee,* 418–419.

973 Collins and Lapierre, *O Jerusalem*, 424–425.

974 Collins and Lapierre, *O Jerusalem*, 424–425.

975 Collins and Lapierre, *O Jerusalem*, 424–425.

976 Museum of the History of Tel Aviv-Yafo,"Tourist Israel, Tourist Israel Tours, https://www.touristisrael.com/museum-of-the-history-of-tel-aviv-yafo/892/.

977 Collins and Lapierre, *O Jerusalem*, 443.

978 Gene Currivan, "Zionists Proclaim New State of Israel; Truman Recognizes It and Hopes for Peace," *New York Times*, May 15, 1948, http://www.nytimes.com/learning/general/onthisday/big/0514.html.

979 Dan Kurzman, "Independence Day 1948: 'The Most Crowded Hours in… History,'" Historama: The Online History Shop, http://www.historama.com/online-resources/articles/israel/story_israel_first_independence_day_14_may_1948.html.

980 Eric Gartman, *Return to Zion: The History of Modern Israel* (Lincoln, NE: University of Nebraska Press, 2015), 123.

981 CBN Documentaries, *The Hope,* 2015.

982 Maxine Dovere, "1948: Not Everyone Was Dancing," *Jewish News Service*, April 4, 2012, http://www.jns.org/latest-articles/2012/4/4/1948-not-every-one-was-dancing.html#.WOKE9E0VDcs.

983 Shelley Kleiman, "The State of Israel Declares Independence," Israel Ministry of Foreign Affairs, http://mfa.gov.il/MFA/MFA-Archive/1999/Pages/Shelley%20Kleiman%20-%20The%20State%20of%20Israel%20Declares%20Ind.aspx.

984 Collins and Lapierre, *O Jerusalem*, 449.

985 Sachar, *History of Israel,* 313.

986 Collins and Lapierre, *O Jerusalem*, 451–452.

987 CBN Documentaries, *The Hope,* 2015.

988 Clifford and Holbrooke, *Counsel to the President*, 19–24.

989 Clifford and Holbrooke, *Counsel to the President*, 19–24.

990 George Lenczowski, *American Presidents and the Middle East* (Durham, NC: Duke University Press, 1990).

991 Devine, *Harry S. Truman*, 114.

992 David Bernard Sacher, "David K. Niles and United States Policy," Senior Honors Thesis, Harvard University, 1959, 1, quoted in Radosh and Radosh, *Safe Haven*, 338.

993 History Channel, *Israel: Birth of a Nation*, 1996.

994 Collins and Lapierre, *O Jerusalem*, 576.

995 "Esther Cailingold," Zionism and Israel Biographies, Zionism & Israel, http://www.zionism-israel.com/bio/Esther_Cailingold.htm.

996 Collins and Lapierre, *O Jerusalem*, 576.

997 Benny Morris, *Righteous Victims: A History of the Zionist-Arab Conflict, 1881-2001* (New York: Vintage Books, 1999), 242.

998 Chaim Herzog and Shlomo Gazit, *The Arab-Israeli Wars: War and Peace in the Middle East* (New York: Vintage Books, 2005), 97.

999 Sachar, *History of Israel,* 343–347.

1000 Ami Isseroff, "Timeline: Israel War of Independence," Zionism and Israel, http://www.zionism-israel.com/his/Israel_war_independence_1948_timeline.htm.

1001 "Israel War of Independence," *Zionism and Israel Encyclopedic Dictionary*, Zionism & Israel, http://www.zionism-israel.com/dic/War_of_Independence.htm.

1002 "David Ben-Gurion," Encyclopedia Britannica, https://www.britannica.com/biography/David-Ben-Gurion.

1003 "Elections in Israel," Israel Knesset, https://knesset.gov.il/mmm/data/pdf/me03504.pdf.

1004 Radosh and Radosh, *Safe Haven*, 342.

1005 "Israel's War of Independence," My Jewish Learning, http://www.myjewishlearning.com/article/israels-war-of-independence/.

1006 My Jewish Learning, "Israel's War of Independence."

1007 Morris, *Righteous Victims,* 248.

1008 "Israel War of Independence," *Zionism and Israel Encyclopedic Dictionary*, Zionism & Israel, http://www.zionism-israel.com/dic/War_of_Independence.htm.

1009 Sachar, *History of Israel,* 336.

1010 "Israel War of Independence," *Zionism and Israel Encyclopedic Dictionary*.

1011 Sachar, *History of Israel,* 333–335.

1012 "Admission of Israel to the United Nations," Israel Ministry of Foreign Affairs, http://www.mfa.gov.il/mfa/foreignpolicy/mfadocuments/yearbook1/pages/admission%20of%20israel%20to%20the%20united%20nations-%20general.aspx.

1013 Sachar, *History of Israel,* 353.

1014 "Israel's Basic Laws: The Law of Return," Jewish Virtual Library, AICE, http://www.jewishvirtuallibrary.org/israel-s-law-of-return.

1015 CBN Documentaries, *The Hope,* 2015.

1016 CBN Documentaries, *The Hope,* 2015.

1017 Bob Cohen, "Bob Cohen introduces the Truman-Jacobson Video," The American Israel Public Affairs Committee (AIPAC), https://www.youtube.com/watch?v=P7f5p42rorg.

1018 CBN Documentaries, *The Hope,* 2015.

1019 CBN Documentaries, *The Hope,* 2015.

1020 CBN Documentaries, *The Hope,* 2015.

1021 Sachar, *History of Israel,* 312.

1022 CBN Documentaries, *The Hope,* 2015.

1023 Collins and Lapierre, *O Jerusalem*, 165.

1024 CBN Documentaries, *The Hope,* 2015.

1025 "Golda Meir," Biography.com, http://www.biography.com/people/golda-meir-9404859#synopsis.

1026 Mary Grey, "Biography: Arthur Balfour 1848–1930," The Balfour Project, http://www.balfourproject.org/arthur-balfour-mary-grey/.

1027 CBN Documentaries, *The Hope,* 2015.

1028 CBN Documentaries, *The Hope,* 2015.

1029 Collins and Lapierre, *O Jerusalem*, 397–398.

1030 "Profile: King Abdullah I of Jordan," Aljazeera, Aljazeera Media Network, February 20, 2008, Http://www.aljazeera.com/focus/arabunity/2008/02/2008525183443732794.html.

1031 Sachar, *History of Israel,* 322.

1032 Morse, *Nazi Connection,* 100–108.

1033 Morse, *Nazi Connection,* 108.

1034 Radosh and Radosh, *Safe Haven*, 346.

1035 Bob Cohen, "Bob Cohen introduces the Truman-Jacobson Video," The American Israel Public Affairs Committee (AIPAC), https://www.youtube.com/watch?v=P7f5p42rorg.

1036 McCullough, *Truman*, 599.

1037 Harry S. Truman, "Truman to Jacobson," June 30, 1955, Jacobson Papers, Truman Library.

1038 Adam Kirsch, "The Truman No Show," *The New Republic*, September 14, 2009, https://newrepublic.com/article/69246/the-truman-no-show.

1039 Adler, "From Dream to Reality," 198–225.

1040 Donovan, *Conflict and Crisis*, 420.

1041 McCullough, *Truman*, 705–707.

1042 David Pietrusza, *1948: Harry Truman's Improbable Victory and the Year That Transformed America* (New York: Union Square Press, October, 2011), 403.

1043 McCullough, *Truman*, 707.

1044 McCullough, *Truman*, 707.

1045 Tim Jones, "Dewey Defeats Truman," *Chicago Tribune*, http://www.chicagotribune.com/news/nationworld/politics/chi-chicagodays-dewey-defeats-story-story.html.

1046 Pietrusza, *Improbable Victory,* 403.

1047 Pietrusza, *Improbable Victory,* 410–411.

1048 Radosh and Radosh, *Safe Haven*, 275–276.

1049 Margaret Truman, *Harry S. Truman*, 416–419.

1050 Harry S. Truman, "Truman Interview," *The 50 Years War: Israel and the Arabs*, A PBS/WGBH/BBC Film, 1998.

1051 Radosh and Radosh, *Safe Haven*, 344–345.

1052 Radosh and Radosh, *Safe Haven*, 344–345.

1053 McCullough, *Truman*, 620.

1054 Radosh and Radosh, *Safe Haven*, 353–354.

1055 CBN Documentaries, *The Hope,* 2015.

1056 Radosh and Radosh, *Safe Haven*, 345–346.

CPSIA information can be obtained
at www.ICGtesting.com
Printed in the USA
LVHW081313100619
620723LV00017B/679/P